Divine Fruitfulness

Divine Fruitfulness

*A Guide through Balthasar's Theology
beyond the Trilogy*

Aidan Nichols OP

THE CATHOLIC UNIVERSITY OF AMERICA PRESS

Published by T&T Clark
A Continuum imprint
The Tower Building, 11 York Road, London SE1 7NX
80 Maiden Lane, Suite 704, New York, NY 10038

www.continuumbooks.com

This edition published under license from T&T Clark, an imprint of Continuum International Publishing Ltd, by The Catholic University of America Press 620 Michigan Avenue, N.E., Washington, D.C. 20064

Library of Congress Cataloging-in-Publication Data
Nichols, Aidan.
  Divine fruitfulness : a guide to Balthasar's theology beyond the trilogy / Aidan Nichols.
    p. cm. – (Introduction to Hans Urs von Balthasar)
  Includes bibliographical references and index.
  ISBN-13: 978-0-8132-1481-8 (pbk. : alk. paper)
  ISBN-10: 0-8132-1481-5 (pbk. : alk. paper) 1. Balthasar, Hans Urs von, 1905-1988. I. Title. II. Series.

BX4705.B163N53 2006
230'.2092–dc22

                                                                            2006021807

Typeset by YHT Ltd, London
Printed on acid-free paper in Great Britain by
MPG Books Ltd, Bodmin, Cornwall

Contents

Preface

With the present work I conclude the five-volume *Introduction to Hans Urs von Balthasar* which has offered readers a series of 'guides' to the different parts of his corpus. In calling this fifth and final instalment a 'Guide to Balthasar's Theology', I mean to institute a contrast with the fourth book in the series, *Scattering the Seed*, which took as subject his early writings on philosophy and the arts. In Balthasar's mature theology we see the seed there sown springing up, flowering and fruiting in an abundance of theological applications. Hence the title of the book to which this is the Preface: *Divine Fruitfulness*. Its subtitle also includes the words, 'Beyond the Trilogy'. To my three studies dedicated to Balthasar's great Trilogy (*The Word has been Abroad* on his theological aesthetics, *No Bloodless Myth* on his theological dramatics, *Say it is Pentecost* on his theological logic), *Divine Fruitfulness* goes further in four respects.

First, while at the opening of my three-part commentary on the Trilogy I offered an introduction to Balthasar's life-story as well as to the works of the Trilogy itself, here in the opening chapter, 'Introduction to the Wider *Oeuvre*', I venture to consider not only other aspects of his literary production but also the Church-political context of his work. How did he see contemporary Catholicism – and, for that matter, how did it see him? Secondly, whereas my studies of the Trilogy touch wherever appropriate on the literally dozens of writers – both Christian and non-Christians – of whom Balthasar makes occasional use, this book identifies the principal origins of his architectonic approach to the structure, content and ethos of theology as a whole. (Hence the overall title given to Chapters 2 to 5: 'Sources'.) Thirdly, though the Trilogy contains, no doubt, Balthasar's richest theological fare, to grasp the bread-and-butter of his theological doctrine the remaining writings are frequently more helpful. To alter the metaphor from gastronomy to optics: the aesthetics, dramatics and logic offer three perspectives on revelation, perspectives that correspond to the three 'transcendentals', the beautiful, the good, the true. But that is not to say that the great affirmations of revelation, and the major motifs of the Christian life, are incapable of exhibition by a multi-focal approach which prescinds from these particular 'formalities' – to use the more precise Scholastic expression in place of the somewhat impressionistic contemporary term 'perspective'. (Hence the overall title given to Chapters 6 to 13: 'Themes'.) Fourthly, while *Say it is Pentecost* included a brief 'Postword', *Divine Fruitfulness* offers a Conclusion to the whole five-part series, asking at greater length the question, What will the Catholic theology of the twenty-first century (and later) owe to this enormously ambitious *oeuvre*?

There are several notable introductions to Balthasar's thought by other writers, and these of course necessarily overlap to varying degrees with the matter I present in this book as in the others in the series. However, it is a feature of *Divine Fruitfulness* that I make use of a good deal of rather inaccessible Balthasar material, published for the most part in Swiss newspapers and magazines, much of which, I think I am right in saying, has not been drawn upon before. My thanks go to Don Willy Volonté, Dean of the Faculty of Theology of Lugano, during my two visits there, for making it possible for me to consult the holdings of the Balthasar study centre housed in that institution, as well as to Frau Cornelia Capol for sending me photocopies of other items in the Archiv Hans Urs von Balthasar in Basle.

Aidan Nichols, OP,
Blackfriars, Cambridge,
Solemnity of St George,
Protector of the Realm, 2006

1

❧

Introduction to the wider *oeuvre*

Personal beginnings

He began as a *Germanist*, a specialist in literature in the German language.[1] He himself wrote an elaborate and highly polished German, which some critics, though, considered in its elegance more like French and certainly not typical of the Swiss. It was, however, among the Swiss that he was born in Lucerne, on 12 August 1905, into a patrician family whose history went back centuries in this historically most Catholic of the Swiss cities and cantons – though on his mother's side there was also Hungarian blood, from the landowning class in the Austro-Hungarian monarchy still flourishing, or relatively so, at the time of his birth. He went to school with the Benedictines, in the glorious sub-alpine and Baroque setting of their abbey school at Engelberg, and less memorably with the Jesuits at Feldkirch in the Austrian Voralberg, before studying German literature and philosophy in the Universities of Vienna, Berlin and Zurich.

Towards the end of his doctoral studies at the University of Zurich his academic investigations of how the German poets and prosists saw 'eschatology' – the ultimates in human existence – were punctuated by a new development in his personal life. While making the *Spiritual Exercises* of St Ignatius, he suddenly 'knew' – he describes it almost in revelatory terms – he should be a priest.[2] His subsequent entry into the Society of Jesus in 1929 set him off on his theological – as distinct from literary-philosophical – journey. While he did not enjoy the Neo-Scholastic teaching he received from the Jesuit study-house in Bavaria, he appreciated enormously the years of his formation spent with French members of the Society at Lyons, from 1933 to 1937. This was at a time when Catholic theology in France was undergoing a little renaissance founded on return to the Fathers and a listening to a wider range of the voices of experience, notably from imaginative writers such as

---

1 I offer here what is to some extent a complementary reading of Balthasar's life and work from that given in the first volume of my commentary on the Trilogy, *The Word Has Been Abroad. A Guide through Balthasar's Aesthetics* (Edinburgh, 1998), pp. ix–xx. The difference lies chiefly (an explanation of his work as publisher aside) on how Balthasar saw both the Church of his day and his own literary production, and, reciprocally, the way his work was viewed by other pertinent parties in the Catholic Church. All works cited are by Balthasar unless otherwise indicated.

2 'Por qué me hice Sacerdote', in J.–R. M. Sans Vila (ed.), *Por qué me hice Sacerdote* (Salamanca, 1959), pp. 29–32, and here at p. 31.

1

those with whom Balthasar was already familiar in the German-speaking context. Unlike some, but by no means all, the French Jesuits, Balthasar never lost confidence, however, in the perennial importance of St Thomas, especially for metaphysics. Part of the reason was the inspiration of one German-speaking Jesuit, the somewhat unplaceably Thomistic Erich Przywara whose interpretation of the analogy of being as, among other things, a thesis about mysticism and spiritual experience – a theological mindset and not just a theorem in metaphysics – influenced Balthasar his whole life long.[3]

The major encounters

It was Balthasar's posting back to Switzerland in 1940, as University chaplain in Basle, which accidentally – or perhaps we should say providentially – fixed his future path. He discovered his gifts as editor, translator and publishing entrepreneur, thanks to his energetic prosecution of a series of works designed to preserve many good things from the Western Christian and humanist heritage – should the outcome of the Second World War, then raging, be, as he feared, a new barbarism.[4] More importantly for theology proper, he met two Basle residents who decisively shaped his future doctrinal thought: the great Protestant dogmatician Karl Barth, and the mystic Adrienne von Speyr whom he received into the Catholic Church in 1940. It was as a result of his involvement with von Speyr in an attempt to create a 'Secular Institute', for consecrated celibates of both sexes, attached to the Jesuit Society but living in the world, that in 1950 he decided to seek dispensation from vows in a Religious Congregation not disposed to grant him his request. The rest of his life he spent as what German-speaking Catholics call a *Weltpriester*, a 'priest in the world', that is, a member of the secular or diocesan clergy.

From this point on, Balthasar's life would be bound up with the fortunes, in every sense, of the publishing house he now founded, the Johannes Verlag. His days were dominated by his work as author, editor and publisher. Though hardly the stuff that Hollywood movies are made of, it was in its own way a colossal feat. As author of some eighty books and five hundred articles, translator of over a hundred works, editor of more than ten essay collections and numerous anthologies, as well as the midwife of the sixty-plus volumes of Adrienne's writing, mostly posthumous, he might be thought to have justified his existence without running a commercial theological publishing house for forty years. And this is without even mentioning his occasional activities as lecturer, preacher and giver of the Ignatian *Exercises*.[5] Setting out his ideal of a Catholic publishing house, he spoke of its enormous responsibility: it acts 'in the name and representation of the

---

3 See Przywara's 1932 study *Analogia entis. Metaphysik. Ur-Struktur und All-Rhythmus* (Einsiedeln, 1962, 2nd edition). An account in English is available: T. O'Meara, OP, *Erich Przywara, S. J. His Theology and his World* (Notre Dame, IN, 2002), pp. 73–83.
4 The *Europäische Reihe* of the *Sammlung Klosterberg* (1942–1951).
5 Though even some of this was published, for instance as *Die Gottesfrage des heutigen Menschen* (Vienna, 1956); ET *Science, Religion and Christianity* (London, 1958). It appeared in American translation as *The God-question and Modern Man* (New York, 1967).

Church'.[6] He made it plain such a house should 'turn to the world' – not by allowing its own Christian attitudes to become 'unclear or ambiguous' but with a view to 'illuminating, evaluating and opening up the world in the radiance of Christian revelation'.[7]

The translations

It is worth mentioning the subjects of his translations: it gives a good idea of the influences he hoped were going to shape the contemporary Church. So what kind of material was he putting out?[8] For patriotic reasons I mention first his English translations: a book on prayer by the Anglican High Churchman Arthur Michael Ramsey, and the Low Church Anglican C. S. Lewis's personal choice of passages from his own Scots Presbyterian 'master', the theological fantasist George MacDonald. Much more significant in terms of his overall output and direction were his translations from the French, and first and foremost the huge amount he translated from the main writers of the early twentieth-century French Catholic literary revival: Paul Claudel (all his poetry, for example), Charles Péguy, and the novelist Georges Bernanos to whom he devoted a lengthy monograph giving it, on its second edition, the significant title 'The Church as Lived'.[9] He established an entire series *Theologia romanica*, dedicated to work produced by the Church in France. There and elsewhere he translated the *Pensées* of Blaise Pascal; selections from Pascal's near contemporary, the seventeenth-century founder of the French School of spirituality, Pierre de Bérulle, and the journals of the lay philosopher from the Modernist period Maurice Blondel. Latterly he added Jean Corbon's 'Liturgy from the Wellspring': a Dominican of the Melchite rite, Corbon had authored the final section of the present *Catechism of the Catholic Church*, its book on prayer. However, the lion's share of Balthasar's translations for the *Theologia romanica* series and its parallels went to his fellow Jesuit, known to him from his Lyons period, Henri de Lubac, whose copious *oeuvre* he also summarized in his study of his old mentor, 'Henri de Lubac. His Organic Life's Work'.[10] When in 1975 Balthasar was made an associate of the Institut de France, he told *les instituticiens*:

> Despite the indifference of a public saturated by mediocre religious publications, I would like to continue this slightly madcap enterprise of presenting to your Eastern neighbours [he meant Germany, Austria and Switzerland] what contemporary France produces that is most

---

6 'Über die Idee eines katholischen Verlages', *Renaissance. Gespräche und Mitteilungen* I (1952), p. 1.
7 *Ibid.*, p. 3.
8 Full bibliographical information about his translations may be found in C. Capol (ed.), *Hans Urs von Balthasar. Bibliographie 1925–1990* (Einsiedeln-Freiburg, 1990), pp. 117–31.
9 *Gelebte Kirche. Bernanos* (Einsiedeln, 1971); ET *Bernanos. An Ecclesial Existence* (San Francisco, 1996).
10 *Henri de Lubac. Sein organisches Lebenswerk* (Einsiedeln, 1976); ET *The Theology of Henri de Lubac* (San Francisco, 1991).

precious in the realm of spiritual thought, all that merits being appreciated and loved beyond her frontiers.[11]

From the Spanish, he translated 'The Theatre of the World' by the seventeenth-century priest-playwright Pedro Calderón as well as, more predictably, the Ignatian *Exercises*. His German anthologies from the Fathers include, from the Greek, substantial, well-ordered extracts from the Apostolic Fathers and Irenaeus, as well as from Origen, Gregory of Nyssa and Maximus the Confessor, on all three of whom he produced entire monographs in the years 1936 to 1942. From the Latin he made new translations of a great deal of Augustine, including the *Confessions* in 1985. This is a representative selection and not an exhaustive account – for which the interested reader must consult Cornelia Capol's invaluable *Bibliographie*.[12]

The works of Balthasar and von Speyr

Preparing for publication von Speyr's biblical commentaries and other spiritual works occupied a great deal of Balthasar's time. He had not finished publishing her posthumous writings by the time of his death. While we can legitimately say that the combination of the Greek Fathers, Thomas and Barth was what shaped most fundamentally Balthasar's general theological outlook, a great deal in his presentation of particular doctrinal areas would have been significantly different without von Speyr's influence. This is especially true of his theology of the Trinity and the Incarnation, including the Paschal Mystery – and notably the Holy Saturday phase of the latter; his Mariology, and theology of the missions of the saints; his account of the sacrament of Penance (Confession), and his teaching on obedience as readiness (*Verfügbarkeit*) and self-surrender (*Hingabe*), on spiritual childhood and on prayer. The synthesis of the more academically recognizable sources and Adrienne von Speyr's meditations is especially apparent in the set of five volumes which collect together the most important of his theological essays, as also in his single most sustained ecclesiological effort, *The Christian State of Life*. Lastly, Adrienne's preoccupations are evident in the final volume of his theological dramatics,[13] mention of which brings me to his best-known works.

For at the heart of his corpus lies his own trilogy: the theological aesthetics, *Herrlichkeit* or 'The Glory of the Lord',[14] the theological dramatics, *Theodramatik*,[15] and the theological logic, *Theologik*,[16] and the separately

11 'Allocution de M. Hans Urs von Balthasar à l'occasion de son installation comme Associé Etranger dans l'Académie des Sciences Morales et Politiques', Institut de France, Séance du lundi 9 juin. No. 13, p. 5.
12 See note 8 above.
13 On which see A. Nichols, OP, *No Bloodless Myth. A Guide through Balthasar's Dramatics* (Edinburgh, 2000), pp. 185–239.
14 *Herrlichkeit. Eine theologische Ästhetik* (Einsiedeln 1961–1969); ET *The Glory of the Lord. A Theological Aesthetics* (San Francisco, 1985–1989).
15 *Theodramatik* (Einsiedeln, 1973–1983); ET *Theo-drama. Theological Dramatic Theory* (San Francisco, 1988–1998).
16 *Theologik* (Einsiedeln, 1985–1987); ET *Theo-logic* (San Francisco, 2002–2005). On this see A. Nichols, OP, *Say It Is Pentecost. A Guide through Balthasar's Logic* (Edinburgh, 2001), pp. 1–194.

published 'Epilogue' to that trilogy.[17] It is to these that the earlier volumes in this series: *The Word Has Been Abroad* (on the aesthetics), *No Bloodless Myth* (on the dramatics) and *Say It Is Pentecost* (on the logic) have been devoted. Taken together, the stars of the trilogy and the planets that circle it in the works 'beyond the trilogy', constitute the most impressive body of distinctively Catholic dogmatics in the twentieth century. The writings of the German Jesuit Karl Rahner are, taken globally, the only possible competitor, but the ethos of Balthasar's *oeuvre* is strikingly different.

A very Catholic dogmatics

One way to put that difference is to say his work is a self-consciously *Catholic* dogmatics not only doctrinally but also in its frame of cultural reference. Unlike Rahner in the later part of his career, Balthasar was not especially impressed by official, never mind wild-cat, ecumenism. Balthasar became irritated in the course of the 1970s by 'a certain sort of Catholic ecumenism', which seemed at the ready to downplay or at any rate abstract from specifically Catholic emphases.[18] That irritation may explain the abandonment of the volume on ecumenics projected for a fairly prominent place in the trilogy as one of the last volumes of the aesthetics. Earlier, however, Balthasar had written one of the best books ever on the Reformed theologian Karl Barth, largely in praise.[19] He had also opened a dialogue with Martin Buber about Judaism, a subject often linked to (inner-Christian) ecumenism as distinct from inter-religious dialogue.[20] The third volume of the aesthetics has lengthy chapters on one Lutheran, Hamann, and one Orthodox, Solovyev. The dramatics contains an exchange with the theology of Luther, and throughout the entire trilogy numerous motifs of Eastern Christian theology are sounded. But it remains the case that this is a very self-consciously *Catholic* dogmatics. Its composition was motivated in large part by the desire not to lose anything of the historic patrimony of the Church – rather than a conviction that, in the context of contemporary ecumenical endeavour, not to speak of epistemological pluralism, one should simplify down to essentials – the predominant tone of the later Karl Rahner. This is one reason why some people are attracted to Balthasar's writing and others are not.

It may be useful, then, in the rest of this introduction to attempt to 'position' Balthasar in terms of how he saw the life of the Church vis-à-vis the contemporary world as well as how the hierarchical Church, and notably the Papacy, saw him.

17 *Epilog* (Einsiedeln-Trier, 1987); ET *Epilogue* (San Francisco, 2005). On *Epilog*, see A. Nichols, OP, *Say It Is Pentecost, op. cit.*, pp. 197–210.
18 The phrase is Iso Baumer's: 'Vermittler des Unzeitgemässen. Hans Urs von Balthasar als Autor, Herausgeber und Verleger', in K. Lehmann and W. Kasper (eds), *Hans Urs von Balthasar. Gestalt und Werk* (Cologne, 1989) , pp. 85–103, and here at p. 99.
19 *Karl Barth. Darstellung und Deutung seiner Theologie* (Olten-Cologne, 1951; Einsiedeln, 1976, 4th edition); ET *The Theology of Karl Barth. Exposition and Interpretation* (San Francisco, 1991).
20 *Einsame Zwiesprache. Martin Buber und das Christentum* (Cologne-Olten, 1958); ET *Martin Buber and Christianity. A Dialogue between Israel and the Church* (London, 1960).

His 'pre-Conciliar' programme

In the immediately pre-Conciliar period, Balthasar certainly belongs with those who considered the median state of Church life and thought it too stuffy, and, like Blessed John XXIII, wanted to open windows. In fact, Balthasar's metaphor was a good deal more aggressive. It was 'razing the bastions', bringing down fortress walls. But as one reads his book of this title, *Schleifung der Bastionen*, one finds that Balthasar is actually arguing that in certain respects this razing has already taken place – by 1952, that is – without the Church really being aware of the fact.[21] He speaks of a 'new Catholic attitude'. On the one hand, this attitude takes the form of solidarity with the aspirations of global humanity. And yet on the other hand it refuses to heed the wish of the Enlightenment that the Church would jettison her universal mission by, for example, treating all religions as equally justified through being complementary approaches to a total truth beyond any of them. Balthasar points out that, in the struggle over Jansenism, the Church of the early eighteenth century had already judged the proposition 'outside the Church there is no grace' to be false, and if that thesis *is* false then by the same token it must be true that outside the Church there is the possibility of salvation, based on the baptism of desire. But this does not affect that *other* truth according to which all salvation is mediated through the Church: both in the sense of coming from God in Christ through the Mother of the Lord as mediatrix of all graces (for Mary is the archetype of the Church) and in the further sense of coming from God in Christ through the 'one, heavenly-invisible and earthly-visible and hierarchical Church'.[22] There is only one Church, which is at the same time in heaven and on earth.

By way of anticipation of major themes of the Second Vatican Council, Balthasar found outside the Church's visible borders not only, in the inner sanctum of human hearts, invisible desires pertinent to salvation but also, on the public square, concrete truths and values belonging by right to the Catholic Church but now spread beyond her borders, perhaps through actions (Balthasar cites the Reformation) that were at one level guilty and yet have been used by the cunning of the Providence of God. One might think that, sundered from her unity, these goods would lose their value. But this is not so. As Balthasar writes, 'What was once Church and supernature cannot return to world and nature'.[23] Catholic Christians, then, can find in the ecclesial communities and world society beyond them what Balthasar terms 'extrapolated awareness', *das extrapolierte Bewusstsein*, of divine truths. (When discussing truths once possessed only by the Church which have now travelled so far abroad as to go beyond the separated ecclesial communities into the civil order simply as such, he typically gives the – papally approved but in more recent years theologically controverted – example of human rights.) The Church's theologians may not yet recognize this development but, Balthasar comments, the awareness of it is moving like the hastening spring among what he calls the 'responsible laity'.[24] A new form of exchange

---

21 *Schleifung der Bastionen. Von der Kirche in dieser Zeit* (Einsiedeln, 1952); ET *Razing the Bastions. On the Church in this Age* (San Francisco, 1993).
22 *Ibid.*, p. 54.
23 *Ibid.*, p. 56.
24 *Ibid.*, p. 57.

between Church and world is coming to be, not by way of secularizing the Church but through sensitivizing her to, as he puts it, 'all those who are genuinely waiting for grace and for the Word that is to be proclaimed to them'.[25]

On this basis, Balthasar expected to see a massive transformation of Christian consciousness, which he sums up in a short formula. It will be a transition from 'privileged person' to 'responsible person', *vom Priviligierten zum Verantwortlichen*.[26] Elsewhere he was writing at the same time that never since the first three centuries had the Church's spiritual situation been so open, promising and well adapted to the future.[27] The Church is so living that she can afford to be a little reckless with her past traditions. There is a 'livingness' about her which transcends all particular traditions from the past 'insofar as responsibility and readiness for the future demand it'.[28]

Yet even in his headiest moments of 'Brave New Church' he did not cease to insist that only *saints* can show the mystery of Christ 'repeating itself' in his Church-body.[29] Divine grace does not consider 'quantity', but only 'the unconditionality of single persons'.[30] Only saints can now 'save Christendom'.[31] Balthasar liked to repeat Péguy's dictum: a couple of saints at the front and a great procession of sinners will follow: 'that is how my Christendom is made'.[32] The way he expressed this position, incidentally, was not so vulnerable to the charge of individualism as might be thought. If for individuals the love command is the highest law, then the equivalent for the social totality can hardly be 'the egoism of reasons of State'. Both individual and society live in the time when Christ is king, his law supreme. 'Reasons of State, *die Staatsraison*, will not fall short if they acknowledge this law.'[33]

Despite the increasing negativity with which he regarded post-Conciliar developments in Catholicism, Balthasar retained a considerable suspicion of the more embattled varieties of Catholic traditionalism. In 1963, while the Second Vatican Council was sitting, he published in the distinguished Zurich daily paper, *Neue Zürcher Nachrichten* an analysis of twentieth-century Catholic integralism, German, French and Spanish, which he described as seeking to win the Kingdom of God by the weapons of the world.

The possible combinations between monarchism, juridicism and the military spirit, secret societies, politics and high finance are endless. The problem remains, whether and how these (very diverse) realms of

---

25 *Ibid.*, p. 58.
26 *Ibid.*, p. 59.
27 'Alte Kirche und junge Welt', *Civitas* 7 (1952), pp. 579–84, and here at p. 584.
28 *Ibid.*, p. 580.
29 'Die eine Kirche und die vielen Kirchen', *Civitas* 7 (1952), pp. 633–39.
30 'Über den Glauben', *Basler Studentschaft* 25 (1944), pp. 69–71, and here at p. 71.
31 'Wer wird die Christenheit retten?', *Pfarrblatt des Dekanates Basel-Stadt* 32. 1 (29 December 1944), p. 134.
32 Cited in *ibid.*
33 'Was ihr dem Geringsten meiner Brüder getan habt', *Einsiedler Anzeiger* 83. 88 (6 November 1942), pp. 1–2, and here at p. 2. Balthasar was here berating his co-nationals for their inadequate response to the victims of repression and war who had sought refuge behind Swiss frontiers. In his version of the parable of the Grand Assize (Matthew 25.31–46), 'I was a refugee, an emigré, and you sheltered me – or did not shelter me'.

value can be placed at the service of Jesus Christ who bore the sins of the world not as a tiger but as a 'lamb'.[34]

Integralism is a 'post-Revolutionary way of thinking and action' which seeks to recover for Christendom the spiritual and political power it held for a thousand years but now can only strive to do so in an 'inner-ecclesial form'.[35] Rather than seek to experience the 'tangledness' of subsequent historical reality from within, integralists judge it sufficient for appropriate action in the world to 'take a look at correct [doctrinal] concepts'. And of course such a unique system of concepts is not found in the human world at large. Typically, then, integralism insinuates that the realm of supernature is closed to nature, as is the realm of nature to it. We shall not hear much from *this* source about paths to God outside the Church, by uncovenanted graces accorded in relation to the 'realm of love'.

Balthasar does not say that all concern with doctrinal systematics implies integralism. What marks out integralism is, rather, the prioritizing of the 'political and social taking of power by the Kingdom', then *subsequently* from these 'citadels' to proclaim the message of Golgotha and the Sermon on the Mount. It is this order of priorities which occludes, in his opinion, the 'humiliated Lamb, the crucified Love'.

This description best fits the movement *Action française* (Balthasar produces a roll-call of distinguished French clerical and lay intellectuals who had belonged to it, but he omits to mention the papal ban on membership which caused such agonies of conscience in the France of the 1920s). Balthasar rebukes integralists for their secretiveness. The *disciplina arcani*, the 'principle of reserve' as Tractarians called it, makes sense in explaining the faith to those outside, but 'within the Church there should be light'. Balthasar criticizes the procedures of the Holy Office, the Papacy's doctrinal organ in this regard. (The Second Vatican Council was taking steps at this time to reform them.)

When, however, he introduces his remarks on concrete examples by saying 'we are solidary with those we criticise', he makes it clear this is no declaration of spiritual war.[36] At least the integralists had ardour, and clarity about the faith: two qualities he was going to find sorely lacking in Western Catholicism in subsequent years. Many of the saints, he admits, tried to achieve spiritual goals by worldly means. And is there much to choose between this 'emphatically static and formal monarchical Constantinianism' and the equally 'emphatic dynamic-evolutionist democratic Constantinianism' of 'Progressive' Catholicism? Pronouncing 'a plague on both your houses' was, of course, a rather negative thing to do. Balthasar would persist in it, notably in the 1969 essay 'Kirche zwischen links und rechts', though he would conclude there, more positively, that Christ was the 'only true

34 'Integralismus: II. Beispiele', *Neue Zürcher Nachrichten* 30 November 1963, Beilage 'Christliche Kultur' 27, 44.
35 'Integralismus: I. Grundsätzliches'. *Ibid.*, 23 November 1963, Beilage 'Christliche Kultur', 27, 43.
36 A number of members of Opus Dei (he had commented quizzically on the spirituality of their founder, Josemaria Escriva de Balaguer, later canonized by Pope John Paul II), wrote to him after the publication of this article. He responded in 'Friedliche Fragen an Opus Dei', *Der christliche Sonntag* 16. 15 (1964), pp. 117–18.

Integralist', since all 'things in heaven and things on earth' are to be 'united' in him (Ephesians 1.10), just as he is the 'only true Progressive', reaching through to the Eschaton, the 'Pioneer of our faith who brings it to completion' (Hebrews 12.2).[37]

Post-Conciliar developments

Balthasar criticized post-Conciliar developments precisely for the way their promoters mistook the genuine change of outlook that *was* required with a parody or caricature of it which, so far from being requisite, was actually disastrous. As an Anglican admirer expressed it:

> He was to live to see the way in which the opening up of the Church to the world which he and others had fought for could easily lead to the erosion of that which was distinctively Christian.[38]

The mistake was a covert acceptance of Enlightenment humanism and the myth of progress. Thence arises an occlusion of the uniqueness of Christian revelation in the plenary form it attains by way not only of Catholic specificity but also of Catholic wholeness. Emphasis on not just the *distinctively* Catholic but the *holistically* Catholic would mark Balthasar's controversial writings in the years following the Second Vatican Council. But even in the early 1950s, being 'responsible' did not mean accepting principles of action commonly recognized in civil society, sharing with others what Hans Küng would term a 'global ethic' for the sake of inter-communitarian good relations. It meant, as Balthasar put it in *Razing the Bastions*, 'vicarious representation, bearing responsibility, sacrifice'.[39] When he looks for an instance of being a responsible person, it is Anthony of Egypt he comes up with, the Egyptian farmer who withdrew to the desert to do battle with spiritual evil. His heroes were not, therefore, modern seekers of consensus across confessional boundaries such as, say, the founders of Christian Democracy.

By 1968, a year of anarchy in France and Federal Germany and in Universities elsewhere, he was commenting on the 'end of conventional Christianity' that, if people were lambasting that Christianity for mediocrity and *embourgeoisement*, it was incumbent on them to say how they would present the Church as a 'sign of authenticity' to the world. Only one way is known, which is when:

> a real saint has broken through into immediacy vis-à-vis the Gospel, has dared to take a headlong leap into the flowing primordial element of revelation.[40]

When a series of recent German television programmes was presented as a 'practical introduction to disobedience' (1968 was also the year of Paul VI's encyclical on sexual ethics, *Humanae Vitae*, the true beginning of doctrinal dissent on a host of issues in post-Conciliar Catholicism), Balthasar was

---

37 'Kirche zwischen links und rechts', *Civitas* 24 (1969), pp. 449–64, and here at p. 464.
38 J. Riches, 'Hans Urs von Balthasar', in D. Ford (ed.), *The Modern Theologians. An Introduction to Christian Theology in the Twentieth Century*, I (Oxford, 1989), p. 248.
39 *Razing the Bastions, op. cit.*, p. 59.
40 'Ende des konventionellen Christentums?', *Schweizerische Kirchenzeitung* 136. 13 (28 March 1968), pp. 197–99, and here at p. 199.

quick to point out the contrast with the saints. For them, obedience to the Church was part and parcel of 'going to God' – even if they also asked from the Church a *kind* of obedience to their own missions and God-given charisms.

Balthasar found there was far too much talk of the Church's (deficient) 'credibility'. What, he asked, of the credibility of God? The real plausibility-structure of Christianity is Chalcedonian. It must do justice to the human, yes. But it must also show the human on its way to self-transcendence in the direction of the divine. The dimensions of the Christian mystery were currently being 'abbreviated', sold short.[41]

On one point, however, Balthasar never shifted from adhesion to one theme of Catholic Progressivism, already adopted in the 1950s. And this was his belief, in part sanctioned by sociological data, that the Church would shrink to a numerical shadow of her former self, and must prepare to enter a diaspora situation where she could still be – and perhaps more effectively be – 'yeast' to the world. Karl Rahner, to select a 'left-of-centre' figure from the late twentieth-century Catholic crisis, would take a similar view. If the consequence of this outer weakening should be that the Church is less respected since she appears less needed (in Balthasar's words, 'the inner light seems weak and wavering because of the light that is dawning outside'[42]), this may conform the Church more fully to Christ by making of her, in Paul's graphic language in First Corinthians (1.18-31), a practitioner of 'folly' for Christ's sake. As Balthasar wrote:

> If this were the key to the present situation of the Church then she would stand closer to the Lord in the active event of redemption than ever before. It would also be true then that her apparent organic weakness, her decline, her division, belong in reality to the mystery of a supernatural weakening corresponding, in its own time, to an exalted supernatural fruitfulness.[43]

In his Passion, Christ poured out his blood uncalculatingly, just as during the ministry he had healed many by the power that went forth from him without always knowing who had touched his garments. So it should be with the Church. There is no reason to think Balthasar ever went back on this – as we might call it – high spiritual justification for the abandonment of Christendom. As he summed up in *Razing the Bastions*:

> Weakness means fruitfulness; and the weakness of the Bride Church in the face of the peoples is a mystery of her fruit-bearing among them, a mystery that remains invisible to eyes outside her.[44]

It is, however, counter-intuitive to suppose that acquiescence in the diminishment of the cultural mission of the Church assists the efficacy of her evangelical mission. Hence the appeal to the mysteric.

---

41 *Ibid.*, p. 199.
42 *Razing the Bastions, op. cit.*, p. 64.
43 *Ibid.*
44 *Ibid.*, p. 67.

The great non-event

Despite the prominence he was ever more surely gaining as theologian and spiritual writer, Balthasar had not been called to participate as a *peritus* or expert adviser at the Second Vatican Council. There is no sure explanation why. If it was more than the luck of the draw, we should probably be correct to link it not so much with any perceived shortcomings in his thought as with the two inter-connected controversial issues of his life, his departure from the Society of Jesus and his sponsorship of the mystic Adrienne von Speyr. Two Conciliar *periti*, Henri de Lubac and Karl Rahner, discussed the matter in print around the time the Council ended. De Lubac described it as 'disconcerting' that Balthasar had not been called but on the whole thought it just as well.[45] Not only would he have been unsuited to committee work but future generations might have been deprived of the theological works he was producing during the Conciliar period (that refers chiefly to the theological aesthetics, complete except for the two biblical volumes by 1965, the year the Council ended). In any case, the most valuable emphases of the Conciliar texts had already been incorporated in Balthasar's own outlook before the Council opened. De Lubac could say this because he regarded the Dogmatic Constitutions of the Council on Divine Revelation and the Church, *Dei Verbum* and *Lumen gentium*, as themselves Christocentric and considers that Balthasar anticipated them. De Lubac identified as the main fruit of Balthasar's work a better grasp of the unique originality of the faith, especially through his Trinitarian presentation of Christ as the opened heart of the Godhead. In fact, Balthasar himself would later complain that the Council had *not* spent enough time on Trinitarian and Christological doctrine, wrongly supposing that these could largely be taken for granted. 'Nothing could be sillier than to make of the Council documents something like a Catechism for our time.'[46]

Rahner was inclined to ascribe Balthasar's lack of wide recognition to a variety of factors: some definitely to Balthasar's credit but others not. Balthasar's readers or potential readers were too bourgeois and philistine to appreciate him. Like, to a degree, the Council itself, they were caught up with 'secondary issues' – Rahner has in mind no doubt issues of pastoralia and the reform of Church structures which left Balthasar cold. But not all the grounds Balthasar provided for his own comparative marginalization were creditable to him, so Rahner opined. Scholastic theologians could reasonably complain that his work lacked conceptual precision. And more people than they were likely to be offended by the not infrequent harshness of his judgments. On the whole, Rahner was inclined to identify as the single main cause Catholic readers' lack of patience with so prolix and complex an undertaking (once again, it was the theological aesthetics Rahner was thinking of). He himself believed Balthasar's work to be seed sown in a field. People would hear more of it in the future.[47] In this Rahner was prophetic.

In point of fact Rahner was also correct in his assertion that the Council

---

45 H. de Lubac, 'Un testimonio di Cristo. Hans Urs von Balthasar', *Humanitas* 20 (1965), pp. 851–69, and here at pp. 851–52.
46 'Reform oder Aggiornamento?', *Civitas* 21 (1967), pp. 679–89, and here at p. 684.
47 K. Rahner, 'Hans Urs von Balthasar', *Civitas* 20 (1964–1965), pp. 601–604, and here at p. 604.

Fathers' choice of themes did not leave Balthasar especially enthused. In an interview in *Theologie und Kirchen* for 1969 he regretted that the Council had spent so long on the value of the person, on psychology, sociology and the mass media, that it had failed to say very much about the 'primordial powers on whose basis everything Christian in its own way is at work in the world'.[48] He included there: the Cross of Christ, the obedience to death which was the ground of his exaltation, and his abiding contemplation of the Father; likewise, the fruitfulness of contemplation and the loving surrender of one's existence to the work and mind of Christ; or again, the place of unceasing prayer, and spiritual poverty: in a word, 'all those things that Christians who know about their Christianity place first; and which alone can lead to a genuine dialogue with other religions'.

In an essay from the year following the Council's closure, 'Reform or aggiornamento?', he expressed perplexity at the prominence given the latter theme. Purification, repentance, renovation, these were all fine motifs, typical of the reforming Church councils of the Middle Ages. The only sense he could give to 'aggiornamento' was that it might be tacitly implied in the great Missionary Command at the end of St Matthew's Gospel (28.18-20). To 'teach all nations' would be capriciously impeded if the Church herself created human obstacles to get in the way of evangelization. But the Missionary Command underlines that what is to be taught is 'everything' Christ commanded the apostles – so distinctly *not* 'a selection of propositions which can be accepted by modern people without any essential constraints or challenges'.[49] True reform is always back to the origins, and entails the intensified conversion of the Church as Bride of Christ with all her members.

Post-Conciliar developments

Balthasar considered the expectations placed on the Second Vatican Council exaggerated. In a 1977 lecture in Sankt Gallen, offering a 'realistic look at our Swiss situation', he remarked that no Council can renew the spirit of believers.[50] At the most it can indicate some 'correct lines' on which renovation may proceed. He also drew an unfavourable contrast with the Council of Trent, which had been 'accompanied by a cloud of saints' in many walks of Church life. There was little apparent evidence the same was true of Vatican II. Balthasar deplored the 'naïve optimism' which had placed such faith in 'structures': committees, councils and synods at all levels of ecclesial organization. Balthasar could see in the upshot only *Gleichschaltung* (a pejorative term since the Third Reich for 'bringing into line') and *Leerlauf*, waste of energy. Renewal will not come from here but from individuals sensitivized to the divine words. Perusal of this essay exposes us to Balthasar's post-Conciliar hard-hittingness: part of the background to his reclamation by John Paul II and the future Benedict XVI for the work of Catholic 'restoration' – though neither of them were ever as negative about the Council events (and texts) as Balthasar could be.

---

48 H. Baur, 'Kirche unter der Autorität Christi. Ein Publik-Gespräch mit Hans Urs von Balthasar', *Theologie und Kirchen* 18 (2 May 1969), p. 27.
49 'Reform oder Aggiornamento?', *art. cit.*, p. 681.
50 'Realisticher Blick auf unsere Schweizer Situation', *Timor Domini* 7. 2 (1978), p. 3.

Balthasar's portrayal of the neighbouring French Church in this period makes painful reading even after thirty years. The only hope he saw for the French Jesuits and Dominicans was that those who currently set the intellectual tone – Marxistic with the Jesuits and 'tending to atheism' with the Dominicans – would leave their respective Orders. 'Over the heads of the hierarchy and then – volens, nolens – together with them', 'a systematic destruction of the faith is at work' (Balthasar produced official catechetical materials as examples). The real villain of the piece in the rise of Lefevbrism is 'the French clergy or the French bishops', who, when an opportunity arose to crush a bishop they had shunned for at least fifteen years, suddenly discovered they were, after all, faithful to Rome. Fortunately, in this battle for the faith in minds and hearts there were groups of laypeople, or individual laity, who were keeping the flame alive. (Balthasar had in mind especially some of the young French academics who collaborated with the journal *Communio*.)

As for Switzerland, he compared the Church's situation to the becalmed vessel in Joseph Conrad's short story *The Shadow Line*. Dead calm, with stress on both syllables. As a good Swiss, Balthasar thought the introduction of a more democratic way of doing things could help the 'circulation of blood' in the Church – but only if there is a spiritual re-awakening and the Church does not drown first in a sea of paper. He lamented the lack of awareness of the existence of the 'great tradition of Christian meditation'. Swiss Retreat houses had become centres of dilettantish aping of yoga and Zen, aiming to give in five hours a wisdom it took Asiatic masters a lifetime to achieve. How could such places, then, be 'centres of radiation' for Christian holiness? And the sort of religious education currently offered in schools – occupied at best with 'friendly ethical and where possible ecumenical things which, so to say, make possible a respectable Christian or at least bourgeois life', how can this elicit such holiness, or indeed vocations to the priesthood come to that?[51] A rather specific account of liturgical abuses follows, and a more allusive mention of the deficiencies of the seminaries. Balthasar found in Switzerland *ein wildgewordener Klerus*, 'a clergy run wild'. What is to be done? He 'well understands' people who no longer go to the churches. But that is not the answer. The answer is to 'go to the centre' where alone there is 'light'. He encourages the faithful laity to use what Newman had called their 'prophetical office' to make the bishops listen. For their part, the clergy must learn or re-learn Christian contemplation to be able to pass it on to their parishes. In such contemplation each discovers personally how they are 'sinners before the merciful grace of God in Christ', and so can rediscover the sacrament of repentance, Confession.[52]

Fortunately, the Lord is still dispensing charisms: Balthasar mentions with great warmth the founder of *Communione e Liberazione*, the Milanese priest Luigi Giussani, and that movement's houses in the Ticino where the theologian of canon law, Eugenio Correcco, soon to be bishop of Lugano, was their great supporter. (By the time of Balthasar's death, the Italian-speaking canton provided his main following in the Swiss church.) In such, the Church lives and is young again. Balthasar's call to action was 'Not traditionalistic,

51 *Ibid.*
52 *Ibid.*, p. 12.

not progressive, but simply Catholic!'[53] He had hope, then, in 'our Christian and Catholic people who ... in the confusion of clerics and theologians ... have the absolute duty to care for the condition of Catholicity, by protest if need be'.[54] (He explained how in Salzburg he had helped the philosopher Professor Robert Spaemann to initiate a petition to do just that.) Of course this presupposes that a significant number of the faithful, whether highly educated or less so, do have a right feeling for the 'proportions' of the faith.

For individuals to find personal solutions does not suffice. Christianity is irreducibly communitarian with claims to make on society at large. The theologians of Latin America have this much at least correct: it is mystical and political at once. Unsurprisingly, this address, and its various published forms, did not make Balthasar popular in all Catholic quarters in Switzerland. Through such media as a conversation with Michael Albus in *Herder-Korrespondenz* his disillusion with Catholic liberalism was also becoming known abroad.

> The Church seems to me to be a little like a watering-can with a hole in it. When the gardener comes to the flower-bed which he wishes to water there is nothing left within. The Church reflects too little on the [parable of the] treasure in the field. She has sold much. But has she really got the treasure in return? She has descended into the valley of democracy. But can she still be the city on the hilltop?[55]

In other ecclesial milieux, such telling the emperor he had no clothes was, by contrast, a message people delighted to hear.

John Paul II on Balthasar

We 'fast forward' now to a very different moment in modern Church history at which indeed Rahner's judgment that Balthasarian thought would have a great future was vindicated. And this is 23 June 1984 when Pope John Paul II made Balthasar the first recipient of the International Paul VI Prize for contributions to Catholic thought. At the risk of attenuating the dramatic contrast this reversal of fortune involved, in all fairness I must mention some inbetween-times straws blowing in the wind. In 1965, the year when Rahner put into print his thoughts on Balthasar's neglect, the theology faculties of the Universities of Münster and Fribourg (both Catholic) and Edinburgh (Barthian Protestant) gave Balthasar honorary doctorates to mark his sixtieth birthday, while the patriarch Athenagoras of Constantinople awarded him the 'Golden Cross' of Mount Athos for his services to Greek patristics. In 1969 Paul VI had ended what many would consider Balthasar's ecclesial isolation by making him a member of the International Pontifical Theological Commission founded in the wake of the Second Vatican Council. And in 1972, he became the prime mover in the setting up of a prestigious journal the *International Catholic Review: Communio*. (It appears in a number of European languages; its English language version is edited in Washington.) But, in

53 'Zur Überwindung der kirchlichen Flaute', *Vaterland* (Lucerne) 150, 1 July 1978, p. 3.
54 *Ibid.*
55 'Geist und Feuer. Michael Albus: Ein Gespräch mit Hans Urs von Balthasar', *Herder-Korrespondenz* 30 (1976), pp. 72–82, and here at p. 78.

terms of Balthasar's ecclesial standing, none of these events compares with his singling out by John Paul II for this unique award.

It is of interest, I think, to know what the pope said on that occasion and how Balthasar responded to it. Granted that Balthasar *might* have been called to the Council but was passed over, choosing him as the first recipient of a theological prize in honour of the principal pope of the Council, Paul VI, could be said to involve a little papal explaining.

In his speech, John Paul II expressed the hope that the expression of esteem involved would 'comfort' Balthasar for 'the toil [he had] carried out'. In these words there is surely at least the ghost of a suggestion of making amends.[56] Balthasar's reflection on the work of 'Fathers, theologians, mystics' had entailed, said the pope, placing his

> vast knowledge at the service of an *intellectus fidei* which would be able to show modern man the splendour of the truth which flows from Jesus Christ.

Like all the sciences, John Paul II went on, theology is a service to truth, that truth which is ultimately a reflection of or even a sharing in God himself, citing St Thomas's commentary on John: there is 'one absolute Wisdom which by its essence is truth, namely that divine being by whose truth all true things are true'.[57] That citation certainly sums up Balthasar's principal foray into philosophy, the 1947 study *Wahrheit*, 'Truth', which later became the opening volume of his theological logic. But, John Paul continued, theology is more specifically a service to revealed truth. 'This does not', he said:

> impede nor even compromise the scientific nature of research, but directs it in an original way and gives it a value which the other sciences do not possess.

And John Paul II proceeded to express that additional value in a way that is definitely congruent with Balthasar's writing if not necessarily shaped by it.

> The truth studied by the theologian is not the fruit of a conquest of his, but the gift which God, in his inscrutable and wonderful plan of love, has made to men by manifesting himself principally through the sacred humanity of Jesus Christ, who is the Mediator and the fulness of all revelation.

What is surely distinctively Balthasarian is when Pope John Paul proceeded to remark that theology's exploration of revealed truth serves it by uncovering, and to the degree possible expressing, that revealed truth's 'harmony', 'unity' and 'beauty'. The choice of those three qualities – harmony, unity, beauty – thus strung together, can hardly be an accident.

In keeping with not only Balthasar's attitude but also the response of his Protestant mentor Karl Barth to the situation of modern-day theology, were John Paul II's succeeding comments which highlight the centrality of respect for and fidelity to the revealed divine Word in the theological enterprise. As he declared:

---

56 'Hans Urs von Balthasar has placed his knowledge at the service of the truth which comes from God', *L'Osservatore romano* 23 July 1984, pp. 6–7, and here at p. 6.

57 Thomas Aquinas, *In Evangelium Johannis*, 1, *lectio* I, no. 33.

No means to which the theologian turns for research, and no revision of
the epistemological structure of theology are acceptable if they do not
fully respect divine truth. No interpretation must ever forget the
supernatural character and the transcendent origin of revealed truth.[58]

For the first time since his opening remarks John Paul mentioned Balthasar
by name when he ascribed to him a special role in reminding theologians that
theology must proceed not only from wonder at the marvellous deeds of God
but also from contemplative praying through the intensification of faith.
Underwriting Balthasar's concept of *betende Theologie*, 'praying theology', or
théologie à genoux, 'theology on one's knees', the pontiff quoted, perhaps
significantly, not the essays in Balthasar's essay collection *Verbum caro*, on
fundamental theology, which deal with this, nor his book on contemplative
prayer, *Das betrachtende Gebet*, another obvious source, but Balthasar's brief
critique of Rahner's notion of anonymous Christianity, *Cordula oder der
Ernstfall*, 'Cordula, or the Crucial Test'.[59] Furthermore, John Paul made his
own Balthasar's maxim that theology and spirituality, when these two are
rightly seen, are indivisible.

In his conclusion, Pope John Paul II emphasized the ecclesial mission of
theologians. Theology is not the 'free practice of just any profession'.[60] Its
ecclesial mission entails that the theologian attend to three dimensions. The
first such dimension is the past. That means: Sacred Tradition, the understanding of revealed truth that has been growing, under the Spirit's gui-
dance, in the Church's history. The second dimension is the present: the
theologian must seek to support the Church in the faith she professes today.
That might lead one to suppose that the third dimension would be the future,
some version of which some Catholic theologians seem to prefer to inhabit.
But actually the pope named as the third dimension requiring the theologian's attention what he termed human experience in the concrete, which
means, he explained, a constructive, but critical, dialogue with modern culture. Of all of these, by implication, he found Balthasar a model to be
followed.

Lastly, as one would expect in a speech devised by a pope and curia, this
ecclesial vocation of theology is said to constitute a service also to the
magisterium of the Church. Citing *Lumen Gentium* 25, bishops too are doctors, if not in the same sense as theologians. The relation of bishops and
theologians should be complementary not antagonistic. Theology helps the
magisterium when it follows it; when it accompanies it; and also when it
precedes it, looking for new paths. It is above all in this last case – when
theology is seeking out new modes of thought – that the theologian should
(in John Paul's words):

take care to unite closely in his heart both the filial devotion of the
disciple and the desire to know ever better and to penetrate more

---

58 'Hans Urs von Balthasar has placed his knowledge at the service of the truth that comes
   from God', *art. cit.*, p. 6.
59 *Cordula oder der Ernstfall* (Einsiedeln, 1966); ET *The Moment of Christian Witness* (New
   York, 1968).
60 'Hans Urs von Balthasar has placed his knowledge at the service of the truth that comes
   from God', *art. cit.*, p. 7.

deeply into the intelligence of the revealed mystery transmitted in the living Tradition of the Church.[61]

Balthasar on Balthasar

How, then, did Balthasar respond? We cannot assume that he had seen this text beforehand, so perhaps 'response' is not the best word. How at any rate did he choose to present himself and his thought at an occasion which clearly represented a turning-point in his fortunes in the Church?

Balthasar began by saying that he conceived his work as simply initiated, not completed. It fell, he explained, into three stages of which the first was for him personally the most important. At his priesting, his Ordination card showed the beloved disciple, St John, embraced by Jesus. The motto beneath was *benedixit, fregit, deditque*: 'he blessed, broke and gave'. The 'breaking', of which, he said, he had had a premonition, came when he was obliged by what he called a 'formal order from St Ignatius' (who had of course died in 1556), to leave his spiritual home, the Society, 'in order [as he put it] to realize a kind of extension of his ideal in the world'.[62] Then it was that St John – he means the beloved disciple – was shown to 'us' – the plural form there certainly indicates Adrienne von Speyr and himself – as the ideal disciple of Jesus. 'Ideal' disciple in what sense? In as many as five senses, judging by the way Balthasar speaks.

First, it was John who grasped that in the community of disciples obedience is based on the Son who by his own obedience revealed the Blessed Trinity. Secondly, John was the disciple who realized that light has to penetrate darkness to its very depths – almost certainly a reference to the Balthasarian–von Speyrian theme of the Descent into Hell and the spirituality they based upon it. Thirdly, it was to this disciple, John, that the Crucified entrusted the spotless Church in Mary. In other words, this disciple alone was given to understand the nature of the bond that makes Mary what Balthasar elsewhere, writing jointly with Joseph Ratzinger, called the 'primal Church'. John stands at the fountainhead of the profoundly Marian inspiration of Balthasar's own thinking about the Church. Fourthly, the 'Gospel of love' which John was inspired to write culminates in an 'apotheosis of Peter': that is, in a high doctrine of the primacy of the apostle Peter as chief shepherd of the Church, archetype of the Roman pontiffs: 'Feed my lambs, feed my sheep' (John 21.15, 17). Finally, from the third and fourth of these considerations Balthasar drew the conclusion that John, while deliberately keeping himself out of the limelight, unites Mary and Peter, and it is by this title that Balthasar and von Speyr made him the patron of the *Johannesgemeinschaft* or Institute of St John that they founded. So what Balthasar is saying is that, from the word 'go', his vocation had been to found with Adrienne that common work. Towards the end of his life Balthasar became anxious that people were increasingly writing about his theology – but without sufficient reference to her

The second phase of his life – perhaps 'theme' would be a better word

---

61 *Ibid*.
62 'Address of Hans Urs von Balthasar', *ibid*.

because the 'stages' concerned are hardly arranged in strict chronological order – involves his translating activity. We have already seen the range of this so there is no need to follow Balthasar in his summary of it. Let us note, however, that he gives two rationales for it, one general and the other more specific. The general purpose of this plethora of translations, whether anthologies of texts or entire books, was what he called

> to make as concrete as possible the meaning of catholicity by the translation of what, in the great theological tradition, seemed to me should be known and assimilated by the Christian of today.[63]

Balthasar had sought, then, to extend the initiative of Henri de Lubac, whose great work 'Catholicism. On the Social Aspects of Dogma', had not only included all aspects of dogma worth mentioning, far beyond the issue of solidarity in creation and redemption (the 'social aspects' the subtitle had in view), but devoted over half its space to a choice of texts from various epochs and languages illustrative of its range. Balthasar's second reason for his translating activity was more specific if also more obscure. He considered the task of making known the 'most spiritual among our brothers and sisters' – he means his fellow Christians of past and present – to be very much in the spirit of St John, who is called, above all in the Greek Christian tradition, *ho theologos*, 'the theologian'. What does this mean? It is a somewhat vatic pronouncement, but we can certainly say that both brotherhood (and so by extension sisterhood) and knowing God in Jesus Christ are high on the list of priorities of the Gospel and Epistles of St John. Possibly that is all Balthasar wanted to say.

And so on to the third stage or rather theme, which is what he terms, 'my own poor books'. Here, unlike in those books, he was brief. They exemplify, he told the pope, three aims. First, he wanted to demonstrate the uniqueness of Jesus Christ, and to show in the way that he did so how all philosophical anthropology – all reflective, natural study of man – culminates in him, and culminates more especially in the way Jesus Christ enables us to transcend our mortal birth by a new birth to 'immortal Trinitarian life'. Showing that would necessarily have the effect of fusing together again theology and spirituality whose disassociation he called in strong language 'the worst disaster that ever occurred in the history of the Church'. Secondly, and more simply, he wanted to overcome theological fragmentation by showing the unity of all the theological treatises – he means by that the compartmental tractates into which Scholastic theology, even restricting oneself to its dogmatics, had come to be divided. Thus, no Christology without Trinitarian theology and vice versa; no Incarnation without the Paschal Mystery and vice versa; none of these without the history of salvation from Abraham to the Church and vice versa. Thirdly and finally, he aimed to show by his writings that the evangelical Counsels – what later became the vows of the Religious life – contain no flight from the world. On the contrary, they involve dedication to the world's salvation by following Christ and imitating his Eucharistic self-giving. This seems a relatively restricted theme to be allotted a third of his rationale for so extensive a theological corpus. But the reason is of course that he wanted once again to justify the establishment

---

63 *Ibid.*, p. 8.

with Adrienne of the *Johannesgemeinschaft* and to end with a reminder of that topic.

We do not know what John Paul II made of the address, except insofar as it can be inferred from his naming Balthasar a cardinal four years later, in June 1988. But on 26 June, three days before he was to be instituted cardinal, this massive figure, giant in the Catholic landscape, died at Basle. Fittingly. After all, it was the city not only of Barth but of Adrienne von Speyr.

PART ONE: SOURCES

2

ᵒᵍ✿ᵧᵒ

Divine Predecessors: the Fathers of the Church

How can we characterize Balthasar as 'interpreter of the theology of the Church Fathers' – to borrow the subtitle of a splendid monograph on this topic?[1] This is a study by perhaps the most distinguished German Balthasar scholar, the Jesuit Werner Löser, and its title – enthusiastically sanctioned, we are told, by Balthasar himself – reads 'In the Spirit of Origen.' So here we have another guiding thread through the labyrinthine ways of Balthasar's many-corridored theological home.

Balthasar's approach to the Fathers

As Löser points out, Balthasar's approach to the Fathers – more pompously, his 'hermeneutic' of the patristic texts – is not the customary one of modern patrology, that subdivision of contemporary academic scholarship. Really, that approach cannot be understood without some grasp of his theological position, because important elements in his approach derive from, notably, says Löser, his 'Christocentric doctrine of grace'.[2] And if Henri de Lubac greatly influenced Balthasar's reading of the Fathers, this cannot be the least of the reasons why. On the whole, progressive theology in modern Western Catholicism has adopted de Lubac's 'gentle harmonization of grace and nature' but sorely neglected the way de Lubac underscores the 'newness and transforming nature of God's revelation in Christ'.[3] (This is, of course, one reason why such theology drifts ever further from the Fathers.) For his part, de Lubac would ascribe to Balthasar a real 'connaturality' with patristic thought. While aware of the limitations of each patristic writer he discussed and even, in certain respects, of their age as a whole, he nonetheless, so de Lubac judged, made their vision his own.[4]

Balthasar was no less informed about the sheerly historical dimension of the subject than other patrologists. His principal aim, however, is to show the

---

1 W. Löser, *Im Geiste des Origenes. Hans Urs von Balthasar als Interpret der Theologie der Kirchenväter* (Frankfurt, 1976).
2 *Ibid.*, p. 3.
3 C. Steck, SJ, *The Ethical Thought of Hans Urs von Balthasar* (New York, 2001), p. 99.
4 H. de Lubac, 'Un témoin dans l'Eglise: Hans Urs von Balthasar', in *idem, Paradoxe et mystère de l'Eglise* (Paris, 1967), p. 200.

value of the patristic testimonies for contemporary Catholic theology. To this end he makes use of what Löser calls a 'theological phenomenology', which does not simply register and analyse historical data but, using a higher measure than the historical-critical method, seeks to identify the holistic form whereby particular aspects of the thought of this or that Church Father are held together as a unity. To present the morphology of a living organism is more than to offer a biochemical analysis of the same.[5] And so, for example, in his anthology of Origen texts, Balthasar claimed to have, as it were, re-composed the face of Origen from the pieces of a mosaic.[6] Again, in the foreword he explained his Maximus book as 'an attempt to grasp intuitively, and to make visible, the shape of his ideas'.[7] And in his exploration of Gregory of Nyssa's writing, he formulated his entire programme of patristic research in terms of 'penetrating to the vital source of [the] spirit of [any given Father], to what directs the entire expression of their thought'.[8] Here, however, a definite theologico-dogmatic option enters in. Since for Balthasar, under first de Lubac's influence and then Barth's, *Jesus Christ* is the centre and foundation of all creation, we can expect Balthasar's ideal reconstructions of patristic theological forms to seek out this key dimension and tease out its implications.

The virtues of the Fathers

For Balthasar the phrase 'the virtues of the Fathers' signifies in particular – here I echo Löser – three things. First, Balthasar stresses the shared sense among the Fathers of the 'positivity of the finite'. The Fathers of the Church had a firm commitment to the goodness of the finite realm – something Balthasar had himself learned, before beginning his patristic studies, in poetic guise from Claudel and more philosophically from Przywara. In Przywara, the goodness of the finite appears as the interplay of essence and existence, of what Przywara calls *Sosein*, being just so, and *Dasein*, being there at all. That interplay confers ontological richness and depth on each and every finite thing while at the same time also pointing to the creature's dependence on God. How pointing? Just because there *is* an interplay of this kind – for a creature, unlike for God, essence is not the same as existence (it is not a creature's essence *to be*) – we are shown every thing's contingency, its not having to be around at all. This is of course the famous 'real distinction' between essence and existence so much prized in the Thomist school. Through the act of existence, a creature's essence is always something received, and this implies, for Balthasar, its temporality. Such temporality is not a negative thing, as Platonism customarily supposed. Rather is it in its own fashion a 'reflection, similitude and imitation of eternal being', precisely

5 W Löser, *Im Geist des Origenes, op. cit.*, p. 11.
6 *Origenes. Geist und Feuer. Ein Aufbau aus seinen Werken* (Salzburg, 1938; 1952, 2nd edition), p. 16. There is an English translation: *Origen. Spirit and Fire: a thematic anthology of his writings* (Washington, 1984).
7 *Kosmische Liturgie. Das Weltbild Maximus' des Bekenners, op. cit.*, p. 12; ET *Cosmic Liturgy. The Universe according to Maximus the Confessor* (San Francisco, 2003), p. 25.
8 *Présence et pensée. Essai sur la philosophie religieuse de Grégoire de Nysse* (Paris, 1942), p. xi. Again, this work has an English translation: *Presence and Thought. The Religious Philosophy of Gregory of Nyssa* (San Francisco, 1995).

in the latter's overflowing life:[9] thus Balthasar in the opening volume of his theological logic, which, in its original version, is more or less contemporary with his patristic monographs. Now if grace truly builds on nature and does not mar it, then this same dynamic structure will surely be taken up by the grace of Christ.[10] To look hard for this theme in reconstructing patristic thought is, clearly enough, to approach the Fathers with the benefit of Thomist hindsight. The same is true when Balthasar adds that the *disponibilité* of creaturely being is at its profoundest a capacity to be disposed for possibilities that transcend the creaturely realm altogether: the famous 'obediential potency' much stressed in Scholastic thought.[11]

Still on the theme of the 'positivity of the finite', we can say more about what Balthasar both discovered from and read into the patristic corpus. In Balthasar's scanning of the Fathers, a key notion is the way man is so very finite that he must seek his completion from beyond himself, from an absolute (and hence capitalized) Freedom. This is really the conclusion, insofar as it has one, of his early work on the eschatology theme in the German poets and philosophers, *Apokalypse der deutschen Seele*.[12] The soul must undergo a conversion by which it recognizes the sovereign freedom of God, or what Balthasar's earliest theological essay, 'Patristik, Scholastik und wir', called the divine *Abstiegsbewegung*, God's movement of descending love. So it is that the soul comes to see itself as God sees it.[13] That explains how Balthasar regards the eros/agape distinction which has earned patristic thought so much disapproval from, especially, Lutherans. 'Eros', desiring love, is a codeword for our striving for the Infinite.[14] By itself it cannot save us. It is too affected by sin. The divine agape, God's charity, by contrast, *can* save us, and yet it does not do so without reference to the eros which is our yearning for God and in its own way an image of the divine loving, God's longing for us. So agape must fulfil eros, not replace it. That – the subject, incidentally, of *Deus Caritas est*, the first encyclical of a papal disciple of Balthasar's, Joseph Ratzinger – is a really important point in Balthasar's espousal of the Greek Fathers in particular. As he would write in *A Theology of History*, speaking of the biblical revelation:

> The 'bodily' union of humanity with God made present in it has been, in a manner beyond all comprehension, presented to us in terms of *eros*,

---

9 *Wahrheit. Wahrheit der Welt* (Einsiedeln, 1947), p. 220.

10 See on this *idem*, 'Patristik, Scholastik und wir', *Theologie der Zeit* 3 (1939), pp. 65–104, ET 'The Fathers, the Scholastics, and Ourselves', *Communio* 24 (1997), pp. 377–96; also, 'Analogie und Dialektik. Zur Klärung der theologischen Prinzipienlehre Karl Barths', *Divus Thomas* 22 (1944), pp. 171–216.

11 'Analogie und Natur. Zur Klärung der theologischen Prinzipienlehre Karl Barths', *ibid.*, 23 (1945), pp. 3–56.

12 *Apokalypse der deutschen Seele*, III. *Die Vergöttlichyng des Todes* (Salzburg, 1939), p. 324.

13 For an account of this essay see A. Nichols, OP, *Scattering the Seed. A Guide through Balthasar's Early Writings on Philosophy and the Arts* (London, 2006), pp. 17–32.

14 For an especially fine statement, see 'Eros und Caritas', *Seele* 21 (1939), p. 154: Eros is 'the general push to break open one's narrow, egoistic sphere and to fly out so as to give oneself to something greater than oneself, to forget oneself and one's poverty in donating oneself to some exalted, attractive, captivating being or aim'.

as the fulfilment of what the Song of Songs had celebrated long before – existence as a 'bridal state'.[15]

A second theme in Balthasar's appreciation of the Fathers is his feeling for the Fathers' distinctive epoch in the succession of times and seasons in the Christian dispensation. The Fathers have a distinctive *Zeitalter*, and it is high in value. Balthasar was wary of Hegel's necessitarian presentation of the dialectically progressive character of the passing of time. (In *Apokalypse der deutschen Seele*, at the end of his account of Kant's eschatology, he found the origins of what he most distrusted about German Idealism in the Idealists' turning Kant's doctrine of Providence into a speculative system about development in history.) But on the other hand, he also disapproved of historical positivism, for which history is 'just one damn thing after another'. His idea of historical epochs as 'temporal forms' (*Zeitgestalten*) was an attempt to steer between these opposing perils. Hints of it can be found in a very early (1928) essay on the art of fugue – in the rhythm of history certain high points furnish measuring-rods for later times.[16]

What that meant to Balthasar is plain from 'Patristik, Scholastik und wir'. The Church, he wrote there, enters the pagan world

> with a maximum of direct, glowing Christian life and instinctive assurance about what is true and determinative for the Christian reality.[17]

This would seem to set Balthasar straightaway on the side of the pure neo-patristic theologians in the incipient debate over 'la nouvelle théologie' already beginning in the later 1930s. But in point of fact, he draws up a balance sheet of loss and gain in a very unpartisan fashion. Emerging as the predominant factor on the debit side is what he perceives as the threat posed by the Platonism of the Fathers to the 'fundamental law' of incarnational Christianity. There are lesser warnings too about the undesirability of an over-enthusiastic embrace of the early Fathers and ecclesiastical writers. Many in the ante-Nicene period (before 325) used formulae which should be regarded as quite *dépassé* and even, in the light of later standards, heterodox. The struggle with the great heresies – Gnosticism, Montanism, Arianism, Nestorianism, Monophysitism, Manichaeanism, Donatism – led the Church of this epoch to restrict the arena for acceptable speculation ever more tightly. Yet, on the credit side, let us not overlook the positive greatness of a period to which all subsequent generations in the Church are in permanent debt. With the help of the Ecumenical Councils, spiritual building goes on that provides foundations for all later Christian theology, and, to change the metaphor from architecture to aquatics, with a fullness from the source that will never be attained again. Nourished by Scripture, patristic doctrine unfolds the content of revelation with marvellous directness. This is the springtime of the Church in the world, a *Jugendzeit* filled with immediacy of response. In Athanasius, Basil, Cyril, Chrysostom, Ambrose, Augustine, life and teaching were one reality. And so the first, the greatest and the most

15 *Theologie der Geschichte* (Einsiedeln, 1959); ET *A Theology of History* (New York and London, 1963), p. 119.
16 'Die Kunst der Fuge', *Schweizerische Rundschau* 28 (1928), pp. 84–87.
17 'Patristik, Scholastik und wir', *art. cit.*, p. 84.

taxing struggle with the spiritual–intellectual powers of paganism was won. All succeeding generations of thinkers, preachers, mystics, must go back to the fountains of the Fathers, to drink and be strengthened.[18]

A final theme to be mentioned, by way of preamble to Balthasar's use of the Fathers, is the 'universality of the catholic', to which, on his reading of the main lines of patristic writing, they bore witness. Here Balthasar was deeply indebted to de Lubac's *Catholicisme*, which had treated patristic theology in just this spirit.[19] Christ is the heart of the world, so no truth is alien to Christian truth, which alone is able to encompass all others. Though Balthasar had mastered the tools of patristic scholarship – and so could make breakthroughs in, for example, the dating and ascription of certain patristic texts, his *forte* will not be detailed historical reconstruction of the thought of the Fathers for its own sake, but the way their great themes can be exploited and integrated in an overall presentation of the faith as a truth so great that none greater can possibly be conceived.

And so on to Balthasar's actual treatment of the Fathers and early ecclesiastical writers themselves.

The Greek Apologists

The earliest he touches on are the Greek Apologists of the second century: Theophilus of Antioch, Athenagoras and the author of the *Letter to Diognetus*. An anthology of their writings emerged from his publishing house in 1958, equipped with suitable forewords both to the individual authors as well as to the group – one can hardly write 'school' – as a whole.[20] Despite the slimness of the literature, Balthasar finds useful lessons in the Christian apologetics of that early 'sub-apostolic' age. Balthasar admires them because, conscious of the 'universality of the Christian', they addressed a non-Christian environment by a twofold programme: arguing for some of the truths of the faith from valid elements already found in pagan thought, and presenting others as persuasively as possible. So they offer a combined apologetics and catechesis treading a *via media* between rationalism and supernaturalism.

> Narrow and shaking bridge! And yet it had to be traversed, between the two chasms of a rationalism of mere philosophy of religion and a supernaturalism that rejects the entire achievement of reason and ascribes access to God to faith alone.[21]

Despite the lack of much obvious Christology in these writings (though in the case of Theophilus that is almost certainly owing to the interrupted transmission of texts), Balthasar held they were motivated by the same Christocentricity as he himself had learned from de Lubac and Barth. And what is the evidence? Simply their awareness that Christ has conquered the world so thoroughly that now all pagan wisdom belongs to him and his Church. This produces not an attitude of condescension, *de haut en bas*, but a

---

18 I make use here of a passage from my *Scattering the Seed*, *op. cit.*, pp. 25–6.
19 H. de Lubac, *Catholicisme. Les aspects sociaux du dogme* (Paris, 1938).
20 *Griechischen Apologeten des zweiten Jahrhunderts* (Einsiedeln, 1958)
21 *Ibid.*, p. 62.

desire to take that pagan wisdom seriously, to engage with it on its own level.

Thus, for example, whereas *Theophilus* regards the revelation of the one true God as made possible only by the inspiration of the hagiographs, the authors of Holy Scripture, he treats certain elements of pagan philosophical thought as veridical even when they deal with the divinity. Sometimes the pagans have hit upon truths by chance; there may also, he thinks, have been borrowing from Hebrew sources. But Theophilus does not rule out – to Balthasar's evident approval – the idea that the best explanation for pagan truth lies in the status of human reason as a divine gift, with 'roots that are in some manner inspired'.[22] (Theophilus's attitude to the Sibylline prophecy suggests he does not restrict charismatic inspiration to biblical revelation either.)

Athenagoras wants to initiate an argument for the resurrection of the body philosophically. That too is fine with Balthasar. Far from implying that Athenagoras considered the resurrection to belong in the realm of 'pure nature', it testifies to his integrated view of reality as nature-under-grace. Instructed by de Lubac, once again Balthasar approves.

The unknown Alexandrian author who wrote the *Letter to Diognetus* appeals to a Balthasar wearing a different hat: Balthasar the co-founder with Adrienne von Speyr of the *Johannesgemeinschaft*. He and the ancient writer share an enthusiasm for 'holiness in the world'. But Balthasar is not content with the lack of dogmatic reference in the *Letter*'s famous account of Christians as the soul – the 'life and soul' one might almost say – of the social bodies where they are present. Christians cannot be 'life-giving and fruitful for the body'[23] in the way the *Letter* says they ought to be unless we factor into its account those ecclesiological and Christological dimensions which the comparison – Christians as soul of the social body – really requires. Christian universality needs a reference to the way the Church is poured into the world as the basis of a new humanity – the 'mystical body of Christ', and, beyond even that, something has to be said about the hypostatic union when the divine person of the Word inserts himself through the 'body' of his human nature into human reality as a whole. Balthasar will have nothing to do with a social ethics separated off from dogma.

Irenaeus

Still in the second century, we move on to a Church doctor from Roman Asia who ended his life in Gaul, as bishop of Lyons. Balthasar discovered St Irenaeus, perhaps the first Catholic theologian in the full sense – an overall presenter of divine revelation – during his study years at Lyons between 1933 and 1937. (At Lyons it was in any case impossible to avoid Irenaeus, whose patronage makes the holder of the bishopric there the honorary primate of the Church in France.) As early as 1943 he brought together a number of Irenaean texts in German translation, giving them the title: 'Irenaeus: the Patience of Ripeness'. If that title is somewhat oracular, the subtitle makes plain the spirit in which Balthasar approached this Christian from Roman

---

22 *Ibid.*, p. 26.
23 *Ibid.*, p. 92.

Asia who was martyred as bishop of Lyons in 202. The subtitle reads: 'The
Christian Answer to the Myth of the Second Century'.[24] In seeking to free
Christianity not only from misconstrual in an alien mythological system,
Gnosticism, but also from sometimes inappropriate Platonic clothing, Irenaeus performed, according to Balthasar, a service to the Church which
makes him a master of continuing importance. Irenaeus demonstrates the
positivity of the finite – and in that sense (Balthasar goes so far as to say) the
truth of the analogy of being – a concept of which, we can be fairly sure,
Irenaeus was quite innocent. Balthasar had no doubt that 'gnosis' – or what
he sometimes called 'gnostic pathos' – was alive and well in modern thought
and sensibility, even if historic Gnosticism was no more. Gnosis could be
found, he wrote, whenever someone sought to 'put in the place of redemption by the God who stoops down to enter the everyday world a self-
redemption through striving to leave that world behind'.[25] That had been his
conviction since his first theological attempt in 'Patristik, Scholastik und wir'.

The book was republished in expanded form in 1956 (and again in 1983,
with in between a second selection in 1981), while a more extended *précis* of
Irenaeus's theology – or, rather, what Balthasar found valuable in it, dating
from 1962, can be examined in the second volume of *Herrlichkeit*.[26] Since I
have dealt with the latter in my study of Balthasar's theological aesthetics *The
Word Has Been Abroad*,[27] it will suffice here to mention the great themes.
Irenaeus keeps united apologetics and dogmatics. He defends against the
Gnostics the structure of created being which in various respects – but all in
the name of spiritualization – they would tear apart. He affirms the earthly
world as not only created by the good God but the true locus of divine
salvation, and holds the two orders – creation and redemption – in unbroken
continuity. (In his early Irenaeus anthology Balthasar calls Irenaeus 'decid-
edly the father of the "realism" of Christian theology'.[28]) Temporality is to be
welcomed not shunned: it enables God to display in history his saving 'art'.
The many-levelled effect of divine acting comes to a perfect climax – Irenaeus's word was 'recapitulation' – in Jesus Christ. The Old Testament,
already pregnant with the Saviour, is at once fulfilled and surpassed in him.
With the founding of the *Catholica*, the emergence of the Church of Christ, we
have the final form of the saving history till earthly time ends. The second
volume of the theological dramatics will rehearse the way Irenaeus shows
the two freedoms, divine and human, as interacting, with divine agency so
invested as to save human agency from its self-ruin. A substantial appendix
on how Irenaeus sees these matters was included within that volume, and is
captured snapshot-wise in my study of the dramatics, *No Bloodless Myth*.[29]

These Irenaean themes are also typically Balthasarian, even though

24 *Irenäus. Geduld des Reifens. Die christliche Antwort auf den Gnostischen Mythos des zweiten
   Jahrhunderts* (Basle, 1943; Leipzig, 1983, 3rd edition). A modified selection of texts
   appeared as *Irenäus. Gott im Fleisch und Blut* at Einsiedeln in 1981, and has an English
   translation: *The Scandal of the Incarnation. Irenaeus against the Heresies* (San Francisco,
   1990).
25 *Irenäus. Geduld des Reifens, op. cil.*, p. 9.
26 *Herrlichkeit. Eine theologische Aesthetik. II. Fächer der Stile. 1.Teilband: Klerikale Stile* (Einsiedeln, 1962), pp. 33–94.
27 A. Nichols, OP, *The Word Has Been Abroad, op. cit.*, pp. 69–74.
28 *Irenäus. Geduld des Reifens, op. cit.*, p. 14.
29 A. Nichols, OP, *No Bloodless Myth, op. cit.*, pp. 68–69.

Balthasar regretted Irenaeus's chiliasm (millenarianism), as well as what he saw as his overly linear, insufficiently dramatic presentation of the relation between Old and New Covenants and – a somewhat anachronistic criticism! – lack of a precision tool-box for historical description. The desire to take seriously the historical events of the life of Israel, of Jesus, and of the apostolic generation joins modern historical critics to Irenaeus, even though at the same time their frequent anti-supernaturalism, and general prescinding from the Easter faith and the apostolic kerygma, distances them from him.

One or two students of Balthasar had noted, in brief format, the elective affinity that joined Balthasar to Irenaeus, not only in the theological aesthetics but in the dramatics too.[30] But a wider claim has also been made, at fuller length. Balthasar's whole project can be regarded as a Neo-Irenaean answer to modern Gnosticism, and (even more strongly) *was* by its author so regarded – totally counter to those critics of Balthasar who have found him a little too close to the Gnostics himself! For Kevin Mongrain:

> Balthasar granted Irenaeus of Lyons privileged status as the quintessential patristic figure whose theology is the standard by which all other patristic theologies should be judged.[31]

This Balthasar did, Mongrain's thesis runs, by reading Irenaeus through lenses supplied by Henri de Lubac, whose *Catholicisme* not only cemented Balthasar's primary bond to the Fathers but treated them as, essentially, apostles of an arch-sacramental Christianity proclaiming a God of incarnational paradox. With this commitment in place, Balthasar's chief intellectual *bêtes noires* could only be modern 'Gnostics': that is, any thinker who opposed the conjunction of eternity and time, matter and spirit, in Christ and his Church-body.

What Irenaeus adds more particularly to the patristic consensus is the theme of the *mutual glorification of God and man* seen as the saving revelation's whole purpose: a theme Mongrain calls 'reciprocal doxology'.[32] This powerfully sounded motif of reciprocal doxology Mongrain takes to be the basic conceptual scheme underlying Balthasar's entire trilogy which he qualifies accordingly as an exercise in 'doxa-logic'.[33]

That 'Ireneaean retrieval' is the only way to 'read' Balthasar's *oeuvre* considered as an exercise in neo-patristic theology may perhaps be doubted. Why, for example, in that case, to take one simple point, did Balthasar encourage Löser to call his survey of Balthasar's *patristica* 'In the Spirit of Origen'? If Mongrain is correct, should it not have been 'In the Spirit of

---

30 E. Falque, 'Hans Urs von Balthasar, lecteur d'Irénée ou la chair retrouvé', *Nouvelle Revue Théologique* 115. 5 (1993), pp. 683–98; K. Tortorelli, OFM, 'Some Notes on the Interpretation of St Irenaeus in the Works of Hans Urs von Balthasar', *Studia Patristica* XXIII (1989), pp. 284–88; *idem*, 'Balthasar and the Theodramatic Interpretation of St Irenaeus', *Downside Review* CXI (1993), pp. 117–26.

31 K. Mongrain, *The Systematic Theology of Hans Urs von Balthasar: an Irenaean Retrieval* (New York, 2002), p. 9.

32 *Ibid.*, p. 100.

33 *Ibid.*, p. 16.

Irenaeus'?[34] Likewise, I am by no means as sure as is Mongrain that the influence of Barth on Balthasar was so entirely a matter of simply confirming intuitions derived from de Lubac, or indeed that the influence of Adrienne von Speyr's mystical materials is so exaggerated, in a mood of misplaced chivalry, by Balthasar himself. The gradual process of assimilating Balthasar's work and its place among the circle of Catholic theologies will probably show, however, that Mongrain's fundamental intuition certainly has some truth. It is notable that in *Unser Auftrag*, looking back from the vantage-point of 1984 at his own intellectual and spiritual development, he places considerable emphasis on the way that little by little Augustine ceded first place in his patristic affections to a quartet of Greek Fathers of whom he placed Irenaeus first. If we are looking for the single most helpful manner in which to approach Balthasar's theology, considering his de Lubac-inspired appeal to Irenaeus is a major contender.

Origen: an approach

But let us forego rashness. In his book 'In the Spirit of Origen', Werner Löser, who has as good an acquaintance as anybody with Balthasar's corpus as a whole, wrote boldly, 'For Balthasar Origen is the key figure of all Greek patristic theology'.[35] This judgment hardly does more than echo Balthasar's own statement in an interview that Origen is his preferred 'interpreter and devotee [*Liebhaber*] of the Word of God'.[36] Half a decade before his 1943 anthology of passages from Irenaeus, he had translated large gobbets of Origen under the dramatic title 'Spirit and Fire',[37] and written a substantial essay on Origen's theological doctrine for a French academic journal. Not until two decades later, however, would he publish this in book form, choosing for its title another couplet of key words: 'Word and Mystery in Origen'.[38]

Balthasar belongs with an attempt by a number of patristically minded theologians in mid-twentieth-century French and German Catholicism to rehabilitate Origen. In his study of the seventh-century Greek Father Maximus the Confessor, Balthasar would write:

> Only if one keeps the entire phenomenon of Origen in mind – the fervent 'man of the Church' who died a martyr, the great lover of both the letter and the spirit of Holy Scripture, the daring theologian who tried to take everything good and positive that Greece and gnosis had conceived and to put it at the service of Christ's truth – only then can one understand how Origen can and must always be a source of new and fruitful inspiration for the Church's reflection.[39]

---

34 It must be admitted that Balthasar contrasts Origen with Irenaeus to the advantage of the latter in *The Scandal of the Incarnation, op. cit.*, p. 8. But that judgment concerns one issue only: the 'spiritualization' common, in very different ways, to Gnostic and Middle Platonist thought.

35 W. Löser, *Im Geist des Origenes, op. cit.*, p. 83.

36 M. Albus, 'Geist und Feuer. Ein Gespräch mit Hans Urs von Balthasar', *art. cit.*, p. 81.

37 Origenes, *Geist und Feuer, op. cit.*

38 'Le mystérion d'Origène', *Recherches de Science religieuse* 26 (1936), pp. 513–62; 27 (1937), pp. 38–64. The book version is *Parole et mystère chez Origène* (Paris, 1957).

39 *Cosmic Liturgy, op. cit.*, p. 33.

Origen had suffered posthumous condemnation at the Second Council of Constantinople, the fifth ecumenical Council, for his speculations, albeit tentatively expressed, on protology (the pre-existence, as he saw it, of the soul) and eschatology (a restoration to integrity of all things, including the damned). He was also criticized for his doctrine of God, notably his sharp differentiation of the life and activity of the Trinitarian persons. This reha-bilitation attempt in the lands bordering the Rhine was a movement which succeeded to the modest extent in getting some passages from Origen's writings inserted into the post-Conciliar Roman-rite Liturgy of the Hours. Western scholars were alert to the possibility – in fact, the likelihood – that some at least of the condemned texts from Justinian's Council were not Origen's at all, but reflected the positions of later, more radicalized, disciples. But any wider rehabilitation struck the rock of the implacable opposition of the Eastern Orthodox, awakening at Rome the determination not to give the East additional unnecessary offence.

Balthasar was quite aware that a 're-Catholicizing' of Origen would almost certainly entail a degree of purification of his texts and tenets, but he held that Origen's loyalty to the Church justified, morally and histori-cally, this retroactive operation. Much in his teaching survived, and, re-contextualized, did great Christian good. Not for nothing does Balthasar hail the doctrine of St Maximus the Confessor, the great synthesizer of tra-ditions among the later Greek fathers, as 'Chalcedonian Origenism'.[40]

Origen: Word and mystery

When Balthasar looked back at the Greek tradition, he could find no better pair of terms for what he had in common with the Egyptian master than 'Word' and 'mystery'.[41] These name, after all, the central realities with which any Christian has to do. Origen's faith, like that of many Christians, was in God's self-communication (his 'Word') and knowledge of that Word enabled Origen, as the Christian at large, to grasp reality as more wonderful, more inexhaustibly significant than we could ever have imagined (it is 'mystery').[42] Balthasar also had good reasons of his own for bringing together these two key terms – 'Word', 'mystery' – so understood.

In the first place, he wished to accept, on the Church's behalf, the chal-lenge laid down by Barth, whose formidable presence on the wider scene he had already registered in the 1930s, before their first encounter in Basle. Balthasar wanted, by a 'Christological concentration' modelled on Barth's, to show how Catholic writers too could display revelation's existential power and intellectual coherence through sustained and searching reference to the divine Word, the Word which became flesh in Jesus Christ and witnessed to itself in the Bible and in Christian proclamation. When he compared Origen's

40 *Ibid.*, p. 317.
41 *Parole et mystère chez Origène* (Paris, 1957).
42 I make use in this section of some material first published in French as 'Préface' in the re-printed: H. U. von Balthasar, *Parole et mystère chez Origène* (Geneva, 1998), pp. 5–9. All subsequent references to Balthasar's work of this title remain, however, references to the original edition.

style to a dry, hot desert wind, he had in mind Origen's utterly unsentimental passion for the Logos, the Word.[43]

But Balthasar rejected the view of some distinguished Protestant historical theologians who treated Origen's Logos-doctrine as quite unsacramental. Balthasar claimed, in fact, exactly the opposite. Since for Origen any creature can be a symbolic expression of the Logos, in incarnation the Word becomes his own symbol. As creature he becomes the symbol of his own divinity. As more specifically a *bodily* creature, he becomes in his bodiliness the symbol of the humanity he has assumed. Furthermore, when the God who is essentially unbounded by space and time takes on such – not only creaturely but bodily – expression, the influence he exerts through his body is not confined by that body's limits, as ours would be. The influence of the Word, specifically as incarnate, extends as far as the creation itself. St Thomas Aquinas will one day explain this by calling the bodily humanity of Jesus the 'conjoined instrument of the Word'.

Under this general heading of the (extended) sacramentality of the Logos we can also note the role the Church and Holy Scripture play in this context. The visible Church is the symbol of Christ's 'mystical' body – his indefinitely extensible body-mediated influence, while Scripture is at its own level a kind of incarnation where the Logos becomes present in the interrelationship of the literal and spiritual senses of the biblical text.

And, in the second place – moving now from 'Word' to 'mystery', along with other theologians committed to a 'return to the Fathers' Balthasar wished to recover, over against a too often dessicated and second-rate Scholasticism, that awareness of the Christian universe as satisfying heart and imagination, as well as reason, and drawing human beings to the heights of union with God, which was so pervasive a feature of the religious sensibility of the patristic age. Hence 'mystery': for, as another representative of *la nouvelle théologie*, Louis Bouyer, was to show, Christian *mysticism* is rooted in the Christian *mystery*.[44] Without detriment to the just demands of intelligibility, we must say that no logic compels the Logos in his self-manifestation, for even via an objective revelation (which the truth-system of Judaeo-Christianity certainly is), it is always a divine subjectivity – divine *personal* being – that – or rather *who* – addresses us.[45]

And yet of course Origen of Alexandria was not a twentieth-century dogmatic reconstructionist (like Barth and the theologians of *la nouvelle théologie* who were to some degree at least Balthasar's models). Origen was an ancient thinker whose concern was to take a – substantially modified – version of the Platonism that served as the vehicle for philosophical wisdom in his environment and put it together with the Holy Scriptures, commentary on which constituted as a catechist his daily work. 'Word' and 'mystery' will look somewhat different, accordingly, in Origen's writing from how Balthasar might present them in his own right. The wonder of *Parole et mystère chez Origène* is the intellectual and spiritual insight with which, from his own

---

43 *Geist und Feuer, op. cit.*, pp. 13–14.
44 L. Bouyer, *The Christian Mystery. From Pagan Myth to Christian Mystery* (ET Edinburgh, 1990).
45 *Parole et mystère chez Origène, op. cit.*, p. 10.

perspective, Balthasar scans Origen's corpus without ever tearing Origen unceremoniously from his own time and place.

Perhaps the key thing to note is that for Origen, as for Balthasar, the Word by his economic humiliation in becoming man, became man on two levels simultaneously – that of flesh, and that of spirit. The entry of the uncreated Logos into the realm of rational spirit, of which his embodiment in human flesh is the expression, renders his incarnate words and actions mysterious in a twofold way. If we are to understand them, we must first move from the 'letter' to the 'spirit', but then, in the second place, we must ascend from created spirit to Uncreated. And even then we have not finished, for the Logos, by his mediatorial role in God, would open to us the infinite space of the *Trias*, the Holy Trinity. History and mysticism, accordingly, are inseparable.

By the same token, the 'embodiment' which the Logos takes on earth must be understood in relation to the universal outreach of God's creative and salvific will. The 'body' of Christ, a multivalent term in both Origen and Balthasar, includes the Scriptures – the corpus (as we still significantly say) of literary texts to be actualized as discourse – which signalize his presence. It also takes in the Church – the social organism – which by predilection he makes the field of his action. The theologian, then, has the task of locating the richly manifold utterances of the Bible in the infinite concrete unity of the Logos. Origen did this by his allegorical exegesis. Balthasar will emulate him by the very different method of reconstituting the unity of revelation as a manifestation of God's amazing glory (aesthetics), of his liberating goodness (dramatics) and his saving truth (logic). The teaching that doctors of the Church dispense in the Church's name is 'Scripture in act' – as Balthasar puts it, paraphrasing one of Origen's homilies – and so Christ speaking to the world.

Balthasar was by no means uncritical, however, of even those aspects of Origen's thought which are in no way formally heterodox. He did not care for the predominance of 'ascending theology' in Origen's mental world. There is not enough *kenosis* in Origen for Balthasar's liking, not enough attention to the divine self-emptying in Incarnation, and its ethical implications for the mimetic discipleship of the Christian. For Balthasar there is nothing so badly wrong with Origen's doctrine of 'spiritualization', the evermore thorough penetrating of the Christian by the Spirit who opens to the soul infinite horizons, *so long as this remain firmly in the context of 'kenosis'*.[46]

Origen: a survey of useful themes

When Balthasar settles down to write his Origen study, approached along the lines suggested above, the themes he takes from this massive – if, through misplaced zeal, sadly truncated – corpus will be remarkably germane to his own mature theological work. We can swiftly enumerate those not already mentioned in my account of the spirit of Balthasar's approach. First, and very briefly: citing the Alexandrian thinker's *Commentary on John* as well as his

---

46 W. Löser, *Im Geist des Origenes, op. cit.*, p. 93.

masterpiece of apologetics, the *Contra Celsum*, Origen's is a metaphysics and mysticism of radiance, not darkness.[47] Balthasar makes the point so as to argue that, whatever his rhetoric of esoteric initiation might suggest, this is a thinker for whom the Christian reality flowers into light – just as Balthasar himself will present matters in the theological aesthetics. All being is, in an extended sense, sacramental: the open book of God.

But secondly, that does not mean we are excused the task of intellectual and moral effort. The right reader of God's first and most general revelation, creation, needs the sort of purification Plato spoke of in his *Seventh Letter*. How much more the recipient of God's second and specific, revelation, found in the Judaeo-Christian Scriptures, and the Tradition of the Church. Balthasar never doubted the cognitive role of such purification, or, to use the language of the Gospels, *conversion*. As he put it in an essay on 'Culture and Prayer', written in the same year as *Parole et mystère*: 'Meta-noia is the epistemological presupposition for the ability to hear the Word and follow it'.[48] All things are sacramental – but we must know them according to the Logos. The explanation, closely pertinent to the entire Trilogy of aesthetics, dramatics, logic, is subtle. All sensuous reality is a 'sign' and 'precursor' of spiritual being whose 'truth', in our apprehension of it, turns on the 'measure of its complete actuation in the order of the three transcendentals' – the good and the beautiful as well as the true.[49] All things should stimulate us to go beyond, in an 'ec-stasy' or standing outside ourselves which alone can lead to our 'en-stasy' or full appropriation of our own identity, which happens, so Origen remarks in the *Homilies on Jeremiah*, when 'our heart does not harden, but rises like incense towards the face of God'.[50] The universal 'openness' of spirit, feared by the pagan Greeks in their clinging to ordered limit, is as dear to Origen as to Balthasar who hails it as man's radical de-centring in favour of God, in a 'movement of transcendence that constitutes our person'.[51] Does the development entailed ever cease? Some Origen texts seem to say so, for faith, hope and the role of suffering, are so strongly underlined. But other passages indicate it is endless, even in eternity – linking Origen on this both backwards to Irenaeus and forwards to Gregory of Nyssa. These are not merely moral realities. Balthasar does not hesitate to speak on Origen's behalf of the 'ontological compenetration of the creature and God',[52] and lays out its contours in the ancient master's own rapturous images: that of 'spiritual senses and their entirely active passivity to receive the [divine] Light, Voice, Perfume, Taste'; that of spiritual nourishment, for as Origen remarks in his treatise on prayer, the Logos himself is our 'substantial bread';[53] and, above all, the imagery of 'nuptial union' – not just for certain advanced mystical states but for the most basic ontology of nature and grace – which Balthasar himself will do so much to re-launch in his own spiritual theology. For the Logos does not relate to us only as our transcendent term.

47 *Parole et mystère, op. cit.*, pp. 15–16, citing Origen's *In Ioannem commentarium* 2, 23, and *Contra Celsum* 7, 44.
48 *Kultur und Gebet* (Frankfurt am Main, 1957), p. 3.
49 *Parole et mystère*, p. 20.
50 Origen, *In Jeremiae librum homiliae* 6, 6.
51 *Parole et mystère*, p. 21.
52 *Ibid.*, p. 25.
53 Origen, *De oratione* 27.

By his own good pleasure, he freely communicates himself to us, to become immanently one with us, as he chooses. That is why each soul must always be ready, listening. Adrienne von Speyr will confirm the key role here given to 'preparedness', *Bereitschaft*. (It is *always* why for Balthasar Christian theology remains utterly dependent on the Word of God – God's speaking, or his silence.)

The third theme Balthasar selects from Origen's corpus is the centrality of the Incarnation, and, within the Incarnation, the Paschal Mystery. Balthasar approves of the way Origen contextualizes his account of salvation in a general anthropology of man in relation to God: he will emulate him in his own *A Theological Anthropology*, the well-chosen title for the American translation of *Das Ganze im Fragment*. For Origen, creation is first and fore-most of spirits (angelic and human), and only the souls that have ceased to live in spirit as iron in fire – red-hot in enthusiasm for their creative Archetype – enter on the carnal pilgrimage which will be, however, their way home. The economy of the flesh is thus not only a sign of punishment, it also indicates a hope of remedy. True, 'the Word of Life who is Charity' can speak within us, adapting himself to the needs of each type of recipient, and indeed of each recipient. (Balthasar regards Origen's account of the differentiation of the Word in his self-presentation to individuals as an answer in advance to the call for a more 'existential' theology in his own time.[54]) But the Word does not save created spirit except through the medium of flesh. Balthasar sums up the message of various homilies by Origen on the Old and New Testaments when he writes:

> This is why the Image, the divine Word, having pity on those who were like him, took on this fallen flesh, so as to purify it in his purity, to transform the carnal body into his incorruptible pneumatic body, and embraced the material world in the spiritual fire of his holocaust.[55]

By his Resurrection, as Origen comments on the sacrificial system of the Jews in the Book of Leviticus, he 'climbed up to the heavens whither fire by its nature is directed'. The 'holocaust of his flesh offered on the wood of the Cross united earthly things to heavenly, human things to things divine'.[56] Everything Origen has to say about Scripture and the Eucharist, the Church and Baptism, must be related to this flaming centre – as Balthasar will seek to do in his own fundamental theology, ecclesiology and theology of the sacraments.

Placing these motifs side by side might well lead us to think that, fourthly, Balthasar will find in Origen a paradigmatic account of the desirable com-plementarity of objective and subjective in Christian faith, life and thought. And so it proves. As he writes apropos of Origen's theology of the Euchar-istic presence and Holy Communion – the realism of which he has just stoutly defended:

> The Logos is only present in act in hearts ready to hear him. That is the locus in the doctrine of the Mystery of the crucial role of 'subjectivity', so broadly developed in his admirable teaching on the inner senses and

54 *Parole et mystère*, p. 36.
55 *Ibid.*, p. 44.
56 Origen, *In Leviticum homiliae* 1, 4.

the discernment of spirits. Without this complement, the 'objective' theology of the Mystery would be deficient.[57]

Balthasar's theology of the saints, like the ecclesiology developed above all in the final volume of the theological logic, will manifest the same desire to do justice *both* to the givenness of the objective, public, embodied economy of salvation *and* to the subjective, inner, invisible economy of grace which is its necessary 'complement'. The notion of the vital interrelation of the 'objective' hierarchy of office and the 'subjective' hierarchy of charismatic holiness issues from Balthasar's – strongly 'Catholicizing' – interpretation of Origen of Alexandria.[58]

Gregory of Nyssa: An aim in view

The fourth-century Cappadocian doctor Gregory of Nyssa is the next of the figures Balthasar tackled as he set out on his trilogy of Greek patristic studies – Origen, Gregory, Maximus. Until the 1920s and 30s, Gregory's writings had received little attention from textual critics. From that standpoint Balthasar calls them, with some exaggeration, 'the most neglected of all the patristic era'. Though German classicists were making reparation, the complaint is the more pointed if we can believe his claim that Gregory was 'the most profound philosopher of the Christian age', as well as an 'incomparable mystic and poet'.[59] Nyssa combines the 'essential' – philosophical investigation of the concepts that encapsulate the nature of things, and the 'existential' – the drama of lived existence.

When Balthasar remarks that, so far, students of Gregory have only done justice to the 'essential', whereas *he* is going to devote at least as much attention to the 'existential', he is announcing a project in Greek patristics comparable to the one the historian of mediaeval philosophy Etienne Gilson was carrying out at the same time for the Latin Scholastics.[60] Just as Gilson tried to prove that Aquinas was an 'Existentialist' *avant la lettre*, so Balthasar will do the same for Nyssa. At the time, Gilson was emphasizing the way the God of St Thomas is Pure Act and therefore beyond our conceptual grasp. So likewise Balthasar emphasizes Gregory's statement in *Contra Eunomium* 12 that God is 'wholly energetic and action', *holon energês kai praxis*, for which reason the knowing soul fails to grasp the infinite divine life. Gilson did not hide the complementary fact that, for Aquinas, the divine essence can be properly 'named' by its attributes (above all, through its identification with self-existent being, 'I Am who Am', the 'metaphysics of Exodus' [3.14]). So likewise Balthasar admits the way that, in Gregory's thought, there is objective knowledge of 'aspects', *epinoiai*, of that essence, notably because God is 'true being', *to alêthôs einai*. God is he who 'by nature has being', *ho tê*

---

57 *Parole et mystère, op. cit.*, p. 63.
58 *Ibid.*, pp. 86–87. The exception is Origen's doctrine of Penance where he refuses to unworthy presbyters the power of sacramental absolution but grants it to worthy laics, *ibid.*, pp. 93–94.
59 *Présence et pensée, op. cit.*, p. XIII.
60 E. Gilson, *Le Thomisme: Introduction à la philosophie de saint Thomas d'Aquin* (Paris, 1942–1944). This was in fact the fifth edition of a much earlier work which lacked this 'Existentialist' emphasis. See also *idem, Being and Some Philosophers* (Toronto, 1952, 2nd edition).

autou phusei to einai echei.[61] Precisely here, though, conceptual shortfall reveals, albeit indirectly, the ungraspable fullness of the divine essence. The conclusion is: 'All "essential" knowledge [of God] already supposes an "existential" faith'.[62] Balthasar is echoing Gilson. The reason for this is plain. It is the desire to seduce the French intelligentsia into believing that, even when compared with Heidegger and Sartre, the God of historic Christianity has all the best tunes. Even if Balthasar's declared (and entirely credible) motive is the wish to put a large quantity of deep blue water between Nyssa and the pagan Platonists, we can hardly mistake the underlying wider apologetic aim.

In point of fact, however, Balthasar's interest in this essay is chiefly focused on Gregory of Nyssa's theological anthopology, the texts for which also provide the Cappadocian bishop's doctrine of grace. There are undoubted riches here – one thinks especially of the Gregorian account of spiritual desire, which grows in the measure that it shares in what it loves, hence for man made in the divine image the life of grace and glory can only be a continuous 'stretching out', *epektasis*, toward God.

> The primal Good being infinite by nature, communion with him on the part of one who thirsts for him must necessarily also be infinite, capable of unending enlargement.[63]

Not till the book's end do we find much of that investigation of Gregory's thinking about the Holy Trinity largely dominant in the modern recovery of his corpus.[64] In compensation, one notes that far more treatises by Gregory are exploited than is the case in later twentieth-century systematics where, with the decline of classical studies as part and parcel of theological formation, dogmaticians are increasingly dependent on available translations. Excessive schematization based on a comparatively small number of texts, a feature of the present-day use of patristic sources by systematic theologians, was not one of Balthasar's vices.[65]

That is not to say that Balthasar's book itself lacks a systematic structure. Far from it. If anything, Balthasar has made of Gregory a systematic thinker in the Teutonic manner. But even scholars who suggest as much concede the profound suggestiveness of Balthasar's study. For example, the Hungarian Cistercian David Balas remarks how the

> deep and original, though somewhat forced, study of von Balthasar is very suggestive for the overall comprehension of Gregory's thought.[66]

As Werner Löser has shown, the book's three parts actually fall into a diptych. In parts one and two – presentations, respectively, of 'becoming and desire' and of 'the image', Balthasar expounds Gregory's account of the

---

61 Gregory of Nyssa, *Vita Moysis*, 1.
62 *Présence et pensée, op. cit.*, p. XXI.
63 Gregory of Nyssa, *Contra Eunomium*, 1.
64 There are some crucially placed remarks, however, in *Présence et pensée*, pp. XVI–XVIII.
65 For an illuminating account of what can go wrong, see for instance, M. R. Barnes, 'Augustine in Contemporary Trinitarian Theology', *Theological Studies* 56. 2 (1995), pp. 237–50.
66 D. L. Balas, Μετουσία Θεού. *Man's Participation in God's Perfections according to Saint Gregory of Nyssa* (Rome, 1966), p. 16.

would-be ascent of man to God – what the Swiss theologian had called, when treating of Origen, *theologia ascendens*. In Gregory's treatment, this is a necessarily incomplete and uncompletable movement. In part three, Gregory – as presented by Balthasar – revolutionizes the perspective. In texts brought together under the Balthasarian heading of the 'philosophy of love', Gregory writes of God's own incarnational descent into the world, there to meet his human creature who vainly struggles to cross the abyss that separates the created from the uncreated realm. Of this *theologia descendens*, Gregory's commentary on the Song of Songs is the *pièce de résistance*. In fact, Balthasar treats the commentary on the Song as the 'centre and high point' of all Nyssa's work.[67]

Gregory of Nyssa: the Incarnation

On Balthasar's ('de Lubacian') Christocentric reading of these Cappadocian texts, the 'descending' theology and philosophy of love means, above all, then, the Incarnation. No longer is it a question of how the soul can approach God but of how in fact God has drawn close to us. For metaphysics Christianity will substitute meta-history, since an eternal reality now gives itself to us within, or from within, an historical fact. No analysis of the soul as image of God could make us suspect the Uncreated Grace who in his own Person will now enter our hearts. And this brings with it a second change to Gregory's 'ascending' account of man rising up toward God through knowledge and desire. Hitherto all was on the level of individuals. But when the external fact whereby meta-history reaches us turns out to be social – the Church, prepared in Israel – we gather that the internal reality is social as well. It is nothing less than the 'mystical body' of Christ. *De facto*, we enter into communion with God only Christocentrically since One who is God, in taking individualized human nature, by that partial contact touched the entire nature of humanity in its indivisible unity and continues so to do. Through a vital union he transmits grace, resurrection and divinization to the whole body.

For Nyssa, so Balthasar points out approvingly, though the Incarnation, and indeed the whole life of the Redeemer, was absolutely prerequisite, the Cross and Resurrection are alone conclusive for our salvation. They mark the point where the Lord extirpates the deepest roots of sin, which sink into the passions, into corporeality and mortality, and indeed into time itself. It is in the *overall* Incarnation – from Annunciation to Ascension – that God the Word, the Only-begotten, takes possession of our nature in its full extent in all human beings, and does so both juridically and ontologically: by right and by being. In his humanity, Jesus is the true 'primal' man who alone realized the state of communion with God from which Adam and his posterity defected. Appropriately, then, he enjoys a primacy in the order of birth by his virginal Conception and in the order of regenerate human nature by his Baptism just as by the Resurrection he will become the firstborn from the dead. Not unfittingly, in the environs of that Event, the Magdalene took the Crucified and Risen One for a gardener. In a 'type' or foreshadowing laid out for us in the Song of Songs, the Bridegroom descended into the garden of the

---

67 W. Löser, *Im Geiste des Origenes, op. cit.*, pp. 102–103.

Bride, since the garden he must cultivate is *ourselves*, our humanity. And as Balthasar stresses on Gregory's behalf:

> To appropriate its new 'nature', transformed by Christ, humanity must become aware of its new centre and operate in him and by him the supreme synthesis of death and life.[68]

For this, each person must make their own the Lord's redeeming death and Resurrection – in signs, yes, notably Baptism and the Holy Eucharist, but this is only a foundation, an introduction to the 'death' which must typify the work of our whole life and become in us more and more complete. For souls who desire to be like the eternal Word, the Spouse – the Church – shows them a way of apparent contradiction. It is the way of assimilation to the kenosis and death of the humiliated Christ. That notion that our salvation, glorification, deification, takes place under the veil of its seeming contrary will be reinforced by Balthasar's study of Karl Barth, who learned it from Luther, and become an enduring feature of his soteriology and notably his theology of the Paschal mystery.

Thus the Church grows by perpetual acts of love for, and imitation of, Christ. True mystagogical initiation is, writes Balthasar, expounding the teaching of Gregory's commentary on the Song of Songs, a sharing in the Church's 'looking' towards her Spouse. Through ecclesial life, our human nature in its spiritual aspect, by which it exists in the divine image, is reconstituted on a higher level, just as Christ himself, the second Adam, has taken the place of the first, the Adam who fell away.

> Being the limit between death and life, glory and ignominy, God and the world, the Church is thereby the very point of contact of opposites, and thus the true mediatrix. She is the truth of the image – the window through which floods of divine life penetrate the creature.[69]

Gregory of Nyssa: the Holy Trinity

Concretely, the revelation of 'the Presence' – the depths of the divine being – is the revelation of the Trinity by the Trinity. The Father, the divine Archer, sends the Son into the world to wound it with love and unite it with Christ in his mystical body. The Spirit does the uniting – always without confusing. The Son, the Sole-begotten Light, can be seen only in the Light of the Father: the Holy Spirit who proceeds from him. Only when illuminated by the glory of the Holy Spirit can we enter into understanding of the glory of the Father and the Son. 'Gregory's mysticism finishes logically and necessarily in a Trinitarian theology.'[70]

Balthasar now takes some elements from Gregory's contribution to the Trinitarian controversies turbulently afoot in his lifetime, to underscore the link between his religious philosophy and his Triadology. The Trinitarian dogma can be summed up as 'Life in the Eternal'. To know the Father is eternal life; whoever believes in the Son has eternal life; to receive the Spirit is

68 *Présence et pensée, op. cit.*, p. 114.
69 *Ibid.*, p. 122.
70 *Ibid.*, p. 133.

to receive a source springing up for eternal life. In God there is no solitude but rather perfect mutual inclusion. The Father is grasped in the Son, the Son in the Holy Spirit. So lifegiving grace originates in the Father, and flows through the Son to those who benefit by the operation of the Spirit. For Balthasar, Nyssa is a proto-Augustinian theologian. At the time of writing *Présence et pensée* he thought Gregory accepted elements of the 'Augustinian' psychological *imago Trinitatis* -- the Triune God mirrored in the created powers of mind, reason and spirit or love. Later, Balthasar changed his mind about the authenticity of the homily on Genesis 1.26 on which this claim is based.[71] But that still left intact another reason for affirming the affinity with the North African doctor. For both, the Holy Spirit is essentially unitive. In his economy, the Spirit tends to integrate all creation in union with God through the perfect eschatological Image that is the 'whole Christ', Uncreated and created in one.

Sources of Maximus the Confessor: Evagrius, Denys, John of Scythopolis

One of Gregory of Nyssa's exact contemporaries was the Origenist monk *Evagrius of Pontus* who played a major, if often subterranean, role in the development of Greek Christian spirituality. Balthasar visited his corpus twice – once to furnish an overview of Evagrius's thought at large,[72] the second time to help reconstruct its textual basis. Specifically, this latter project was an ambitious attempt to recreate Evagrius's work as exegete of Holy Scripture, for Evagrius had left behind, either in fragments or under the cloak of anonymity, commentaries on various biblical books – the Psalter and Proverbs, Genesis and Numbers, the Books of the Kings, Qoheleth, Job and the Song of Songs, and, in the New Testament, the Gospel according to Luke.[73] Balthasar's attribution to Evagrius of a Psalm-commentary hitherto ascribed to Origen was spectacularly confirmed twenty years later by a find in the Vatican Library.[74] Balthasar's general view of Evagrius – he was more 'Origenistic', in the sense of the anathemas against Origenism launched by the emperor Justinian, than was Origen himself – would have the support of later scholars, especially after the discovery of what appears to be the original, uncorrected version of Evagrius' 'Gnostic Chapters', the *Kephalaia gnostika*.[75]

Scholia or commentaries on *Denys's* writings were long passed down under the name of Maximus the Confessor. To Balthasar belongs the honour

71 It can be found in *Patrologia Graeca* 44, cols 1327–46.
72 'Metaphysik und Mystik des Evagrius Pontikus', *Zeitschrift für Askeze und Mystik* [Innsbruck] 14 (1939), pp. 31–47.
73 'Die *Hiera* des Evagrius', *Zeitschrift für katholische Theologie* 63 (1939), pp. 86–106 and 181–206.
74 M.-J. Rondeau, 'Le commentaire sur les Psaumes d'Evagre le Pontique', *Orientalia Christiana Periodica* 26 (1960), pp. 307–48.
75 A. Guillaumont, *Les six Centuries des 'Kephalaia gnostica' d'Evagre le Pontique. Edition critique de la version grecque commune et édition d'une nouvelle version grecque, intégrale, avec une double traduction française* (=*Patrologia Orientalis* 28, 1, Paris, 1958).

of restoring them to their rightful author: the early sixth-century John, bishop of Scythopolis.[76] Balthasar realized that a Syrian translation (in the British Museum, now British Library) of part of the Greek Dionysius *scholia* could only be John's. Internal criteria suggested that by far the greater part of the Greek text stemmed from the same source. Balthasar had no *parti pris* against Denys – great, if anonymous, Syrian theologian on whose work he had poured praise in *The Glory of the Lord*.[77] There he had applauded Denys as doyen of aesthetic theologians, since in his work aesthetic transcendence – where we look via a sensuous appearance to a spiritual content thus become manifest – provides the formal scheme for understanding all theological (and mystical) movement from the world to God. In Balthasar 'beyond the trilogy', admiration for Denys is postponed till we deal with that synthesizer of the Eastern patristic tradition Maximus the Confessor, in whose overall vision Denys, as Balthasar explains, played a major part.

Among Denys's other sources, Balthasar had a good deal more time for *John of Scythopolis* than for Evagrius. He considered him 'a great scholar and no mediocre philosopher'.[78] He praised his many-sided theological and humane interests. John is a good example of a defender of the 'positivity of the finite' and the 'universality of the catholic' – two main qualities Balthasar found inspirational, as we saw above, in the Fathers at their best. In Balthasar's broad definition of the term, John can also be said to represent the principle of the 'analogy of being' as well. This he did in Christology, by emphasizing the complete integrity of the humanity assumed, but above all in the cosmology for which his commentaries should be most admired. Cosmologically, John excludes pantheism, allowing the finitude and multiplicity of the world positive meaning.

> He worked out the positive meaning of material multiplicity and of the mind's 'turn to the appearances' ... along lines Maximus never took and, in some ways more clearly than Maximus; as a result, he avoids the danger, very real in Maximus, of a one-sided spiritualism.[79]

John likewise avoided emanationism, presenting the creative Ideas of things as, quite simply, the thoughts of God who in knowing things knows their natures in himself. John stressed the resurrection of the flesh with a frankness worthy of Irenaeus. In the exalted Christ the body too reaches God's right hand. Balthasar was delighted to be able to note, under the heading of the 'universality of the catholic', *scholia* which showed how at home John was in the Greek classics and his desire to 'translate' the Hellenic achievement into Christian terms.

Introducing Maximus, the Byzantine Aquinas

Balthasar's Maximus study was of major importance in setting this towering figure of Greek patristics in perspective – as he fairly noted in the foreword to

76 'Das Scholienwerk des Johannes von Skythopolis', *Scholastik* 15 (1940), pp. 16–38, reprinted as 'The Problem of the Scholia to Pseudo-Dionysius', in *Cosmic Liturgy, op. cit.*, pp. 359–87.
77 *The Glory of the Lord*, II, *op. cit.*, pp. 144–210.
78 *Cosmic Liturgy, op. cit.*, p. 366.
79 *Ibid.*, p. 374.

the second edition of 1961.[80] Balthasar's brilliant intuition was that Maximus offered a synthesis. Despite the occasional, unsystematic character of his writing, he was not merely – as a number of earlier scholars had thought – 'at best a reservoir of disparate traditions'.[81] For Balthasar, Maximus was '*the* philosophical and theological thinker who stands between East and West', revealing their convergence. This convergence was not, for Balthasar, between Byzantium and Rome, merely. Maximus unified in a certain fashion Asia and the whole Western world – an extraordinary, but sincerely intended, claim.

Balthasar's animus against the very idea of the *Reichskirche*, the 'imperial Church', his disapproval of the role of the emperor at Councils, and his sympathy for the Antiochene theologians who suffered a *damnatio memoriae* at the Second Council of Constantinople (552), inclined him to call the age of Maximus a bleak epoch in Church history. In the context, thus interpreted, Maximus's task was to set the springs of Christian reflection flowing again. For Balthasar, this has four aspects. First, Maximus re-presented Denys the Areopagite as a Church theologian of the first rank. Though, as Balthasar's researches attested, John of Scythopolis had been Denys's enthusiastic commentator, it was largely among educated humanists in Monophysite circles – and so not in the Great Church – that Denys was read and approved. Secondly, Maximus recovered great tracts of the teaching of Origen, doing so by the simple device of reviving interest in a figure steeped in the latter's thought and sensibility, the impeccably orthodox Gregory Nazianzen, one of the three 'holy hierarchs and universal teachers' of the Eastern church (the others being John Chrysostom and Gregory of Nyssa's brother Basil). Thirdly, and more daringly, Maximus had an attempt to rescue for Christian thought what was worthwhile in the teaching of Evagrius. For, despite his alarmingly innovatory metaphysics (they have been compared with features of Buddhism), Evagrius offered analyses of the development of the moral and contemplative life which synthesized Alexandrian thought and the practical wisdom of the desert fathers: no mean undertaking. Fourthly and finally, though the masters of the school of Antioch were beyond formal rehabilitation, Maximus was able to do justice to their concern for the humanity of Christ by his own emphases on the reality of the Saviour's human – and not only divine – will. Balthasar calls that:

> the man Jesus' own active doing and willing – not a passive human nature dependent on the activity of a personal divine Logos, as the Monothelites imagined.[82]

Balthasar presents Maximus as defender – over against early Byzantine Caesaropapism (the term 'Caesaroprocuratorism' would probably be preferable) – of the faith tradition of Peter's chair in Rome. Balthasar's account of Maximus's trial for sedition presents the position in somewhat unnuanced terms, namely those of

---

80 *Cosmic Liturgy, op. cit.*, p. 23. For an overview of modern Maximian scholarship, see A. Nichols, OP, *Byzantine Gospel. Maximus the Confessor in Modern Scholarship* (Edinburgh, 1993), pp. 221–52.
81 *Cosmic Liturgy, op. cit.*, p. 25.
82 *Ibid.*, p. 37.

a single decision: for Rome, the refuge of free, evangelical faith, against Byzantium, the bulwark of politico-religious integralism.[83]

Rome was 'the refuge of orthodoxy guaranteed by the Gospel itself', even if it also needed the theological 'treasures of the Christian East – Dionysian, Origenian, Evagrian, Antiochene'.[84] That explains how Latin Rome (not that, in this period, Rome was consistently or consciously Latinate) and Byzantine East come together in Maximus's work. But what of that wider 'Asia' Balthasar has spoken of? Maximus treats Evagrian thought (and behind Evagrius the elements in Origen's corpus on which he drew) as distinctively 'Asian' in the sense that they represent a widespread approach to the great issue of the One and the Many as found in different ways in the various religiosities of Asia. (So this has nothing to do with the 'Roman Asia' of St Irenaeus and what patristic scholars generally designate 'Asiatic theology'.) The manner in which Balthasar describes 'Asia', painting with a very broad brush, is reminiscent of his polemical picture of Platonism in his first theological essay: 'Patristik, Scholastik und wir'.[85] The world-renouncing passion of Asia:

> is a way of stripping off form, in order to find the infinite Absolute in a state of formlessness. The world, compared with God, is unreality, a falling away from the eternal unity. Expressed in terms of this picture of things, an incarnation of God can only mean a concession, the gracious descent of God into multiplicity, into the realm of matter, in order to lead what is multiple back into unity. In the end, it is not so much a synthesis of the One and the Many as a gesture of the One towards the Many, beckoning it home into the One.[86]

But where, asks Balthasar, does this leave the ontology of created being? How much of this natural 'Asian' religious impulse can be integrated with Christianity without endangering the Gospel? Or to put it in more Maximian terms, by bringing Christ into the very centre of the theology of creation can the duality of God and world be rendered 'bearable' for 'Asian' thought?

It was Maximus's achievement to bring into Chalcedonian Christology the 'whole Asian mystique of divinization' – not on the 'lower' level of natural 'dissolution and fusion' (this was where Monophysitism stumbled) but on the 'higher' level of the biblically disclosed mystery of the personal synthesis of the humanized God. Into this framework, everything worthy in Origen and Evagrius could fit. Philosophically, Maximus was helped by Aristotle and Denys. From Aristotle, he borrowed his notion of the

> irreducible, ultimate substance of a thing, with its inner field of meaning and power defined in terms of potency and act.[87]

From Denys, by contrast, he learned that the finite world, both as a whole and in its individual members, enjoys an 'indissoluble autonomy ... in relation to the infinite reality of God'. So Maximus was fortunate. In terms of

83 *Ibid.*, p. 43.
84 *Ibid.*, p. 44.
85 See A. Nichols, OP, *Scattering the Seed, op. cit.*, pp. 17–32.
86 *Cosmic Liturgy, op. cit.*, p. 45.
87 *Ibid.*, p. 49.

ideas and sources he was admirably placed to marry scholasticism and mysticism, all on the basis of a profoundly meditative reading of Scripture. Balthasar considered Maximus's metaphysical (and Christological) clarity a major desideratum for inter-religious dialogue today.

Maximus among the doctors

If any single one of these sources is more constitutive than the rest for Maximus's overall vision, that would be – on Balthasar's reading – Denys. Balthasar has a wonderful account of Denys's picture of the cosmos, his:

> ecstatic vision of a holy universe, flowing forth, wave upon wave, from the unfathomable depths of God, whose centre lies always beyond the creature's reach; his vision of a creation that realizes itself in ever more distant echoes, until it finally ebbs away at the borders of nothingness, yet which is held together, unified, and 'brought home', step by step, through the ascending unities of an awestruck love.[88]

Yet Maximus's world is firmer, stabler: he 'envisages a naturally lasting cosmos as the supporting ground of all supernatural divinization'.[89] However, Maximus does not stop at correct theory. As a committed Christian monk, he seeks 'the transformation of a merely contemplative embrace of all things into a living, concrete love', and one that is psychologically informed – acute, indeed – where the parodies of love we call the vices are concerned.[90] For Maximus, tutored by Chalcedon:

> Love, which is the highest level of union, only takes root in the growing independence of the lovers; the union between God and the world reveals, in the very nearness it creates between these two poles of being, the ever-greater difference between created being and the essentially incomparable God.[91]

And so the Maximian synthesis could be put in place.

> All things, for him, had become organic parts of ever-more-comprehensive syntheses, had become themselves syntheses pointing to the final synthesis of Christ, which explained them all.[92]

The preamble to the *Mystagogia*, Maximus's commentary on the Divine Liturgy, shows the Chalcedonian formula expanding into an entire metaphysics, with nature and grace a synthesis that 'unites creatures by distinguishing them and distinguishes them by uniting them'.[93] And here comes the most decisive comparison, which is with the thirteenth-century Dominican St Thomas Aquinas:

> Maximus is a real predecessor of Aquinas, anticipating his concern to preserve the essence of every thing, or better, to set each thing's integral

88 *Ibid.*, p. 58.
89 *Ibid.*, p. 61.
90 *Ibid.*, p. 62.
91 *Ibid.*, p. 64.
92 *Ibid.*, p. 66.
93 *Ibid.*, p. 69.

completeness within an openness and a readiness for union that allows
it to be elevated and brought to fulfillment.[94]

Maximus's theological doctrine

Balthasar follows up a chronological account of Maximus's life and works
with a spirited recreation of Maximus's specific doctrine under four headings: his teaching on God, on the divine Ideas as foundation of the world, on
the being of the cosmos, and on humanity – where he introduces a dramatic
element since humankind now lives under the regime of sin, yet is poised
between Paradise and Parousia. *Cosmic Liturgy* will be rounded off by a
presentation of two great Maximian 'syntheses': the 'synthesis' of Christ
himself, and the 'synthesis' of Christian existence, the Christian life.

On *God*: thanks to the biblical revelation it was possible to see that God's
absoluteness and the world's finitude and relativity do not exclude each
other, since God's transcendence makes possible an immanence whereby his
presence nurtures things precisely in their difference. The God of Maximus is

> the mystery of a supreme, self-contained simplicity, fully co-existing
> with the twofold, incomprehensible and irreversible self-opening of
> this unity to both the world as a whole and the world in all its
> particulars.[95]

He lies beyond both affirmation and negation – which is why no neutral
concept of being can 'span the realities of both God and creature; the analogy
of an even-greater dissimilarity [shades of Przywara!] stands in the way'.[96] It
is also why 'distance grows with increasing nearness', and '[f]ear, hesitation,
and adoration grow with love'.[97] 'Notice', invites Balthasar:

> how far into the realm of mystical speculation the echoes of the Chal-
> cedonian formula have penetrated! The highest union with God is not
> realized 'in spite of' our lasting difference from him, but rather 'in' and
> 'through' it. Unity is not the abolition of God's distance from us, and so
> of his incomprehensibility; it is its highest revelation.[98]

This the Incarnation attests.

Still, and here Maximus's Trinitarian realism comes into view, owing to
the fact that the history of salvation is 'the history of the triune God in the
world, ... the real restoration of the creature to the Father through the Son
and the Spirit', the Christian faithful nonetheless find themselves 'truly "in"
the Trinity'.[99] Though Maximus imposes on himself far greater 'restraint'
than would be the case among the doctors of the Latin West, eschewing all
systematic explanation of the Trinitarian processions, he teaches that the
mystery of God is 'pregnant with a life of ineffable fruitfulness'.[100] That

94 *Ibid.*, p. 71.
95 *Ibid.*, p. 86.
96 *Ibid.*, p. 89.
97 *Ibid.*, p. 92.
98 *Ibid.*, p. 92.
99 *Ibid.*, p. 100.
100 *Ibid.*, p. 103.

metaphor of fruitfulness, borrowed from his favourite Romantic writers, was so dear to Balthasar that it comes as something of a surprise to see that here it is pure citation from Maximus himself. In the *Ambigua*, Maximus's exposition of problematic passages in St Gregory the Theologian (Nazianzus), we hear of God not only teaching the mind caught up in encounter with him 'the reality of his own monadic existence', but spurring it on to be 'receptive to his divine, hidden fruitfulness, as well': 'whispering' to it that 'this Good can never be thought of without the fruit of the Logos and of Wisdom', that is: the second and third Trinitarian persons.[101] This 'intrinsically fruitful God' is the God of love beyond intelligible being.

On the '*Ideas*': these are for Maximus 'the basic outlines, in God, of his plan for the world', or again, 'the preliminary sketch of the creature within the Spirit of God'. The Word incarnate – never far from Maximus's mind – will bring together in his own unity 'the identity of all the world's ideas in God's essence and their identity with each other as creatures (that is, in *not* being God)'.[102] Once more, even in this highest realm of ontological discourse about being, the Chalcedonian formula is king – and takes us beyond what philosophical Platonism could dream of. The element of truth in (heretical) Origenism is that there *is* a prehistorical world crucial to our story – not, however, as ante-natal actual existence but as the timeless 'superexistence of all beings in their divine idea'.[103] This entry of the world into God is only fully achieved, however, by the Incarnation and Paschal Mystery, which are not just the centre of history but central to the world's foundational scheme. Thus the great text in Maximus's *Centuries on Knowledge* whose key character Balthasar highlighted in his work.[104]

What of the *being of the cosmos* and of *humankind*? Balthasar terms Maximus's notions of these 'synthetic': the reiteration of this adjective (or its noun) is surely intended to make the claim that Maximus achieved what Hegelianism failed to bring off. The first and most fundamental of Maximus's theses is 'the synthesis between being and motion, ultimately between eternal being and the finite being that moves out from it and on toward it'.[105] That must be seen in the total evangelical context Maximus gives it:

> [T]he goal God sets for the world is now not simply dissolution in him alone but the fulfillment and preservation also of the created realm, 'without confusion' [*asunchutôs* [one of the celebrated adverbs of the Chalcedonian Definition]], in the Incarnation of his Son.[106]

As the ultimate basis for created being as such, this 'synthesis' enjoys primacy. It is the basis for all the further 'syntheses' Maximus identifies in the structure and working of the world, and notably, as Balthasar presents them: generality and particularity, subject and object, intellect and matter. Human life is marked by 'an unconfused mutual indwelling of opposites', a supreme version of the pattern of created being.[107]

---

101 Maximus, *Ambigua* at *Patrologia Graeca* 91, 1260 D.
102 *Cosmic Liturgy, op. cit.*, p. 122.
103 *Ibid.*, p. 133.
104 Maximus, *Centuries on Knowledge* 1, 66–67.
105 *Cosmic Liturgy, op. cit.*, p. 153.
106 *Ibid.*
107 *Ibid.*, p. 176.

Maximus on the drama of redemption

So far, says Balthasar, we have been looking at the world as a 'play of powers, tensions, and balances'. But the world is more than just the setting for such interplay. It is also a 'drama' set in history.[108] Impossible *not* to think at this juncture of the 'theological dramatics' which will be, in the later 1970s and 80s, Balthasar's chief contribution to Catholic dogmatic thought. In Maximus's case the drama is not detailed: he has no highly developed interest in the variety of history. Nonetheless it is real and turns on three acts: the Fall, the Incarnation, the final Parousia – which is, remarks somewhat generally the Balthasar who, throughout his life, seems to have had little feel for the Second Coming of Christ *as such*, 'God's final presence in the world'.[109] If Maximus presents these events as more like overlapping stages, each recognizable in some way in the creature's life, that is not so different from the approach Balthasar himself will follow in his 1977 study *Christlicher Stand*, 'The Christian State of Life'.[110]

As Balthasar interprets him, Maximus has two distinct but not incompatible interpretations of the Fall. What did it mean when the first human couple transgressed the divine command by eating the fruit of the tree of the knowledge of good and evil? In one way, it meant they (disastrously) 'jumped the gun'. God had postponed the moment when they might without danger 'see through creation along with God'[111] to after their moral and spiritual development had confirmed them in virtue and the reception of the gift of divinization. In another way, in choosing this 'tree' rather than the other offered them, the tree of life, they elected to be nourished by material nature, not God, and so committed themselves 'not to dependence on God but to dependence on the senses and on material things'.[112] This is not so much misplaced zeal as insubordination and pride. The sensuous world for Maximus is not only God's good creature, it is also 'reshaped in its inmost being by the human weakness resulting from the fall'.[113] For Maximus, the emotions – the passions, considered as natural impulses, are not of themselves blameworthy, and yet they stand in 'a hidden and indestructible relationship with that sensual egoism that is the basis of sin'.[114] Of all the consequences of the Fall, lust enjoys for him the closest bond with *philautia*, self-seeking love. But at this point Maximus surprises us. Though sexual desire is a sad reminder of the Fall ('an "efficacious sign" of sin', Balthasar calls it on Maximus's behalf),[115] married union – the natural marriage covenant, with sexual congress a key feature – is nonetheless for this extraordinary Byzantine thinker:

---

108 *Ibid.*, p. 179.
109 *Ibid.*, pp. 179–80.
110 *Christlicher Stand* (Einsiedeln, 1977; 1981); ET *The Christian State of Life* (San Francisco, 1983).
111 Words taken from the prologue to the *Quaestiones ad Thalassium* at *Patrologia Graeca* 90, cols. 257D–260A.
112 *Cosmic Liturgy, op. cit.*, p. 183.
113 *Ibid.*, p. 191. Here the comparison between Maximus and Aquinas limps badly.
114 *Ibid.*, p. 195.
115 *Ibid.*, p. 199.

the first level of the progressive syntheses by which the world is unified and brought to its perfection in the unity of God ... In this union lies a first, still confused hint and representation of the unity and unifying love of God, even though it may be misused and twisted.[116]

Only, however, with the Incarnation will the condition of incorruptibility be thrown open to us once more. Not the 'sexual synthesis' but 'Christ the synthesis' will

restore the balance again, by bringing the proud intellect low and by lifting up the flesh that had been hollowed out by passion and death.[117]

Maximus as Christocentric thinker

Evidently, in *Cosmic Liturgy*, Balthasar is enthused by St Maximus as a theologian of *synthesis*, and that not only, or mainly, in the sense of one who integrates into a new unity his own sources of reflection, though the Confessor certainly did this. Maximus takes the Chalcedonian formula of the Word incarnate's own 'synthetic' being as the key to a reading of the world as a whole in the light of faith.[118] The Mediator makes possible the ordered flow of the world's being towards the Father in a movement which Balthasar likens to that of Liturgy: hence the title of his book. Held together in the 'synthetic hypostasis' of the God-man (who synthesizes two ways of existing, divine and human, in his single Person), are God and world, infinite and finite, eternal and temporal.[119]

It is certainly the Word becoming flesh, considered 'from above', who is the power behind the synthesis [of God and world, eternity and time, q. v.]; he is this power, both in his freedom as a person and in the absolute reality of his divine being that is inseparable from that freedom.[120]

---

116 *Ibid.*, pp. 199, 200.
117 *Ibid.*, p. 202. Balthasar finds it a weakness in Maximus's thought that he can find no place for the sexual synthesis in the synthesis of Christ. A reflection of this – suggests Balthasar – is the rather modest place the New Eve, the Bride of Christ, finds in his overall doctrinal view: *ibid.*, p. 204.
118 'For Maximus ... a synthetic understanding of Christ became a theodicy for the world: a justification not simply of its existence but of the whole range of its structures of being. All things for him had become organic parts of ever-more-comprehensive syntheses, pointing to the final synthesis of Christ which explained them all.' *Ibid.*, p. 66.
119 *Ibid.*, pp. 235–36 on eternity and time. For the understanding of 'synthetic' hypostasis, see pp. 245–46, and the note below.
120 *Ibid.*, p. 253. Balthasar stresses, then, that the phrase 'synthetic person' should not be taken in the sense of 'being a passive product of two natures that have simply come together'. Rather, 'the divine Person realizes this unification in and through himself, in the highest freedom, so that he is called "synthetic" [in the first instance] in the sense of being the cause of synthesis', *ibid.*, pp. 249–50. At the same time, this Person – as 'both the divine act of being and the unlimited personal freedom of the Son' – gives 'hypostatic form to the synthesis' human side', where it is a synthesis of body with soul (and vice versa) and between human nature as a whole and the Son himself, *ibid.*, pp. 253–55.

This gives a good idea of the ultimate source of Balthasar's interest in Maximus. It is their common concern with the unity of God and the world, eternity and time, as achieved in the God-man, Jesus Christ. 'The figure of the Redeemer stands in the centre of Maximus' theology', writes Balthasar, just as it does in his own.[121]

And yet, as is shown by Maximus's strenuous engagement in the struggle to defend the two wills, not only divine but human, of the Redeemer, this is so understood as at all times to safeguard the integrity of the human in its unconfused union with God.[122] The two freedoms or spontaneities, divine and human, in the Word incarnate are without separation (to this extent we can speak justly of Christ's 'theandric' action), but they are also without mixing. The Agony in the Garden is for Maximus the keypoint of salvation history. There it was that

> the cosmic struggle between the nature of God and the nature of the world took place ... [The Garden of Olives] is not only the centre of Christ's work but also the core of the syntheses that were intended to achieve the redemption of all creation by drawing it step by step towards God.[123]

By his victorious Passion the Lord became the shining 'sun of all the ages' through whose warming light the harvest of the world ripens into unity with God.[124] Finally, with the Ascension, the whole world comes to dwell – daringly, Maximus uses the technical term for the relations of communion in the Trinity, *perichôrêsis* – in the God of all.[125] This is why Maximus can say that whoever knows the Cross and Sepulchre knows the essence of all things, whoever knows the Resurrection knows the goal for which all things were made.[126] Expressed in more frankly ontological and less lyrically symbolic a vocabulary, the redeeming work establishes fresh syntheses between: man and woman, earth and heaven, sensible and intelligible, and ultimately created and uncreated. Balthasar sums it all up in a statement which puts in a nutshell the message of the theological aesthetics on which he was working when the second edition of *Kosmische Liturgie* appeared, and indeed of his mature dogmatics as a whole:

> The Incarnation – put more sharply, this means the descent into suffering, the Cross, and the grave and the resurrection of the creature who has been burned out in death and so has become transparent for God – is thus the final form of the world, the one that reshapes all other natural forms. Everything takes its decisive meaning and its ultimate justification only from here.[127]

---

121 *Ibid.*, p. 207.
122 *Ibid.*, pp. 256–59. Balthasar attaches to Maximus's soteriology the tag 'Heilung als Wahrung', 'salvation as safeguarding [or, "preservation"]'. Maximus presented the cosmic Logos ever more humanly and evangelically, *ibid.*, p. 207.
123 *Ibid.*, p. 271.
124 *Ibid.*, p. 272, citing Maximus, *Ambigua*, at *Patrologia Graeca* 91, col. 1356C.
125 Maximus, *Ambigua*, at *Patrologia Graeca* 91, col. 1308C.
126 *Ibid.*, at col. 1045AB.
127 *Cosmic Liturgy*, p. 278.

Augustine: man of the Church

It is time to turn to the Christian West for its own sake, and more specifically that North African West where Maximus spent one of his sojourns in exile – learning, so it is thought, something about Augustine of Hippo in the process. In his study of Balthasar's patristic exploration, Werner Löser presents Balthasar's Augustine as above all *vir Ecclesiae*, a 'man of the Church'.[128] Balthasar's basic conviction was that Augustine's profile had suffered distortion. He had been seen through the lens of modern religious subjectivity, rather than treated as what he was, a figure from the ancient Church. The remedy was to replace the *Confessions* in the framework of his writing – and, above all, preaching – as a whole. In the course of the twentieth century, depth psychology, Existentialism and the phenomenological analysis of time certainly underlined Augustine's 'dramatic religious existence', but at the expense of his image as a man of the Church. In the introduction to 'The Face of the Church', his series of extracts from the sermons, Balthasar declares Augustine's fate typical of our era, which 'privileges seeking over finding, the way above the goal'.[129] Augustine the *baptizatus*, Augustine the ascetic, the priest, the bishop, was not that interested in his own 'I'. He was passionately interested, however, in giving up the limits of that 'I' to the 'ever deeper known and experienced Church'.

As to the *Confessions* themselves, the book was written from essentially ecclesial motives – to continue the defence of Catholicism against the Donatists who had cast aspersions on the integrity of his conversion, and to meet the wishes of his friends in the Church (prominent among them, Paulinus of Nola).[130] This is not the story of a private individual but that of a theologian-bishop. And in any case, as its contents make clear, it goes beyond the confines of the psychological or even biographical realm. It is confession of sin and praise of God. The meaning of Augustine's life, as it emerges from these pages, is 'mission in the space of the Church'.[131] The 'biographical' books (I–IX) have to be seen as on their way to the theologically contemplative books (X–XIII), whose subject Balthasar describes as 'the contemplation, in the light of the Word of God, no longer of this one creature but of the creation at large'.[132] In this emphasis on *vir Ecclesiae* Balthasar is not

---

128 W. Löser, *Im Geiste des Origenes, op. cit.*, p. 133. The foundations of this claim are Balthasar's anthologies of Augustine's discourses on the psalms, where he comments on Augustine's way of interpreting Scripture (Aurelius Augustinus, *Über die Psalmen* [Leipzig, 1936; 2nd edition Einsiedeln, 1983]), and of his preaching at large, where Balthasar stresses Augustine's understanding of spiritual perfection and the action-contemplation relationship (Aurelius Augustinus, *Das Antlitz der Kirche* [Einsiedeln-Cologne, 1942; 2nd edition 1955]). Important too in this perspective is his choice of passages from *The City of God* (*Die Gottesbürgerschaft* [Frankfurt am Main-Hamburg, 1961] ; a second edition appeared under the title *Der Gottesstaat* [Einsiedeln, 1982]). One ought also to mention the comments that accompany his editions of the *Literal Commentary on Genesis* (Aurelius Augustinus, *Psychologie und Mystik* [Einsiedeln, 1960]), and the *Confessions* (Augustinus, *Die Bekenntnisse, op. cit.*) – as well as the substantial essay in the theological aesthetics *Herrlichkeit. I. Fächer der Stile. I. Teilband, op. cit.*, pp. 100–44.
129 'Einleitung', in Aurelius Augustinus, *Das Antlitz der Kirche, op. cit.*, p. 11.
130 Augustinus, *Die Bekenntnisse, op. cit.*, p. 214.
131 *Ibid.*, p. 215.
132 *Ibid.*, p. 216.

simply pointing to the proper context of the *Confessions*, a work too often read
as soul-narrative. He is concerned also with the use and misuse of Augustine
in such heretical movements as Jansenism, Lutheranism and Calvinism.
'Augustinus totus noster' is a saying of the Reformed, but for Balthasar the
post-Augustine 'Augustinianism' that withdraws from the *Catholica* has no
right to appeal to the bishop of Hippo.[133]

This approach makes Augustine's ecclesiology an especially important
topic for Balthasar. It was the subject of his 1942 sermon collection, but it was
already anticipated in the 1936 anthology from the *Enarrationes in Psalmos*. In
the Psalms, Augustine hears the voice of the 'total Christ', but also the dialogue of the Church-Bride with her Spouse. Balthasar calls the Psalter, as
Augustine reads it, the 'Book of Hours of the *Christus totus*'.[134] For Löser, the
interrelation of the two chief Pauline determinations of the Church (body,
bride) is what raised in Augustine's mind the question of the Church's
boundaries. As the North African bishop recognized, those boundaries do
not coincide in any simple fashion with the borders of the Kingdom of
God.[135] In Augustine's own lifetime, the problematic lay at the heart of the
Donatist crisis. As Balthasar reports, in Augustine's ecclesiology, the relation
of 'universal grace' and 'ecclesial form' is essentially incomprehensible, thus
making the Church a 'reflection of the divine incomprehensibility itself'.[136] To
Balthasar's mind, however, Augustine's own ecclesiological limitations are
shown in the paucity of his remarks on 'Mary and Peter', the Mariological
and (Roman-) Petrine dimensions of the Church.[137]

Where Augustine scores is in the historically dramatic character of his
ecclesiology, as shown in the theology of ecclesial history in the *De Civitate
Dei*. For Balthasar indeed, the *Confessions* are but the 'introductory chamber
music to the great orchestra of the *Civitas Dei*'.[138] Balthasar's introduction to
the Johannes Verlag *De civitate Dei* explains that Augustine is not so much
concerned with the history of the City of God as with its historicity, and the
presuppositions and implications of this *Geschichtlichkeit*.[139] Only the four
central books of the work consider the historical 'appearing' of the eternal
divine Kingdom which thereby finds itself in a condition of estrangement –
or, more kindly put, a pilgrim situation. Augustine smooths out the various
phases of the history concerned because this contrast – and not any relative
differentiations within it – is what is really uppermost in his mind. Using
Heideggerian language, Balthasar remarks that Augustine treats time, death,
judgment and Paradise as *Existentialen* – abiding 'existential' dimensions – of
the Kingdom in its pilgrim state.

But of course there are two 'communities' (or 'citizenships', *Bürgerschaften*)
in Augustine's account – the society of God and the society of the world.
Whether men belong to the first or the second is a matter of their choosing.
What is happening, as Balthasar sees it, is that Augustine has taken up a
biblical theme, the theme of decision (familiar from, for example, the 'Two

133 'Einleitung', in Aurelius Augustinus, *Das Antlitz der Kirche, op. cit.*, pp. 13–14.
134 'Einleitung' in Aurelius Augustinus, *Über die Psalmen, op. cit.*, p. 9.
135 'Einleitung' in Aurelius Augustinus, *Das Antlitz der Kirche, op. cit.*, p. 16.
136 *Ibid.*, p. 18.
137 *Ibid.*, pp. 19–21.
138 Augustinus, *Die Gottesbürgerschaft, op. cit.*, p. 16; idem, *Die Bekenntnisse, op. cit.*, p. 217.
139 Augustinus, *Die Gottesbürgerschaft, op. cit.*, p. 15.

Ways' literature of the Old Testament) – and taken it up with such seriousness as to lend it protological and eschatological dimensions, reference to an absolute beginning and an unconditional end. Augustine sees such 'decision' as remotely prepared, from eternity indeed, and with resonances stretching out ahead indefinitely, world without end. This is how he came to develop his theology of predestination which 'for Balthasar, oversteps the limits of what the Christian can know in faith'.[140] What he thinks went wrong was that Augustine clothed the biblical theology of decision in the garments of a Hellenic – effectively, a Neo-Platonist – cosmology. In other words, too much necessity attaches to the preparation and outworking of such decisions. In Balthasar's eyes, Augustine's protology and eschatology need 'decosmologizing' before they can play their proper role in the Christian life. Balthasar claims that Augustine anticipated to some degree such a reading of his work. That is so inasmuch as he

> relocated the unavoidability of decision for or against God in the most inner and hidden essence of the individual and developed the idea of world historical event only as an *indicator* or *indirect* echo of the most inner and hidden decision, never as its open and direct representation.[141]

Augustine on time and the Eternal

Clearly, Balthasar was going to be highly interested in Augustine as a theologian of the temporal in relation to the eternal. And this indeed is what we find. Balthasar's principal reflections on *time* – as distinct from the related but by no means identical topic of *history*[142] – unfold by way of an exposition of the thought of St Augustine, and more especially of Book XI of the *Confessions*.[143] Balthasar opens his account by situating Book XI within the *Confessions* as a whole.[144] In the first nine books of the work, Augustine has told us his life story up to the time of writing, a story which is (negatively) the confession of Augustine's weaknesses and (positively) the confession of God's greatness – and especially of the greatness of his mercies. This has been the 'story of a life full of guilt and vanity, but recalled and converted by the grace of God'.[145] The story ends with the death of St Monica, and that is appropriate, says Balthasar, not only because his mother's life was itself fulfilled by the conversion of her son as these nine books have described it but also because Monica's death enables Augustine to introduce the theme of the relation between time and the Eternal which will preoccupy him in the

140 W. Löser, *Im Geiste des Origenes, op. cit.*, p. 145.
141 Augustinus, *Die Gottesbürgerschaft, op. cit.*, p. 24.
142 We could say that human time is the *structure* of the medium in which history takes place whereas history is the *content* with which that medium is filled.
143 'The Fragmentary Nature of Time', in *idem, Man in History. A Theological Study* (ET London and Sydney, 1968), pp. 1–42. The title of the collection in the original German gives a clue as to how Balthasar understands the notion of time's 'fragmentariness' in this essay: *Das Ganze im Fragment. Aspekte der Geschichtstheologie* (Einsiedeln, 1963): in a fragment *the whole* may appear.
144 See also on this E. P. Meijering, *Augustin über Schöpfung, Ewigkeit und Zeit: das elfte Buch der 'Bekenntnisse'* (Leiden, 1979).
145 *Man in History, op. cit.*, p. 1.

remaining four books of his work. As she lay dying, Monica 'directed her love upward to "the eternal Jerusalem", "our Catholic mother", "which thy people sigh for in their pilgrimage from birth until they come there"'.[146] It is the tension constituted by the polarity between this earth in its pervasive corruptness and that true home, the heavenly Jerusalem, which will henceforth be engaging Augustine's attention.

Balthasar makes the observation, and it is an acute one, that Augustine is not here changing the subject. The *Confessions* do not consist of an autobiography followed by a study in philosophical theology, as though it were almost accidental that the two ended up within the same binding. What Augustine is doing in the closing books is to explore the pre-conditions that throw light on how it was possible for there to be just such a story of sin and grace, creation and redemption, as the one he has set forth. The twin mysteries of man's fall and sanctification: these furnish the context where he will locate an account of, precisely, *time.*

Crucial is the basic contrast with which Augustine works. On the one hand there is the immutability of God, God with his eternally abiding Word in whom heaven and earth were created. On the other hand, there is a mutable world which by its creation moves out from God, passing into the non-divine. Within that world live similarly mutable rational species that not only move out from God but also, alas, move away from him in what we term 'sin'.

Augustine acknowledges that humans, animals and angels experience different modes of duration.[147] Still, these have it in common that the creature who knows duration is 'of time' with the deficient 'collectedness' or being 'gathered together' this implies and, in that way, embodies the tendency towards non-being which 'of-time-ness' entails. Later, in his commentaries on the Book of Genesis, which provide us with his theology of the cosmos, Augustine will speak more generously of the being of the animal creation in this regard, remarking how 'the beauty of cosmic time is woven out of the passing away of things, generation succeeding generation'.[148] For man, however, as for the angels, it is necessary to have an unchanging will that is 'endlessly and unfailingly united to [God]'[149]. Man, then, must go beyond all temporal mutability.

In language reminiscent of the psalmist Augustine laments the instability and disorientation that the temporality of the human condition involves.[150] Our rescuing from this state of affairs – being as we are, creatures and, more specifically, fallen creatures – can only lie in our re-discovery of how, through the world, we may return to the truly Abiding. Fortunately, God is our Origin in no merely temporal sense which would make him now past in relation to us. '*Thus* it is that He is the Beginning: unless He remained when we wandered away, there should be no abiding place for our return.'[151]

It will not surprise readers of Balthasar's trio of studies of the Greek Fathers to learn that this 're-discovery' is – so it now turns out – divine gift.

146 *Ibid.*, citing Augustine, *Confessions*, IX. 13.
147 Augustine, *Confessions* X. 17; *idem, In Genesim liber imperfectus* 8.
148 *Idem, De Genesi ad litteram,* I. 14.
149 *Idem, Confessions* I. 34.
150 *Ibid.,* XI. 29.
151 *Ibid.,* XI. 8. Italics added.

The *world at large* cannot empower our return to the Source, our access from time to the Eternal. Only the Mediator who joins the world to God in coming from the Father can do this. In a passage which combines reference to Psalms 17, 25, 26 and 62 in the Old Latin version of Scripture as well as to the Letter to the Philippians, Augustine finds Jesus Christ to be the key to conversion from the temporal to the Eternal.[152] The introduction of the figure of the Redeemer does not alter the fact that for Augustine the concept of time is philosophically and theologically inseparable from that of eternity. It is *because* we need to reach the Eternal that we need Jesus Christ. In the Mediator – the incarnate Word – the temporal and the eternal, so Augustine implies, enter into a saving synthesis. This is the notion Balthasar found in St Maximus in fuller form and took to be the heart of the Byzantine confessor's theology of both Christ and the salvation he wins for us.

It struck Balthasar that this notion of a resolution of time through reversion to the Origin gives Augustine's thought a formal similarity to Hindu, Buddhist and Gnostic concepts of time. Similarly, the questions Augustine considered most important in the philosophy of time: What is the distance between the temporal and the eternal? What is the measure of this distance?, link him to Plotinus. But what a vast difference between the Catholic bishop and either the Neo-Platonist master or the Oriental systems the notion of *God's elective love* introduces! As Balthasar writes:

> The philosopher has nothing but a mortal existence which searches for immortal love and, in the form of eros and *philosophia*, thirsts for the unattainable, at best something once grasped and now lost, now longed for. The Christian, with Augustine, can know that which is longed for as the reality of agape, which is *theologia*, the self-communication of eternal love, which has received, in grace, a time-transcending, fully true, answer.[153]

Balthasar understands that love in a full-bloodedly *Christological* way. Going beyond Augustine in a theological elaboration of his own he says:

> The sequence of events within time – fall, sin, lost being, and lost time – is always already contained in the first predestined man, who is also the last Adam, the Alpha and Omega of all times, and expressly in his blood, which blots out everything else, that is, in his passage through time and death. The time-transcending point as the point of Christ lies not only 'over', 'before' and 'after' time; it transcends it in such a way that it simultaneously contains it.

The predestined Lamb both transcends time and contains it not in the fashion that God may be said to be transcendent and yet immanent vis-à-vis his creation but through the *event* of his Incarnation, Death and Resurrection whereby he *takes time into himself*. And so Balthasar concludes:

> This descent of the Son into the eternally 'beneath' of the earth, in order to ascend from there into the eternally 'above' of all the heavens (Ephesians 4.10), is the comprehensive measure of all vertical time, that

152 *Ibid.*, XI. 29.
153 *Ibid.*, p. 19.

measure within which alone every individual reversal of time [he means by that every conversion] ... can take place. This is necessary for the establishment of true, fulfilled time.[154]

When we realize the full extent of human sin (something which we can only do by adverting to the Cross and Descent into Hell) we see how the sinful time of the creation had, by Calvary, run its course. And yet it was just then, at that 'point of greatest antithesis' between the world and God, that the 'spotless eternity' of the incarnate Word turned that 'point', by his sacrifice of love, into the 'place of the most intimate loving union between Father and Son'.[155]

Balthasar's use of patristic themes as a launching-pad for further theological reflection brings us conveniently to the first of the three major twentieth-century inspirations to be dealt with at length in this study: his debt to Henri de Lubac.

---

154 *Ibid.*, p. 33.
155 *Ibid.*, p. 36. I have made use in this final section of some material originally published in 'Approaching the Eternal: Balthasar on Time', *Second Spring. A Journal of Faith and Culture*, 2 (2002), pp. 43–9.

3

༺❀༻

Divine Mentor: Henri de Lubac

Balthasar's study of de Lubac was published as an act of homage for de Lubac's 80th birthday in 1976 but, as he himself explains, his reflections on the Lyonese master had long been maturing. What was their background?

Introduction to an oeuvre

As early as 1944, von Balthasar singled out de Lubac along with – in the far past – Goethe, and – among his contemporaries – Erich Przywara, Adrienne von Speyr and Karl Barth, as the 'constellation' of intellectual lights that guided his ideas and his mission.[1] No more than Przywara was de Lubac among the young Balthasar's Jesuit professors. But he was nonetheless his mentor. Whereas Przywara functioned philosophically in this way for Balthasar at Munich, encouraging him to reach on that level Augustine, Thomas and Newman and with their aid to confront modern philosophy, de Lubac's services were theological. In an era, in Jesuit scholasticates, of somewhat insipid Neo-Scholastic pedagogy, de Lubac opened Balthasar's mind to the Fathers and, indeed, the entire wider tradition of theology in the Church. As a result of de Lubac's inspiration, so Balthasar explained:

> 'Patristics' meant for us a Christianity whose thought was turned towards the infinite spaces of the Gentiles, and which still hoped for the salvation of the world.[2]

If de Lubac provided the impetus that led Balthasar to conceive his own Greek patristic trilogy – on Origen, Nyssa, Maximus – he also awakened Balthasar's love for Irenaeus and Denys. In the company of three Latin doctors, these two figures, one from Roman Asia, the other Syrian, would be the subject of his soundings in theological aesthetics, 'clerical style'. The specific themes Balthasar took from de Lubac, so the Italian Balthasarian scholar Giovanni Marchesi persuasively opines, were fourfold. First, there was the ordering of creation to redemption. Second is surely the emphasis on the Church as mystery and notably as Christ's spotless Bride. Third must be mentioned the encounter of the Christian 'given' – God's absolute truth – and modern unbelief. And, easier to overlook, Balthasar borrowed from de Lubac

1 *Die Weizenkorn. Aphorismen* (Einsiedeln, 1944; 1958, 3rd edition), p. 34.
2 *Rechenschaft* (Einsiedeln, 1965), p. 5.

the category 'expression' (*Ausdruck*) as perhaps the best term we have for the relation between the Trinitarian reality and the human flesh of Christ.[3]

An overview of the whole

On almost the eve of returning the proofs of his de Lubac study to the printers (this at any rate is the impression, perhaps over dramatic, Balthasar conveys), its subject put into his hands the manuscript which would become de Lubac's intellectual autobiography. The *Mémoire à l'occasion de mes Livres* proved a storehouse of material on de Lubac's life, studies, enthusiasms, friendships.[4] Not that Balthasar reconceived his own essay. De Lubac's book was patterned by chronological order, Balthasar's by a choice of themes. While de Lubac stressed the occasional nature of his writings,[5] Balthasar believed they possessed nonetheless a manifest 'organic unity'.[6] In a sense, so Balthasar thought, the key to de Lubac's output lay in his – largely unwritten – book on the 'essence' of Christian mysticism. Though de Lubac could find for such a book no satisfactory literary form, and eventually felt an adequate survey of its subject to be in every sense beyond his powers, Balthasar considered that the *idea* of it – the attraction of its idea – mastered all de Lubac's investigations into very diverse realms. The notion of a literary *oeuvre* as a series of advances on a central redoubt itself never actually reached was one that appealed to Balthasar anyway. That, we might surmise, was one reason he sought publication for the enormously rambling *preambula fidei* that is *Apokalypse der deutschen Seele*.[7] We can gain a glimpse, however, of what de Lubac's mysticism book might have contained through the substantial preface he wrote for someone else's work.[8]

For his part, Balthasar opens his own study by identifying an irreplaceable key idea in de Lubac's thought, an 'objective base concept' there. What is this concept? It is that of

> an undeniably positive dynamism, in the knowing and willing of the creature, that tends through all finite intra-worldly reality but also, through all the negations of a 'negative theology', toward a goal that cannot be reached 'from below' but is nevertheless necessary.[9]

Though something like this 'basic idea' can hardly be missed when reading de Lubac on the relation of natural and supernatural, its application goes way beyond that single theme.

Balthasar proceeded to attend to de Lubac's sources. In the early 1920s, when the war-wounded de Lubac was finishing his studies, the star of three Francophone intellectuals swung high in the firmament. These were the

---

3 G. Marchesi, SJ, 'L'influsso di Henri de Lubac su Hans Urs von Balthasar', *Gregorianum* 78. 4 (1997), pp. 719–34, and here at p. 727.

4 H. de Lubac, *Mémoire à l'occasion de mes Livres* (Namur, 1989); ET *At the Service of the Church: Henri de Lubac reflects on the circumstances that occasioned his writings* (San Francisco, 1989).

5 Compare *idem, Théologies d'occasion* (Paris, 1984).

6 *The Theology of Henri de Lubac, op. cit.*, p. 10.

7 See A. Nichols, OP, *Scattering the Seed, op. cit.*, pp. 33–244.

8 'Préface', in A. Ravier, SJ, *La Mystique et les mystiques* (Paris, 1965).

9 *Ibid.*, p. 12.

philosopher of action Maurice Blondel, the philosopher of mysticism Joseph Maréchal and the reinterpreter of Thomas in 'intellectualist' (some would say Idealist) terms Pierre Rousselot.[10] De Lubac took from them nothing especially systematic but rather a 'fundamental *élan*': a basic orientation or uplift. He took the *spirit* of their work for his own in collating the texts of St Thomas, by that date the preferred 'classic' of the Society of Jesus quite as much as for the Dominicans – though the Jesuits had long seen Thomas through the eyes of their Baroque systematician, Francisco Suárez. Balthasar's description of this *'élan'* sounds remarkably like his definition of de Lubac's 'objective base concept'.

> The paradox of the spiritual creature that is ordained beyond itself by the innermost reality of its nature to a goal that is unreachable for it and that can only be given as a gift of grace.[11]

This approach necessarily got de Lubac into hot water with the 'tutioristic scholastic theologians' who played safe (that is the point of 'tutiorism') by echoing the formulations of the approved commentators on Aquinas in the post-mediaeval centuries, rather than trying to look again, with new eyes, at Thomas's texts.

Balthasar lets the historian of mediaeval thought Etienne Gilson speak for de Lubac's supporters on the issue of the natural and the supernatural. Gilson deeply disapproved of the sixteenth-century Dominican Thomas of Gaeta ('Cajetan') whose influential commentary on Thomas's *Summa theologiae* was often treated as decisive by de Lubac's critics. Gilson treated the problem as a lack of humanistic *finesse*. Unused to nuance, unaware of the oblique, Cajetan and company were not at the level of the delicate intellectual adjustments needed. This can hardly be the whole story: Cajetan was not an anti-humanistic Scholastic but a considerable humanist in his own right. De Lubac's own 'take' on the matter was that Cajetan had imposed on Thomas a quite inappropriate grid taken from the fifteenth-century theologian Denys the Carthusian. For Denys (to be carefully distinguished from his patristic namesake!), had human nature not being given a supplementary supernatural end, in no sense would men and women have desired the vision of God. Denys also knew perfectly well that his teaching was opposed to Thomas's.

Balthasar takes the view that, in the famous quarrel over the 'new theology', the Jesuits surrendered to the more rigorist Dominicans for fear of appearing doctrinally soft-focus – just as in the eighteenth century, for fear of appearing laxist, they had reacted to Jansenist criticism by a policy of out-Heroding Herod. In neither case did it do them lasting good. De Lubac was perfectly right to reject any 'dichotomy' of nature and grace, and to espouse the view that a sound philosophy will always tremble on the verge of becoming theology, just as a sound theology will always possess philosophical backbone. For Balthasar, the ultra-orthodox Dominicans of the 1950s

---

10 For de Lubac's debt to Blondel see A. Russo, *Teologia e dogma nella storia* (Rome, 1990); for his use of Rousselot's work, see J. M. McDermott, SJ, 'De Lubac and Rousselot', *Gregorianum* 74. 7 (1997), pp. 735–59.

11 *The Theology of Henri de Lubac, op. cit.*, p. 13.

are, despite the seeming contrast, forerunners of the secularistic Christians of the 1970s who sold out the faith to 'sciences' of various sorts.

De Lubac's integration of philosophy/theology, nature/grace recaptures for Balthasar the attitude of both the Fathers and St Thomas. Unlike some supporters of the 'new theology', Balthasar insists that Aquinas is fundamentally one with the Fathers – even the Greek Fathers and ecclesiastic writers, such as Origen – in his most basic positions. Thomas's thesis that nature desires the vision of God but only grace meets the desire is nothing more or less than the precipitate of patristic theology as a whole. Whether the historical St Thomas would have recognized this thesis when put in quite such bald terms remains a matter of debate among students of Aquinas' work.[12] But Balthasar is right to say that the background of most of *la nouvelle théologie* was not simply such non-Thomistic sources as Newman, the writers of the Catholic Tübingen school, Blondel and the nineteenth-century French philosophers of spirit. It lay also in certain currents in Thomism itself. There come to mind, for instance, Ambroise Gardeil's insistence that theological work must always be homogeneous with the 'revealed given' in all its concrete historicity, and more widely the new image of Thomas as reader of the Fathers purveyed by the historical theologians who were Gardeil's successors in the northern French Dominican study house, *Le Saulchoir*.[13]

Pope and Curia – who had never intervened in de Lubac's case – eventually made up for their benign neglect of him during his consequent difficulties with the Jesuit Society. That was when John XXIII named him a consultor of the theological commission preparing for a new General Council. Like his election to the Institut de France, this was some compensation for the humiliation of seeing his books withdrawn from the open shelves of Jesuit libraries or recalled from bookshops. But Balthasar points out that, in reality, de Lubac's stock stood no higher in his native France after the Council than before it. Progressive-minded intellectuals, who dominated post-Conciliar Catholicism in that country, treated him as yesterday's man. The bishops, some of whose policies he had criticized, were distinctly cool. He was charged with pessimism about developments in the Church; Balthasar defends him by saying he simply remained faithful to his vision of authentic Catholicity.[14]

Nor was this an idiosyncratic vision. The ample – for some, too ample – references with which his work was freighted witness de Lubac's wish to make his writing as impersonal as possible. As Balthasar remarked polemically but not wholly inaccurately of de Lubac's flagship work, *Catholicisme*,[15] de Lubac's book was 'a tapestry', a composition formed from selections of the 'oldest theology, which could only appear as new theology to certain reactionaries'.[16] Balthasar compares the role of de Lubac's sources to the

12 J.-H. Nicolas, OP, 'Les rapports entre la nature et le surnatural dans les débats contemporains', *Revue thomiste* XCV (1995), pp. 399–416.
13 See on this F. Bertoldi, 'Appunti sul rapporto tra von Balthasar e la Nouvelle Théologie', *Communio* 105 (1989), pp. 108–23.
14 See *Henri de Lubac, Viaggio nel Concilio; Hans Urs von Balthasar, Viaggio nel Postconcilio. Interviste con Angelo Scola* (Milan, 1985).
15 H. de Lubac, *Catholicisme. Les aspects sociaux du Dogme* (Paris, 1938; 1983, 6th edition).
16 *Prüfet alles – das Gute behaltet* (Ostfildern, 1986); ET *Test everything. Hold fast to what is good* (San Francisco, 1989), p. 14.

voice of the chorus in Greek tragedy. To some extent this compromises his point if the role of the chorus is to represent the dramatist's own view. Actually, de Lubac by no means lacked personal intent, as Balthasar well knew.

True, the topics of de Lubac's theology – from mediaeval exegesis to Buddhism, from nineteenth-century French socialism to the Christian Platonism of the Renaissance – seem to defy general description. But Balthasar held that all becomes plain if the surveying eye takes de Lubac's *Catholicisme*, his first and single most influential book, as its vantage point. The intention is to show Catholic Christianity as a fullness so great that it amounts to understanding's widest horizon. Narrowness is the Church's true opposite. Alas, modern rationalistic humanism begins in anti-theistic reaction, thus occluding for culture the real orientation of the world. For Balthasar, de Lubac's desire to win back terrain from a false naturalism explains almost everything in his output. It explains the re-instatement of the wider symbolics, patristic and early mediaeval, of the Eucharist; the controversial defence of Origen and his own confrère Teilhard de Chardin; the recovery of the integrated vision of Church, world, Kingdom, in the Fathers and High Scholastics.

The challenge of Godlessness, West and East

One of de Lubac's specialties was showing how seeming antinomies can be resolved in a higher synthesis – at any rate in the true Church! Balthasar picks this up when he introduces de Lubac's *Catholicisme* as an answer to the conflicting atheisms of Western Europe and East Asia. The first offers a social and collectivist answer to the problems of human beings (evidently, de Lubac was writing in an epoch when the principal organized atheism in the West was Communism); the second offers to the same problems a solution that is interior and individualist. But Catholicism is *both* inextricably social *and* interior; the one gains in direct, not inverse, proportion to the victories of the other.

For enlightenment on de Lubac's picture of Western atheism the reader must turn to three works: *Le Drame de l'Humanisme athée* of 1944; *Proudhon et le Christianisme* (on nineteenth-century French Socialism and its implications), which followed it the next year, and finally, much influenced by certain passages in the Second Vatican Council's Pastoral Constitution on the Church in the Modern World, *Athéisme et le sens de l'Homme* in 1968. But the first of these books – 'The Drama of Atheistic Humanism' – is the crucial one. De Lubac shows no sympathy for either Karl Marx or Friedrich Nietzsche, the prophet of non-Marxian atheism in the West, while reserving severer censures for their positivist contemporary Auguste Comte. It is, however, Ludwig Feuerbach, the German philosopher of systematic atheism, who is his chief bête noire. It was Feuerbach who launched the first two, at any rate, of these thinkers directly or indirectly on their careers. Without Feuerbach, would they have accepted the dictum that what is given to God is subtracted from man? In Marx, French socialism, English political economy and German metaphysics might have mixed as a very different soup, while without Feuerbach's influence on Arthur Schopenhauer and Richard Wagner Nietzsche would have been a different man. Nietzsche intrigued de Lubac (he would return to him in 1950 in *Affrontements mystiques*). On Balthasar's interpretation, de Lubac makes Nietzsche a strange kind of European Buddhist for whom *samsara*, the flux of change, and *nirvana* with its bliss, can be made to coincide in the enlarged awareness of the *Uebermensch* – the 'superman' to whose emergence Nietzsche looked forward. De Lubac was not very happy, though, with the professional anti-atheists of the nineteenth century – Dostoevsky whose work, he thinks, teems with ambiguities except at a few luminous points (the figure of Alyosha in *The Brothers Karamazov*, the death of Raskolnikov in *Crime and Punishment*), and Kierkegaard who did not realize the possible services a *converted* Hegelian could do for the faith. Balthasar, by contrast, was a lifelong admirer of both Dostoevsky and Kierkegaard, as *Apokalypse der deutschen Seele* bears witness. And as to Hegel, while *Apokalypse* was much more muted in its bestowal of esteem, Balthasar made his own, discreet, use of Hegel, chiefly in ecclesiological matters, in the last volume of the theological logic.

How, then, to evaluate Asiatic atheism which, for de Lubac, is what *au fond* Buddhism is – despite the emergence in the Amida Buddhism of Japan of a kind of theology of grace. For Balthasar, the Buddhism which emerges from de Lubac's three studies, is very much as Vladimir Soloviev (another hero of the theological aesthetics) considered it to be: the purest mysticism that has ever existed – but with no space for the living God.[17] What Schopenhauer approved in Buddhism – ascetic love without an object – is what makes it ultimately a dream. Only esoteric Buddhism (like the Amida version) finds an object, but Amida's saviour-figure is without historical foundation, providing no firm basis for a grasp of a merciful God. Fortunately, the grace of Christ can be efficacious even in a putative way of salvation that is objectively insufficient: a claim that *Catholicisme* went out of its way to affirm.

Both atheisms, the Western and the Eastern, are out of step with the recognition of *persons* and their irreducible value, the atheism of the West because it is collectivist, the atheism of the East because it is monistic.[18] This is an important reason, Balthasar thinks, why de Lubac championed Teilhard: his evolutionism, whatever its metaphysical weaknesses, is fundamentally personalist. It is in persons, the level of the personal – personal agency, personal will in love – that for Teilhard the cosmos comes to its climax.

Balthasar notes the seemingly fortuitous origin of de Lubac's Buddhist essays in the curriculum he was obliged to teach to at Lyons. But, despite a willingness to identify occasional affinities between other religions and the Gospel, the conviction of Christianity's uniqueness went back far in the story of de Lubac's mind. As long ago as 1912, one of his earliest Jesuit teachers, Joseph Huby, had edited a remarkable handbook on the history of religions called, provocatively, *Christus*. In his introduction, Huby dealt with the issue of likeness and unlikeness in terms which anticipate de Lubac's predominant concern in the quarrel over the 'supernatural'. The mistake made by

---

17 H. de Lubac, *Aspects du bouddhisme* (Paris, 1951); *idem, La rencountre du bouddhisme et de l'Occident* (Paris, 1952); *idem, Amida. Aspects du bouddhisme, II* (Paris, 1955).
18 For Balthasar's critiques of these religious and philosophical world-views, see R. Gawronski, SJ, *Word and Silence. Hans Urs von Balthasar and the Spiritual Encounter between East and West* (Edinburgh, 1995), pp. 5–40.

Christianity's opponents, Huby opined, had to do with that very thing. As he wrote:

> Some deny it a priori; others, by a misunderstanding reminiscent of certain apologists more zealous than they are informed, seem to imagine the world of nature and the world of grace to be total strangers the one to the other. They happen upon some points of contact between Christianity and other religions, and straightaway congratulate themselves on having undermined all transcendent revelation. This is to disregard the fact that in Catholic doctrine the order of supernature and the order of nature are neither disparate nor contrary, that the supernatural goes beyond the natural through enlarging and deepening it, that the supernatural pre-supposes in us root capacities and basic possibilities that it actualises and perfects. What is so astonishing about noticing analogies and contact between these two orders? The sophisms [of Christianity's critics] consist in concluding from these partial coincidences and material similarities, to a total, vital identity.[19]

One might just as well suppose, Huby concluded, that man is no more than an animal since animals and humans alike show signs of sense-related activity.

The supernatural

Still sticking to his plan of treating *Catholicisme* as the departure point of all de Lubac's work, Balthasar now seeks to show the way three main literary projects stem from it: the enquiry into the supernatural, the books on mediaeval exegesis, and the various defences of Teilhard. It is something of a tour de force of interpretation, but by no means an unnatural one. We can begin with the way *Catholicisme* pre-contains the writings on the supernatural. Those writings ask, how can man in his natural order be interiorly ordained to the order of the perfection of grace without in the least being able to demand it for himself? For Balthasar, de Lubac was a 'young David' pitted against the 'Goliath' of the modern rationalization – 'logicization' – of the Christian mystery. This is a dig at Neo-Thomists of a certain stamp. We shall see, however, that Balthasar is not impervious to the force of their criticisms of de Lubac's theology of grace.

In the opening historical section of *Surnaturel* the argument is put forward that by abreaction from the (condemned) views of the Louvain theologians of the seventeenth century to the effect that the grace of original righteousness was 'owed' to Adam for the perfection of his nature (Baius) or was the means for him to exercise his freedom (Jansen), an equally erroneous understanding of the texts of Augustine (and Thomas) emerged.[20] The essence of man was located in the sheerly natural goal of a created spirit. This, comments Balthasar, is the thesis in the genealogy of errors that de Lubac will not cease to

19 J. Huby (ed.), *Christus. Manuel d'histoire des religions* (Paris, 1912), p. x, cited in H. de Lubac, SJ, 'Un inédit. Mémoire sur mes premières années, II', in *Bulletin de l'Association Internationale Cardinal Henri de Lubac*, II (1999), pp. 6–28. On Huby, see de Lubac's 'In memoriam. Le Père Joseph Huby', *Recherches de science religieuse* 35 (1948), pp. 321–24.
20 H. de Lubac, *Surnaturel. Etudes historiques* (Paris, 1946).

defend against all comers. It re-surfaces in the books de Lubac published on the same subject once the crisis over the orthodoxy of his doctrinal position had subsided: *Augustinisme et théologie moderne* and *Le Mystère du surnaturel*, both from 1965. Material quarried from Thomas's account of human freedom sought to show from that angle too that Aquinas was largely uninterested in any other goal for created spirit than the supernatural one. Raids on the history of the vocabulary involved strongly suggest how a systematic use of the language of the 'supernatural' much postdates Thomas. It would result in modern times in a distinct treatise, *De Deo elevante*. In itself, such research into philology and pedagogy proves nothing. But it is indicative.

More widely: for de Lubac, man is a paradox. He is the being that tries to reach the total good though he cannot – cannot without outside aid, that is: namely, without the help of God. In what de Lubac regards as a key text for theological anthropology, Thomas too sees such a being as more noble than one that, by its own inner resources, can reach a goal, but only of a limited kind.[21]

But this text is not entirely unambiguous. For his part, Balthasar insists we have to get beyond a view of grace as simply a means to fulfil our natural aspirations. The entire natural order is located *within* the supernatural order of God's primary intent in the creation of man. In saying as much, he offers de Lubac a Barthian corrective. We were not brought into existence just for the sake of our own beatitude but for the glorifying of the God of gracious love. (That might also be called an Irenaean corrective: shades of Mongrain's 'reciprocal doxology'.) Basing himself on two passages from *Surnaturel* Balthasar exults:

> Beatitude is service, vision is adoration, freedom is dependence, possession is ecstasy.[22]

In the realm of absolute love, only the 'law of self-expropriation' holds.

Now by the time of writing 'Augustinianism and Modern Theology' where de Lubac sought to clarify his intentions and meet objections, he had another byroad in the theology of grace to consider. And this was Karl Rahner's view of the graced 'horizon' of created nature as laid out in his theory of the 'supernatural existential'. Balthasar was well known as a critic of Rahner's 'anonymous Christianity', itself a concept made possible by his wider theology of grace. So he does not let pass the opportunity to distinguish de Lubac's view from Rahner's own.

For de Lubac the human soul cannot be treated as just one instance of nature in general. It is created immediately by God and exists in a similarly equal immediacy of relation with him. Moreover, the capacity of the human spirit to take in all reality after some fashion *positively excludes the idea of a final goal for it within this world.* (Here de Lubac capitalizes on Thomas's concession that a life of contemplation of God in creation can only be for humans a *provisional* goal or end.) Taking in all reality after some fashion would surely mean taking in after some fashion God in himself – but that God lies beyond this world. Nor is it enough to say, with Maréchal, that the human spiritual creature for ever and a day approaches asymptotically the vision of

---

21 Thomas Aquinas, *Summa theologiae*, Ia.IIae., q. 5, a. 5, ad ii.
22 H. de Lubac, SJ, *Surnaturel, op. cit.*, pp. 483; 494.

God. (Tantalizing, but Tantalus was a sufferer in Greek mythology, so not a pleasing option.) Still, de Lubac is emphatic – and this is what differentiates him from Rahner – on one key point. In this capacity for the divine, which constitues our innermost essence, *there is not as yet any trace of supernatural grace*. Knowledge of what the human spirit 'really wants' is in no way given with our natural condition. It is solely the result of the free call of God. In *Le Mystère du surnaturel*, de Lubac remarks that, in the 1950 encyclical *Humani generis*, Pius XII was perfectly right to say man could have been created a spiritual creature *not* called to participation in God. But then this would be a very different world.[23] With all this Balthasar is clearly in agreement. In conversation with Angelo Scola, later patriarch of Venice, he called *Surnaturel* 'nothing else but the simple recovery of an important aspect of Augustine and Aquinas'.[24] But while he accepts that de Lubac has successfully distinguished the free offer of a share in the divine life from our created endowments, he is not at all so sure that justice has been done to the equally necessary distinction between the creation of spiritual being and the supernatural finality of our nature. God created in man a spiritual being ordered to participation in his own divine existence, but *this does not as yet imply that we have as our goal the intimate sharing of the divine Trinitarian friendship* – which is now the proper end of our humanity. Does this radical deification in its utter unexpectedness come across adequately in the distinctions de Lubac draws? Unless there had been some *lacunae* somewhere, could de Lubac's correctives have been misused in the way – unintended by their author – Balthasar deplores?[25]

The interpretation of Scripture

If *Catholicisme* announces de Lubac's deep interest in the theology of grace in its relation to nature, it likewise heralds his work on mediaeval biblical interpretation. For it asks, in what measure are prophecy and typology, the content of the Old Testament, ordered to the New, while all the time leaving to the latter its sheer novelty – in other words, without the content of the New Testament being grasped in advance in the Old. Balthasar points out that de Lubac always treats Scripture *theologically*. This makes his interest in patristic and mediaeval exegesis intelligible, and partially explains (if it does not wholly excuse) his lack of interest in twentieth-century biblical scholarship.[26] De Lubac's base affirmation amounts to something like this. The Word of God which became flesh in Jesus Christ prepared his Incarnation in Israel not only by shaping a history but by providing an economy of words to interpret that history. That is why there *is* an 'Old Testament', a body of literature with that name, and not just an 'Old Covenant', a set of dealings of God with Israelite humanity. In Scripture, Old Testament together with New, the Word abides in his fullness because Scripture is ever animated by the Holy Spirit. De Lubac liked a little formula from an anonymous

23 H. de Lubac, SJ, *Le Mystère du surnaturel*, *op. cit.*, p. 105.
24 *Test everything*, *op. cit.*, p. 14.
25 *Ibid.*, pp. 14–15. For de Lubac's last thoughts see his *Petite catéchèse sur nature et grâce* (Paris, 1980).
26 H. de Lubac, *Exégèse mediévale. Les quatre sens de l'Ecriture* (Paris, 1959–64, 4 vols).

patristic writer, the Pseudo-Ambrose: 'The divine Scripture always speaks and calls'.[27]

The notion of the senses of Scripture, dear to de Lubac's heart, might easily be written off as a curiosity from the theological past. In modern accounts (which are not without mediaeval forebears) we generally encounter it tidied up into a fourfold hermeneutic theory. A quartet of senses, or ways of interpreting texts, are playing together: the literal or historical sense; the typological (sometimes called 'allegorical') or Christological sense; the tropological or moral sense; and the anagogical or mystical (sometimes called 'eschatological') sense. Balthasar will not accept the relegation of this approach to a lumber room in the theological attic. Seeking to illuminate de Lubac's interest in it, he calls it 'an instrument for seeking out the deepest articulations of the story of salvation'. He recalls how, in an encomium on de Lubac, the newly enthroned archbishop of Paris, Jean-Marie Lustiger, put together de Lubac's enthusiasm for early mediaeval exegesis with the disdain for much of the biblical scholarship of our own time.

> The Middle Ages served for him as a sort of protected laboratory for investigating this great crisis of positivist thought in matters of exegesis from which Karl Barth tried to extricate himself . . .[28]

This comment neatly joins Barth and de Lubac, two congruent influences on Balthasar's thinking. It also suggests the momentous issues for the identity and intelligibility of doctrine this seemingly arcane subject opens up.

Now de Lubac's first love among exegetes was Origen.[29] Balthasar, we have seen, shared this love. Origen prepares the way for the developed mediaeval treatment of the senses of Scripture. One important service de Lubac's Origen studies performed was to clarify just how the Alexandrian master understood the issues. Origen uses two schemes, each with three senses. The first, which follows the Jewish philosopher Philo's analysis of the make-up of the human being as body, soul and spirit, proposes a trio of historical, moral and mystical senses of Scripture, corresponding to these three human powers or aspects. This is, explains Balthasar, an 'ascensional' scheme, which bears in mind the individual's need to follow a path of purification if he or she is to have real knowledge of the divine mysteries.[30] (The anthropology it houses is, incidentally, still very much that of Eastern Orthodox writers.) Contrary to what is sometimes alleged, it remained in use in the Latin West, in unsystematic fashion, until at least the end of the Middle Ages. Balthasar stresses on de Lubac's behalf that at any rate for Origen this scheme is at the service of another one which, accordingly, enjoys the primacy. This second scheme is not so much historical, moral and mystical as it is historical, allegorical and moral (often called on this version of things

27 Cited in *ibid.* II., p. 485.
28 J.-M. Lustiger, 'Intervention', in 'Conférence de presse inaugurant les Oeuvres complètes du cardinal Henri de Lubac aux Editions du Cerf, Institut de France, le 11 décembre 1998', *Bulletin de l'Association Internationale Cardinal Henri de Lubac* II (1999), p. 57.
29 H. de Lubac, *Histoire et Esprit. L'intelligence de l'Ecriture d'après Origène* (Paris, 1950).
30 Indeed, following Origen's lead, the spiritual life and the spiritual understanding of Scripture are coterminous: thus W. F. Murphy, Jr, 'Henri de Lubac's Mystical Tropology', *Communio* 27 (2000), pp. 171–201.

'tropological') – with which latter sense 'anagogy' is associated. Here the 'history' is the Old Testament, the 'allegory' is the mystery of Christ, and the 'morality' is the life of the Church. The associated 'anagogy' is the eternal fulfilment of all the preceding, where it is the corporate destiny of humanity, and not simply the individual soul, that is at stake. So the way this second scheme is constructed has nothing particularly to do with anthropology, the make-up of the human being with his or her various powers or capacities. It has everything to do with the plan of God, the unfolding stages of salvation history.

But even this is not the whole story. The life of the Church now and the Kingdom hereafter can be regarded as phases that are internal to the total mystery of Christ. In which case, the second trio really reduces to a duo, a duo that is absolutely commonplace and basic to the mind of the Fathers. There is the 'letter' or 'type', the Old Covenant, and the 'spirit' or 'truth', the New.

Balthasar applauds the merits of the patristic and early medieval scheme or schemes. He likes the way they treat all the dimensions of meaning – the 'senses' – as indissociable one from another. He approves of the manner in which the second scheme, at any rate, treats the pullulating plurality of the Bible by reference to the single normative centre that is Christ. He finds plausible de Lubac's account of what happened to the scheme in the High Middle Ages and afterwards. For de Lubac, the emergence of the *Summa* genre with its pretensions to systematizing, precipitated a crisis in the biblical hermeneutics of the mediaevals. The 'letter' now tended to generate an autonomous science of exegesis – something which will of course continue till our own day. 'Allegory' found its future in 'dogmatics'; tropology and anagogy in 'spirituality'. De Lubac has a soft spot for Erasmus, who, he thinks, bravely tried to relaunch spiritual exegesis at an unpropitious time. Not that de Lubac is in some unqualified way banging an antique drum. He accepted that the likelihood of theology explicitly reverting to the early mediaeval scheme was slim. Nonetheless, he wanted theologians to affirm the permanent validity of the main lines of thought the scheme represented and to open themselves to a fullness and unity of meaning, in the interpretation of Scripture, such as we find that verified in the approach of the Fathers and the writers of the early mediaeval Latin Church.

Placing the unplaceable: Teilhard de Chardin

For Balthasar, *Catholicisme* has already in mind the problem faced by the Teilhard books.[31] What relation do the macro-mutations of the evolutionary process – especially the transformation of the pre-human body into the human – actually bear to that definitive transformation which is the entry of man into the divine life? In what way is the glorified Christ of the Parousia

31 H. de Lubac, *La pensée religieuse du Père Teilhard de Chardin* (Paris, 1962); *idem, La prière du Père Teilhard de Chardin* (Paris, 1964; 1968, 2nd edition); *idem, Teilhard missionaire et apologiste* (Toulouse, 1968); *idem, L'Eternel féminin. Etude sur un texte de Teilhard de Chardin* [includes *Teilhard et notre temps*] (Paris, 1968; 1983, 2nd edition); *idem, Teilhard posthume. Réflexions et souvenirs* (Paris, 1977).

the determinative goal and end (Teilhard will write, the 'Omega Point') of all evolutionary history?

De Lubac's real purpose in writing the Teilhard studies, so Balthasar believed, was to prevent Teilhard's work from being consigned to the Index of Prohibited Books (still operative until some point in John XXIII's pontificate). This was correct. De Lubac was commissioned for the task by the Jesuit General and the four Jesuit Provincials in France. Teilhard's aim, so de Lubac argued, was to counterpose to the godless scientism of the West and the impersonal mysticism of the East a view of the emerging cosmos which saw it as converging on God in Jesus Christ. Teilhard was a scientist for whom, nonetheless, spirit was 'more real' than matter, Christ than the world. This, Balthasar thinks, touched a chord in the de Lubac of 'History and Spirit in Origen', and indeed of *Corpus Mysticum*, a study of how the early mediaevals saw even the transformed elements of the Eucharist as ordered to something more wonderful still – the union of Christ and his members in the eternal Church.[32] The world is united from above and beyond itself. It is united only divinely. It reaches coherence only through the Omega Point that is Christ.

Conscious of the widely shared criticisms of *Teilhardisme*, de Lubac sought chiefly to defend him, thought Balthasar, on two particular points. First, Teilhard had to be exonerated from the charge that he is an immanentist thinker, for whom the universe, through grounding in God, spontaneously brings forth its own divinization. De Lubac admits that there is for Teilhard a kind of *immanent* Omega or final goal in the world's intrinsic tendency to maturation, its inbuilt direction or 'teleology'. But Teilhard did not accept that this abolishes the need for a *transcendent* Omega, which can only be thought from above, from the side of God in revelation and salvation. At a critical point in the world's maturing, so he affirmed, the initiative passes altogether to God. The world's work is to prepare its own sacrifice, as it enters finally the crucible of the Parousia. Balthasar emphasizes the importance to Teilhard in such contexts of the idea of *passivity*. That lies at the opposite pole from self-divinization. Then secondly, de Lubac, while conceding the unsatisfactory nature of Teilhard's attempts at metaphysics, stresses Teilhard's horror of doctrinal Modernism. For Teilhard, to abandon the dogmatic principle would be to give up the attempt to write a specifically Christian cosmology. This is fair enough comment, but the question is whether Catholic doctrine can play its role in cosmology without the maieutic help of a consistent metaphysic worked out in the twofold light of both reason and revelation. Here, despite certain outdated elements in his scientific culture, Thomas remains more useful than Teilhard.

In 1963, when the German edition of Teilhard's *Le Milieu divin* appeared, Balthasar would add his own, rather more tough-minded comments, writing both in the Viennese theological journal *Wort und Wahrheit* and the widely read Zurich daily, the *Neue Zürcher Nachrichten*. Though Balthasar opens both of these articles by praising *Le Milieu divin* as a book which, owing to its author's passionate Catholic spirituality, has a real power to illuminate and convert, he cannot avoid entering some serious criticisms as well. Though he accepts de Lubac's point about Teilhard's anti-Modernism, Balthasar considered

---

32 *Idem, Corpus mysticum. L'Eucharistie et l'Eglise au Moyen Age. Etude historique* (Paris, 1944; 1968, 3rd edition).

Teilhard's evolutionism – which represents for the Jesuit palaeontologist not simply a hypothesis about the development of species but a total *Weltanschauung* – has become the motor driving his spirituality along.[33] Unfortunately, this distorts his notion of God and of Christ. Where God becomes the 'central Monad' of the world, and ceases to be the 'totally other', his Word can no longer be heard as coming from *the Lord* to Israel and the Church.[34] Teilhard's emphasis on energetic achievement in world-making contradicts the principal idea he hoped to commend: that our destiny and that of the cosmos lies in the 'amorisation of the world', imaged in the Cross of Christ. In this relentless concern for successful developmental efficacy the disinterestedness of love, indeed its 'groundlessness', actually disappears from view.[35] If we are going to have a Christian thinker for whom evolution is the chief category, then we should do better to stick with Vladimir Soloviev, who at least does not 'take all the wind from godless Zarathustra's sails'.[36] Somehow, Teilhard has unwittingly imbibed a dose of Nietzsche, and it was the wrong medicine. Balthasar counsels his readers to remain 'under' God. Let us build no castles in the sky, not even pious ones, lest they prove towers of Babel.

By 1969 Balthasar was even less enamoured of Teilhard's eschatology, though he forbore from mentioning him by name. He now rejected outright any notion of 'convergence' between inner-worldly teleology and a divine 'Day Omega'. The 'postulate of such a convergence', he wrote, harshly:

> is nothing other than the erection of a new myth and idol in the room of Christian faith … It is a myth which walls man up within a closed inner-worldly horizon, in place of leading him toward the true freedom of the children of God.[37]

Creature and paradox

A writer much of whose time is spent expounding the thoughts of other people (such as de Lubac, and indeed Balthasar, but scarcely Teilhard) prompts us eventually to ask, Yes, but what do *you* think about things? For a graphic reply, Balthasar turns to three short works by de Lubac, *Paradoxes* of 1945, *Nouveaux Paradoxes* of 1954 and, in between these two, *De la connaissance de Dieu* (1948) which became in 1956 *Sur les chemins de Dieu*. Perusal of these essays – the first two are really just collections of aphorisms or *aperçus* – leads Balthasar to find the heart of de Lubac's original contribution in *theological epistemology*. For de Lubac, rationalism is the illegitimate domestication of the human spirit. Yet for all that, de Lubac is hostile to the evisceration of theological reason by appeal to mysticism. The intellectual and the mystical must go hand in hand or they will not 'go' at all. We have, de Lubac thought, a capacity for affirmation that extends beyond our faculty

---

33 'Die Spiritualität Teilhards de Chardin. Bemerkungen zur deutschen Ausgabe von *Le Milieu divin*', *Wort und Wahrheit* 18 (1963), pp. 339–50, and here at p. 341.
34 *Ibid.*, p. 342.
35 *Ibid.*, p. 346.
36 *Ibid.*, p. 344. Balthasar repeated this criticism when he re-wrote the piece as 'Zum Göttlichen Bereich Teilhards de Chardin', *Neue Zürcher Nachrichten*, 4 May 1963, Beilage *Christliche Kultur* 27. 18.
37 'Die Struktur der Kirche in einer säkularisierten Welt', *Vaterland* 44, 22 February 1969.

for representing reality or arguing about it. We shall not practise negative or apophatic theology aright unless we have seen that 'in the *positio*' – in the statements of affirmative or cataphatic theology – there is 'already present', as de Lubac put it, 'an *"eminentia"'*, which shows criticism the way.[38] By 'eminence' there he meant a quality of affirmation which can survive, and triumphantly survive, the necessary qualifications introduced by the demands of critical reason in negative theology.

An example of what de Lubac meant by the intellectual and the mystical needing to go hand in hand is found in his most basic account of God. For him, the proofs of the existence of God are necessary instruments of thought. And yet the concept of God they show to be instantiated is not itself gen-erated by reason. Such thinking about God is but one example of the 'paradoxes' in those of de Lubac's books which blazon that word in their titles. Another example leads on to Balthasar's last main subject which will be de Lubac's account of the Church and her faith. Speaking of the theolo-gical concept of Holy Tradition de Lubac wrote:

> The living mystery expresses itself in historical forms and ... the mystery always transcends these [same] forms.[39]

The Church and her faith

Balthasar treats de Lubac's 'fundamental theology' – his theological inves-tigation of the historic revelation, and the act of faith which registers and receives it – as an aspect of his ecclesiology. This is feasible because for de Lubac the Church, and not the individual, is the primary subject of the act of faith, the chief agent involved in actually carrying out the act of believing. First of all though, he comes to grips with the mystery of the Church in and for itself.

Even that is late in the day in de Lubac's writing. As with the Fathers, remarks Balthasar, until late on the Church was the hidden presupposition of de Lubac's theology. True, it was not to the fore, but neither was it on the margin. It was the atmosphere in which all else was seen. This is why Bal-thasar can call de Lubac's *Méditation sur l'Eglise* the spirituality which cor-responds to the theology in *Catholicisme*.[40] In terms of lived experience of the realities *Catholicisme* describes, the Church is essential. Balthasar reports on *Méditation* that in this work 'the mystery of the Church rises up as the existential centre of the entire mystery of salvation'. The Church is itself mysteric: a community convoked by God and not simply a congregation of men, and hence eternal as well as temporal, invisible as well as visible.

In succeeding chapters of *Méditation* other aspects come to light. For de Lubac the Mass is at the heart of the Church. The Church makes the Eucharist but the Eucharist makes the Church (that is why, comments Bal-thasar, the Eucharist can be true only in the Church). The Church is ineluctably related to God as well as to the world – hence the Church and its culture cannot be absorbed by State or nation. The Church is the sacrament of

38 *The Theology of Henri de Lubac, op. cit.*, p. 95.
39 *Ibid.*, p. 102.
40 H. de Lubac, *Méditation sur l'Eglise* (Paris, 1953; 1975, 4th edition).

Christ, and so can never be reduced to sociology. Over against the twelfth-century abbot-theologian Joachim of Fiora who predicted a new, charismatic Church of the Spirit: the Church's constitution, being divinely originated, can never be transcended.[41] Balthasar treats the last three chapters encomiastically. The seventh chapter wonderfully evokes the 'man of the Church' and hence unwittingly portrays de Lubac himself, who accepted the blows other Churchmen dealt him peacefully, for love of the Church. The eighth chapter manifests a wisdom that for Balthasar blows away all the hyper-criticisms of the Church by acidulous post-Conciliar commentators – in advance! The ninth and last chapter is a lyrical explosion: a meditation on the affinity of the Church with the Mother of God.

What befell, then, this ecclesiology after Vatican II? De Lubac's *L'Eglise dans la crise actuelle* dates from 1969. Written at the height of the worst troubles of the French Church, which was besieged by ultra-traditionalists on the one hand, ultra-progressivists on the other, the book sought to show the doctrinal continuity between the documents of the Second Vatican Council and the preceding ecclesial tradition. It is instructive to see which parts of it Balthasar singles out for special mention. First, there are de Lubac's criteria for authentic renewal. Without a genuine love for Jesus Christ, and love too for the unity of the Church, there would, so de Lubac predicted, be no true renewal of Catholicism. He warned against a theology that was unilaterally political (these were also the years when the 'political' theology was, in warmer climes, turning Liberationist), or indeed exclusively charismatic (the 'Charismatic Renewal' was taking off about then as well). Next, Balthasar drew attention to the way this collection of essays applies to ecclesiology de Lubac's epistemological ideas about paradox in its relation to primordial intuition. The Church contains aspects which are contrasting, and may seem contradictory. But the contradictions are resolved when the paradoxes we note send us back to the original mystery, Christ in the Church. Finally, Balthasar highlights the chapter on the religions of the world in patristic perspective. In fact, de Lubac uses this essay to present a view of world religions as in a state of mutual contradiction – which in itself shows they cannot *per se* be means of salvation willed by God. It follows from the approach adopted in *Catholicisme* that world history turns on a single axis, not multiple ones. But the axis is such that it can give shape to all the truths genuinely embodied in the other religions.

To the 1971 study *Les Eglises particulières dans l'Eglise universelle* (whose case Balthasar sums up baldly as 'agin' national Bishops' Conferences), de Lubac added a piece on the motherhood of the Church which reiterates, in the post-Conciliar context, a theme of his earlier ecclesiology. Only where the Church is understood comprehensively as our Mother, can the ecclesial mandate of bishops and priests be understood as real fatherhood (and not just institutional administration). The decline of these living symbols of supernatural generation through the Church was a major preoccupation of Balthasar's own writing in the 1970s and afterwards.[42]

---

41 *Idem, La postérité spirituelle de Joachim de Flore* (Namur-Paris, 1979–1981, 2 vols).
42 Cf. the presentation of this theme, with debts to de Lubac, by A. Nichols, OP, 'The Bishop as Bridegroom of his Church: a Roman Catholic Contribution', in J. Baker (ed.), *Consecrated Women? A Contribution to the Women Bishops Debate* (Norwich, 2004), pp. 157–63.

But what would the Church be without the faith of the Church? In turning to that topic in *La Foi chrétienne, essai sur la structure du Symbole des Apôtres*, de Lubac in a sense reversed the terms of the enquiry and asked, What would the faith be without the Church of the faith?[43] He insists – this is Balthasar's prime contention – that faith is not simply Christian, it is ecclesial. The ultimate subject of faith – i.e. the ultimate agent in the act of faith – is not the individual believer but (as we have mentioned) the Church herself. The individual must be educated to share in the Church's act. In terms of faith's material object (as Aquinas would say), faith centres on the triune God in his movement towards the world in Christ. But in terms of its formal object – the perspective in which it engages with this content, faith for de Lubac is the Church's welcome to this movement. Faith is perfect *subjectively* in Mary the Mother of the Lord who is also Mother of the Church. It is perfect *objectively* in the mission with which the Church is invested and for which she is guaranteed the integrity of Word and sacrament.

The study culminates for Balthasar in its account of the unity of faith. De Lubac teaches that there is in the end only *one* dogma, the mystery of which needs to be explained in its many aspects. Here we can detect the hand which, perhaps, was most responsible for the presence in *Dei Verbum*, the Dogmatic Constitution on Divine Revelation of the Second Vatican Council, of the statement that Christ is not only the Mediator of revelation but also its 'fulness':[44] words to which Pope John Paul II alluded in giving Balthasar the Paul VI Prize. Synthetic, Christological, concentration, then: these are shades – or anticipations – of Karl Barth. It is notable that when de Lubac wants to defend the notion of dogma ('the dogmatic affirmation [he wrote], without constituting by itself alone the act of faith, is essential in order to nourish and orient the latter'), it is to the example of Christology that he turns. Maintaining the primacy of objective being over 'personal meanings and appropriations' is vital because 'everything depends on what Jesus Christ, the Son of God, was'. Unless we assert this primacy, i.e. know through dogma who Christ is in himself, faith will become 'an illusory dream or an anthropocentric withdrawal'.[45]

A Renaissance conclusion

Balthasar ends his study, somewhat abruptly, with some remarks on de Lubac's study of the Renaissance Christian-Platonist and Lay Dominican Pico della Mirandola.[46] Leaving aside the banal consideration that *Pic de la Mirandole* was the last of de Lubac's books to reach Balthasar, the reason for

---

43 H. de Lubac, *La Foi chrétienne, essai sur la structure du Symbole des Apôtres* (Paris, 1970).
44 See *idem, La Révélation divine. Commentaire du préamble et du chapitre I de la Constitution 'Dei verbum' du Concile Vatican II* (Paris, 1983, 3rd edition), pp. 43–48. However, de Lubac himself notes the statement in Pius XI's encyclical *Mit brennender Sorge* , 'In Jesus Christ, the Son of God become man, the fulness of divine revelation has appeared'. He also counselled in this study against a 'pure' or unqualified Christocentrism (Christ is the Word of the Father), but nonetheless claimed that Christocentrism is indeed the best way of linking the mysteries as called for by the First Vatican Council.
45 H. de Lubac, SJ, *The Christian Faith. An Essay on the Structure of the Apostles' Creed* (ET San Francisco, 1986), pp. 102–103. The second citation is actually taken, approvingly, from the Scots Presbyterian theologian T. F. Torrance.
46 H. de Lubac, *Pic de la Mirandole. Etudes et discussions* (Paris, 1974).

choosing this finale was probably the – altogether admirable – way Pico combined spiritual independence with catholicity of attitude. His anthropology begins from human freedom, but this is no closed humanism: the goal of that freedom is the supreme peace of all things in union with God. Pico's attempt to combine Plato and Aristotle (hardly the first in history, Thomas Aquinas had, if not explicitly, the same project!) exemplifies the spirit de Lubac approved: treating concepts as indispensable yet limited, as tending to point beyond themselves. Pico treats man as essentially an ecstatic being who must model himself on Thrones and Seraphim (shades of *Surnaturel*). His gleaning husks of pagan wisdom (the *prisca theologia* he sought among the ancients, classical and otherwise) puts one in mind of de Lubac's raids on Asiatic wisdom as well. A Renaissance man can form the climax of a study of – and by – a modern priest-student of the Catholic tradition in all its length and breadth, height and depth, precisely because Balthasar shared the view that the Renaissance was not anti-Catholic, un-Christian or essentially atheistic, but simply 'a period in which men were trying to find a new, more personal piety, and new expressions of religious thought'.[47] So why *not* end with Pico as, like de Lubac, a wonderful *homo ecclesiasticus*, 'man of the Church'?

---

47 R. Pfeiffer, *History of Classical Scholarship, 1300–1850* (Oxford, 1976), p. 19.

4

❀❀❀

Divine Interlocutor: Karl Barth

Getting a grip

Balthasar's book length study of Barth, a triumph of sympathetic interpretation, was published in 1951.[1] This date stands in evident relation to ten
extremely well-attended lectures Balthasar gave in Barth's presence over the
winter of 1948–9 at the Basle *Verein für christliche Kultur*. (In pre-ecumenical
days, this event must have been *piquant*.) His foreword explains the rationale
of the work. A number of Catholic writers – including some highly distinguished ones such as Karl Adam, Erik Petersen, Jérôme Hamer, Gottlieb
Söhngen and Erich Przywara (Balthasar thought especially highly of the last
two) – had tried to come to terms with Barth's work. But this was before
Barth's *Kirchliche Dogmatik*, his great *Summa theologiae* setting out his mature
views, was much advanced, if indeed when some of these authors wrote it
had even started. Balthasar himself had earlier ventured comments on Barth's would-be theological revolution: both before the Second World War in,
for example *Apokalypse der deutschen Seele*;[2] and during or after it, in substantial articles in *Divus Thomas* – the house journal of Germanophone
Thomism – and the *Revue de Science religieuse*.[3] In 1939 he had already
attempted, in brief compass, an overall view of Barth for Catholic readers in
the Viennese *Theologie der Zeit*. The simple clarity of the resulting article, 'Karl
Barth und der Katholizismus', gives us an orientation.

Barth, we read, is the 'most significant Protestant thinker of modern times,
and perhaps indeed since Luther and Calvin'.[4] After his Calvinist opening
(evidently, that is how at this point Balthasar saw Barth's *The Letter to the
Romans*), Barth has built more and more Catholic material into what is still,
however, basically a Protestant dogmatics. But the way Barth presents his
Catholic stuff – in the perspective of his own distinctive concept of theology

---

1 An abridged English translation appeared almost twenty years later as *The Theology of
Karl Barth* (New York, 1971). Another twenty years elapsed before a full English text
became available: *The Theology of Karl Barth. Exposition and Interpretation* (San Francisco,
1991).
2 *Apokalypse der deutschen Seele* III, *op. cit.*, pp. 316–91. See my account in A. Nichols, OP,
Scattering the Seed, *op. cit.*, pp. 219–29.
3 'Analogie und Dialektik', *art. cit.*; 'Analogie und Natur', *art. cit.*; 'Deux notes sur Karl
Barth', *Revue de Science religieuse* 25 (1948), pp. 92–111.
4 'Karl Barth und der Katholizismus', *Theologie der Zeit* (1939), pp. 126–32, and here at p.
127.

as the confession of God's grasp of the world in his revealing action – allows him to treat it as all grist to Evangelicalism's mill. The *difference* between Barth and the Catholic Church boils down to two things. The first is how to understand the relation of a sinful world to the God of grace. The second is how to understand the relation of the world of nature to the God of revelation.

Barth's idea is that the world's values are worth nix in the eyes of God, because man's revolt against God cancels out their positive charge. How would a king view even the virtues of a general who had raised the standard of revolt against him? Only a sublime act of pardon could reinstate him. Balthasar replies that, following Paul, Augustine and the (sixth-century) Second Council of Orange, Catholicism also considers the grace of God to be bestowed on human beings by his free sovereign mercy and that alone. But, unlike Barth, it treats Paul's descriptions of the negative divine judgment on human aspiration *not* as what actually is the case but as what would be the case *had God not shown the world mercy*. But he has, and so everything looks different. Christian humanism now makes sense after all.

What, then, about the second issue: 'nature' and the God of revelation? That is Balthasar's way of saying, 'nature and supernature'. And why does he put it like that – nature and *revelation*, rather than 'nature and grace'? Because we get the idea of nature – theologically speaking, this is nature as what stands in relation to super-nature – by, precisely, looking at nature in the light of revelation. When through revelation we learn of God's 'ever and essentially unowed, infinitely free and sovereign communication of the inner, intimate and personal divine life', we draw a line by contrast around our own circumscribed spiritual powers.[5] In other words, we get the point the Catholic Church is making: super-nature is more than nature, while – however, and this is the bit Barth seems to miss – super-nature presupposes the free independent spiritual being on which to lavish all this wondrous gift. In the 'drama' (this insight will be the nucleus of the later theological dramatics) between God and the creature, there is a real dialogue: a natural word, as well as a supernatural supreme word. 'Pantheologism' – where everything divinely worthwhile is comprehended within the word of grace – just cannot be right. Barth needs to shake himself free from the delusion that created nature and a sinful world are much the same thing.

Fortunately, says Balthasar, not only has Barth never drawn all the logical consequences he might from this thesis. As his writing has developed, he has also attenuated its force – conscious that it must otherwise lead eventually to 'a denial of the Incarnation, the Church, justification, and even to letting the world disappear completely into God'.[6] Increasingly, Barth recognizes not only an objective Church and objective sacraments, but also the real action of human freedom and rationality within grace – and therefore what Latin theology has called 'created grace', where grace and nature meet and kiss. That said, Balthasar appreciates the *ethical* impulse behind Barth's positions (or hesitations). What, rightly, Barth wants to neuter is that pride of life whereby thinking driven by original sin presents itself theologically as an angel of light, and the Cross of Christ is emptied of its power. From the

5 *Ibid.*, p. 129.
6 *Ibid.*, p. 131.

standpoint of 1951, Balthasar treated these early efforts at evaluation not as superseded by Barth's own development (in fact, they all post-dated the first volumes of the *Church Dogmatics*) but as constituting first drafts of the book to hand.

The aims of Balthasar's Barth book, and his admiration for Barth

In his book, the aim is, first, to expound the basic structure of Barth's thought – what in German is called the relevant 'teaching about principles', *Prinzipienlehre*, as distinct from what Barth may have to say on this or that theological topic. Then in the second half of the book, Balthasar will set out to offer a Catholic response. Balthasar stresses that the latter cannot of course be in any sense official. And yet it will not, he thinks, be eccentric or idiosyncratic. Just before Balthasar published, Pius XII had promulgated the hard-hitting encyclical on current temptations in Catholic theology, *Humani generis* (1950). Balthasar notes the two most relevant complaints for his project: an irrationalism which disdains the contribution of the Scholastics (Barth would never countenance that), and 'false eirenicism' – i.e. in regard to non-Catholic Christians and their distinctive ideas. That, surely, was a more pertinent temptation. Somewhat strangely, Balthasar claims that the material he will deal with in Barth is situated only at a tangent to the main Protestant–Catholic divide, even though that material will include sin and grace, and the doctrinal role to be given the idea of nature. Yet all these are highly germane to any evaluation of the 'magisterial Reformers'.

Balthasar's ostensible aim in writing was to understand, from a Catholic angle, a Protestant thinker of exceptional quality and depth. But a clue to his wider ambition is found in the following statement in his 'Overture' to the work:

> According to a well-known position of Newman, the Catholic Church can see herself as the embodiment of wholeness and totality only when she has done all in her power actively to incorporate the riches of all partial points of view.

What the Fathers did with ancient springs, what Aquinas did with all sorts of wisdom, that (we are to understand Balthasar as saying) he himself would like to do – doubtless, not singlehandedly – with the 'immense intellectual accomplishments of ... Protestant theology' as well as of a (very generally intended) 'modernity'.[7]

But why choose *Barth* in particular as interlocutor? For Balthasar, Barth offers at one and the same time

> the most thorough and penetrating display of the Protestant view and the closest rapprochement with Catholicism.[8]

Here, in 1951, Balthasar wants to regard Barth *both* as more obviously Protestant *and* as more potentially Catholic than he had in 'Karl Barth und der Katholizismus' back in 1939. What Balthasar means, surely, is that Barth represents the most coherent statement of the spirit of Protestantism – and at

---

7 *The Theology of Karl Barth, op. cit.*, p. 12.
8 *Ibid.*, p. 23.

the same time a marginalization of its letter. The magisterial Reformers are not exactly relegated but they are relativized: thanks to the new prominence Barth gives not just the Church Fathers but the mediaevals too. Balthasar also indicates his enormous admiration for the *manner* in which Barth writes, his passionate concern with the theological object, God himself in his revelation. This is passionate objectivity, in the service of the Word that bathes nature in its radiance, fulfilling and super-fulfilling the world's promise. What Catholic theologian could *not* profit from studying this – not least (so the present writer adds) – studying to imitate in turn?

> Who besides [Barth] in the last decades has so understood how to read Scripture: neither 'exegetically' nor 'biblicistically', neither by recon- structing hypothetical events nor by indulging in florid or pastoral rhetoric? Barth focuses on the Word, fully and exclusively, that its full splendor might radiate out to the reader. Who but Barth has gazed so breathlessly and tirelessly on his subject, watching it develop and blossom in all its power before his eyes?[9]

Balthasar thinks one would need to go back to Aquinas to answer this – not *entirely* rhetorical, then – question. Though Barth admired and learned from Kierkegaard he could not agree with the latter's severance of the reli- gious from the aesthetic. For Barth, the religious is aesthetic because it is religious! This was an old preoccupation of Balthasar's as well. Readers of his early essays on the relation of religion and aesthetics will not be surprised to find that he wanted almost immediately to qualify this statement of iden- tity.[10] Barth's 'frescoes' run the danger of all sacred art: translating the Eternal into terms of the temporal can distort, not least by exaggeration. Overall, though – this was Balthasar's judgement – Barth obtained purity of design and beauty in execution by taking 'objective theological realities', the themes of divine revelation, as constraints that set him free.

The principles at stake: analogy and Christocentrism

But these are all *stylistic* qualities of Barth's theologizing, which, at least in theory, could be shared by many others (Balthasar, not least). What about his particular standpoint in the choice of *Prinzipien* to govern his theological work? Balthasar's description of where Barth stands strongly suggests that, for all his appreciation of his fellow-Jesuit Erich Przywara, there was a clear sense in which taking Przywara's work as representative of Catholicism had led Barth astray. Przywara's first hostage to fortune consisted in treating Catholic Christianity as a *via media* between a pantheistic naturalism and a 'theopanistic' Protestantism. (By 'theopanistic' is meant: where what is cre- ated has no intrinsic value since all – in the Greek, *pan* – value is deemed to inhere only in God. Przywara had Barth's own *early* theology in mind here.) According to Balthasar, this line of Przywara's suggested a strategy to Barth. Barth could present his own mature theology as a similar middle way between on the one hand Liberal Protestantism – above all, the Protestantism of the early nineteenth-century Romantic theologian Friedrich Daniel Ernst

9 *Ibid.*, p. 26.
10 See A. Nichols, OP, *Scattering the Seed, op. cit.*, pp. 9–16.

Schleiermacher, with his privileging of religious *experience*, and on the other hand Catholicism with its claims that grace and infallibility can be built into the created order – really possessed by human beings (grace by the saints, infallibility by the hierarchy, and especially the pope). Actually, as Balthasar points out, Barth does not really take seriously Przywara's trope of the 'middle way', but regards these two positions as defining by contrast what is essential in his own. (Indeed, if anything, Barth is likely to suggest, ironically, that Schleiermacher's 'pious subject' and Catholicism's sacred persons are so fundamentally similar that they might well consider an alliance: Pietist Lutheran subjectivism plus the pope!) No, it is a second gambit of Przywara's that caused the real trouble by seriously damaging Barth's theological perception of Catholicism. In seeking an intellectual tool whereby to work out his *via media* between naturalism and theopanism, Przywara hit on the idea that perhaps the *principle of analogy* might do the trick.[11]

Indisputably, the principle of analogy was important to later Thomism as a tool of theistic metaphysics. It was, however, by no means so prominent in Thomas himself. Nor did it enjoy a comparable role in other schools of Catholic thought (indeed, the Scotists were, if anything, allergic to it). Serving well Przywara's turn, it did little to increase Barth's respect for Catholicism since, considered as a philosophical principle, *it could perfectly well be stated without reference to the name of Christ.* The notion that the basic contours of the God-world relationship could be established in a non-Christological way was anathema to Barth. The upshot is that, whereas Barth can agree with more of the specifics of Catholic doctrine than we would expect, he considers the Catholic 'system' to be vitiated as a whole. Where he disagrees with particular doctrines, this tends to be because he regards them as symptoms of something wrong in a wider outlook. Basically, Barth

> accuses [Catholicism]... of possessing an overarching systematic principle that is merely an abstract statement about the analogy of being and not a frank assertion that Christ is the Lord.[12]

So far Balthasar has only defined Barth's standpoint negatively. There are two reasons for this. One is, quite simply, that half of the ensuing book will take Barth's positive principles for its theme. But the other reason is that Balthasar wants now to note, albeit in a preliminary way, a Catholic theologian's view of Barth's view of Catholicism. This might be self-indulgent if the purpose of Balthasar's study were sheerly descriptive. But he has already declared that the work will open a dialogue. It is not only exposition, *Darstellung*. It is also interpretation, *Deutung*, and that from a Catholic point of view.

For his part, Balthasar asserts there is no reason why a Christocentrism as resolute as Barth's should *not* be the organizing principle of a Catholic theology. While not accepting that the analogy of being functions as the systematic formal principle Barth claims, Balthasar treats that principle as innocuous, or even helpful – once seen as an *auxiliary* to the work of Christian theology as a whole. So far from trying to remove God's transcendence, it is meant to secure it. The analogy of being does not only claim

11 Especially in E. Przywara, *Analogia entis, op. cit.*
12 *Karl Barth, op. cit.*, p. 37.

that the world's creaturely being – truth, goodness, beauty, unity – is in some way like God's uncreated being. It also says that it is *un*like God's – the Fourth Lateran Council of 1215, an important Council for high mediaeval theologians who used the idea of the analogy of being, would say: *far more unlike than like.* That of course had been much of the point of Przywara's mystical interpretation. For Pryzwara, applying the analogy of being to the spiritual life, the more we grow towards God, the more we realize how much further than we thought we need to grow. Distance between God and ourselves, for Przywara, increases as a result of greater proximity. Introducing Przywara to a new readership after his death, Balthasar would declare indeed that:

> The truth … of the analogy of being [in Przywara's version] was … most clearly related to Barth's own pathos: both stand against Kantianism and Hegelianism, against the methods of immanence of either Scholasticism or Modernism, against every form, whether pious or impious, of trying to get control over the living God.[13]

But the thing Balthasar wants to stress about a formal principle – whether this be the analogy of being or any other – is that it will be found at work *in* the content of theological doctrine, in 'material dogmatics'. The 'dialogue' with Barth will have to proceed, accordingly, both in terms of specific themes of Catholic dogma, for these are outworkings of formal principles, and in terms of those principles themselves, since without them the specific themes will not be seen aright. This see-sawing between 'a posteriori' and 'a priori' approaches is the hallmark of Balthasar's book.

Meanwhile he can offer a first shot at an answer to Barth's charge that Catholicism makes the free creature 'self-subsistent' vis-à-vis God's grace and thus, in effect, licenses human autonomy which is pretty close to pride, and therefore sin. The Tridentine Church was compelled – by the misconstruals entailed in the Protestant revolt – to emphasize 'works' and indeed the Church 'institution'.

> But this was done [Balthasar explains], not as a counter-concept to free grace; rather, works and institution were understood as its highest form, the most daring deed, the most breathtaking venture of grace itself.

With this perfect back-hander to Barth's opening serve, Balthasar can go on to say that, from Trent on, human being and work were to be fully affirmed while honouring God's grace 'in everything'.[14] Balthasar makes it apparent that he intends to treat this theme – grace *in* human freedom, the Word *in* the institutional Church as Christologically – indeed, as Christo*centrically* – as Barth himself. Christ's 'form' *is* the form of revelation *and indeed of creation itself* as it was meant to be and is destined to be.

---

13 'Erich Przywara', in L. Zimmy, *Erich Przywara: sein Schrifttum, 1912-1962* (Einsiedeln, 1963), p. 6. Balthasar also notes how Przywara though distrusting 'system' rejected with abhorrence 'all philosophies of experience that dispense with structure and substance', *ibid.*, p. 8.
14 *Karl Barth*, pp. 53–54.

Barth's early 'dialectical' theology

Balthasar also makes it clear he will treat Barth's thought as a developing whole. The early so-called 'dialectical' theology, which re-creates the strangeness of the revelatory event in a fallen world, must not be counter-posed against the mature theology of the *Church Dogmatics*. True, the latter are composed in limpid classical German, the former in turbulent, expressionist 'Existentialese'. But the continuities are at least as striking as the discontinuities, not least because a central category – perhaps *the* central category of Barth's ontology – remains that of *Ereignis*, 'event'.

Now Barth's early theology took the form of two successive and very different commentaries on St Paul's *Letter to the Romans* – the New Testament text where in Barth's opinion the issues of the human knowledge (and ignorance) of God, and of grace (and therefore sin) were best raised and answered. Balthasar brings out the qualities of Barth's commentaries in prose as full of fireworks as their own. The first of Barth's two attempts at representing the Paul of Romans is expressed in a powerful yet eclectic philosophical language drawn from Plato, Hegel and others; the second, while making use of Existentialism, keeps closer to biblical terms. Both have as their theme what Balthasar calls 'dynamic eschatology' which he defines as

> the irreversible movement from a fatally doomed temporal order to a new living order filled with the life of God, the restoration ... of the original ideal creation in God.[15]

The last phrase in that sentence is key to the *first* edition of the commentary, where in the course of blowing to smithereens an emasculated, sentimental reading of the Pauline Letter, Barth goes to an extreme. 'Sin' becomes any distancing from God where the 'I' is treated as seeking to enjoy a life of its own. In effect, as Balthasar remarks, for Barth at this juncture there are only two possibilities: identifying (human) nature with the Holy, or naming it as sin. (The difficulty, or rather the impossibility, of stating this in plain terms is one major reason why Barth invokes here the notion of 'dialectic' – on which more anon.) This mystical–apocalyptic choice between 'ecstasy' and 'catastrophe' does not prevent Barth from simultaneously launching a (socialist) political programme. Balthasar sums up the latter starkly. 'As reflection, subjectivity is individualism.'[16] Our unholy individuality is to be replaced by organic incorporation into the universal humanity now appearing in Christ, when everything personal about us – and not just our property – will be expropriated for the common good. That idea of our expropriation into the communion of saints will subsequently play a part, incidentally, in Balthasar's theological dramatics and his hagiology, or theological reflection on the mission of the Mother of God and the saints.

The second edition of the Romans commentary seems less weird. Under Kierkegaard's influence, Barth is affected by the thought of the 'infinite qualitative difference' between divine and human. He eschews 'Romantic immediacy', with its attempt to expunge this 'difference'. These pages express his famous assault on 'religion' as the covert form of man's would-be

15 *Ibid.*, p. 64.
16 *Ibid.*, p. 67.

self-divinization. The wayward promise in the Garden, 'You will be like God!' (Genesis 3.5), is the essence of sin. (In *Scattering the Seed*, my guide through Balthasar's early writings, it was shown how Balthasar's first essay in dogmatics accepts that starting-point for a theology of sin and grace.[17]) However ineradicable religion may prove, the Christian is not to exemplify *homo religiosus* but to take up an eschatological posture, beyond all human possibilities. But Balthasar finds in the second edition of Barth's Romans commentary much that smacks of the first. The themes of lost immediacy to God, and self-consciousness as already a fall from grace are presupposed if not actually sounded. Balthasar's most searing indictment comes in the following statement:

> The coincidence of the concept of nature and grace necessarily leads to the coinciding of the concepts of nature and sin . . . : the law of life, the entelechy of nature, is 'Eros', the 'concupiscence' of sinful, instinct-driven, love. Once more the lines of the Gnostic East meet up with those of the Reformation: they become one in the concept of 'pathos', which equates guilt and nature, drive and decadence.[18]

These are, of course, the same reservations Balthasar had noted on the eve of the Second World War.

Balthasar finds much that is real Paul in Barth's 'Romans', version two. What alarms him is how much there is that is not. The trouble lies with the way Barth *applies* to the Letter his idea of 'dialectics', implying as he does so an aboriginal seamless unity of Creator and creature. The problem is not so much, then, with the idea of dialectics *in and of itself*. In fact, Balthasar finds the idea of dialectics really rather a good one. What is good about it? First, the idea of dialectics is epistemologically astute. In objective knowledge, while we meet the real as it is, we do not possess it wholly. Emphasizing dialectical argumentation is a reminder that we should not rest on our laurels as knowing agents, but constantly seek to 'fill out' our knowledge, refine our concepts. Secondly, it is ontologically attentive. As real, the object itself – any object – is greater than its objectification. We should be open to 'possible surprises' coming from its side. Thirdly, it makes possible due regard for the difference being a person entails. Methodical dialectics enables us to draw a useful distinction between objects that are also subjects and objects that are not. When dealing with a free subject, dialectics has to undergo a metamorphosis and become a *dialogue*, an inter-personal exchange. A fourth possible advantage is that dialectics, so understood, may be able to reach an acme in the knowledge of God. It may turn out that, to raise the question of God, even in natural theology as when we ask after the status of the world as a divine epiphany, will be to 'crown' this ascending series of senses of the term 'dialectics' or 'dialogue'. That was the view of the influential inter-war phenomenologist Max Scheler. (In dialogue with Barth and Barthians Balthasar could not, at this stage, be too assertoric on the point.) Here – if this possibility is verified – the enquirer is opened to nothing less than the divine itself. Be that as it may, Balthasar is clear that once we enter the realm of revelation, the idea of dialogue becomes, as Barth proposes, a necessity for

17 A. Nichols, OP, *Scattering the Seed, op. cit.,* pp. 19–23.
18 *Karl Barth, op. cit.,* p. 71.

thought. Most of these points owe something to Balthasar's study of Gregory of Nyssa, and all echo the first volume of Balthasar's theological logic, *Wahrheit. Wahrheit der Welt*, published just four years previously, in 1947.

In revelation, the divine Word expresses itself freely yet decisively, definitively, and in so doing it arouses the response of faith. Here if anywhere is an Object which must be approached dialectically for it is unique in fullness, an Object that is supremely Subject and therefore to be engaged in dialogue and not just by arguments. The Word of God uses human 'concepts and percepts', but is always more than them for it is divine. Balthasar cites a little maxim from St Gregory Nazianzen, 'Appearing, he is hidden; hidden, he appears'.[19] Theological method must have built into it, then, some dialectical safeguard: it must ask so as to receive answers, but use those answers to ask again. It cannot rest content until theology be thoroughly moulded by the Word, while recognizing that this will also require the fullest 'existential commitment' : the sort of thing one expects from witnesses. It will allow God's speech to fill up its own.

But to Balthasar's mind, Barth should not have implied that dialectics must become the *whole* of theology. The real task of dialectics in theology is, rather, to guard dogmatics from premature closure, to warn it against presumption, and – above all – to point to the two divine attributes dearest to Barth: God's incomparability and his 'aseity' or sovereignly independent being. As it happens, Barth found the language of being not wholly sympathetic; or rather, he interpreted statements about the being of God in revelation as accounts of the sheer 'act' that God is, as *actus purus*. God as 'sheer act': that was interpreted by Barth, and increasingly by Balthasar, as God's ever-eventful actuality. Barth was right to insist on the abyss between Creator and creature over which the divine Word calls. He was also correct in asserting that the creature thus divinely called to dialogue is itself a guilty creature, one that has said No! to God, has lived by active opposition to him, and has thus negatived its own relation to God. And yet he was wrong and incorrect to make this the whole story. An exclusive use of Barthian dialectics could only reinstate the weaknesses Balthasar detected in the first commentary on Romans. Without jettisoning dialectics, Barth needed another tool. And as subsequent efforts showed, he found it in the much-derided concept of *analogy* – analogy not now of *being*, but of *faith*.

The transition to analogy: Barth's rediscovery of Chalcedon

The phrase – the analogy of faith – is Pauline (Romans 12.6); the use of it Barth's own. He came to it when, in the course of the later 1920s, the disadvantages of what Przywara had labelled 'theopanism' and Balthasar 'pantheologism' were borne in on him as he struggled with various issues of culture and philosophy, ecclesiology and ethics. He needed to accord the world a relative self-subsistence vis-à-vis God if the world were really to be *another* in relation to God. Thus, writing of culture and philosophy in 1926 Barth asserts that

> when the Word of God is spoken and heard in the world of sinners, it strikes against a potential in the world of nature, history and reason

19 *Ibid.*, p. 75.

that sin has not destroyed ... That is an indispensable presupposition for this Kingdom to dwell among sinners.[20]

In this connexion, Balthasar devotes much attention to Barth's 1927 study *Prolegomena zur christlichen Dogmatik: die Lehre vom Worte Gottes* ('Prolegomena to Christian Dogmatics: the Doctrine of the Word of God'), as well as to some contemporary essays from one of which the foregoing citation is extracted. In Balthasar's view, there are telltale signs here of a personal intellectual struggle going on throughout the 1920s. Its issue was almost as much a breakthrough for Barth as had been the first edition of Romans. If the latter – the Romans commentary – marks Barth's emancipation from Liberalism, the former – the *Prolegomena* – embodies his gradual discovery of a 'genuine, self-authenticating theology' fit to serve the Trinitarian revelation, in Jesus Christ, of the Word of God. Why were the earlier writings *unfit*, on Balthasar's view, to serve it? Because Barth's earlier 'monism' of an invasive divine Word makes the world

> look so forlorn and hopeless under this harsh glare that one might just as well wish it did not exist ... Barth finally came to feel the deeply unchristian tenor of such a panorama.[21]

Balthasar's passionate conviction that the Barth of the Romans commentaries had been remiss in speaking in dualistic pairs – body and soul, nature and spirit, subject and object, internal and external – as though these sets of terms lack all synthesis, is borne not only of his commitment to the theology of St Maximus the Confessor, for which the synthesizing of polarities was key to the divine plan but was also owed, more widely, to his delvings into the Idealist and Romantic philosophers, dramatists, poets. Whatever else one may say, theologically or philosophically, against those varied figures, that many of them really sought such synthesis, wherever and whenever, can hardly be gainsaid. In itself – and leaving aside the vagaries of their various odysseys – this could only be congenial to a Catholic mind.

The decisive shift in Barth's development came with a re-evaluation of Incarnation. Though the 1927 *Prolegomena* express his adherence to Chalcedonian Christology (and exhibit other straws in the wind that blow toward the future), his 'mistrust' of 'every form of continuity' – might it not give the impression that revelation is simply 'out there', waiting to be picked up off the pavement, or the market stall? – led him to downplay the Incarnation's force. Here Barth stresses the freedom of the Word in Incarnation, rather than the plain fact that the Word became man. As Bruce McCormack has pointed out, in Barth's Göttingen lectures (just before his move to Münster and the writing of the *Prolegomena*) it is plain that the Incarnation happens only as a series of discreet divine acts and *not* through the definitive moment,

20 K. Barth, 'Die Kirche und die Kultur', in *idem, Die Theologie und die Kirche* (Munich, 1938), pp. 374–75. The article, originally written in 1926, anticipates Barth's mature position on this point in volume II/2 of *Kirchliche Dogmatik*, after he had overcome his fears that his fellow-Evangelical Emil Brunner, with his positive doctrine of the image of God in man was affirming a self-subsistent relationship between God and the trio of nature, history and reason that circumvented the Incarnation.

21 *Karl Barth, op. cit.*, p. 94. Barth had already declared his adherence to the Chalcedonian Christology in the *Prolegomena zur christlichen Dogmatik: die Lehre vom Worte Gottes*. Balthasar notes this in *Karl Barth* at p. 88.

constitutive of everything that follows, that is Jesus' Conception: what Catholic tradition calls the 'Annunciation'. Nor does the Incarnation mean as yet for Barth that the 'antithesis' of God and mankind is 'overcome' in the human nature assumed. Their 'antithesis' is transcended for him only in the act of Atonement on the Cross. McCormack draws the appropriate conclusion:

> The overcoming of the antithesis [between God and man] in the Person of the Logos in no way sets aside the antithesis on the level of the relationship of the natures … The faithfulness of God triumphs [through the Paschal Mystery and not before] in the Person of Christ over the unsublated antithesis of God and humankind.[22]

As this judgement indicates, there was still some way to go. Barth's controversy with his fellow Protestant Emil Brunner over whether there was any sense at all in which man, without the supervention of the Word of God, has genuine religious potential after the Fall showed as much. So did the distinctly unnuanced character of his continuing disapproval of the *principles* (and not just the disputed doctrines) used by Catholic theologians.

But little by little, his discovery, or rediscovery, of the Chalcedonian dogma, which proclaimed how in the God-man Jesus Christ, divine nature and human nature were united without confusion gave him the means to construe that relative self-subsistence of the created order he had earlier minimized or dismissed. It enabled him to do full justice to the somewhat isolated theological optimism of the 1926 essay in which he had proclaimed 'The human race has been restored to life through God's active reassertion of his claim in Jesus Christ'.[23] It also made possible his partial but real *rapprochement* with Catholic theology. On Balthasar's interpretation, Chalcedonian Incarnationalism would give Barth the key to the whole *Church Dogmatics* as, from the mid 30s at any rate, that multi-volume work unfolded. As Barth himself put it in volume II/1, published in 1940:

> Even the Incarnation ratifies the creature as a distinct reality from God. The very event of the Incarnation indicates that, while making God and the creature one, it also reveals that God and the creature are in themselves two and distinct. Even the creature has its own reality in relation to God.[24]

Barth's move from dialectics to analogy – or, better, from dialectics alone to dialectics with analogy – was fuelled by this belief.

Analogical thought in the 'Church Dogmatics'

Balthasar speaks about the 'centrality' of analogy in Barth's mature thought, while having to confess that in volume I of the *Church Dogmatics*, the first part – a book in its own right, as with all the volume-divisions – fails to mention it

22　B. L. McCormack, *Karl Barth's Critically Realistic Dialectical Theology: Its Genesis and Development, 1909–1936* (Oxford, 1995), pp. 365–66.
23　K. Barth, 'Die Kirche und die Kultur', *art. cit.*, p. 376. As Balthasar writes, 'Only from Christ will Barth learn that there is room for a genuine and *active* human nature alongside God', *Karl Barth, op. cit.*, p. 106.
24　K. Barth, *Kirchliche Dogmatik II/1. Die Lehre von Gott* (Zurich, 1942), p. 579.

and the second part seems merely to note it. But beginning with II/1, from which quotation has just been made, it 'starts to take definitive form, so that the doctrine of analogy unfolds more and more clearly with each succeeding volume'. In the last volumes, it has at last become the 'central theme of his theology'.[25] So what does it amount to?

The brief mention in the opening volume is already instructive. There *is* a similarity of the creature to God (as well as an infinitely greater dissimilarity). That similarity is founded on divine action as the Word takes hold of the creature. Yet in so taking hold of man, entering human thought and human language, what results is not something utterly alien to the human. There is an imaging relationship of *Abbild* to *Vorbild*, copy to archetype, in what transpires. Thus: though it is by his own revelatory act that God chooses certain human truths to express his own divine truth, this is no arbitrary action (as Nominalism would have it), since by virtue of creation man's truth is already God's own. Barth now takes seriously the reality and basic goodness of the creature in its freedom and relation to God. As Balthasar sums up:

> The creature can respond [to God] because it has received the ability to do so. And it responds in such a way that its 'autonomous' response remains the highest instance of its receptivity. And that implies theological analogy.[26]

So the 'analogy of faith' moves to centre stage where, inceasingly, it is given a Christological foundation. The analogy is ultimately based on the grace of Christ through whom the world is made as well as redeemed. Because Jesus Christ, God and man – Barth now begins to abandon the less focused phrase 'the Word of God' – is the true measure of all things, God and the world are not *simply compatible*. Rather, they boast a kind of compatibility so intense that no contradiction can possibly dissolve it. Natural humanity is *per se* good, the human will *considered as a constituent of human nature* (what the Scholastics termed *voluntas ut natura*) is ordered to the good. Classical Hellenism, for instance, though the bugbear of so many Protestant dogmaticians, offers in many respects a desirable vision of the human essence and colours thereby not only the picture painted by the Fathers but that of the New Testament itself. To say as much is not, for Barth, to embrace (mere) humanism. Why? Because all of this is made possible only by the grounding of creation in the divine Son who himself cannot be thought of save in his unity with the man Jesus.

Pointing out how useful Barth found the concept of 'presupposition', *Voraussetzung*, in this context, Balthasar shows how for the great Evangelical theologian the order of salvation in Christ is *presupposed by* the order of creation, and vice versa. In a famous Barthian formulation, the order of nature is the 'external ground' of the order of Incarnation and redemption – 'the Covenant', but the order of the Incarnation and redemption is the 'internal ground' of creation. Thus these orders are unified but never conflated. In the pre-existent Word who cannot be thought without reference to his incarnate life as Jesus – in this Lamb slain from before the beginning of

---

25 *Karl Barth, op. cit.*, p. 107.
26 *Ibid.*, p. 113.

the world, the creation has been given a promise. It will never founder, since it is built on him. The human essence will never be altered unrecognizably, because it inheres in its Head, the Word become human as Jesus Christ. The creation is not itself grace. But it is ordered to grace. Was it through learning this from Barth's writings of the late 1930s and 1940s that Balthasar proved able to steer so easy a course in the choppy Catholic waters churned up round comparable notions by Henri de Lubac and the 'nouvelle théologie'?

Be this as it may, one delightful consequence of Barth's approach for Balthasar lay in the quite unexpected way it ratified the symbolist theology of the Alexandrian school – including his old favourite, Origen (but of which, in 'Patristik, Scholastik und wir', Balthasar had been unduly suspicious). Everything in the cosmos may have some capacity to symbolize salvation history, and the coming redemption, since the creation covenant lies *within* the covenant of God with the world in Jesus Christ. Being as it is internal to the covenant of the Incarnation, the world's meaning can only be gauged by reference to the covenant of salvation which gives creation its final sense.[27] In particular, the first Adam, our proto-parent, is the prototype of the second Adam, who is himself the archetype of grace. Human nature, like human reason, has its foundation in the uncreated truth of the Word, the Word who from before all time the Father elects to be humanized as Jesus Christ, and to be known as such in the decision of faith. By the time Barth got to Volume III of the *Church Dogmatics*, and especially III/2, writes Balthasar:

> He saw the whole of nature and the order of creation from the beginning as nothing but the potential for receiving the act of revelation ... The essence of creation ... is defined by its capacity for perceiving and accepting the Word of God and for being the stage for the event of the Incarnation of the Son.[28]

Nature is the *presupposition for grace*, a presupposition 'decreed by and derived from the Word of God himself'.[29] In this fashion, Barth intended both to allow nature (and reason) its proper integrity and yet take away all cause for thinking nature (and reason) can ever either stand alone or contribute positively to the covenant of salvation. No property or power disposing one to grace and revelation inheres in nature (or reason). Rather, explains Balthasar on Barth's behalf:

> creation's capacity to join in a covenant with God, its orientation to its already established goal, its instrumental availability is ... an adaptation devised by God to make it suitable for God's plan. There is nothing in the creature that is inherently suitable to be the point of contact. Rather, the whole creature, with its light and shadow, has become the fitting occasion for that unheard of surpassing of nature that took place

---

27 *Ibid.*, pp. 124–25.
28 *Ibid.*, p. 165. Note, however, that Barth's doctrine of the image of God in man – the foundation of any theological anthropology worth the name – is Trinitarian not Christological. Balthasar will accept Barth's view that man is in the image through the way human relationality (first, of man and woman, but then in any form of human communication) reflects the eternal mutuality of the divine Persons, *ibid.*, pp. 125–26.
29 *Ibid.*

in the Passion, death and Resurrection of Jesus Christ. And this is why creation in the final analysis was called 'very good'.[30]

As Balthasar writes, he is trying to understand Barth's position: not, in the first half of his book, either defending or attacking it. But the alert reader will notice an internal discrepancy in the last citation. If there is no natural point of contact for grace and revelation in the creature, in what sense is the creature a *fitting* occasion for the surpassing of nature in Jesus Christ? This will be an issue Balthasar must address. But for the moment, and rightly, he does not want to disguise the *strangeness* – to more conventional textbook Scholastic thinking – of the main lines of Barth's thought. (Not that it is any stranger in that regard than some of the thought patterns of the Fathers!) For Barth, man's openness to relation with God is a constituent of his human nature but *only* through the '*de facto* revelation in Jesus Christ, [which is] the very basis of creation'.[31] Without wanting simply to *deduce* human nature from the order of redemption, Barth is firm that it cannot theologically be described on the basis of its own immanence. Our nature cannot be understood without a grasp of where salvation history is going.

But it is above all in relation to human rationality – as distinct from any of the other powers of man – that Barth's schema is so striking. First worked out in his study of St Anselm, *Fides quaerens intellectum*,[32] Barth presents a view of the faith/reason relationship where the organ for registering absolute truth can only be some kind of faith ('proto-faith' might be, thinks Balthasar, a suitable name here), since what grounds all 'logic', all valid thought, is not in fact a 'what' at all. It is a 'who': the divine Logos.[33] Accordingly, all authentic rationality rests on the freedom of the Word. Faith is the venturesome 'decision of the human mind to live in and from the truth of God'[34]. In such faith, the human mind is saturated by the light of the Logos. As, on Barth's interpretation, the *Proslogion* of St Anselm set out to prove, 'Whatever is thought is thought from this event'.[35] As Balthasar cites the opening part of the volume of the *Church Dogmatics* devoted to the topic of creation:

> Just as everything that exists outside the Creator owes its existing to him and to him alone, so too all knowledge about existence that takes place outside of him can only occur because he has not hidden his infallible knowledge of his own existence as the ground of all other existences. ... *Because* God has said, 'I am!', we can and must say back to him not only, 'Yes, you are!' but also the rest of the declension, 'I myself am!' and 'this about me [the others – he, she, they and it] is also what is with me!'. The ontological order holds its own in the noetic order.[36]

30 *Ibid.*, p. 166.
31 *Ibid.*, p. 127.
32 K. Barth, *Fides quaerens intellectum* (Zurich, 1931); ET *Anselm. Fides quaerens intellectum* (London, 1960).
33 This perception provides the basic theme of the second, Christological, volume of Balthasar's *Theologik. Wahrheit Gottes* (Einsiedeln, 1985).
34 *Karl Barth, op. cit.*, p. 141.
35 *Ibid.*, p. 144.
36 K. Barth, *Church Dogmatics* III/1, pp. 399–400; cited *Karl Barth, op. cit.*, pp. 138–39.

As a perception, *Wahrnehmung*, literally a 'taking of truth', *wahr-nehmen*, such proto-faith concides with the primal act of reason itself.

However, the key point taken by Balthasar – and not merely taken but absorbed by him, so it becomes a *Leit-motiv* of all his subsequent theology and philosophy – is this:

> Only in conjunction with the revelation of absolute truth can all the relative truths of creation be known and recognized.[37]

Balthasar goes for this Barthian thesis hook, line and sinker. *Nothing is understood properly until it is understood in relation to divine revelation.* Barth's manner of *explaining* the state of affairs to which the thesis draws our attention is another matter. For Barth, there is no way up from 'analogous truth' to 'absolute truth' *unless* the revelation of the latter – God's own truth, in itself – is accepted in its proper form: by faith. Then and only then can any question of the analogy of being be raised. Indeed, 'the Fool' of Anselm's meditation in the *Proslogion* is a fool precisely because he tries to abstract from the event in which God's Word is disclosed and 'consider concepts as if they were immanent moments of thought'.[38] He chooses not to believe at one level what, at another level, having heard the Name of God, he cannot but believe.

For Barth, philosophy can manage on its own only when considered as an *inconclusive* enquiry. Abstraction does not lie so long as it does not mistake itself for ultimate concretion. But a philosophy that tries to have the last word – as, say, a comprehensive metaphysics, or an enquiry into natural theology, or (favoured in some Catholic circles in this period) a 'Christian philosophy' – will always be found to have taken out a loan from theology somewhere along the line. Only from within the encounter with the Word of God can we establish the nature, possibilities and limits of the natural knowledge of God. Though not the standard teaching of contemporary Catholic Scholasticism, from a Catholic doctrinal standpoint this is certainly a marked improvement on Barth's horrified root-and-branch rejection of any and every *Anknüpf-ungspunkt*, 'point of contact', between the Word and the natural man in his controversy with his fellow Protestant dogmatician Emil Brunner.[39] As the concluding section of *Karl Barth* will show, it is also an *Anknüpfungspunkt* with Balthasar himself.

Balthasar has said that he wants to regard Barth's theology as a developing whole. But such is the clear blue water that Barth is putting between the *Church Dogmatics* and his earlier dialectical writing that he now regards creation's difference from God not only as no evil (whereas the second of his *Romans* commentaries saw it precisely as evil) but, to the contrary, a positive good. And the reason – which Balthasar will formally adopt in his own theology, most notably in *Theodramatik* – is Trinitarian. The 'standing over against one another' which is a presupposition of the communion of the Trinitarian Persons, revealed in God in Christ, proves that, theologically, *difference can be divine*. Of course, despite the Incarnation (itself a testimony to the positive value of difference, as the divine assumes the human without annulling it), there is still such a thing as sin – and, to that extent, no mere

37 *Ibid.*, p. 144.
38 *Ibid.*, p. 145.
39 K. Barth, *Nein! Antwort an Emil Brunner* (1934).

difference from God but contradiction to him. Yet, since Christ has made peace reign between God and the world, this contradiction is now 'bracketed' by the truth of the Redeemer.

The question now arises for Balthasar: what becomes of Barth's studied hostility to analogy-of-being thinking if Barth no longer denies the value of the spontaneous quality of human cognition (the 'agent intellect'), and recognizes that reason can be actively receptive to faith? In point of fact, Barth now opposes only the attempt at a 'neutral' employment of that analogy (or any concept of being), recognizing that the analogy of being may indeed have a place in Christian theology – but *only within the analogy of faith*. That means: if we accept that all knowledge of God rests on prior revelation, with its centre in Christ, such that the human potential for knowing God is actualized only in faithful assent to the claims of that divine Word, then we can safely posit a 'correspondence' between divine and human being, the Archetype and the image. Balthasar brushes aside Barth's protestations that he has not accepted the analogy of being. He may *say* he has not, but what else can we think when he writes, for instance, in his Anselm book:

> ... other beings ... possess only imperfectly (and always will) what God had perfectly (by nature and not by gradual achievement): existence.[40]

Balthasar was, and would remain, enough of a Thomist to think this a crucial concession.

How to think of Barth

That really concludes Balthasar's positive exposition of the mature Barth's thought. As he would be the first to admit, it does not provide an overview of Barth's dogmatics. Indeed, not all the volumes of the *Kirchliche Dogmatik* were finished at Balthasar's time of writing. So how could it? What Balthasar has done is to identify the main neurones in the organism of Barthian thought. This sometimes means detecting neuralgia: a dysfunction in neural connexions. Balthasar has critical questions to put to Barth. But more fundamentally, it means tracing the pathways of the living nerves in their vitality. Balthasar wants to recognize not only how far Barthianism has become compatible with the body-tissue of Catholicism but also how health-giving its inspiration could be for Catholic theology.

Balthasar praises the beauty of the emerging *Church Dogmatics*. 'Rarely has Christendom heard God's love sung with such infinite, melodious beauty.'[41] Balthasar was clearly moved by it in the writing of his own theological aesthetics. What a plan of sovereign love Barth lays out – doing justice to the elements of drama Balthasar will later explore in his theological dramatics. In words which anticipate Balthasar's own theology of history:

> The matrix of the world is not closed in on itself ... It is open to God's action, which does not annul or rend the fabric of [its] history but gives it its true form.[42]

40 K. Barth, *Anselm. Fides quaerens intellectum, op. cit.*, pp. 179–80.
41 *Karl Barth, op. cit.*, p. 169.
42 *Ibid.*, p. 170.

He is enthusiastic about Barth's recovery of the New Testament – and patristic – orientation of the doctrine of election (or predestination) to the figure of Christ. In Christ, the Father chooses his own Word, but in the form of a creature, to lead the world back to God in a 'primal election' that is the 'foundation for the whole epic of divine providence'.[43] Moreover, by letting the beloved Son take on himself the deserved reprobation of guilty creatures, God makes the Gospel message news of unalloyed joy. Barth's re-working of the standard (Protestant and Catholic) theologies of election was deeply to influence Balthasar. Not only did it confirm his determination to write dogmatics, wherever possible, Christocentrically. It steeled him to maintain the concept of substitutionary exchange – and so no mere 'Christ the Representative' in his theology of the Atonement. It inspired him to write in dark, Goya-esque shades – far from the bright colours of Byzantine Easter icons – his theology of the descent of Christ into Hell, notably in *Mysterium Paschale*. It lies behind his reluctance, in the closing eschatological volume of the *Theodramatik*, to permit tragedy to cloud the *Commedia* of the Trinitarian homecoming. It explains his corresponding willingness (despite warning criticism from more rigorist spirits) to entertain the hope that all human beings may be saved, while never (despite the encouragement from more liberal spirits) asserting that they are.[44] He had learned too well Barth's lesson that it has not been given us to anticipate the exact range of redemption. God's will to save is not a 'natural process that absorbs all opposition'.[45]

It would also be hard to overestimate the influence of Barth's doctrine of election on Balthasar's theology of mission, which permeates at all points his account of grace. Barth inserts ecclesiology between the God of electing grace and the individual Christian. The Christian's vocation belongs with the mission of the Church to 'the many' – and, so long as the time of the Church lasts, that many refers 'not to a determinate, but to a dynamic and open number'.[46] Electing grace, mission, apostolate: these are coterminous terms, even, adds Balthasar, for enclosed nuns, even for mystics hardly heard of by the world. Thus Balthasar's studies of St Thérèse of Lisieux and Blessed Elizabeth of the Trinity.[47]

Balthasar now feels able to state the fundamental form Barth's mature theology takes. His first stab at defining it might be described as an attempt to identify its *philosophical principle of order*, its root philosophical idea. Balthasar sees it as the notion of the *concretissimum* – maximal concreteness in the fullest unfolding of the possible. Concreteness – on the one hand, that calls to mind a positive quality Balthasar had identified in the shift of focus from the mediaeval world-view to modernity. On the other hand, *concretissimum* was, as it happened, a mediaeval term, which commended itself

---

43 *Ibid.*, p. 175.
44 The American translation of *Was dürfen wir hoffen?* (Einsiedeln, 1986), published under the title, *Dare we Hope that 'All Men may be Saved'?* (San Francisco, 1988), includes for good measure Balthasar's *Kleiner Diskurs über die Hölle* (Einsiedeln, 1987), and an article 'Apokatastasis' from the *Trierer Theologische Zeitschrift* 97 (1988), pp. 169–82.
45 Cited from Barth's *Kirchliche Dogmatik* II/2 in *Karl Barth, op. cit.*, p. 185.
46 *Ibid.*, p. 183.
47 *Therese von Lisieux. Geschichte einer Sendung* (Olten, 1950); ET *Thérèse of Lisieux. A Story of a Mission* (London, 1953); *Elisabeth von Dijon und ihre geistliche Sendung* (Cologne-Olten, 1952); ET *Elisabeth of Dijon. An Interpretation of her Spiritual Mission* (London, 1956).

insofar as Balthasar wants to emphasize the traditional nature of Barth's approach – despite all evidence to the contrary. That is also why Balthasar (where necessary) converts Barth's language of 'event' into the vocabulary of 'act', with its long pre-history in ancient and mediaeval thought. That 'being exists for the sake of act and must be interpreted from the perspective of action'[48] may seem to turn on its head the method of the Schoolmen, with their preoccupation with essences. But – quite aside from asking, *Which Schoolmen?* (a question unaddressed by Balthasar), we need to read aright Barth's intentions. When we do so, we appreciate that his approach – the 'form' of his theology in this regard – is far from antipodean to theirs.

> Barth does not mean to dissolve nature into a pointillist series of dis-
> crete and discontinuous momentary events but to begin with the notion
> of 'fullest realization' and make that the standard and measure of the
> meaning and interpretation of being.[49]

Of course, the act in which a being is most fully realized has its ontological conditions. But a thousand conditions do not make one event. This principle, once explored, turns out to yield us the *theological principle of order* in Barth's thought likewise. Where the *concretissimum* of man meets the *concretissimum* of God is in the encounter with the revealing Word which is simultaneously God's *action* – in creation, reconciliation, redemption. Here, above all, and incorporating whatever has been meant by 'nature' and 'supernature', is *reality*. As Barth writes, 'Everything general is contained in this particularity'.[50] If we are to grasp the truth – the true essence – of human nature, we must never forget that man has been allowed to inhabit this mystery of God's own concreteness, the loving freedom in which he is and acts as Father, Son and Spirit. Abstraction, neutrality, ahistoricity: these are Barth's conceptual enemies. Human beings only exist because the divine creative, reconciling, redemptive action has embraced and is embracing the entire race in Jesus Christ. For this reason, Balthasar accepts Barth's own sobriquet for his thought: 'intensive universalism'.

This conclusion leads Balthasar to uncover – as he believes – the main taproot of Barthianism in its formal method. Despite all Barth's criticisms of Friedrich Schleiermacher, the Father of modern Protestant theology in its Romantic–Idealist–liberal mode, the basic schema of his thought is indebted to Schleiermacher, even if the content is very different. In each theology, everything turns on 'one point of highest intensity'. For Schleiermacher access to this is given by the famous 'feeling of absolute dependence', Schleiermacherian faith; for Barth, access to the 'point of highest intensity' is given through encounter with the divine Word. Balthasar tries to show how it is common to both men to work by positing a duality subsequently overcome by a further 'intensification'; to treat the 'point of absolute intensity' as grounding all exercise of reason, though lying beyond it; to see that point as approached – though never attained – by dialectical thinking, and, lastly, to take this 'point of unity' – for Schleiermacher, the subject–object unity that is God, for Barth the unity of God and man in Christ – as at the

---

48 Karl Barth, *op. cit.*, p. 191.
49 *Ibid.*
50 Cited from *Kirchliche Dogmatik* II/2, in *Karl Barth, op. cit.*, p. 193.

same time a 'point of totality' from which all reality can be comprehensively explained.[51] Balthasar's analysis is rendered more persuasive from the standpoint of historians of theology by the admiration Barth several times expressed for the way Schleiermacher, unlike the Reformers, really tried to bring all theological motifs and subject matter into a single interrelated whole.

As already indicated, Balthasar accepts that the *content* of Barth's theology is utterly different from Schleiermacher's. The narrative of the primal history of God's elective dealings in Christ replaces Schleiermacherian transhistoricity: what could be less like Schleiermacher's unity of feeling or experience than Barth's unity through obedient faith? But, Balthasar now asks, Does 'utter' difference mean *unconditional* difference? The question leads him to uncover, he believes, some continuing traces of Idealism in Barth's thought which *could* be worrying if they are not merely *auxiliary ideas* in which to express a theology shaped by revelation but, rather, *active surrogates* for that theology. And that cannot be excluded, not given the way Idealism can function as a secularized theology, as 'observers have so often pointed out'.[52] What had happened was this. Balthasar had noticed that the way Barth relates the original, protological unity of man and God to their eschatological unity bears a curious resemblance to the way Idealist accounts of the world-process fuse 'the Proton and the Eschaton' – notably in Hegel's account of 'Spirit'.[53]

Balthasar's verdict is a qualified 'not guilty'. Barth's account of pre-destination may suggest a God's-eye view but how can it be called reducing revelation to a system when he insists revelation can only be received in the decision of faith? Symptomatic of the 'existential' quality of his thought is the role played in it by ethics, where

> Each article of faith has a corresponding ethic, not as a practical 'corollary', but as the equally essential 'decision-side' of [its] truth ...[54]

Barth's theology neither 'anticipates God' nor 'truncates revelation', but holds together the boldness of faith and the humility of its calling. There *are* a few traces of Idealist influence in Barth – notably the way he draws the doctrine of the Trinity from the sovereignty of God in his revealing Word; his tendency to contrast being and act; and even his idea of the angels as potencies of the divine essence. All of these infelicities could be construed as the result of nervousness about the divine objecthood, bête noire of the Idealists. But they hardly register, so Balthasar feels, compared and contrasted with Barth's

> firm will never to understand God in the manner of the Idealists as merely a further extension of the subject (reflecting on itself) but to see

51 *Ibid.*, pp. 201–203.
52 *Ibid.*, p. 201.
53 *Ibid.*, p. 207. Balthasar found rather suspicious the evident relish with which Barth expounded Hegel's philosophy in his survey, *Die protestantische Theologie im neunzehnten Jahrhundert* (Zurich, 1947).
54 *Karl Barth, op. cit.*, p. 222.

God all the more as a genuine Other, a real Thou present in the continued existence of the world.[55]

But we are not quite out of the woods yet. People say, But is not Barth's dialectical manner, continuing even into his mature period, typical of Idealism, which 'as an intellectual method, undertook to interpret the essence of being as nature and spirit through contradiction and its dynamic overcoming'?[56] Balthasar replies on Barth's behalf: not so, because for Barth 'thesis' and 'antithesis' mean simply God's Yes and God's No, and between these no 'synthesis' is possible. And despite Hegelian echoes, Barth's account of the *concretissimum* does not rest on a philosophy of the development of 'the Idea' in history but on a Christ-centred theological eschatology drawn from Scripture.

Balthasar's questions to Barth

Does this mean, then, that Balthasar finds no problems with Barth at all? In fact, he has several probing questions to put to him. The questions fall under a single general rubric. Is Barth's use of Idealist categories, careful and critical though it may be, governed by 'certain intra-theological proclivities and tendencies', which go on to 'generate a dubious and one-sided view of revelation', and then find expression in the philosophical outworks of his thought?[57] In other words, even though the explicitly Idealist elements in the way Barth clothes revelation conceptually may be largely anodyne, and sometimes downright helpful (something Balthasar never denies), could they also be symptoms of a *theological* – rather than philosophical – faultline which actually *is* worrying?

Where might this faultline run? We shall not be surprised to learn it issues from a failure on Barth's part to give creation its full due. His passion for Christocentrism is altogether praiseworthy. Christ is indeed the goal of creation. But this does not necessitate the narrowing of outlook on creation Barth sometimes exhibits.

> Revelation does not presuppose creation in such a way that it equates it with the act of revelation. In giving ultimate meaning to creation, revelation does not annul creation's own proper and original meaning.[58]

And Balthasar adds for good measure:

> Revelation does not say that just because everything comes from Christ and returns to him we are justified in marshalling everything into a speculative system or that other, freer versions of christocentrism are excluded.[59]

---

55 *Ibid.*, p. 226.
56 *Ibid.*, p. 228.
57 *Ibid.*, p. 241.
58 *Ibid.*, p. 242.
59 *Ibid.*

That is, of course, a further point. In the way he orders his Christocentric doctrine of predestination, Barth tends – in Balthasar's eyes – to overstep the boundaries of revelation, laying down principles which require conclusions not consonant with Scripture. (Balthasar says this notably of the joy – of all things – with which for Barth Christians should approach the Last Judgement.) And then finally, Balthasar doubts whether Barth leaves a spacious enough place for the Church, which for Barth is principally the external representative (only) of faith in the Word. Writing, we must again note, in 1951 – and thus before the completion of the *Dogmatics* – Balthasar suspects that hostility to an institution which will not confess its own relativity is what really lies behind Barth's distance from Catholicism. Perhaps – subconsciously at least – a systematic Christocentric predestinationism attracted Barth precisely for its power to rule out such a fate.

A Catholic response

Balthasar turns now to the constructive part of his study which is to suggest a Catholic version of Barth's enterprise, by way of accepting and celebrating, yet also correcting and supplementing, what Barth has achieved. At this stage of his writing career, Balthasar does not want to propose a Catholic manner of theologizing analogous to Barth's which would be at the same time an original and distinctive – a distinctively Balthasarian – response to him. With the advantage of hindsight, we can say that the whole of Balthasar's theological output is going to be precisely that – but the best part of forty years will elapse before this project is completed. In the meanwhile, Balthasar wishes to offer a *generic Catholic response* which will consider three main issues: the structure (philosophical and theological) of Christian thought; the idea of nature in its relation to grace; and Christocentrism – with a coda on an issue flagged up, merely, in this account: grace and sin. The rationale of this choice is obvious to anyone who has followed Balthasar's reading of Barth's work.

(i) A philosophy without theology
First, then, the structure of (Catholic) Christian thought. The noblest fruit of human understanding is *philosophy*. When, however, *revelation* – the greatest truth conceivable – is given to man, it taxes philosophy to the utmost. From the encounter there emerges a 'philosophia perennis', but this should not be thought of as a form of truth completed once for all at any point in the history of thought. Rather is it, says Balthasar, a 'form of truth in vital development, adapting and offering itself as such to the vessel of revelation'.[60] In this section of *Karl Barth*, Balthasar is not only advising Barth on how Catholic theologians would understand the role of philosophy in theology. He is also indicating his own position – a mediating one, we can call it – in the battle, then raging, between classical Thomists and revisionists.[61] This was the quarrel of the *nouvelle théologie*, already touched on, which in the year immediately before his Barth book was published had elicited Pope Pius

---

60 *Ibid.*, p. 251.
61 See on this A. Nichols, OP, 'Thomism and the *nouvelle théologie*', *The Thomist* 64 (2000), pp. 1–19.

XII's encyclical on questionable tendencies in modern thought, *Humani generis*. Balthasar's *via media* is highly apparent when he writes of the theologian who best displayed the possibilities of the gradually accumulating philosophical tradition of Catholicism:

> What Thomas Aquinas built is a form – and he displayed this form so widely and convincingly that not only elements of the past but also those of the future could have room in his thought, either by being able to incorporate the new into itself or by being fruitful enough to let itself be transformed *by* the new.[62]

In the 'new theology' dispute, revisionists like Jean Daniélou would almost certainly *not* have wished to say Thomism was capable of absorbing any philosophical novelties, while classicists like the Dominican Michel-Marie Labourdette would have baulked at adding that it might also 'let itself be transformed' by them. Balthasar tries to hold the two ends of the chain. Since revelation, the self-revelation of the Logos, is 'the highest *ratio*', it can and must attract 'all the forms of the worldly *logoi* of truth in order to present its inexhaustible fulness'.[63] (This was the insistence of the supporters of *nouvelle théologie*.) Yet in no way can revelation take as its servant a philosophical mish-mash of disparate and quasi-contradictory propositions. (This was the counter-insistence of the Pope.)

Still, the upshot is that Catholic theology will always 'burst the confines of any specific and limited structure of thought'.[64] Catholicism is not expressible in a single system of thought. The Church's dogmatic pronouncements are an attempt to produce no such thing. Their object is revelation, not philosophy, and from the latter they draw terms to be used only in the most 'generally accessible' way. There is no single principle – not even the analogy of being – in use so as to build up a systematic whole. Indeed, citing the *second* volume of Przywara's *Analogia entis* (much more to Balthasar's liking in this regard than its predecessor):

> Rightly understood, the analogy of being is the destruction of every system in favour of a totally objective availability of the creature for God and for the divine measure of the creature.[65]

Paradoxically, it is in an article with a title perfectly suited to confirm Barth's worst fears – it could be translated 'The Broad Range of Analogy as the Basic Form in Catholicism' – that Przywara writes what should most fully allay Barth's anxieties. In the single, concrete actual order of God's world, said Przywara, 'there is for the real existent no purely natural religion, no purely natural philosophy'. Everything, whether 'consciously or unconsciously, in full measure or in paltry reflections, bears the one 'God in Christ in the Church as its final form'.[66] Barth is quite wrong, not only about the analogy of being but also about Catholicism in general as a closed system of thought.

---

62 *Karl Barth, op. cit.*, p. 252. Italics in original.
63 *Ibid.*, p. 253. Balthasar was almost certainly influenced in this formulation by the work he was doing quasi-contemporaneously on St Maximus the Confessor.
64 *Ibid.*
65 Cited in *ibid.*, p. 255.
66 E. Przywara, 'Reichweite der Analogie als katholischer Grundform', *Scholastik* 3 (1940), p. 527, cited *Karl Barth, op. cit.*, p. 257.

That does not mean, however, that the question of the role of philosophy –
or philosophies – within theology is not an interesting or important question.
Barth did well to raise it. The Fathers themselves used elements of philosophy: their theology was not simply a presentation of the saving events. With
the Scholastics the role of those elements grows larger – without, of course,
losing contact with the divine acts in history. Contrasting Schoolmen and
Fathers in this regard, Balthasar puts it very well:

> Here we find a certain age-old tension between two types of theology: a
> more concrete and positive theology that builds upon the historical
> facts of revelation and thus makes greater use of the categories that
> apply to *events* (although it is not always aware of doing so); and a
> more speculative theology that steps back into a certain contemplative
> distance from these immediate events and takes for its object the
> events' rationality or the implied connections between the individual
> truths of revelation.[67]

It is hardly a question, then, of comparing the refreshingly philosophy-free
with the depressingly philosophy-burdened. *Act*, as Barth recognizes, is itself
a concept calling out for philosophical exploration whether the categories
used be more existential or more 'essential'. One cannot force people to
choose between the 'actualistic and dramatic' on the one hand and, on the
other, a theology of 'prior capacities and essences'. These two approaches
necessarily interpenetrate – as they do in the world, in human thinking, and
in revelation itself which is both action and contemplation, both faith as deed
and faith as vision. Balthasar's trilogy, in combining theological dramatics
and theological aesthetics, and understanding the interrelation of these by a
theological logic, might be called an extended commentary on this short
passage in his book *Karl Barth*.

But since vis-à-vis Barth Balthasar is defending the second, more Scholastic, kind of theology and its rightful use by an interpreter of the Gospel, he
quite naturally underscores its virtues. He defends it as a tribute to the
contemplative dimension of the Gospel. What Scholastic theology provides
is:

> an intrinsic and inseparable dimension of the event of revelation itself,
> giving it room and distance and stillness, enabling it to be itself ... a
> serene meditation on this event in contemplative distance.[68]

Now, if we can suppose that it is above all the theology of *Thomas* Balthasar
has in mind here (and the succeeding pages of his study confirm that
impression), then Barth's own theology bears it an uncanny likeness. Both
theologies – Thomas's and Barth's – turn on a version of the well-known
exitus-reditus scheme, whereby all things flow forth from the One – in biblical
terms, have their '*Genesis*' from it, and in some way return to the One – in
biblical terms, come under, at the End, the reign of God (in Barthian terms,
this concerns above all the theme of predestination). What the disciples of
Thomas and Barth himself are doing here is pressing into a service an
ordering principle which brings out something crucial about theology's subject

67 *Ibid.*, p. 258.
68 *Ibid.*

matter. They are not forcing revelation down onto a bed of Procrustes into whose hard form it will never fit. To call the theology of Thomas basically a natural theology with a little light revelatory sugar thrown atop is an historical nonsense. The very concept of natural theology did not emerge until the late sixteenth century.

What Balthasar grants, though, is that Thomas occupies a transition stage in the history of Catholic thought. For Aquinas, the natural and supernatural orders were still interwoven – even if not as seamlessly so as with the Fathers of the Church. Behind Thomas lies the single concrete spiritual order of patristic theology; ahead of him there is looming the twofold natural and supernatural order of the makers of the First Vatican Council. What was comparatively new in Thomas was the way he appreciated the distinct formalities and ways of working of philosophy and theology – not so as to sever these from each other but so that each should appreciate the other for itself. Since this can lead to an intensification of their mutually beneficial effects, we should, says Balthasar, welcome it.

That is not to say, however, that Balthasar is *never* placed on the defensive when he considers Thomas. In accordance with the then prevailing scholarship, he holds that the doctrines of the Trinity, of Christ, and of the Church, are less structurally important for Aquinas than those of the One God, and the abiding pattern of creation. Modern Thomist scholars are unlikely to agree with him when he remarks that Thomas

> focussed on the lasting structure of the universe, in contrast to which the temporal nature of salvation history as standard setting *singularia* receded into the background.[69]

Present-day historical theologians would be more likely to hold that the lesson Balthasar considers Barth can teach – the synthesizing of 'the mere historical fact and purely transhistorical doctrine'[70] – is already there in Aquinas. The issue will return when Balthasar turns to the topic of what might become in a Catholic context of Barthian Christocentrism.

(ii) Nature and grace
If Thomas is posed halfway between the Fathers and Neo-Scholasticism in matters of theological method, he occupies the same intermediate position on the topic – crucial, in any dialogue with Barth – of *nature and grace*. Entering this particular arena, so far as Thomas interpretation is concerned, resembles stepping into a minefield. Balthasar is fully aware of the possible range of views among even historically minded students of Thomas (let alone those who are not!). However, he considers one proposition to be inescapable. In Thomas's doctrine of humanity, 'the nature of created spirit is directed beyond itself'.[71] Though there are various ways of understanding that statement, all such understandings, if properly text-based in Aquinas's writings, are in agreement on one thing. Thomas 'never entertains, *even hypothetically*, a final goal that could be unmoored from the supernatural

69 *Ibid.*, p. 264.
70 *Ibid.*, p. 266.
71 *Ibid.*, p. 268. A sample of such an approach is T. Weinandy, D. Keating, J. Yocum (eds), *Aquinas on Doctrine. A Critical Introduction* (London and New York, 2004).

vision of God'.[72] Now faced with the challenge of Michel du Bay, 'Baius', the Louvain divine for whom grace was a strict requirement of human nature, a hypothesis along those lines – the hypothesis of a pure nature with its own, non-supernatural last end – began to be so entertained, but only *as* an hypothesis deigned to protect the gratuity of grace. Until, that is, certain thinkers detached the concept of 'pure nature' from its original theological presuppositions and set up shop with it, giving it a life of its own.

Balthasar is entirely favourable to the late seventeenth-century Papacy's condemnation of Baian theology. It was as necessary as the condemnation by the Church of the fifth century of Christological Monophysitism and for the same reason. At Ephesus, a Council had once spoken of the 'one natural reality' of Christ and no one had batted an eyelid. At the Second Council of Orange – only a local council but one whose teaching has been treated as authoritative by the Church – formulae close to Baianism were passed without demur. But in each case, subsequent discussion made plain the demerits of these locutions. In the Christological case, Christ was one reality all right, but to bring out the saving significance of that reality one had to speak of him as a single personal subject of two natures. So likewise on the soteriological issue. Adam was a unity of creaturely essence and the gift of grace in a single 'nature' all right, but to bring out the way that synthesis was no necessary one, one had to speak of creaturely essence as just that – *creaturely*, that is: *not in and of itself exalted to a new order by grace*. In a little formula of his own, Balthasar calls the human creature by nature the *servant* of God: not God's *friend*.

So far this is, it may be said, a fairly standard defence of modern Catholic teaching. But Balthasar now moves on to some refinements all his own. We ought to distinguish, he thinks, between a philosophical concept of nature and a theological one, accepting that the two are linked, yes, but only by analogy. Appealing to both ancient and mediaeval philosophy, Balthasar describes a created nature as (a) what is conveyed by something's coming into being, (b) considered especially in that existent being's principles of action, (c) and its goal, (d) and not excluding the environment its life presupposes. Looking at things purely from a philosophical angle, there is no adequate reason for ruling out the possibility that human nature (so defined) might include a vocation to be the friend of God, called to an intimate share in his inner life. It is only by revelation that we know this *not* to be so – that our vocation to the beatific vision is not a consequence of our human essence but, rather, the upshot of God's grace. Evidently, then, the *theological* concept of nature, revelation-dependent as it is, will not coincide with the philosophical. The theologian knows that human nature now exists concretely only in the gracious order whereby God wills for us friendship with the Trinity. When, accordingly, the theologian studies nature, as a reality distinct from grace, he or she will be seeking to grasp the subject (or recipient) of grace – a subject which though it has been altered by grace and now exists 'otherwise' (the Latin term would be *aliter*) is not other than nature, not a different reality (the Latin phrase would be: *non alter*).

Theologically speaking, we can only find it exceedingly difficult to say just what aspects of humanity in the concrete are owed to 'pure nature', and

72 *Karl Barth, op. cit.,* p. 269. Italics original.

Balthasar is tempted by the view that it may be better not to try. In our *de facto* world we know only man's supernatural goal. Yet we must continue to work with the contrast nonetheless. Only so can we say, marvelling, that the servant has become the friend. Put more technically, we must insist on the difference between the *formal* concepts of nature in philosophy and theology respectively – even though we can have no assurance as to the extent of the difference in the *material* concepts concerned. Balthasar says:

> Of course, philosophy does have a *formal* object, that is, the nature of the creaturely world as such. But it has no purely isolable material object, because the actual world of creation actively participates *de facto* in the Word of revelation, either positively, in grace, or negatively, in sin.[73]

Theology can add to philosophy, though, a crucial truth – and it is by 1951 an old one in Balthasar's writing. The closer humanity's union with God through the Word, the clearer becomes our understanding of the natural distance between them. Under grace, that distance is now the locus of a 'genuine and fruitful conversation'.[74] And in the final analysis the explanation for that must be *the mystery of the Holy Trinity* where the 'distance' (i.e. difference) between the Persons is the condition for the perfect *perichôrêsis* of their loving communion.

Congruently with what has just been said, Balthasar makes an important summary statement on the issue of the natural (as distinct from supernatural) knowledge of God:

> Our natural capacity for knowing God is incorporated as an inserted moment in the ultimate, supernaturally relevant knowledge. Accordingly, even the Creator's natural and indirect revelation in the world is not annulled in his revelation of grace but is fulfilled and surpassed in the direction of Christ's humanity. For his [Christ's] human nature is the total sacramental sign of grace.[75]

That is a statement which also sets out a programme for his future theology.

(iii) Christocentricity (and sin and grace)

This brings us, of course, to the topic of *Christocentricity*. Balthasar claims that classical Catholic thought, historic and modern, is in fact Christocentric, and that the only way to make sense of this is along the lines he has just stated. Thus his position on nature and grace is confirmed (and with it, Barth's, if appropriately deprived of what Balthasar terms a certain over-rigidity in formulation). Thomas, Scotus, Suárez, despite differences of formulation of the 'motive' of Incarnation, share a single basic perspective. In the words of Emile Mersch, the great proponent in Balthasar's lifetime of teaching on the 'whole Christ', Christ the Head and Christ in the members:

> The Incarnation remains essentially a means of salvation against sin … But at the same time, the Incarnation was willed for its own sake, for a redemptive Incarnation is nothing else but the ultimate radicality of

73 *Ibid.*, p. 291.
74 *Ibid.*, p. 292.
75 *Ibid.*, p. 318.

incarnation itself: the Incarnation itself is the act in which God sur-
renders himself entirely.[76]

But more widely, Balthasar brings to the witness stand a whole host of
modern Catholic writers for whom Christ must be the very meaning of
nature and creation, since supernaturally exalted nature was the first thing
God willed in creating. As the Munich dogmatician Michael Schmaus put it,
God 'willed nature as the presupposition of the supernatural', so as to have a
'place' where 'he could let his own life pour forth'.[77] Again, the inter-war
Italo-German writer Romano Guardini, in his *Wesen des Christentums* – a book
to be placed in a long line of German attempts since Harnack to state the
'essence of Christianity', protests that the essence of Christianity is Christ –
and from his account of union with Christ Guardini derives his theology of
grace and from an account of grace his theology of the ultimate meaning of
nature.[78] Przywara, who might be thought, from Barth's disapprobatory
remarks, the least likely source of consolation on the point, teaches that
'everything that might be a way to God or an image of God is only a dim
reflection or a first intimation of what alone is revealed in Christ' – words
taken from Przywara's brief précis of his thought, *Summula*.[79]

It coheres with this that the thinkers Balthasar commends as not unre-
presentative of modern Catholic thought try to marry thinking about the
'essences' of things with historical thinking – a theology of, in Barth's terms,
the *event*. They seek to see together the immanent historicity of humankind
and the transcendent historicity of the Lord of history who in his incarnate
Word so enters time as to become the norm of the histories of both individuals and the world at large. (Here Balthasar lays the foundation for his own
study *Theology of History* which we shall be considering under the heading
'Time and History' in part two – *Themes* – of the present study.) Once again,
the key is Christ, in whom the two historicities, immanent and transcendent,
are joined in Jesus' two natures.[80] In this perspective, Balthasar considers
some of the critics of Neo-Scholasticism in the Modernist period to have been
misunderstood. Figures like Lucien Laberthonnière and Maurice Blondel
simply wished to 'be pioneers of the concrete and historical aspects of
ontology'.[81] God is, with the Thomists, pure Act – but he is act, those writers
stressed, as fulfilling history and spirit. We see him being by acting as well as
acting by being.

On the other hand, Balthasar criticizes (without naming them) the French
writers of *la nouvelle théologie*. Though de Lubac's historical research is

---

76 E. Mersch, *Théologie du Corps mystique* (Paris, 1946), I., p. 170.
77 M. Schmaus, *Katholische Dogmatik* II (Munich, 1949, 4th edition), p. 186.
78 R. Guardini, *Das Wesen des Christentums* (Würzburg, 1940, 2nd edition), p. 68.
79 E. Przywara, *Was ist Gott? Eine Summula* (Nuremberg, 1947), p. 18.
80 Something Balthasar did not foresee was the renewal of Christian cosmology at the end
   of the twentieth century – with consequent criticism of the anthropocentric implications
   of Christocentricity of a certain kind. By treating nature, with Barth, as a theatre brought
   into being as the setting and instrument for realizing man's eternal election in Jesus
   Christ, Balthasar risked aligning himself at this point with the most anthropocentric
   theology since Origen, diminishing to that degree the serviceability of his theological
   aesthetics for a renewed theology of the cosmos in its biodiversity. See H. P. Santmire,
   The Travail of Nature. The Ambiguous Ecological Promise of Christian Theology (Minneapolis,
   1985), pp. 151–54.
81 *Karl Barth*, p. 341.

unassailable, the appropriate conclusion to be drawn from it is simply that the encounter of grace fulfils man's truest essence – *not* that such fulfilment can be compelled by any natural necessity. Balthasar felt the 'new theologians' might be compared in this respect to members of the nineteenth-century Catholic Tübingen school who also experienced 'temptations' along these lines. We cannot get beyond the paradox of the 'pure otherness of grace that comes from above' and the 'imperfectability of the world and of culture ... when deprived of grace' – a formula whereby Balthasar paraphrases the theology of culture of the little-known inter-war Austrian theologian Oskar Bauhofer.[82] He makes the historically interesting aside that the two chief factors moving twentieth-century Catholic theologians to share Barth's thinking on the priority of Christ vis-à-vis creation were recourse to pre-Augustinian patristics (possibly Irenaeus was especially in mind), and also social philosophy, which wanted to stress that solidarity in Christ is more primordial than the fracture of solidarity in Adam. So, like Barth, modern Catholicism has to struggle with the eschatological implications of such a protology. Dare we hope that all may be saved? This is, of course, the issue of sin, ubiquitous among us, and the even more abounding grace thereby made available.

Conclusion

Does this mean, then, that Balthasar considers he has proved Barth to be compatible with Catholicism and Catholicism with Barth? Not really. First of all, his entire approach has been restricted to the three related issues of creating, gracing, redeeming – in more Barthian language, creation and covenant. In no way has he addressed directly those issues of ecclesiology and sacramental theology from which the Protestant Reformation began. But secondly, even in the theology of creation and covenant there is no perfect accord. Balthasar finds in Barth's denial of any theological pertinence to the philosophical understanding of God a narrowing of Christian wisdom, and remains concerned that, without a proper doctrine of nature, Barth cannot do full justice to the human response to the divine Word. Furthermore, there is one issue in the theology of grace where no accord seems likely. As Balthasar explains, Catholic theology could never accept Barth's – characteristically Protestant – denial that justifying grace brings about an ontological change in the human creature (and not just an upgrade of its credit). God's gift of grace to us is a participation in his inner life, 'neither purely forensic nor purely eschatological ... [but] real, internal and present'.[83] As the saints, we might add, have not only known, but shown. One wonders what Balthasar would have made of the Joint Declaration on the theology of justification signed between Catholics and Lutherans at Augsburg in the year 2000.[84]

---

82 *Ibid.*, p. 347.
83 *Ibid.*, p. 377.
84 On the difficulties of reaching a satisfactory common statement with Protestantism on this topic, see A. Nichols, OP, 'The Lutheran-Catholic Agreement on Justification: Botch or Breakthrough?', *New Blackfriars* 82 (2001), pp. 375–88.

In the course of his subtle discussion of this final (and, for the moment, irresoluble) difficulty Balthasar gives an early statement of his controversially dramatic theology of the Atonement whereby it was Christ on the Cross – not justified human beings – who was *really* in Luther's famous phrase *simul justus et peccator*: at once the Just and Holy One and the substituted Representative of sinners. But the issue of inherent justification aside (not that it is a bagatelle), Barth's theology of creation and salvation lie open to a Catholicizing interpretation. Balthasar feels he has shown that *to this extent* the claim of Protestant dogmatics to warrant the schism by a different (and better) theology of the foundations of Christianity falls to the ground.

The distinctively Catholic doctrines in Western Christendom (on magisterium, the sacraments, the veneration of the Mother of God and the saints) do not follow from some unhappy amalgam of theology and philosophy leading to an overestimation of human powers, as Barth fears. Balthasar has proved there simply is no such amalgam determining the Catholic view of revelation from the bottom up. There is only 'God's free use of man and human realities in Christ'.[85] This is the grace of God in its wondrous descent – its *Abstiegsbewegung* – 'assuming hierarchical and institutional forms ... the better to lay hold of man, ... a being bound by nature, structure, law'. And likewise it is grace taking shape through personality traits and circumstances in order to confer a 'charismatic mission or vocation' to transform the individual for God's purposes.[86] In Balthasar's most favoured metaphor, it is grace making the vine-branches fruitful in bringing forth grapes.

In his 'afterword' to the second, 1961 edition of *Karl Barth*, Balthasar, now aged 55, enumerates the sides of his own later work which, basically, Barth and his own reactions to Barth, inspired. These included much in his patrological efforts: notably the study of St Maximus, in its final (1961) form, and his approach to Augustine, as indicated by his anthologized *De civitate Dei*. Here Balthasar brought to interpreting the mind of the Fathers some principles he had laid out in his contribution to the *Festschrift* for Barth's seventieth birthday under the title 'Christian Universalism'.[87] His study of the nineteenth-century Carmelite mystic Elizabeth of Dijon, which appeared in the year following *Karl Barth* was meant to show the affinities between her understanding of predestination and Barth's.[88] And the way Balthasar prioritizes the ecclesial, 'missionary', significance of charisms in the Elizabeth book – rather than merely exploring, à la Schleiermacher, 'Christian subjectivity', is anticipated in his study of Elizabeth's better-known contemporary Thérèse of Lisieux (which appeared a year before the first edition of *Karl Barth*) and continued in his account of the twentieth-century French novelist Georges Bernanos (published three years after it). Like *Elisabeth von Dijon*, Balthasar gives his Thérèse book a title that includes the word 'mission', *Sendung*, thus incorporating mystical hagiography into a dogmatics of

---

85 *Karl Barth, op. cit.,* p. 387.
86 *Ibid.*
87 'Christlicher Universalismus', in *Antwort: Karl Barth zum siebzigsten Geburtstag 10. Mai 1956* (Zollikon-Zurich, 1956), pp. 272–86, reprinted in *Verbum Caro. Skizzen zur Theologie I.* (Einsiedeln, 1960). An English translation can be found in *Explorations in Theology* I: *The Word made Flesh* (San Francisco, 1965), pp. 241–54.
88 *Elisabeth von Dijon und ihre geistliche Sendung, op. cit.*

the commission given by the Word of God.[89] This is the only way one *could* commend mystics to a Barthian. That emphasis may not be so apparent in the Bernanos book.[90] It is indicated, however, in the closing chapter on the existential significance of the sacraments in Bernanos' writings: the sacraments as lived show God's grace energizing the Church as act. Again, exactly the same Barth-stimulated preoccupation – to show how the mystical dimension is not private interiority but ecclesial grace – declares itself in Balthasar's contribution to the standard twentieth-century German language commentary on Aquinas's *Summa theologiae*, which dealt with Thomas's treatise on special gifts of grace and the distinction between the active and contemplative lives.[91]

Balthasar implies – somewhat surprisingly – that his most Barthian book so far was his theology of contemplation, *Das betrachtende Gebet*, where he set out to combat formlessness and unattunedness to God's sovereign beauty just as had – in a vastly different mode – Karl Barth.[92] But of course his theological aesthetics, *Herrlichkeit*, still under way at the time of these comments of 1961, would take this much further. The most obviously Barthian of Balthasar's later writings is really his *Theologie der Geschichte*, though by 1961 he was discontented with what he considered a certain narrowness in it (for which he blamed Barth!) and directed his readers' attention to his forthcoming essay collection, which actually appeared as a quasi-unified book: *Das Ganze im Fragment. Aspekte einer Geschichtstheologie*.[93] (The third volume of Balthasar's essays would consider, rather, the Holy Spirit.)[94]

In the ten years since he produced the original version of *Karl Barth*, had he progressed any further in *rapprochement* towards what Barth represented? Indirectly, yes, and in two ways: first, in his ecclesiological essays by opening doors to a wider inner-Christian ecumenical dialogue (this two years before the Second Vatican Council opened);[95] and secondly, and more subtly, by trying to bring out 'all the implications of the analogy of being in the analogy of faith' – by which he meant doing increasing justice to the human medium of revelation and salvation. Having criticized Barth on the score, he could hardly escape self-criticism with integrity. This judgment directs us to some of the essays on revelation in *Verbum Caro*[96] and to his continuing interest in the figure of St Maximus. At the close of *Karl Barth*, he presents Maximus as the desirable complement to the Cyril of Alexandria who was Barth's chief Christological inspiration. The dyophysite, dyothelite doctor of Jesus' full human nature and will could still play a part in modern Chalcedon-inspired dogmatic thought.

He re-visited the topic of Barth's overall significance three times: for Barth's seventieth birthday in 1956, for his eightieth birthday in 1966, and on his death in 1968. On the first occasion, in a brief celebration in a Basle daily,

89 *Thérèse von Lisieux. Geschichte einer Sendung, op. cit.*
90 *Bernanos, op. cit.*
91 *Thomas von Aquin: Besondere Gnadengaben und die zwei Wege menschlichen Lebens. Kommentar zur 'Summa Theologica' II/II* (Heidelberg, 1954).
92 *Das betrachtende Gebet* (Einsiedeln, 1958).
93 Cf. *Das Ganze im Fragment. Aspekte der Geschichtstheologie, op. cit.*
94 *Spiritus Creator. Skizzen zur Theologie* III (Einsiedeln, 1967; 2nd edition 1988).
95 *Sponsa Verbi. Skizzen zur Theologie* II (Einsiedeln, 1961; 2nd edition 1971).
96 *Verbum Caro. Skizzen zur Theologie* I, *op. cit.*

Balthasar described Barth as better serving the common cause of Christianity, despite his 'many warlike remarks about the Catholic Church', than many Protestants who adopted 'a more eirenic and ecumenical tone'.[97] Samson-like, Barth had single-handed shaken the 'temple of liberal Protestantism' and as good as laid it in ruins. He praised Barth's recovery of a forthright confession of the divinity of Christ. As a consequence of his convictions, Barth was cold-shouldered by many Germanophone Protestants until his international fame made a continuance of this attitude impossible. Barth's hostility to ecumenical 'diplomacy' did not make Balthasar think any the worse of him (indeed, he implies rather the opposite). His *Kirchliche Dogmatik*, Balthasar was sure, would feed preachers, researchers and ordinary layfold with good, nourishing diet for generations to come.

Ten years later, writing in the German weekly *Christ und Welt* in the context of Protestant Neo-Liberalism and Catholic Neo-Modernism, Balthasar ascribed to Barth (not unreasonably) his own disappointment at the direction both Protestant and Catholic theologies were taking in the 1960s. Thinking no doubt of the Second Vatican Council's Pastoral Constitution on the Church in the Modern World – at the time and afterward the most generally controversial of its documents, he imagined Barth's displeasure at the way in that document the Council had seemed, so far as possible, to place on the same level the Word of God on the one hand and considerations based on natural law, psychology, sociology and religious phenomenology on the other – exactly the sort of false equivalence Barth had spent his whole life combating. Balthasar considered Barth was ending his days a saddened man.

Not that this was likely to interfere with his message, which is, wrote Balthasar admiringly, 'ever more clearly and classically spoken'.[98] And what is that message? Balthasar tells us in a single sentence of lucid German theological prose. It is:

> that Jesus Christ is the Lord of man and of the world, that this Word brings the old man down to death, in order with his divine power to let a new man rise from the grave; that for man salvation lies exclusively – beyond mankind itself – in this saving Word; that man should be gripped by the grace of faith; that the Word of God as Scripture and proclamation present it to us, is powerful enough to interpret itself for man and make itself intelligible to him, and so carries its measure in itself, and is not required to be measured by human standards if human beings are to comprehend it.[99]

After the subleties of *Karl Barth*, that is a simple statement, and its simplicity is not just a function of the semi-popular organ in which it appeared. It

---

97 'Karl Barth siebzig Jahre alt', *Basler Volksblatt* 84. 108 (9 May 1956). Balthasar had paid the same compliment a decade previously *in re* the ecumenical assembly presided over by Archbishop Nathan Søderblom of Uppsala, 'We are thankful to Karl Barth for, with us, rejecting on dogmatic grounds every relativising kind of religious conversation (as was conducted in Stockholm) and that he considers it a virtue of the Catholic Church never to have participated in this type of discussion': 'Über Sinn und Grenzen christlicher Kontroversie', *Gloria Dei* I (1946–1947), pp. 205–18, and here at p. 205.

98 'Ein unbequemer Partner. Karl Barth zum achtzigen Geburtstag', *Christ und Welt* XIX. 18 (1966), p. 14.

99 *Ibid.*

reflects Balthasar's realization that in the doctrinal (and moral) confusion of the 1960s, some straight talking about what (he and) Barth represented was necessary. He now resumed his earlier appreciative comments on Barth's style of writing. Not only does the high quality of his prose mean he will bulk large in any future history of Swiss literature but also particular qualities that generate that overall standard of writing are perfectly suited to their religious content: the sober yet passionate objectivity, the sense of concreteness in dealing with *das Allerkonkreteste*, God in Jesus Christ: 'the most concrete of all'. Compared with this, the food of state-of-the-art theological writing in the 1960s struck Balthasar as thin gruel. Barth can afford to wait, thought Balthasar, till the waters of a humanistic theology trickle away into the sand. His refusal to seek the verdict of those scientific exegetes currently most in fashion before daring to venture on biblical interpretation was praiseworthy. Scientific exegesis has its place, but as a method for grasping for the revealed divine word in the human words of Scripture it is itself unscientific. Balthasar picked out for special approval Barth's theology of the divine attributes ('fully biblical'), his 'functional' (not over against ontological) Christology and his teaching on election (predestination). He is an 'uncomfortable ecumenical partner' (a phrase that gives Balthasar's article its title), but his objections are always worth hearing. Balthasar repeated his objections to Barth's theology on certain points: the refusal of a natural knowledge of God weakens his theology; his opposition to any creaturely sub-mediation of grace shows an insufficient confidence in the divine gifts. But the *Church Dogmatics* as a whole are living proof that the instinct of faith can be found in individuals no matter what their Christian community (*Gemeinde*: for Catholic doctrine the Reformed congregations are not in the full sense 'churches'). The Holy Spirit may choose his instruments as he will.

Two years later Barth was dead. In his local Catholic paper in Lucerne, Balthasar contributed a final appreciation.[100] It is more expansive about Barth's attitude to Catholicism – partly on the basis of personal knowledge – than any other comment Balthasar published. It describes how touched Barth was by the interest Catholic dogmaticians, beginning in the 1930s, took in his thought; how he considered them to have, often, a better understanding of his writing than his Protestant peers. Balthasar records how not only he himself but others on the Catholic side also saw how close they could approximate to Barth on many points – and how all were agreed that Barth had misunderstood the analogy of being which, whether he liked it or not, was an internal requirement of his own favoured 'analogy of faith'. The more the Bultmannians marched through the German Universities and took over the Protestant faculties, the closer the sympathy Barth felt for Catholic theology – and this was intensified still further by the renewal of teaching found in the great majority of the texts of the Second Vatican Council. Balthasar discloses Barth's comment to him that, had he been born a Catholic Christian, he doubted very much whether Protestantism would attract him now. Three days before his death, Barth had proposed a double essay, by Balthasar and himself, to be dedicated to the Pope (Paul VI), and expressed to Balthasar his sorrow at the troubles which immediately post-Conciliar

100 'Karl Barth. Eine Würdigung', *Vaterland* 292 (1968), pp. 560–61.

Catholicism was encountering (the defection of priests and Religious, and other trials).

Balthasar does not hesitate to draw a lesson from the confrontation of Barth's work with the post-Conciliar crisis. In a frightening manner, Progressive Catholicism was justifying the accusation of the Barth of the early volumes of the *Church Dogmatics* that Romanism and Liberal Protestantism were, appearances notwithstanding, natural bedfellows. Neither took with full seriousness the Word of God. Balthasar appealed to his Catholic readers to heed Barth's warning: study the history of Liberal Protestantism, inwardly digest and draw the necessary lessons, and do so now before it is too late.

The fullness and fervour with which Barth led Balthasar to approach the main dogmatic themes was confirmed by his more or less contemporaneous encounter with the mystic Adrienne von Speyr.

5

֍

Divine Helpmate: Adrienne von Speyr

Adrienne von Speyr was the other great discovery of Balthasar's years as chaplain in Basle. She was also probably the twentieth century's most remarkable mystical theologian: a mystic, namely, become theologically articulate. Though her place in the history of Catholic theology is, thanks to her influence on Balthasar, entirely assured, her life and teaching are of considerable interest in their own right. For our purposes, we need to note Balthasar's own declaration that it is impossible to understand his work 'unless one takes seriously the influence of Adrienne von Speyr'.[1] Indeed, he devoted the greater part of his account of the *Johannesgemeinschaft* to an analysis of their convergent paths and common theological inspiration. The title, significantly enough, was *Unser Auftrag*: *'Our* Mission'. Nor was this simply a matter of their joint founding of a 'secular institute' (*Weltgemeinschaft*) for people vowed to celibacy but living out a professional life in the world.[2] It also concerned Balthasar's theology. After 1941, he wrote, 'my books were greatly influenced by her ideas'.[3]

---

1 M. Albus, 'Geist und Feuer. Ein Gespräch mit Hans Urs von Balthasar', *art. cit.*, p. 73.
2 See, for example, 'Das Ärgernis der Laienorden', *Wort und Wahrheit* 4 (1951), pp. 485–94, where he regretted the scant respect shown to the newly emerging Secular Institutes – 'allotments on the city's edge' compared with the historic Orders, with their 'ancient noble park from the *Barockzeit*', and entered a plea for the Institutes' combination of chastity with obedience but hardly poverty since 'Christ did not live ... a dirty poverty', p. 490; and, two years later, 'Wandlungen im Ordensgedanken', *Schweizer Rundschau* 52 (1953), pp. 679–84, which argued that though the Church, owing to her access to 'eternal powers', is not fully submitted to laws of cultural senescence, each Order is in some way bound to the moment of its foundation. Today, in a modernity where the Christian of the future will be less faithful to the Church, receive the sacraments less frequently, obey the pope and clergy less, it is all the more important to have 'lay monks' who will undertake the task of penetrating the world. See too: 'Neue Gemeinschaftsformen in der heutigen Kirche. Zur Entwicklung der "Weltlichen Institute"', *Universitas. Zeitschrift für Wissenschaft, Kunst und Literatur* 13 (1958), pp. 167–77, which places the development of the Institutes in the context of various Church initiatives of the period 1920 to 1945 intended to cope with the 'contemporary upheavals in the area of human organisation and civilisation', p. 167.
3 *Unser Auftrag, op. cit.*, pp. 49–50.

Her life

She was born the second of four children on 20 September 1902 in Switzerland, at La Chaux-de-Fonds, in what was at that time the French-speaking
region of Canton Berne (now Canton Jura).[4] Her father, an eye surgeon, came
from a Basle family distinguished for doctors, (Protestant) clerics and busi-
nessmen. Her relationship with her mother was bad, but to compensate she
enjoyed what Balthasar calls 'a totally childlike existence in God and for
God'.[5] On such matters as how to be with God in prayer, and the value of
sacrifice and renunciation, she was instructed, we are told, by an angel.
Though she lived all her life in an academic milieu, worked as a professional
woman and had as her confessor and biographer the most learned Catholic
theologian of the century, we cannot make sense of Adrienne's mysticism
unless we accept that, to her awareness, angels and saints were constantly
coming and going in her life, and behind these the Holy Trinity itself.

Adrienne von Speyr enjoyed a good relation with her father, who allowed
her to go with him on his hospital rounds in order to visit sick children.
Similarly, in the holidays, when she stayed with an uncle who was director of
a psychiatric hospital near Berne, she was found to have a great gift for
calming the patients, getting through to them, and cheering the depressed.
From these experiences came her resolve to become a doctor herself, though
her own health was below par. She was often ill, and had recurrent back-
aches caused by inflammation of the vertebrae. She always became ill before
Easter: 'because of Good Friday', the angel told her. In her prayer, she looked
for ways to share the suffering of the sick, and offered herself to God for that
purpose.

Despite her mother's opposition, she attended a secondary school (the
only girl in her form) so as to obtain the necessary qualifications for beginning medical training. Balthasar tells us that her 'charming disposition,
indomitable sense of humour, and incorruptible judgment in matters of
ethics and religion made her the leader of the class'.[6] In November 1917 the
Protestant schoolgirl had a vision of the Mother of God surrounded by angels
and saints, among whom she recognized Ignatius Loyola. After this experience she found she had a small wound under the left breast over the heart:
she referred to this as her 'secret', a wonderful sign that she belonged physically to God.

Some very difficult years followed. Her father, who had overtaxed his
health in an effort to get a medical professorship at Basle, died. Her mother
became paranoid about money and insisted that Adrienne attend a business
college as well as high school. The teenager developed tuberculosis in both
lungs and was given less than a year to live; she felt that, in the circumstances, nursing would be a more reasonable ambition than medicine. She
began training at a deaconess hospital in Canton Vaud, but overwork soon
brought her to a state of collapse. Her mother moved the family to German-

---

4 She herself has left numerous materials for a biography: notably *Aus meinem Leben,
  Geheimnis der Jugend*, and her journals, the *Tagebuchbände*. All her writings are made
  available by Balthasar's Einsiedeln publishing house, the Johannes Verlag.
5 *Erster Blick auf Adrienne von Speyr* (Einsiedeln, 1968); ET *First Glance at Adrienne von Speyr*
  (San Francisco, 1981), p. 19.
6 *Ibid.*, p. 23.

speaking Basle, even though Adrienne herself could not at this time communicate adequately in German. She appears to have been tempted to suicide soon after this period though, once this crisis was over, her resolve to study medicine quickened. Since her family refused to support her, she financed her medical education by tutoring less advanced students. Her teachers noted the facility with which she grasped all subjects concerned with living persons, as distinct from anatomy, as also her complete satisfaction when finally allowed to work with the sick.

In 1927, when Adrienne was twenty-five, she inherited some money; holidaying at San Bernardino, an Alpine village in Canton Tessino, she met a history professor from Basle, Emil Dürr, who promptly fell in love with her. Unsure whether she should enter marriage, owing to her 'secret', she hesitated, but the couple were duly wed. But Emil died suddenly in 1934 and a distraught Adrienne seemed again but a few steps from suicide. However in 1936 she married one of his pupils, Werner Kaegi, an expert on the Renaissance historian Jakob Burckhardt. It was a union where the spouses lived as brother and sister. Kaegi would outlive her, dying in 1979.

Adrienne had met Hans Urs von Balthasar in the autumn of 1940. He was still a Jesuit at that time, thirty-five years old, and had only recently been appointed student chaplain at Basle. She told him she would like to become a Catholic. The experience of instructing her (she was actually received at All Saints, 1940) was, for Balthasar, an extraordinary one. To begin with, though she had no theological education, he had only to give her the merest outline, hardly more than a suggestion, of a subject and she would come at once to a profound understanding of it. But secondly, in his own words:

> Immediately after her conversion, a veritable cataract of mystical graces poured over Adrienne in a seemingly chaotic storm that whirled her in all directions at once. Graces in prayer above all: she was transported beyond all vocal prayer of self-directed meditation upon God in order to be set down somewhere after an indefinite time with new understanding, new love and new resolutions.[7]

If the conclusion of that quotation seems a lame because vague finale to Balthasar's account, we can add that Adrienne had numerous visionary experiences of the Mother of the Lord and the saints, either individually or in groups, and was taught by them whether verbally or by means of brief symbolic scenes. That, whatever else one might think of it, is scarcely indefinite. Several of the saints particularly prominent in the Latin Catholic piety of the period – the Curé d'Ars (Jean-Baptiste Vianney), the Little Flower (Thérèse Martin) – were involved, but so too were the apostles and many of the Church Fathers whom Balthasar, as a patrologist, was able to identify. On one occasion, driving home from work, Adrienne saw a great light in front of her car, whereupon a nearby pedestrian jumped aside. She stopped to hear a voice say (and Balthasar describes this as the key for all that was to follow): 'You will live in heaven and on earth'.

There were also more external charisms connected with her medical practice: inexplicable cures that became the talk of the town. She herself was terrified by one happening, in the spring of 1941. An angel at her bedside told

7 *Ibid.*, p. 33.

her, 'Now it will soon begin'. In the nights that followed she was asked for a consent to God so total that it would embrace blindly everything God might ordain for her. What in fact 'began' was a series of re-livings of the Passion of Christ and, above all, of Holy Saturday, the Descent into Hell. As Balthasar explains:

> These passions were not so much a vision of the historical scenes of the suffering that had taken place in Jerusalem – there were only occasional glimpses of these, as if for clarification – rather, they were an experience of the interior sufferings of Jesus in all their fulness and diversity. Whole maps of suffering were filled in precisely where no more than a blank space or a vague idea seemed to exist.[8]

These initiations into the spiritual meaning of the events of Good Friday and Holy Saturday, registered in her diaries and later published by Balthasar under the title *Kreuz und Hölle* ('Cross and Hell'), were accompanied by the reception of the stigmata, a common feature of Passion mysticism since Francis of Assisi.[9] The wounds were small, but Adrienne was extremely anxious that they should not be noticed. She felt ashamed that something happening to her, a sinner, might have to do with the Lord's own Passion. In contrast to many other mystics, she avoided any language that might suggest identification, or even participation, speaking instead of, at most, 'proximity'.

Throughout these years she was commenting on the books of Scripture: notably the Gospel and Letters of St John, some of the Letters of St Paul, the Letters of Peter, James and Jude, the Apocalypse and parts of the Old Testament.[10] The commentary on the Apocalypse was especially important for Balthasar, and plays a considerable part in his theological dramatics. Adrienne began it, we can note, after a vision of the Woman with the messianic Child in chapter 12 of St John's text. This was a vision she had experienced at the Dominican monastery of Estavayer in Canton Neuchâtel, during the Retreat Balthasar preached for the founding of the *Johannesgemeinschaft* in the summer of 1945. These commentaries were not written out by her but dictated, at first hesitantly but later in word-perfect form. She was also coming to an understanding of what mysticism itself is. It is a particular mission or service to the Church which can be carried out only in a complete movement of self-forgetfulness, and of receptivity towards the Word of God. For Adrienne, personal states of soul are, as such, of no interest: for her, psychologizing introspection is a deviation from the mystic's true concern, the Word of God, and so a distortion of his or her mission.[11] As already remarked if any mysticism was to commend itself to Karl Barth, which is not perhaps likely, it could only be – as the last chapter has indicated – of this kind. In *Unser Auftrag* Balthasar calls the 'mission' implied by the particular form of mysticism in which she was caught up 'a mission of explication'. That formula throws light on the complementary mission of Balthasar himself in her regard. She spoke on the basis of extraordinary charisms, 'in the Spirit', much

---

8 *Ibid.*, p. 35.
9 A. von Speyr, *Kreuz und Hölle* I. *Die Passionen* (Einsiedeln, 1966). These texts are the fruit of her experiences on Good Friday and Holy Saturday in the years 1941–63.
10 For a bibliography of her writings, see *First Glance at Adrienne von Speyr, op. cit.*, pp. 104–10.
11 *Ibid.*, p. 36; pp. 87–90.

of the time describing visionary material, but attempting to excogitate its doctrinal content. She would continue to do so until Balthasar, with his sophisticated theological culture, understood the message involved.[12] She insisted that his transmission of her inspirations, in the form of edited dictation, had to be 'ecclesially precise'. That is why, explained Balthasar, his own style cropped up there from time to time. But Balthasar rejected the accusation that he had 'ghosted' the resulting texts: her theological originality and the coherence of her insights, despite the great diversity of themes, should exclude that suggestion. However, he did not reject the possibility that 'the interaction of her intelligence and love with the clarity of certain notions learned from me may have played a role'.[13] For those who pooh-pooh Adrienne's contribution – to Balthasar's thought and the spiritual literature of the twentieth century, it may be sobering to note that among those who corresponded with her Balthasar lists: Romano Guardini, Gabriel Marcel, Charles Journet (later cardinal), the Dominican Orientalist Pierre de Menasce, and three Jesuit intellectuals, Erich Przywara, Henri de Lubac and Hugo Rahner.[14]

During the 1950s Adrienne became increasingly ill. Her heart weakened and she developed diabetes. Chronic arthritis set in and after 1954 she had to abandon her work as a doctor. Up until 1964, when she began to lose her sight, she devoured novels in French, especially Bernanos, Mauriac and Colette, as well as many women authors. She also read scholarly books about the ocean, where God in nature was very present to her. At night, except for two or three hours of sleep, she gave herself to prayer. Balthasar records that Adrienne's prayer was universal, directed to all the concerns of God's kingdom, and an offering of self for its needs. Anonymity and availability were two of her favourite concepts in this connexion: letting oneself be absorbed in the universality of spiritual humanity. This must be understood of her, so the literary sources maintain, in an utterly concrete sense. In prayer, she was transported, she claimed, to innumerable places where her presence was needed: during the Second World War into the concentration camps; and afterwards into Religious houses, especially contemplative ones, where fervour for the divine Office or prayer itself had grown cold; into confessionals were confession was simulated or lukewarm, or the priest was not up to the needs of his penitents; to seminaries; frequently to Rome, to the offices of the *Curia romana*; and into empty churches where no one went to pray. She felt herself to be in these places both spiritually and physically, and returned from these strange 'journeys' dog-tired. At the same time, she was also organizing the Community of Saint John, whose members were people living the evangelical counsels but with professional jobs in the world. She spent a lot of time in anonymous almsgiving, notably to poorly off contemplative monasteries and to women without means. These alms she had sent off by letter from different parts of Switzerland and found it delicious to imagine the bewildered delight of those who received them.

Between 1964 and 1967 Adrienne's condition deteriorated. Though she could get down the steps to her study, she had to be carried back. Her

---

12 *Unser Auftrag, op. cit.*, p. 16.
13 *Ibid.*, p. 53.
14 'Aus dem Leben der Kirche. Adrienne von Speyr (1902–1967). Die Miterfahrung der Passion und Gottverlassenheit', *Geist und Leben* 58 (1985), pp. 61–66 and here at p. 65.

eyesight was so poor that she sometimes wrote and posted long letters without realizing that the ink had run out from her pen, and so the pages were blank. For many years she had experienced a vicarious dying, as an aspect of her substitutionary suffering for the suffering of others, their sins or their purgatory. According to Balthasar, her joyousness, courage and child-likeness (she loved children's books and doll's houses, and frequently had them refurbished to give to children) continued till the end. Adrienne von Speyr died on 17 September 1967 – in German-speaking countries the feast of St Hildegard of Bingen, a mediaeval mystic and theologian who had been, like her, a medical doctor. Her last words were 'Thank, thank, thank'. She was buried on her sixty-fifth birthday.

On Balthasar's own account in *Unser Auftrag*, there were numerous theological motifs in his writings which must be ascribed, at least in their final form, to her. The short set of lyrical Christological meditations, *Das Herz der Welt*,[15] Balthasar describes as the fruit of his first living through with her the Holy Week experiences described above. Wherever he subsequently makes reference to the Descent into Hell – in various eschatological essays, in *Mysterium Paschale* (his study of the Easter events), and in the theological dramatics, her contribution must be presupposed. In the rather unlikely context of his phenomenological metaphysics, *Wahrheit*, he considers the 'Johannine' notion of truth – truth as measure, and as love – to be their common discovery.[16] *Der Laie und der Ordensstand*, Balthasar's essay on Secular Institutes, reflects the thought they put into their shared foundation, the *Johannesgemeinschaft*.[17] (Various of the collected theological essays would follow up its themes.) The 1950 book on St Thérèse of Lisieux would never have seen the light of day without her since the theology of mission which dominates it is entirely hers,[18] and Balthasar would use the same hagio-graphical 'method' in his study of Thérèse's fellow Carmelite, Elizabeth of Dijon.[19] *The Christian State of Life*, an investigation of the interrelation of vocations to the priesthood, the Religious life, and the Christian life at large, had been under preparation since 1947 but only saw the light of day twenty years later.[20] The claim that there are only two intrinsically valuable states of life in the Church – consecrated virginity and marriage – was included at Adrienne's insistence. The curious speculations on the character of pre-lapsarian sexual intercourse which crop up in the book from time to time Balthasar ascribed to the combined effect on him of Adrienne and Gregory of Nyssa. She had contributed by prayer and penance to the writing of his 1951 book about Barth in the hope that it would win Barth's sympathy for Catholicism.

Balthasar's investigation of the Existentialist theme of anxiety in *Der Christ und die Angst* drew on her experiences of 'supernatural anxiety' as well as the

---

15 *Das Herz der Welt, op. cit.*
16 *Wahrheit. Wahrheit der Welt, op. cit.*
17 *Der Laie und der Ordensstand, op. cit.* Balthasar later regretted the second part of the title: it was not so much the 'state' of 'being in an Order' they were concerned with as the 'state' of living out the evangelical counsels.
18 *Thérèse von Lisieux. Geschichte einer Sendung, op. cit.*
19 *Elisabeth von Dijon und ihre geistliche Sendung, op. cit.*
20 *Christlicher Stand, op. cit.* Balthasar's Jesuit superiors had found the doctrine of divine call there excessively complicated – not without reason!

imaginative fiction of Georges Bernanos.[21] Looking back, he found her understanding of mission a factor in the universalistic tendencies of his (still) controversial critique of traditional Church life, *Razing the Bastions,* a work described in the opening chapter of the present book. It was predictable that he owed her a debt in his much reprinted essay on 'Theology and Holiness', which first appeared in both German and French in 1948.[22] To the extent that this essay gave Balthasar his particular perspective on the novels, plays and journalism of Bernanos, she played an indirect role in that book too. Their common efforts to guide professional people considering vows of chastity in the *Johannesgemeinschaft* made him sensible to the theme of conflicting loyalties in his other major exploration of a twentieth-century Catholic literary figure, Reinhold Schneider.[23] Balthasar's willingness to write a commentary on relevant questions in Aquinas's *Summa theologiae,* was 'entirely due' to Adrienne's charismatic experiences – even if only the first seven of the these questions deal with 'prophecy and other charisms', the remaining four concerning themselves with the distinction between the active and contemplative lives.[24] In the background of his book on contemplative prayer were her Scripture commentaries, which themselves speak of a wider project: her desire that a theology of prayer should be approached on the basis of obedient listening to the Word of God in the two Testaments.[25]

Rather more surprisingly, Balthasar finds the shadow of Adrienne in his two theological studies of humanity in its historical setting, *A Theology of History* and *Man in History,*[26] notably in the account of the Forty Days (between Easter and Ascension), the 'universalization' of Christ's work by the Holy Spirit, and the topics of mission and Tradition. Most importantly, Balthasar found her presence in the Trilogy. Her key theme of the glorification of the Holy Trinity in the destiny of Christ, stated in the journals as early as 1948 and recurrent in her commentaries on the Gospel according to St John, underlies the whole concept of the theological aesthetics, while Adrienne managed to hit on equivalents of Balthasar's Thomasian expressions *lumen* and *species* in her little work entitled *Das Licht und die Bilder.*[27] Another crucial theme of Adrienne's, mission, becomes in the theological dramatics the principal organizing theme of all Christology – and hence of the divine drama at large. Finally, remarks Balthasar, anywhere he has

21 *Der Christ und die Angst* (Einsiedeln, 1951).
22 'Theologie und Heiligkeit', *Wort und Wahrheit* 3 (1948), pp. 881–96; 'Théologie et sainteté', *Dieu vivant* 12 (1948), pp. 17–31.
23 *Reinhold Schneider. Sein Weg und sein Werk* (Cologne-Olten 1953, 2nd edition). This work was expanded in a revision prepared just before Balthasar's death as *Nochmals:Reinhold Schneider* (Einsiedeln-Freiburg 1991); ET *Tragedy under Grace. Reinhold Schneider on the Experience of the West* (San Francisco, 1997).
24 *Thomas von Aquin. Besondere Gnadengaben und die zwei Wege menschlichen Lebens. Kommentar zur 'Summa Theologica II.-II, 171–182, op. cit.,* pp. 252–464. Balthasar explains he wanted, on the basis of her experience and proposals, to take issue with Thomas when he maintains that extraordinary charisms (*gratiae gratis datae*) do not imply sanctifying grace.
25 *Das betrachtende Gebet, op. cit.* He followed this lead in his *Thessalonischer- und Pastoralbriefe für das betrachtende Gebet erschlossen* (Einsiedeln, 1955).
26 *Theologie der Geschichte, op. cit.,* and *Das Ganze im Fragment. Aspekte der Geschichtstheologie, op. cit.* Incidentally, the American edition bears a different title from the British: *A Theological Anthropology* (New York, 1967).
27 A. von Speyr, *Das Licht und die Bilder. Elemente der Kontemplation* (Einsiedeln, 1955).

spoken of the Blessed Virgin Mary in relation to the Church or of a spirituality for priests, the reader can assume Adrienne's signature on the work.

This is a formidable list, and yet to select one theme as pre-eminent is not
really a difficult task.

Adrienne and the Atonement

The single most important theme she passed onto Balthasar was undoubtedly her mystical penetration of the events of the Atonement, the Paschal
Mystery. Balthasar made this patently clear in the essay he wrote on her for a
multi-author book on 'Women of Faith', which carries the subtitle 'The Co-
experiencing of the Passion and Divine Abandonment'.[28] Balthasar recalls
that, from 1941 onwards, Adrienne re-lived each year – as already mentioned
– the suffering of Christ. These experiences took place during Holy Week,
with Lent as their usual preparation. Balthasar, who was by her side
throughout this time, was struck by the diversity within the suffering of
Christ as Adrienne described it. At the Mount of Olives and on Calvary,
Christ knew different kinds of fear, shame, humiliation, outrage. The
'abundance' of his physical pain is obvious; he also related himself in different ways to the sin of world, experiencing its Godforsakenness from different angles. Each year on Good Friday afternoon Adrienne went into a
death-like trance interrupted only by the lance-thrust described in St John's
Gospel. Shortly afterwards there began the most characteristic feature of her
Passion mysticism: the Descent into Hell, which lasted until the early hours
of Easter Sunday morning.

As she understood things, the Descent is the culmination of the Son's
obedience to the Father. Moved by that obedience, he enters the realm where
God is absent, where the light of faith, hope and love is extinguished, where
God is cast out of his own creation. Moving through the formlessness which
is the world's sin, the divine Son experiences its spiritual chaos. Balthasar
describes what Adrienne told him as 'more horrible than the Hell depicted
for us by the mediaeval imagination'; a being engulfed in the 'chaotic mire of
the anti-divine'.[29]

How did she herself describe the *Triduum*, the 'Three Days' in which the
mystery of the Atonement was enacted? Barbara Albrecht, in her study of
Adrienne, provides a helpful anthology of texts on this theme drawn not
only from *Kreuz und Hölle* but from her Scripture commentaries too.[30]

Adrienne stressed as the chief presupposition of the Atonement the Son's
ability to experience the gravity of human sin in a variety of distinct but
interrelated ways. The incarnate Son experiences sin as God from out of his
absolute purity feels it, but also, since he possesses the integrity of Adam
before the Fall, as humanity would have felt it had man never sinned. But
through the Father's gift he also feels and knows the difference which such
sin works in man: how sin is projected, and what it is like not to repent it

---

28 'Aus dem Leben der Kirche. Adrienne von Speyr (1902–1967). Die Miterfahrung der
   Passion und Gottverlassenheit', *art. cit.*, reprinted in P. Imhof (ed.), *Frauen des Glaubens*
   (Würzburg, 1985), pp. 267–77.
29 *First Glance at Adrienne von Speyr, op. cit.*, p. 67.
30 B. Albrecht, *Eine Theologie des Katholischen. Einführung in das Werk Adrienne von Speyrs. I.
   Durchblick in Texten* (Einsiedeln, 1972).

once committed; how too I feel when I sin in such a way that my sinful action is in dissonance from my character, but also when the sin reveals my character and makes it transparent through and through.

Like other women mystics – Catherine of Siena, Julian of Norwich – Adrienne von Speyr tries to make her meaning intelligible through homely examples: surgical practice, swimming lessons.[31] For there is a mystery here: as she stresses, Christ does not take over the experiences of individual sinners directly – rather does he possess them first and foremost from out of the 'space' between the Father and the Son, and the Holy Spirit who 'circles' there makes them actual in him. He sees the guilt of the world, in its bloatedness, and in its implications *von jeher* – from the perspective of the Eternal. As she remarks in her *Das Wort und die Mystik*:

> As representative of fallen humanity, the Son is introduced by the Holy Spirit to the permanent knowing of the offence of which the Father is the object ... And that all the more so in that he was sent to glorify the Father and do his will.[32]

Perceiving the alienation of human beings from the Father he nonetheless lives among them as man, dwells with the alienated, in a world which by the mere fact of his coming is in no way altered. But in his Passion he who recognizes (*erkennen*) the sin of the world for what it is also confesses it (*bekennen*). Recognition and confession are linked not only by a German wordplay but by Christology: for everything the Son has and knows belongs to the Father. Dying on the Cross, he makes for all our sins a perfect confession, and simultaneously, as he represents them all in their unity before the Father, does penance for them all. The Cross, for Adrienne, is the Son's confession, with Easter the Father's responding absolution.[33] This provided Adrienne with her understanding of the sacrament of reconciliation in her study *Confession: the Encounter with Christ in Penance*. As a follower of Christ, the sinner tries to bring to light his own sins, inseparable as these are from the sin of the world, so as to share experientially in the great absolution of Easter.[34]

In order to experience the more starkly the distance which separates sinners from God, the Son on the Cross lays down his divinity before the Father. The Spirit takes from the hands of the dying Son the offering of his Godhead so as to place it for ever in the bosom of the Father. Or, as Adrienne re-expresses this in less imagistic and more classical doctrinal language: the Spirit allows the hypostatic union of divinity and humanity in Christ to take such a form that it expresses the difference between God and man to the uttermost degree. (Incidentally, this chimes with Balthasar's paradoxical statement in his early programmatic essay in 'Patristik, Scholastik und wir' that the Incarnation of the All-powerful in the impotent one of Bethlehem and Calvary reveals the 'greatest separation' of God and man.) Out of love for the Father, so von Speyr proposes, the Son *renounces the experience of that*

31 *Ibid.*, pp. 90–92.
32 A. von Speyr, *Das Wort und die Mystik*, II. *Objektive Mystik* (= *Nachlassband VI*, Einsiedeln, 1970), p. 176.
33 B. Albrecht, *Eine Theologie des Katholischen, op. cit.*, pp. 92–93.
34 A. von Speyr, *Die Beichte* (Einsiedeln, 1960); ET *Confession. The Encounter with Christ in Penance* (London, 1964).

same love, and renounces too his understanding of that privation.[35] Here we begin
to see the invasion of her theological doctrine by the mystical experience she
had each year on the first two days of the *Triduum*. Going beyond what is
explicitly authorized by Scripture, she insists that the Son, in giving up the
Spirit, gave over to the Father him (the Spirit) who bound him (the Son) to
him (the Father). In tones of fearful negativity and harshness, she speaks of
the dying Christ as only the target of an obedience he no longer knows or can
reflect on, for the object of reflection has been withdrawn and the abandonment (*Verlassenheit*) is complete. All signs of the Father's acceptance fail:
the very being and content of the Father's will are veiled to him. Jesus' self-
offering becomes a saying 'Yes' which can no longer hear its own voice. All
'translation' of heavenly truth into earthly now breaks down for this
'abandoned man on the Cross'; there is no longer any conformity or even
accommodation between above and below. No parables are of any use
now.[36]

Yet while the Son seeks in vain for the face of the absent Father, this
heart-rending openness to the Father is outstripped by the Father's own in
the silence where the Father accepts the sacrifice of the Son. This night of
consummate suffering, where the Son, as Word of the Father, falls dumb is
in fact the fulfilment of the compact between Father and Son, the pact they
have made in love, and so the fulfilment of the innermost being of the
Godhead. This is Adrienne's comment on John 16.25: 'The hour is coming
when I shall no longer speak to you in figures but tell you plainly of the
Father'; this suffering is 'the ultimate that man can surmise of the greatness
of God'.[37] As she puts it in *The Countenance of the Father*, a work from her
Nachlass:

> What [the Father] bequeathed to the Son – his mission with its path
> through the world – has now become fully the Son's possession,
> something the Son has accomplished so utterly that the Father's will
> has been fully realized and made apparent in the Son, while the Father
> himself withdraws into absence, so as to enable all the light to fall upon
> the Son, indeed, so as to take undistracted cognizance of what the Son
> is. The divine unity of essence is not for one moment shattered; the
> Son's equal standing with the Father is fully evidenced and not for one
> moment called into question; while the distinctness of the Persons has
> never been more clearly revealed than in the relationship between the
> Son who is abandoned and the Father who abandons him.[38]

But this is no mere binitarian exchange. Adrienne does not forget, even in
the depths of this commerce between Father and Son, the role of the Holy
Spirit. During Jesus' ministry, the Spirit was, in her favourite term, the 'rule'
of the Son's acting; accordingly, Jesus was, in the words of the Gospels, 'led
by' him.[39] But now, at the moment when the Son's relation as man with the

35 B. Albrecht, *Eine Theologie des Katholischen, op. cit.*, p. 93.
36 *Ibid.*, pp. 93–96.
37 *Ibid.*, p. 96.
38 A. von Speyr, *Das Angesichts des Vaters* (Einsiedeln, 1955, 2nd edition 1981); ET *The
Countenance of the Father* (San Francisco, 1997), p. 82.
39 Matthew 4.1; cf. Mark 1.12; Luke 4.1.

Father reaches its highpoint, the roles are reversed. The Spirit obeys the Son as the latter embarks on that sending forth of the Spirit he will complete at Easter: a sending first 'to the Father' and then to the Church and the world.[40]

On the Cross the Son was, moreover, 'no hermit'.[41] Though Adrienne von Speyr rejects all mitigation of the Son's subjective isolation on the Cross, she stresses that the unique suffering of the Atonement was not, objectively speaking, absolutely alone. In a mysterious way, real, yet offering no lightening of his burden, the Son had co-sufferers. For the believers of the Old Covenant, summed up, for von Speyr, in Job, the Son also suffered, 'rounding off' their sufferings by his own; yet at the same time, he took up all the initiatives involved in their faith, suffering and 'readiness' (*Bereitschaft*, another key word in her vocabulary) and sent streams of grace flowing over them from the Cross. On the Cross, the Son, implicitly, thanks the Father for the predecessors of his new and everlasting covenant, and by fulfilling their attempts as redemptive suffering, makes them into saints of that new covenant of his.

And with these spiritual presences, there stood at the foot of the Cross, Mary his mother. Adrienne's entire spirituality is so Marian that it would be unlikely for her to overlook the Lady of Sorrows in her visions of Calvary. Her first book, *Handmaid of the Lord*, was devoted to Mary,[42] and is dominated by the motif of Marian consent: for Balthasar the fundamental attitude which pervades all von Speyr's mission.[43] In virtue of her unique election, Mary alone among human persons can exclude from her 'Yes' to God every limitation, whether conscious or unconscious. In the Lord's Mother, love, which Adrienne associates with St John, and obedience, which she links with St Ignatius, can coincide, since Mary's love expresses itself in the *fiat*, the will to obey. That is how she became sheer receptivity to the Incarnation of the Word. Such a perfect readiness can be moulded into many figures, as in the great Marian titles. Most importantly, this is how the Church, as Bride of the Lamb, can be formed from her. While time lasts, the Church never fully attains to Mary's perfect consent. Yet the Church carries that perfect consent within her as her determining form, striving towards it as best she can. In the duality of love and authority in the Church, redeemed sinners share in the 'pre-redeemed' consent of Mary – a reference to the Catholic doctrine of the Immaculate Conception, which in the general Resurrection will become the consent of the entire people of God. Mary's consent is the archetype of Christian fruitfulness, and in its light the contemplative life – the attempt to remain entirely open for the Word of God – can be seen as the necessary foundation for the active life as well. At the Cross, Mary shares in the way proper to her as mother in the universality of the Son's crucifixion. According to Adrienne, Mary on Calvary abdicates all right to private intimacy with her Child. She lets into the space between the Son and herself all those for whom she suffers, since he has so bound her co-suffering to his Passion that he will not work out the universal redemption without her.[44] This is, of course, von

40 B. Albrecht, *Eine Theologie der Katholischen, op. cit.*, p. 97.
41 *Ibid.*, p. 102. Cf A. von Speyr, *The Countenance of the Father, op. cit.*, p. 83.
42 *Idem, Magd des Herren* (Einsiedeln, 1948); ET *Handmaid of the Lord* (San Francisco, 1985).
43 *First Glance at Adrienne von Speyr, op. cit.*, pp. 51–54.
44 B. Albrecht, *Eine Theologie des Katholischen, op. cit.*, pp. 99–100.

Speyr's version of the notion of Mary as *auxiliatrix, adiutrix* and even *med-iatrix* of the Atonement.

More original is Adrienne's teaching that in the relation of Mary and John created by the Saviour from the Cross there originates the religious (or monastic) life in the Church. In Mary, the Lord reaches back to the aboriginal consent of mankind to his coming, so as to set flowing the new fruitfulness of the vows from that source. To John, the Beloved Disciple, Christ gives, in the Cross itself, the loveliest gift he has. Here, then, love, fruitfulness and the three forms of self-surrender expressed in the traditional vows are bound together, under the shadow of the Cross, as an inseparable unity.[45]

Moving from Good Friday to Holy Saturday, this moment of the *Triduum* is for Adrienne von Speyr 'the day when the Word falls dumb', a day which she compares, daringly, to the pre-natal dwelling of the Incarnate One in Mary's womb.[46] Resting in her purity, the Christ-child's nearness to his Mother in the womb took the form of reclusion and silence; now, in the womb of Sheol, what harbours him is all that is unclean, and his nearness to the mystery of the Father takes the form of separation and wordlessness. In sheer obedience, the divine Son seeks the Father where he cannot be, in all that is opposed to him. If the Atonement lacked the experience of Holy Saturday, the suffering of the Redeemer would be in some way comparable to that of other men, since his death was, after all, a human dying. It is the fact that the Son must go through Hell in order to return to the Father which gives this death its uniqueness. In Hell, the Son encounters sin in its sheer objectivity, by contrast to this world where, through its embedding in human circumstance, it always has nuance, shadow, outline. But now sin loses that circumscribed character which makes it in some way bearable. At the same time, the Son also meets sin in its sheer subjectivity: the sense in which personal subjects nourish sin with their own substance, mix it with their 'I', lend it their strength. And lastly he encounters it in its aspect of sheer actuality: deep, radical potency now actualized as evil. On the Cross, the Lord suffered sacrificially, by a productive love. But in Hell there is nothing in any way worthy of love: Hell is negative infinity. Behind every sin, the Son sees only one thing: the not-being-there of the Father. But this too is a saving event. As Adrienne puts it:

> The Son took sin upon him in two senses. On Good Friday, up to the moment of his death, he carried it as the personal sin of each individual human being, bearing it atoningly in his divine-human Person by an action that was, to the highest degree that he could make it, for the sake of sinners, the action of a subject. At that moment, every sin appeared in its connexion with the sinner who had committed it, and bore his or her features.

But on Holy Saturday, she explains, things are different. As she goes on:

> By contrast, on Holy Saturday, in his vision of the sin of the world from the standpoint of Sheol, sin loosed itself from the subject of the sinning, to the point that it became merely what is monstrous, amorphous, that

45 *Ibid.*, pp. 100–102.
46 *Ibid.*, p. 109.

which constitutes the fearfulness of Sheol and calls forth horror in the one who sees it.[47]

Both belong equally to the Son's 'confession'.

The body of the Son's passion and death Adrienne calls his 'confession body', for in it he had to carry not only the personal sin of each individual human being but also original sin, and sin as such. Turning now to the climax of the *Triduum*, Easter, she affirms that Christ's risen body is his 'absolution body'. As the body laid in the grave gathered to itself all confession, so the body raised from the tomb bestows itself as pure forgiveness. Hitherto the access of the Father to this earth was barred, because through sin humanity was turned away from him. The Son has turned once again to the Father the face of creation. And so the Father, who had to turn from sin, can turn again to the world. On Easter Day the Son rises visibly as man so as also to arise in the invisibility of God. In the Resurrection, in other words, the Son does not just gain a new relation to the world, to his fellow-humans in their cosmic setting. He gains a new relation to the Father too. The Son, awakened by the Father, presents to him his work. He stands before him in his created humanity which is now in a definitive way the finished creation of the Father. The Son, who in rising receives into himself the Father's life, turns wholly to the Father, since – specifically as the Incarnate One and not just the Pre-existent One – he now lives altogether in him and from him. The risen Son is, in Adrienne's phrase, 'earth in heaven'. From now on, the eternal Word is meant to house all the words of this world, to be the home of all the experience of humanity. Through the sending out of this Word we become believers; through his suffering we are re-made; through his Resurrection we too are raised up in the Word; through his journey home to the Father we too can so speak the Word of the Son to the Father as to reach the Father's heart. Through the Son's work, the Father has become '*Our* Father'. And since the Son's return is accomplished in the Holy Spirit, that Spirit is given to us, for now the *Kreislauf*, the 'circling course' of the love between the Father and the Son, runs through the world and encloses the world in itself.[48] This is very much the scene Balthasar himself will set out in the final, eschatological volume of his theological dramatics.

A comment

Of the religious power of Adrienne von Speyr's understanding of the Atonement there can be no question. What some will, forgivably, find strange is her account of the Descent into Hell. If it is reminiscent of Balthasar's theology of Holy Saturday in *Mysterium Paschale* there can be little doubt that the source is Adrienne rather than the other way round.[49] At the Colloquium

---

47 *Ibid.*, pp. 122–23.
48 *Ibid.*, p. 124.
49 *Mysterium Paschale. The Mystery of Easter* (Edinburgh, 1990); cf. *First Glance at Adrienne von Speyr, op. cit.*, p. 13. Note, however, Balthasar's pre-war interest in this clause of the Apostles' Creed as shown in the Christological references in *Apokalypse der deutschen Seele*, on which see A. Nichols, OP, *Scattering the Seed, op. cit.*, pp. 225–27.

of September 1985 on the 'ecclesial mission of Adrienne von Speyr' – which, held as it was at the papal summer residence of Castel Gandalfo, and addressed by the pope himself, marks the Roman acceptance of her work – Balthasar went out of his way to show the consonance of her Holy Saturday mysticism with the wider tradition of Catholic theology, in the Fathers, the iconography and the already accredited mysticism of the Church.[50] The question was, Is Adrienne's account of the Descent more indebted to the Protestant Reformers of the sixteenth century than to anything in the Catholic (or Orthodox) presentation of the Atonement? Even he, so committed to her as he was, finished by encouraging his hearers to leave her speculation to the theologians, but to imitate the practice which her vision of the Lord's descent sealed in her life: bearing the burdens of others and praying with fervour, notably in works of penance, that none of our brothers and sisters be finally lost.

Yet Balthasar was himself the last person to wish to sever theory, the Church's theological doctrine, from practice, her ethico-spiritual existence. In the course of the development of Catholic dogma, devotion and mysticism have played a considerable part in unfolding the glories contained in the apostolic teaching.[51] It may be that, in the Church's understanding of the Paschal mystery, Adrienne's voice will have a wider resonance in the ecclesial body of Christ. We shall be returning to her again when we consider Balthasar on 'Prayer and Mysticism'. A final comment for now may be left to the English theologian John Saward who, in the steps (it must be said) of Balthasar himself[52] compares the 'double mission' of Balthasar and Adrienne to those of Francis de Sales and Jeanne Françoise de Chantal, or John of the Cross and Teresa of Avila:

> a mission in which the distinctive gifts of a man and a woman, are blended, in purity, for the greater glory of God and the good of the Church.

And he concludes combatively but not necessarily unjustly:

> At a time when eroticism and feminism threaten to overthrow the sexual order of creation and the sacramental order of the Church, this witness by chaste charity to the complementary fruitfulness of male priesthood and Marian prayer is a God-given sign of hope for us all.[53]

Some questions about Adrienne's inspiration – beyond the Descent – remain. Of course, it would be incautious to maintain that Reformed theology, where it does not conflict with Catholic teaching, can add nothing of

50 'La théologie de la Descente aux enfers', in H. U. von Balthasar, G. Chantraine, A. Scola (eds), *La mission ecclésiale d'Adrienne von Speyr* (Paris, 1986), pp. 151–60.
51 See, e.g., A. Nichols, OP, *From Newman to Congar. The Idea of Doctrinal Development from the Victorians to the Second Vatican Council* (Edinburgh, 1990), pp. 190–93.
52 *Unser Auftrag, op. cit.*, p. 16. As Balthasar points out, Adrienne had in any case already sown the seed of the idea in her journals.
53 J. Saward, 'From a terrace on the Rhine. Adrienne von Speyr, 1902–1967', *Thirty Days* (November 1990), pp. 76–78, and here at p. 78.

value to the Church's patrimony of thought. The example of Barth indicates otherwise. But there can also be less helpful residues from a Protestant childhood of a doctrinally severe kind. Some, perhaps, remained lodged in her heart and mind.[54]

---

54 Thus for instance, the unfortunately entitled article 'The Dubious Adrienne von Speyr' by Anne Barbeau Gardiner suggests that in the ultra-realism of Adrienne's Eucharistic teaching she is unconsciously reproducing *attacks* on what Catholics believe about the Real Presence overheard in childhood: thus *Christian Order* 45. 6/7 (2004), pp. 49–64. Naturally, this does not impugn von Speyr's dogmatic intention in seeking to defend that Presence. In her review of Adrienne von Speyr's *Geheimnis des Todes* (Einsiedeln, 1953), now translated into English as *The Mystery of Death* (San Francisco, 1989), Anna Rist writing in *The Canadian Catholic Review* [January 1990], pp. 23–24, notes Adrienne's use of the phrase 'total sinfulness' for post-lapsarian man as a probable residue of Calvinism.

In this chapter I make use of some material originally published as 'Adrienne von Speyr and the Mystery of the Atonement', *New Blackfriars* 73. 865 (1992), pp. 542–53.

PART TWO: THEMES

6

Divine Conceiving: Revelation and Theology

With these sources as aids to the construing of revelation as transmitted by scripture and tradition, Balthasar's theology 'beyond the trilogy' expressed itself in a series of distinctive themes. To begin, we must go back to basics.

Foundations of theology in revelation

What is the basic situation from out of which, so Balthasar supposed, Christian doctrine is produced? In effect, an answer to this question will give us Balthasar's picture of fundamental theology – for this can be understood as any account of how humankind is situated where revelation is concerned. Balthasar is best known for his great trilogy – the theological aesthetics, the theological dramatics and the theological logic – but prior to considering revelation as an artwork, a drama and a logic, he possesses a more straightforward account of what it is for men to be in possession of a revelation at all. That broad topic will occupy the lion's share of our attention, though we must also attend to how Balthasar regarded the particular situation in which in his lifetime the practitioners of such fundamental theology might proceed.

First, then, how does Balthasar treat revelation in its most fundamental sense? How does he see the human being as inhabiting a world where the thinking of revelation is possible, necessary and historically well-grounded (to use the language of classical apologetics, worked out as that was with peculiar clarity in the eighteenth century).

The human situation that makes revelation desirable

Balthasar's most general account of revelation begins from a description of human nature, as concretely lived in human existence, and more especially from an analysis of the way that human nature, while remaining rooted in the life of the cosmos, also exceeds or transcends the rest of the world as we know it. On the one hand, man is a microcosm of the macrocosm, a little world which reflects and sums up the great world of the universe inasmuch as all the principal stages of natural evolution go into the making of the human being. On the other hand, man is not only the 'synthesis' of the world; he is also raised above it by his possession of mind, and indeed of person-hood. Might we call that 'pure Maximus'?

Along with other metaphysically minded religious philosophers, Baltha-sar connects mind with openness to being at large, an orientation to being in general. That we should regard as a characteristically Scholastic, and in par-ticular Thomistic, element in his thinking. And he connects personhood with what might seem the antithesis of the foregoing – the uniqueness of the human individual. That he himself considered a distinctively modern feature of his thought. Now since in both these ways – mind, personhood – the human being transcends the world and is other than it, his or her fulfilment or perfection cannot be sought simply in the fulfilment or perfection of the material world – in biological or technological progress, say, or indeed in the fulfilment or perfection of the human species, merely (for instance, by what Balthasar terms, with an eye – no doubt – on the thought of Pierre Teilhard de Chardin – a 'theologico-mystical evolution').[1] This was an area which the research behind *Apokalypse der deutschen Seele* rendered him eminently fit to study.

The peculiar position occupied by this personal, spiritual animal places him or her in a situation fraught with contradiction. Each person is, to a greater or lesser extent, torn between nature and spirit, and in different degrees pulled apart by the centrifugal forces which would have them move *either* to the greatest possible concentration on the uniquely personal in their life – notably, by the potentially all-absorbing experience of human love, *or* to the maximum possible diffusion of their energies in the service of being in its universality – concrete examples would be dedication to scientific research and scholarship or humanitarian and other work-projects on a grand scale. So the deepest needs of man can only be met, if at all, by what Balthasar terms 'absolute' or 'unconditional' or 'ultimate' being, the being of God – which alone is capacious enough to embrace all these dimensions simulta-neously: our relation with cosmic nature through our physicality; our inti-mate but all-demanding relations with other human individuals through our personality, and our universal and equally demanding relations with reality in its widest scope through our mentality or intellectuality – our being not only bodies but also minds or spirits.

But the question is – and here the issue of revelation at last raises its head, *is* there any way absolute being *could* 'complete' or bring to a satisfactory unity this fragmented and contradictory being, man? (In *Apokalypse der deutschen Seele* Balthasar had explored at enormous length how quasi-impossible it was for non-Christian philosophy in the West to answer this question – for example, as raised by Kant.) Or in Balthasar's own words in *Das Ganze im Fragment*, his study of revelation in history (which is also, then, his theological anthropology):

> How could God, infinite, hence in need of nothing and blissful in himself, help the integration of this creature which, from the whole structure of its being is obviously incapable of being integrated? For its being is not only finite and in the world; it is mortal. Death, it would appear, is the great rock thrown across the path of all thinking that

1 'The Perfectibility of Man', in *idem, Man in History. A Theological Study, op. cit.,* p. 45.

might lead to completeness. Even if one regards its terrible aspect as
something which was a subsequent development in original nature, the
ending of man's earthly life poses one insistent question: How can a
natural being, which must necessarily die (as he must as part of a genus
and a race), be conceived as united, to the point of identity, with an
infinite spiritual and personal being with infinite claims of knowledge
and love?[2]

The fact that man is a riddle to himself, that to all intents and purposes he is
'uncompletable', suggests that if he *is* ever to be integrated, unlikely as that
seems, this will only be from beyond both himself and also the universe – his
relation to whom, after all, is part of the problem in the first place.

Such a way of being integrated in all our dimensions is beyond us,
undiscoverable by us. All we can see is the *direction* in which to look, which
must be towards absolute being. We cannot construct the *character* such an
integration might take. And that is as it should be if we are to do justice to the
'prevenience' or primacy in initiative which Christian tradition ascribes to
God in his revelation of his saving plan.

> The manner of integration is left open and, indeed, must be left open, if
> the relationship between God and man is to be determined and shaped
> in dramatic dialogue by God alone.[3]

We shall return to the topic of how God communicates to man his proposed 'integration' of the human mosaic. Meanwhile, let us notice the fashion
in which Balthasar presents the challenge of revelation. He does so by means
of a contrast between what he calls the 'Christian way' on the one hand, and
'human ways out' on the other. Essentially, he believes there are, outside the
Church's doctrine, only two ways to salvation worth considering. All religions and philosophies, he thinks, boil down to one or other of this pair. Even
though ultimately unsatisfactory – because unable to put together the separated limbs of the all-round human being – they are worthy of respect since

> both in their inventive conception (theory) and in their existential living
> out (practice), they represent the boldest conceptions and most exalted
> endeavours of the human spirit, borne throughout history by indivi-
> duals and peoples prepared to sacrifice their lives for them.[4]

Catholic theologians, says Balthasar, have to agree with Barth that Judaeo-
Christianity is not to be compared, theologically, with the other world religions and philosophies since it alone is the disclosure of God's Trinitarian
Word and so alone *is* revelation. Nonetheless they cannot agree with Barth
that, for this reason, all the traditions of religious wisdom which take their
rise from outside the ambit of revelation are necessarily idolatrous and even

---

2 *Ibid.*, p. 48. Balthasar had learned from his investigation of German (and other) poets and
   philosophers in the modern period (and notably here Scheler, Heidegger and Sartre) that
   what defines man's distinctive *Geiststruktur* is the 'immanence of death in the human',
   otherwise called 'the finitude of the human spirit': thus 'Der Tod im heutigen Denken',
   Anima. Vierteljahrschrift für praktische Seelsorge 11 (1956), pp. 292–99, and here at p. 298. In this
   respect, there was a consonance between the Old Testament and twentieth-century thought.
3 *Man in History, op. cit.*, p. 49.
4 *Ibid.*, p. 53.

diabolical though they *are* ambiguous. Balthasar writes of this ambiguity of the non-biblical traditions:

> As serious attempts to discover salvation, they may contain redeeming grace hidden within them, yet as human creations they may involve man still deeper in his corruptions.[5]

The 'way of appearance' and the 'way of tragic conflict'

So what are the two 'ways' that are the only fundamental alternatives to the biblical revelation? Balthasar calls them 'the way of appearance' and 'the way of tragic conflict'. The first is typical not only of the religions of India but of much Greek metaphysics. It regards the difference between God and the world, unity and multiplicity, as basically a contrast between true being and false, and – appropriately enough, on such presuppositions – proposes to abandon the realm of earthly existence as hopelessly contradictory and find its home instead in the supra-mundane realm of divine power. Here all individuality, all separateness, is declared to be mere appearance. By following this way, the human spirit can confirm its relation to universal truth. But the price to be paid is a heavy one: not just the loss of enjoyment of sharing in the cosmos as one physical being in relation to others but also the renunciation of personal satisfaction in love, whether that love be for a finite other or for the infinite Other that is God. For on the way of appearance

> what can still be called love is fidelity to the 'thou' not in its difference but in its ultimate identity with the loving self.[6]

Such is the way of ecstatic mysticism among the pagans, not without connexion to that 'solution' to the human riddle Balthasar had earlier called 'Dionysian', after the ancient Greek god of that name.

The alternative way – here we are still placing ourselves outside the sphere of revelation – is not to attempt escape from the contradictions of human existence but rather to glory in them. This is the way of tragic conflict. We saw how in the picture Balthasar paints of the human condition, we are pulled in various directions at the same time. Inevitably, we suffer. Standing as we do at the intersection of physical, intellectual, personal, we are inescapably tragic beings. In Greek tragedy and the heroes of Germanic legend – in the Mediterranean world, then, and in the North – human greatness is found only in struggle. This heroic or aristocratic view of salvation – 'heroic' because only the strongest can attain it, 'aristocratic' because only the best can – commonly takes as its necessary background a dualistic metaphysics, like that of the Zoroastrians in ancient Persia and modern India, or the Cathars in mediaeval Europe. Rather in the manner of Nietzsche, the way of tragic conflict rejects any transcendental offer of salvation and counsels people to find their fulfilment by exploiting such resources as are available in the here and now and, for the rest, accepting pain's inevitability. Clearly, this 'way' bears some relation to what in *Apokalypse der deutschen Seele* was termed the 'Promethean principle'.

5 *Ibid.*, p. 54.
6 *Ibid.*

The drawbacks of this second way are also apparent. If the first effectively abolished the good in the human situation along with the evil, the second implicitly eternalizes the evil.

Might there be, then, a 'third way'? The mythologies of various less sophisticated peoples hint at such without their being able to devise world-class religious or philosophical systems. In their halting way, they produce mythical images of reconciliation by expiation, projected onto an eternal horizon of the gracious mercy of a god or gods, so that, for them, in Balthasar's words:

> The ethico-political order of the earth with its active virtue is made possible by a transcendental relationship to a believed [in], hoped-for, and (in loyalty to the god promising it) loved salvation.[7]

Though such mythopoeic constructions decline in cultural importance as philosophy rises, they disclose far better than either of the two 'ways' previously considered that essential law of human nature which is the push of the fragmentary towards its own wholeness.

How can a torn being come to wholeness?

But the answer to the question, How can so torn a being come to wholeness?, does not arrive with mythology. It arrives with revelation. As we shall see, however, the biblical revelation does not simply annul the (other) religions and philosophies. In accordance with a principle that the revelation carried by the Church is the greatest possible totality of truth, goodness and beauty – than which no greater can be conceived (an extension to the theology of revelation of Anselm's celebrated definition of God) – Balthasar will argue that important elements of the rejected alternative 'ways' are in fact retrieved and confirmed by Christianity.

Balthasar has already said that, if there is to be full integration of the bits and pieces of the human jigsaw, this can only come from beyond the world. Only God can take an initiative of this kind, and it will be, then, a *dramatic* initiative. That is, it will not be just 'in place', available, as an intrinsic and abiding feature of the human condition. (Were that to be the case man would only *seem* to be fragmentary and contradictory.) Rather, God's initiative will take man by surprise. It will eventuate at a particular point or points, as the course of human self-experience, and with that our experience of the world and the divine, unfolds in time. Ever since Lessing, philosophers have doubted whether a universal truth about the human condition could be brought about by an historical contingency. But if there is to be a transcendent resolution of the human condition it must by the very logic of the case be the consequence of an intervention in history. And since man is the only fully historical animal, the only one sufficiently detached from natural rhythms to embrace novelty, this divine historical intervention will have to make use of the expressive register the human creature, and no other, puts at the Creator's disposal.

Granted the fact of human freedom, however, God could not use man in

7 *Ibid.*, p. 61.

order to communicate this supreme answer to the human question without obtaining man's willing obedience to be so used.

> God ... uses man in all his [man's] existential doubtfulness and fragility and imperfectibility as the language in which he expresses the word of redemptive wholeness. God, therefore, uses existence extended in time as the script in which to write for man and the world the sign of a supra-temporal eternity. Hence, the man Jesus, whose existence is this sign and word of God to the world, had to live out simultaneously the temporal, tragic, separating distance [from his own origin, i.e. God] and ... the conquest [of that distance] through ... elective obedience to the choosing will of the eternal Father.[8]

Only so could Jesus bring about an essentially unbreakable 'wholeness' within a 'fragment' hitherto incapable of completion. God could give wholeness to the human condition only *in* and *as* man, as a human being.

The centrality of the Resurrection

What this means for Balthasar's presentation of Christian doctrine is that, in company with other twentieth-century theologians (one thinks of the French Catholic François-Xavier Durrwell and the German Lutheran Wolfhart Pannenberg), he places the Resurrection at the very centre of revelation theology. The ways of appearance and tragic conflict are not without their nuggets of truth – the Word made flesh does indeed, as *the way of appearance* might suggest, come forth from the One, the Father, and at his Ascension return to the One, albeit as Head of his disciples, and, as *the way of tragic conflict* had primed us, it is through his super-heroic combat with the power of chaos and hell that he reconciles the world. But neither of them had divined the resurrection from the dead. And precisely this is why they had not been able to 'place the finitude and temporality of historical man in the lap of God's eternity'.[9]

One might think that the Resurrection is a peculiarly difficult element in Christian doctrine to render persuasive and not, therefore, the best biblical theme to choose as the organizing centre of a fundamental theology. How might Balthasar's self-justification proceed? The essay 'Approches christologiques' of 1982 furnishes the start of a reply. What is essential in approaching the person of Christ is the capacity to 'see his indivisible form' – a key motif, that, of the theological aesthetics. Vis-à-vis the 'unique, analogy-less, phenomenon' that is Jesus Christ, the historical–critical method has very definite limits.[10] His *Gestalt* cannot be grasped unless one sees his earthly life, his death and his eternal life as a single if threefold articulation. Balthasar compares Jesus' 'pre-Easter' life and work to the first syllable of a word that only becomes intelligible when we hear the last syllable pronounced. If the crucified Jesus *did* rise, then his earthly life cannot have its own definitive meaning within itself. His 'figure', in the three successive facets it shows in

---

8 *Ibid.*, p. 63.
9 *Ibid.*, p. 64.
10 'Approches christologiques', *Didaskalia. Revista da Faculdade de téologia de Lisboa* 12 (1982), pp. 3–12 and here at p. 3.

his life, death, resurrection, is really 'a communion of life with the entire Word of God in history and creation'.[11] But as Balthasar points out, even if people feel impelled to reject the truth-claims of the Resurrection as too extravagant and therefore implausible, they should be able to see the value of the Resurrection faith as an answer to the question of existence.

And that is so because the Resurrection resolves precisely the contradictions within the human being Balthasar has analysed. First, it resolves the contradiction between nature and spirit – man's cosmic, and his intellectual–spiritual dimensions. In the Resurrection, spirit bursts the bounds of nature without in any way contesting nature's dignity and necessity for man.

> In Christ [who rises not only as spirit but also as nature] eternal love and loyalty became possible without the laws of the physical and mortal heart condemning this love as imagination and as falsehood.[12]

Secondly, the Resurrection also resolves the contradiction between man as an essentially personal being that thirsts for love and man as a spirit determined only by being at large, the generality of things, their universal flow. For the Resurrection shows how the love which brought to his death the man on the Cross 'streams directly into the boundlessness of divine love', the love which encompasses all reality and 'is a full and complete answer to it'.[13] The love displayed on the Cross seemed 'intransitive': what on earth could have been its object? But from the 'abyss of total futility and abandonment' his love corresponded to the 'absolute gratuitousness of God's love for the world'.[14] And so Balthasar can write that

> Man's way to unity with God is now no longer separate from the way of the man with the bleeding heart.[15]

In Christianity, human finitude is not obliterated by the all-encompassing One, as on *the way of appearance*, since so seriously is man taken in his difference from God that God actually becomes man in order to meet human needs from the inside. On the other hand, man is not enclosed within his own limitations, as in *the way of tragic conflict*. He is not, in Balthasar's words, 'absolutised in his tragic difference', for the Spirit of God takes up everything that is positively distinctive about man's difference from other beings as well as the differences which distinguishes one human being from another, and in perfecting them preserves them. Balthasar actually writes that the divine Spirit 'enfolds' them – his term for the loving differences found within God himself where the Father is not the Son nor the Father and Son the Spirit but the Father makes room for the Son to receive and give back love in freedom, and the Spirit, emerging as their eternal Fruit, only unites them in maintaining their everlasting distinction.

11 *Ibid.*, p. 8.
12 *Man in History, op. cit.*, p. 65.
13 *Ibid.*, p. 66.
14 *Ibid.*, p. 66.
15 *Ibid.*, p. 70.

The advantages of his approach

Balthasar's basic option in revelation theology is, we have seen, a decision formally to introduce the concept of revelation by means of a discussion of how human integration is attained. It has various advantages, at least at its time of writing. In the first place, in a period before the words 'New Age' or 'eco-theology' were invented, thought and sensibility were essentially anthropocentric, human-centred, as perhaps, when push comes to shove, is, even in the early twenty-first century, still largely the case. In that context, to link the question of revelation to questions about human welfare and happiness shows immediately the relevance of the Church's dogmatic faith to human affairs. One might regard a revelation so 'marketed' as incredible but one could hardly dismiss its focus of interest as peripheral.

Then in the second place, Balthasar's chosen approach allows him straightaway to mark the position of divine revelation on the chart of the world's competing ideologies. At least in outline we can see where it diverges from one, goes beyond another, ratifies in some respect a third. His approach to fundamental theology enables him to put forward the twofold claim that revelation acts as a helpful criterion for the due criticism of other religions and philosophies and that, at the same time, it locates what is ethically worthwhile or epistemically convincing in those other religions and philosophies within its own more comprehensive view.

And finally, in the third place, this approach by way of the idea of human integration – understood not psychologically, merely, but metaphysically so as to do justice to all the constitutive dimensions of man – makes it possible to take up a clear position in the debate over the relation between nature and super-nature which was the dominant preoccupation of Catholic theology, in one form or another, throughout the twentieth century. In the theological debates that immediately preceded the Second Vatican Council – as the case of de Lubac shows – that discussion was usually couched in terms of the interpretation of texts from St Thomas, and Balthasar is no exception to this rule. His own view is that, in and of himself, man remains most painfully imperfectible. The idea of a possible purely natural integration for this fragmentary, contradictory species has, for Catholic theology, 'no more than a completely hypothetical character'.[16] Here Balthasar is the faithful echo of de Lubac.

> The natural goal of which he [Aquinas] sometimes speaks he regards as the best that a mortal man can achieve in this earthly life, but one which would never suffice to justify the existence and the particular nature of mankind. As an Aristotelean he does not even hesitate to ascribe an inner sense of direction to 'nature' which informs it about its own powers and possibilities in relation to something which is essentially unattainable by it. St Thomas even sees in this apparent disproportion a mark of the dignity of man: 'that nature is of a nobler kind which can attain the perfect good, *even if it needs help from outside to do so*, than that nature which cannot attain the perfect good but attains only to an imperfect good for the achievement of which its own powers are sufficient'.[17]

16 'Theological Reflections on Human Wholeness', in *Man in History, op. cit.,* p. 84.
17 *Ibid.,* p. 82, with an internal citation of *Summa theologiae*, Ia. IIae., q. 5, a. 5, ad ii. Italics are of course added.

For Balthasar's Thomas, as for de Lubac's and for Balthasar himself, there is only one, supernatural goal for human nature. For Balthasar, that truth must be even more important than for Thomas (or de Lubac) since his entire exposition of man's imperious need for revelation turns on this point. This is thanks to the Barthian – and behind the Barthian, the Irenaean – in Balthasar. The first Adam is made for the sake of the second Adam in whom the entire human mystery will be laid bare.[18]

From the starting-point of this conviction Balthasar sets out his account of man's need for the gift of revelation and its media of reception: that inter-related trio of God-empowered dispositions we call the 'theological virtues' of faith, hope and charity. This need is pressing indeed if man is ever to become aware of, and move toward, his own final and supremely integrating end.

Cognitive powers needed to register revelation

Our cognitive powers are well suited to communicating with, or evaluating, fellow-creatures in the concourse of natural being. But they are insufficient for receiving a more-than-natural communication from God. Thus when God reveals himself to man he must give human beings not only his truth but also *the capacity to receive that truth*. In Balthasar's preferred idiom, God must 'bathe' the object of his self-revelation (the medium in which he communicates his truth) and the receiver of that revelation (the people who are meant to apprehend that truth) in a common 'light'. Now to render something common between God and men is to make human beings in some fashion connatural with God – sharers, not by right, but by an extraordinary privilege, in God's own way of being.

When we think of what that involves we can do so either in terms of how it affects our being, or in terms of how it affects our awareness or both. When we think of it in terms of how it affects our being we call it (in the Latin tradition) the habitual sanctifying grace that gives us a share, amazingly, in God's own reality as well as the actual graces that help us to live and act from this new life. When we think of our connaturality with God in terms, rather, of how it affects our awareness, we speak instead of the virtues of faith, hope and charity, which enable our minds and wills really to tend to the self-revealing God as, in his revelation, he truly is. For Balthasar, the theological virtues, seen as our response to revelation on the basis of habitual and actual grace, are reciprocally conditioning. Each one of the three – faith, hope, charity – promotes the others. Sometimes indeed he speaks of them as a single attitude with three aspects, an attitude of

> preferring God to everything that is one's own because he is himself (love) and therefore is absolutely in the right, even against me (faith), and my salvation lies in this (hope).[19]

---

18 'He is intelligible only in the final figure of the dying and resurrecting Son of God', *Man in History, op. cit.,* p. 86.
19 *Ibid.,* p. 95.

The context of doing revelation theology 'today'

To a degree Balthasar was influenced in his selection of a basic theological approach to the notion of divine revelation by his reading of the cultural scene in the middle decades of the twentieth century. He had to take into account, he thought, a shift in culture, both general and philosophical, from a primarily cosmos-centred to a primarily human-centred view of things.[20] Rightly or wrongly, he believed that philosophy 'will ever more clearly find its centre and form in a total anthropology' – a statement influenced, no doubt, by the efforts of Catholic thinkers from the 1930s onwards to integrate the contributions of phenomenology and Existentialism into the Scholastic tradition of the *philosophia perennis*. At the same time, he thought this would not render altogether superfluous an older, more cosmological style of thinking where man is given his place on the ladder of being above the non-rational animals but below the angels. For the 'total anthropology' he wrote of would be impossible without the accompaniment of a

> growing consciousness of [humanity's] ... own history which retains in a living memory even what it once was but can be no longer, just as a man cannot reach total maturity without a living memory of his youth.[21]

Balthasar is not asserting that the truth-claims of divine revelation must be tailored to suit the reductionistic attitudes of a post-metaphysical age, or what Mgr Ronald Knox called 'what Jones will swallow'. He is not proposing theological liberalism. As he put it in *Die Gottesfrage des heutigen Menschen*:

> Christianity ... cannot be derived from the nature of man; ... it is a phenomenon that rests wholly on the historical fact of the appearance of Christ. .... Its basis is ... the existence and self-revelation of Christ as the God-man and Saviour, hence trusting faith in him is the organ that mediates the knowledge of this truth.[22]

On the other hand, since Christianity is undoubtedly both a world-view and a religion, it cannot but enter into relation, whether positive or negative, with the philosophical and religious elements found in culture at large – and so must address itself to meeting their agendas in a given age. That had been his conviction ever since his first properly theological essay, 'Patristik, Scholastik und wir'. Hence:

> though the fundamental formal relations between science, philosophy and Christianity are unalterable, their concrete connexions are subject to a law of changing phases and nuances. History reveals the various aspects of the one human nature, and through these changing aspects the one and objectively uniform revelation of Christ can present itself in new shades of its interior richness.[23]

Now the factor most affected by change in the development of mankind is, so

---

20 Thus his *Die Gottesfrage des heutigen Menschen* (Vienna, 1956); ET *Science, Religion and Christianity* (London, 1958, republished at New York in 1967 as *The God Question and Modern Man*).
21 *Science, Religion and Christianity, op. cit.*, p. 13.
22 *Ibid.*, pp. 1–2.
23 *Ibid.*, p. 10.

Balthasar affirms, man's relation to nature. Man's technical mastery of nature means that he can no longer regard the cosmos with quasi-religious veneration. He is monarch of the world, though he must be a monarch who serves, since the world is entrusted to his care. This predicament, Balthasar optimistically opined, will inevitably teach man to look for God.

> Just because he has matured into technical man without any other home save his own technical being, he is predestined to become religious man.[24]

As these words demonstrate, Balthasar was among those reform-minded Catholic theologians of the decades immediately before the Second Vatican Council who were sanguine about the evangelical possibilities of a secular society – and by implication, then, hostile to attempts to re-sacralize the human sense of the cosmos and indeed to sustain the remnants of Christendom in public culture at large. (A glance at *The Razing of the Bastions* in the opening chapter of this book had already told us as much.) From the perspective of the European early twenty-first century, hindsight might warn us from following him here. What remains valuable is Balthasar's analysis of those features of the human condition which, taken in conjunction, suggest the congruence of the saving revelation with the permanent needs of humankind.

Revelation transmitted: in Scripture, in the Church

But where in the concrete is this revelation found? Balthasar's answer is not terribly original. It runs: 'In Scripture, in the Church'. And yet his way of presenting the *manner* in which Scripture, in the Church, gives us access to the revelatory fullness – Christ as the form at once of God and of man, and so the form of the God/man relation in which the latter receives its norm – *is* original.

Essentially, and like de Lubac, Balthasar accepts Origen's account of the biblico–ecclesial mediation of the Christological fullness: Christ's three 'bodies' in their unity yet differentiation. And these are: the 'body' of Christ which is Scripture (an archaic, Alexandrian way of speaking, which, having found it in Origen, Balthasar wanted to revive); the 'body' of Christ which is the Church (a never abandoned locution), and that body of his (for once inverted commas are unnecessary) which was taken from blessed Mary and in its transfigured, paschal condition is given us in the Blessed Sacrament. In their different modes, each is the single Christ-form as communicated to the world. Balthasar's most extended discussion of the Bible and exegetical method – seen, however, in close connexion with the mystery of the Church – occurs towards the end of the opening volume of the theological aesthetics, and its essence is set forth in my guide thereto, *The Word Has Been Abroad*.[25] Here, then, it will suffice to present the crucial upshot.

The biblical Canon serves the Holy Spirit as a vehicle for the Spirit's

---

24 *Ibid.*, p. 27.
25 *Herrlichkeit. Eine theologische Ästhetik. I. Schau der Gestalt* (Einsiedeln, 1961); *The Glory of the Lord. A Theological Aesthetics: I. Seeing the Form* (Edinburgh and San Francisco, 1985), pp. 531–56; A. Nichols, OP, *The Word Has Been Abroad, op. cit.*, pp. 47–50.

actualizing the 'total historical form of the revelation of salvation'. The Spirit puts the Canon to use by, first, transforming the Old Testament Christologically through its unification with the New. That means we should never practise exegesis of the Elder Covenant – the Old Testament – simply as though we were Jews. The Holy Spirit uses the Canon, secondly, by transposing the literal sense (of the New Testament as well as the Old) into that spiritual sense which is the Christ-event as life-giving *for me*. That is the lesson taught by de Lubac's investigations into the exegesis of the Fathers and the Middle Ages. And that in turn means we should never practise any exegesis as though we were not Christian believers. There is nothing objectionable, writes Balthasar, about Bultmannian existential interpretation of the Bible in terms of the *pro me* principle – Bultmann thought I should be asking what the message means 'for me', just as the early Lutherans had said I should be asking what Christ did as Saviour 'for me' – so long as we add that the 'me' in question is an ecclesial 'me'. It is the 'me' of the Christian who is a Christian 'only in the Church and through the Church, … only in faith and in anticipation of the eschaton'.[26]

There is a remarkable coincidence of view here with that of the relevant sections of the 1992 *Catechism of the Catholic Church* ('CCC'), which also cleaves to 'interpretation in the Spirit' based on the criteria of 'the content and unity of the whole Scripture' (CCC 112); the 'analogy of faith' (CCC 114) and 'the unity of God's plan' of which 'Christ Jesus is the centre and heart' (CCC 112). Since 'Sacred Scripture is written principally in the Church's heart' (CCC 112), it should be read within the 'living Tradition of the whole Church' (CCC 113). In his study of the Petrine office, Balthasar wrote, citing the early nineteenth-century Johann Adam Möhler:

> [Thus] 'Holy Scripture, when abstracted from tradition and the Church', which existed before Scripture and determined its canon, and which possesses an original understanding of its total meaning – could not subsequently bring forth the Church by and from itself. As Möhler aptly said, 'concerning the relationship of ecclesial exegesis to erudite scientific exegesis of Holy Scripture', it is not by exegesis that the Church gains an overall grasp of the revelation that she 'heard from the mouth of Christ and from the apostles', and which 'by the power of the divine Spirit is indelibly imprinted in her consciousness or, as Irenaeus says, in her heart'. If the Church had to obtain her dogmas through self-research, she would become enmeshed in the most absurd contradictions and would annihilate herself. Since the Church herself would have to conduct this research, her presence would have to be presupposed, yet at the same time she would have to be regarded as non-existent, still waiting to attain her own being … through divine truth.[27]

---

26 *The Glory of the Lord. A Theological Aesthetics: I. Seeing the Form, op. cit.*, pp. 548–49.
27 *Der antirömische Affekt. Wie lässt sich das Papsttum in der Gesamtkirche integrieren?* (Freiburg, 1974; 2nd edition Einsiedeln, 1989); ET *The Office of Peter and the Structure of the Church* (San Francisco, 1989), p. 85, citing J. A. Möhler, *Symbolik*, ed. J. R. Geiselmann, I (Cologne-Olten, 1958).

The relation between Scripture and the Church's teaching authority

The diversity of ways in which suitable interpretation could be accomplished points to something Protestantism has often failed to notice. The validity of the Canon of Scripture, far from excluding a reference to ecclesial teaching authority positively *in*cludes it. Since John Henry Newman, the customary fashion in which to express the relation between Scripture and the magisterium has been by ascribing to the latter a power to judge putative developments in the understanding of the former. That seems to be how, through the teaching authority, the Church's tradition reaches doctrinal expression. Balthasar concurs, even to the point of sometimes embracing the metaphor of organic development which, after Newman, was seen as central to the 'theory'.

And yet he also shares with much twentieth-century Eastern Orthodox theology a wariness of over-enthusiastic appeal to 'development' of a kind that might reduce to pygmy status the understanding of the Gospel enjoyed by the apostles and prophets. As he explained in *Martin Buber and Christianity*:

> If the idea of development is applicable and useful in some form or other where the Church is concerned, it can only be in a secondary sense: the fullness once attained cannot, as such, develop – and while people talk somewhat loosely of the development of doctrine they really mean the reflective unfolding of depths of truth already present . . .[28]

Or, as he addressed the same issue in *Razing the Bastions*: 'Revelation is "closed" [with the death of the last apostle] only because the infinite fullness can no longer grow . . .'. But, he added, revelation can, however, 'radiate forth its fullness into infinity, and under its sun everything can grow to full maturity'.[29] For Balthasar, then, time will bring no major shifting of the centre of gravity for the Church's contemplation of revelation in Scripture. There will be no seismic upheaval to alter the proportions of this Scriptural image. 'Ecclesial vitality' in the interpreting of Scripture means that new ideas are always coming up, but not every new idea is a good idea. So, through the grace of biblical inerrancy, the 'light' of the canonical form of Scripture is shed over the Church, allowing us, precisely, to test later developments against this original form. Indeed, in the 1961 essay 'Kerygma und Gegenwart', Balthasar roundly declared that:

> The apostolic kerygma which persists throughout the Christian ages, is beyond question always the same. It does not develop, since it is already the fulness and the end of time.[30]

And he goes on to explain that there is no question of its adaptation to new needs in various historical epochs. All that is in view is those epochs

---

28 *Martin Buber and Christianity, op. cit.,* p. 94.
29 *Razing the Bastions, op. cit.,* p. 36.
30 'Kerygma und Gegenwart', *Wort und Wahrheit* (Vienna) 16 (1961), pp. 9–15 and here at p. 9.

'discover[ing] in its sameness ever new aspects', rather like a camera lens playing over a statue by Michelangelo and finding there 'ever new living lights and shadows'.[31]

Here as everywhere in revelation, Christ is the centre. As with the French Dominican Yves Congar, for Balthasar *ressourcement*, going back to the sources, is useless without what Congar called *re-centrement*, re-centring on Christ as the manifestation of the Holy Trinity. It is because Scripture is not its own centre that the many inner-biblical theologies can co-exist without detriment to its coherence, and the even more numerous extra-biblical theologies come to be, in the service of ecclesial thought, without jeopardizing its originality.

Accordingly, the chief task of the magisterium is not so much to generate new theological forms (though Balthasar does not entirely exclude this) as it is to protect the primal form against distortion in one or more of its aspects. It is perfectly suitable that the magisterium's pronouncements should be founded in the thematic jumble of Denzinger's *Enchiridion* for the magisterium does not intend to produce an overall form of his own. (Balthasar did not live to see the promulgation of the post-Conciliar *Catechism of the Catholic Church* though naturally he would have known its Tridentine predecessor.)

These remarks are not intended to exalt theology at the expense of the teaching office. No more than the magisterium is theology to substitute a form for that which is found in revelation. In the crisis of post-Conciliar Catholicism, which combined a disintegration of theological tradition with a questioning of the standing of the magisterium, Balthasar looked to a reconstitution of sound theological method through the acknowledgement of the essentially ecclesial nature of theology – something the magisterium exists to guard and serve. In the 1969 essay 'Lehramt und Theologie', Balthasar asserted strenuously enough that theologians must decide: is the object of theology 'sheer philosophy of religion', or is it the faith of Christ's Church?[32] The theologian's act of faith (*fides qua*), like that of every member of the Church, is aimed at an object (the *fides quae*) adequate to the act of faith of the entire Church. Otherwise it is gnosis, and not obedience to Gospel truth. In her own responsible obedience to her Head, the Church from the beginning sought to gather the plurality of kerygmatic, catechetical and theological expressions into that unity which the Fathers term the *regula fidei* and that 'rule of faith' it is the task of bishops and pope to represent, 'insofar as this was and is the point of unity of the believing consciousness of the Church'.[33] All magisterial clarifications of individual issues start from here.

A theologian, Balthasar considered, should strive in his thinking for 'beauty of form' – and this entails a re-presentation of the apostolic deposit. But he should do so precisely as service of the Church, and homage to the Church's Lord – not as an 'improvement' on the revelation dominically given. So long as the theologian is faithful to these marching orders, Balthasar is happy for him to emphasize various qualities in theological style – system, it may be, or conceptual clarity, or depth of intuition, or simply practical usefulness to the magisterium. These properties remain, on the

---

31 *Ibid.*
32 'Lehramt und Theologie', *Schweizerische Kirchenzeitung* 137. 22 (29 May 1969), pp. 317–22.
33 *Ibid.*, p. 322.

Balthasarian view of things, ancillary rather than essential. They cannot compete with the more primordial attributes of holiness, contemplation and *sentire cum Ecclesia* - thinking with the Church. These last are the principal qualities at which the theologian should aim. The mind of the saint, of the one who best prays, and the mind of the total Church in her supra-personal transcendence of the individual: these are the twin aspects of the theologian's epistemic goal.

The concept of theology in its relation to holiness

Though Balthasar had a good deal to say about theological method, its heart lies in Balthasar's own 1948 essay on the topic which appeared simulta-neously in French as 'Théologie et sainteté', in the French journal *Dieu vivant*, edited by his fellow-Jesuit Jean Daniélou, and in German in the Viennese journal *Wort und Wahrheit* – and subsequently was reprinted in the first volume of Balthasar's collected articles.[34] In this essay, Balthasar stresses that for the New Testament truth is always truth in practice: we possess truth by walking in a certain 'way'.[35] The great claim of the Church Fathers upon us, explains Balthasar, is the fashion in which they exemplify this approach, entertaining revelation as they embody it spiritually. As he puts it, and the note of criticism is apparent not only of a theology self-divorced from spirituality but also of a self-absorbed spirituality in later times:

> The Fathers found straightaway the appropriate dogmatic clothing for their very personal experience; everything became objective, and all the subjective conditions, experiences, fears, strivings, the 'shock' in a word, were made to serve a fuller understanding of the content of revelation, to orchestrate its great themes. Every form of spirituality, of mysticism was seen as serving a function in the Church. Like sanctity itself, they were above all tasks within the Church.[36]

People had not yet forgotten how Paul, without in any way marginalizing or undermining subjective charisms had nonetheless saved them from idio-syncrasy by subordinating them to the Church's objective structure for, in truth, their goal does not lie in themselves. Balthasar deeply regrets that many later Western saints feared to practise 'dogmatics' in their spirituality, not realizing that, for the Fathers, dogmatics *is* the contemplation of the realities Scripture reveals. Many of the early modern and modern mystics are too interested in telling us about their psychological states under grace to focus on the object of faith as expressed in the dogmas. We really cannot allow, he thinks, a Scholastic and a kerygmatic theology to carry out their distinct enterprises in parallel (this was the idea of a number of Germano-phone theologians in the 1940s). To do so would only confirm the disastrous Kantian or post-Kantian split between the true, *verum*, and *bonum*, the good.

---

34 'Théologie et sainteté', *Dieu vivant* 12 (1948), pp. 17–31; 'Theologie und Heiligkeit', *Wort und Wahrheit* 3 (1948), pp. 881–96. There is an English translation: 'Theology and Sanc-tity', in *The Word made Flesh. Explorations in Theology* I, *op. cit.*, pp. 181–209.
35 Compare John 8.31-32; *ibid.* 7: 18; 1 John 2.4; 2 John 1.4; 3 John 3-4. The main study of this is Jutta Konda's *Das Verhältnis von Theologie und Heiligkeit im Werk Hans Urs von Bal-thasars* (Würzburg, 1991).
36 'Theology and Sanctity', *art. cit.*, p. 190.

Balthasar reminds us of theology's due content and suitable form. He reminds us, first, that the centre of dogmatics is the same as the centre of spirituality. Dogmatics does not rest on a relation between revelation and a secular nature, reason, philosophy that is essentially alien to it. The creating God always intended human nature and human thought to find its true centre and definitive realization in the Word incarnate as Jesus Christ. Balthasar reminds us secondly that the form of dogmatics must betray, as it did with the founders of dogmatics, the holy Fathers, the attitude of prayer of a thinker docile by his faith in the presence of the Object of his reflection. Only the attitude of prayer before the mystery can express a love that waits and does not pre-empt the divine truth that would show itself. The understanding borne of prayer can no more leave prayer behind than for Christianity gnosis can rank as more than an interior form of agape. In other words, what intellectual achievement could there be, in the context of Christian revelation, that found itself unable to receive its mould from *caritas*? The primacy of agape over gnosis would remain one of Balthasar's most constant preoccupations (despite the high and elaborate cognitive claims of his own theology) *not only as regards the predisposition of theologian-subjects but as regards the presentation of the theological Object as well.*

> Dogmas which we now know only from the outside, as the 'content of the faith', ... we must try to see from within again: as the manifestation of the one, single, indivisible truth of God. Supposing that this truth has presented itself to us as the eternal love which surprises us and lays its claims on us temporal creatures: Will not the basic articulations of the so-called Christian 'doctrine' – Trinity, Incarnation, Cross and Resurrection, Church and Eucharist – become the immediate radiations of the glowing core of this truth? How should God, the One and Absolute, be eternal love, if he were not triune? And how, if he did not prove this being love to the end in the Church and Eucharist for the world, which he created out of love, and if he did not take the world up, in Church and Resurrection, into the eternally moved rest of the exchange of love? Dogmas must be nothing other than aspects of the love which manifests itself and yet remains mystery within revelation; if they are no longer this, then gnosis has triumphed over love, human reason has conquered God, and at this instant – first in theology, then in the Church, then in the world – God is 'dead'.[37]

Wonderful citation.

---

37 *Convergences, op. cit.*, pp. 13–14.

7

꙳꙳꙳

Divine Providing: Time and History

Introduction

So much for how a revelation in history arises and comes to be reflected in theology. In his *Theologie der Geschichte*, 'Theology of History', Balthasar shows us how he sees the revelation given us actually illuminating the historical process.

Just as Balthasar's theology of revelation at large is Christocentric inasmuch as it is Christ's Resurrection that renders the Christian answer to the human question the definitive one, so likewise – we shall not be surprised to hear – his account of revelation in history is Christocentric too. An account of revelation in history which accepts the claims he makes in fundamental theology must show how Christ is the centre of history, the key to history's meaning, and the key, therefore, to the meaning of each and every individual life-story which is, so to speak, history in the microcosm: history writ small.

Balthasar's *Theology of History* belongs with a series of mid-century attempts by Catholic theologians – as indeed by Protestant and Anglican – to describe not merely the history of revelation – from the call of the patriarchs, through the history of Israel, to the climactic moment of Jesus Christ and the registering of that moment in the apostolic Church – but also the *manner* in which the fullness of revelation, thus achieved, throws light not only on salvation history but on history at large. In its own way, this enterprise reflected an anthropocentric turn Balthasar describes in *Science, Religion and Christianity* – another version of his account of the shift from the mediaeval to the modern based on the new prominence given the concrete, particular *and historical*, as well as to the personal. But so historically minded a 'turn to the human' was typical of the nineteenth and twentieth centuries, rather than of, say, the Renaissance or the Augustan age. Conscious of the way human beings are shaped by historical agency, for good or ill, many mid-twentieth-century theologians adopted as their maxim, We are all historians now. Where Balthasar differs is in the insistence that the cosmic dimension of humankind (our relations with the rest of the physical universe) and the metaphysical dimension of man (the way that, owing to mind's openness to being, the soul is, in the Scholastic tag, 'in a certain way all things') be well and truly integrated with the historical – something, he thinks, only a really theological theology, centred on God in Christ, can bring off. And, incidentally, only such a theology, we might add, can integrate the patristic and

143

mediaeval as well as modern patrimony of Catholic thought, as Balthasar described that in his earliest – but always relevant – theological effusion, 'Patristik, Scholastik, und wir'.

The life of Christ as 'norm' for all history

Balthasar's *Theologie der Geschichte* studies the life of Christ as the plenitude of history, such that all history – and here he means both salvation history and the general history of the world – is related to the history of Christ as a promise might be to its fulfilment. The life of Christ, he continues (even more audaciously) is the 'norm' for all history whatsoever. As he put it in a more popular presentation, for contemporaries the coming of the Messiah felt like the end of time – and they were right!

> Over and above the being and deed and word of Christ what have we to expect on earth? Everything that God has to reveal to the world, his living depths, his innermost heart, his love for us until death, his will to make us eternally happy in his house as creatures of spirit and body alike, all lies open. Everything sayable is said, everything 'doable' is done.[1]

At the same time, however, the fullness of time which breaks through at the first Christmas, is 'not the end of time but the opening of time's womb to receive the divine seed'.[2]

The concept of 'norm' in *A Theology of History* is something we would more customarily associate with ethics, with moral striving towards perfection by respecting the laws that tells us, Do good, or at least avoid evil, and you will move further towards – or at any rate not move further away from – your fulfilled flourishing as a human being. But for Balthasar that concept is covertly present in any concept of fulfilment. We can hardly regard something as fulfilled unless we have at the back – or the front – of our minds some relevant 'norm' whereby to judge it. That makes possible, then, a *twofold treatment* of Christ as judge of history in all its forms. First, Balthasar investigates what it is in Christ that makes him the norm – his universal relation to history. Secondly, he looks at the implications for human beings, for ourselves.

In the introduction to this work, Balthasar states the basic problem of theorizing in philosophical mood about the historical, and this is the 'tension' between, on the one hand, the 'historical and concrete' and, on the other, the 'abstract and rationally ordered'.[3] For discursive thought, which is the rational glory of Western man's Hellenic inheritance, the necessary and universal (and therefore *abstract*) enjoys the authority of a law that rises above any one individual case and determines it for good or ill. But this triumph does not go unchallenged. Empiricism enters what Balthasar clearly considers a desirable protest, for here the individual fact can all too easily appear disvalued, whereas:

---

1 'Die Gegenwart der Zukunft', *Der christliche Sonntag* 52. 12 (25 December 1960), p. 417.
2 *Ibid.*
3 *A Theology of History, op. cit.*, p. 21.

What is real is the unrepeatable, the concrete, the historical – and abstract laws of being spring from an inadequate attempt on the part of our limited powers of thought to cope with a factual world which we can never really master.[4]

But in another way empiricism, or an exclusive emphasis on the particularity of the concrete, represents a dereliction of duty on the part of thought. We can admire, in a sense, Hegel's sharply contrasting effort to interpret the 'whole sequence and constellation of facts in nature and in human history', seeing them as the manifestation of an 'all-embracing rational spirit, rational precisely in its factual manifestation'. Here reason was paying its tribute to historical facts, treating them not as mere phenomena, beyond the power of 'law-giving reason' to order, but as themselves a 'meaningful presentation of reason'. Nonetheless, Balthasar rejects the Hegelian solution (readers of *Apokalypse der deutschen Seele* will not be surprised to learn) on the grounds that it can equally well be seen as the ultimate devaluation of the historical, beyond anything the Greeks could have dreamed of. Reason disposes of history, leaving no room for creative freedom to play in the acting person.

Approaching the task of interpreting history as a whole

This does not mean, however, that Balthasar is going to set aside the entire enterprise of *interpreting history as a whole*. Taking it for granted that this is a proper task for a Christian thinker, he begins in a breathtakingly *a priori* fashion. All such interpretation requires

> some subject which works in and reveals itself in the whole of history and which is at the same time a being capable of providing general norms.[5]

This 'subject' can only be either God or man. The philosopher working in a non-theocentric mould will naturally prefer the second of these options. But Balthasar deems it untenable. One particular human being can hardly dominate history as a whole. So if we are to speak of man as furnishing a norm for history it must be the human essence we are thinking of. Thanks to the communication, and so communion, possible between free persons solidary with each other through sharing a common essence, one *could* think of that essence as realizing itself historically in the form of 'a common destiny for all the persons who constitute it'. And yet the human essence is found concretely only in individuals. And here we return to the objection already made. Surely it is

> philosophically impossible for one human person, who as such is nothing other than one specimen of the human genus or species (the species whose dignity it is that all its members are unique persons) – it is impossible for one such person to be raised to a position of absolute dominance and hence fundamentally to become the centre-point of all

4 *Ibid.*, p. 6.
5 *Ibid.*, pp. 7–8.

persons and their history; still less possible for him to raise himself to that position.[6]

If the redemption of the human race *were* to be ascribed to a single human liberator it could only be as a result of such a one's pointing out to others a universal way of salvation, unconditionally valid, objectively grounded in the essence of man, in human destiny and the destiny of the cosmos as a whole. And how, on humanistic criteria – prescinding, namely, from the idea of a man who was the envoy and plenipotentiary agent of the ultimate divine reality – could this claim be rendered plausible? Clearly, it could not.

Again, supposing we move onto Balthasar's second option, and propose that *God* might be the basis of history, the response, *pace* Hegel, must be this: since God does not require history so as to communicate himself to himself, what possible reason could there be for treating history as having an objective goal and norm based on the divine essence?

So it looks as if we may have to abandon the idea of history having any *overall* interpretation (other than one illicitly foisted thereon by human projection). But, says Balthasar, not so. Throwing in the towel is premature. Chalcedonian Christianity tells us otherwise. Nothing could overcome the impasse we have reached save:

a miracle undiscoverable and unguessable by philosophical thought: the existential union of God and man in one subject: a subject necessarily, as such, absolutely unique, because the human personality is here, without any strain or breakage, assumed into the divine person who incarnates and reveals himself in it.[7]

This does not mean, so Balthasar insists, the translation of a normal individual embodiment of human nature to a higher level of being. That would be an error akin to Arianism, for which the Word is a superlatively exalted creature, not the Creator-in-the-creature. Rather than speaking, in the first place, of the Incarnation as the ascent, by divine assumption, of a human being, Balthasar – as all along in his career – prefers to think primarily of the descent by self-emptying of the redeeming God. This 'kenosis' reaches such a pitch that God binds himself to enter one human being who, despite the ensuing exaltation, does not cease to be solidary with fellow-humans. Balthasar's fear is that the incarnate Word may be regarded as so unique *qua* sharer in human nature that Christ's unity with the human family could only be regarded as a distant analogy of the unity of the human family with itself. Though admiring Barth's Christological distinction between on the one hand human beings at large as 'men with men' and on the other Christ as the 'man for men' (for Barth, Christ's human nature is monopolized by the redeeming action of Christ and must be understood in terms of it), Balthasar fears that, if this distinction prevents Christ's innumerable brothers and sisters from participating in God's action in Jesus, it would rule out of court the Catholic understanding of how salvation is communicated to people through their fellows in the Church. And so he wants to say that

6 *Ibid.*, p. 9.
7 *Ibid.*, p. 10.

the ascent of human nature into God must be more deeply grounded in the descent of God into human nature. Only then does the inclusion of the redemption of the many within the uniqueness of Christ become intelligible.[8]

Here we are entering into soteriology – not irrelevant to fundamental theology because revelation is always saving revelation. But more immediately pertinent is the fact that the Chalcedonian faith, so understood, solves the dilemma with which Balthasar started. A particular human body and soul, like all human beings 'relatively' unique, is now appropriated by the 'absolute' uniqueness of God himself. A concrete individual united with the Absolute is certainly a case of the specific, the particular, becoming the norm of concrete history. But since what is in union with this individual is the Absolute, this will be without prejudice to the values found in generic or universal realities and truths, even though now – with the Incarnation – these change their significance, and indeed their character, to some degree. As Balthasar puts it and here we see how, to his mind, natural law thinking must be profoundly affected by supernatural revelation and can no longer stand on its own:

> Insofar as Jesus Christ is true man, the universal validity of those normative laws which are grounded in human nature has, with him and *in him*, been assumed into union with the divine Word. This elevation means neither that the universal validity of these laws is destroyed (for after all, human nature is to be redeemed, not annihilated), nor that it is merely preserved, side by side with, but unaffected by, the concrete norm which is Jesus Christ: it is rather that, without being nullified, the abstract laws are, in him, integrated and subordinated within his Christological uniqueness, and formed and governed by it.[9]

The principle is clear. When the norm for all humanity is at last given in Jesus Christ, human nature is both preserved in its integrity yet re-aligned in accordance with the God-man. But *the application of the principle*, so Balthasar admits, is variable.

Applying the principle involved

Not indefinitely so. Three courses of action can at once be ruled out. The first is to carry on with natural metaphysics, ethics, jurisprudence and historical study as though no Incarnation had happened. The second is to treat secular studies and theological studies as parallel affairs, parallel lines which never meet, so that something might be false in philosophy but true in theology, and vice versa. The third is to declare the theological queen-bee so much the mistress of the realms of knowledge that all secular study of the natural world is absorbed into her voracious maw. Balthasar's position is what remains when all these are set aside – and all of them are unthinkable having read Barth and responded critically to him in the way Balthasar has.

8 *Ibid.*, p. 12.
9 *Ibid.*, p. 13.

Precisely because Christ is the absolute, he remains incommensurable
with the norms of this world. The refusal of any such agreed demar-
cation on the part of theology, though it may look like and be called
arrogance, is really no more than respect for the methodological
demands of its subject.[10]

Balthasar surmises that sometimes the Christological re-integration of general laws will involve the God-man assuming them totally into his person, re-
orienting them on him, and at other times leave them practically untouched,
the object of (as he puts it) 'occasional indirect supervision' – language
reminiscent, and probably deliberately so, of the terms in which such post-
mediaeval commentators as Robert Bellarmine saw the role of the Vicar of
Christ, the Petrine office-holder, in international affairs.

Balthasar now draws three crucial inferences from what has been said.
First, Christ is the unique norm for all creation (including then all history) not
in his teaching merely but *in his very existence*. His words belong only within
his total life as a self-giving for the Father's truth and love that was faithful
unto death. Without the sacrifice of Calvary, and its Eucharistic oblation, life-
summating actions as those are, his words would not be that testimony to the
Father which, so the Jesus of St John's Gospel claims, contains within it the
testimony of the Father too (John 8.18). Without his universally salvific self-
giving on the Cross, continued in the kenosis of the Church's Eucharist, his
verbal message would not be

> that two-in-one christological word which reveals the life of the three-
> in-one [the divine Trinity] and which bears within itself a sovereign
> claim to belief and obedience.[11]

The 'Christo-logic' embodied in Jesus' total existence (we are close here to the
gestation of the second volume of Balthasar's theological logic, on Christ as
the Truth) is 'penetrable to those who do not close their eyes to it'. Interestingly, in this perspective, Balthasar regards the 'proofs' of Christ's divine
legateship found in traditional apologetics – namely, the fulfilment of prophecy and miracles – as one and the same. The concordance between prophecy and fulfilment cannot be shown without his eschatological marvels,
the wonderful works to be done by the Messiah.

The second crucial inference Balthasar wants us to draw from his basic
account of the relation between the world's history and Christ's is that the
truth of Christo-logic is not just an *illustrative* truth. It does not merely
exemplify, in however dramatic a fashion, a truth that in principle could
already be known. Its content does not come from the universally human, as
would be the case were it deducible, with whatever difficulty, from the
universal pattern of human existence. Nor can it be reduced to simply the
general relationship between God and the world. In a nutshell, the truth of
Jesus Christ is not just a truth of creation. And the deepest reason is that

10 *Ibid.*, p. 14.
11 *Ibid.*

God wills to maintain his relation to the world only with Jesus Christ as the centre of that relationship, the content and fulfilment of the eternal Covenant.[12]

This is of course the message Balthasar learned from Barth – and having learned it, found it echoed in the best nineteenth- and twentieth-century Catholic theologians as well. It follows that no category drawn from the world can frame Jesus Christ. But then Balthasar is sceptical of all univocal application of general concepts typical of the 'study of religions' to the crucial figures of biblical history. Asking rhetorically whether those biblical figures are but members of wider classes or categories, he maintains

> The answer to all these questions must be no; not because there is no analogy between the general human law and the special Christian fact, but because this special fact, by virtue of Christ's uniqueness, is so constituted as to be, in all its historical singularity, the concrete norm for the abstract norm itself. In the case of the prophet or the apostle, for example, one can clearly register the point of transition, where the content of the general category recedes and fades to such a degree that, in face of the unique historical fact, it becomes practically without importance; although [he adds, in acknowledgement of a recognized Thomistic maxim about the nature/grace relationship] the universal significance is not destroyed ... but perfected and elevated.[13]

The third lesson we should draw from the way he has discussed how the revelation given in Christ fulfils history is that in Jesus Christ *fact and norm are necessarily one*. The God-man is both the actual manifestation of God (fact) and the divine–human pattern for us to follow (norm). We cannot separate out the theology from the history. The historical life of the Word made flesh (up to and including his Resurrection) is the translation into the finite of the infinite truth whch gives all history its norm.

These prolegomena in place, Balthasar turns his attention to the substantive case. There are four dimensions to explore: first, Christ's own 'mode' of time; secondly, the 'inclusion' of history within the life of Christ; thirdly, the person of Christ as the 'norm' of history, and fourthly, history under the norm of Christ.

Christ's mode of time

Christ's mode of inhabiting time can only be understood from the angle of his personal being as the Father's Word who receives everything he has and is sheerly from the Father. As the Christ of St John's Gospel makes clear in numerous references about how his will and his honour are not his own but the Father's:

---

12 *Ibid.*, p. 16.
13 *Ibid.*, p. 18. This passage is almost pure Kierkegaard, from his essay, which greatly intrigued Balthasar, 'On the Difference between Being a Genius and Being an Apostle': see *Kultur und Gebet, op. cit.*, pp. 8–9.

> The Son's form of existence, which makes him the Son from all eternity
> (17: 5), is the uninterrupted reception of everything that he is, of his
> very self, from the Father.[14]

This is what gives him the Sonship by which he can respond spontaneously
to the Father in utter reciprocity of giving. His communion with the Father,
unlike ours, is a communion in the 'eternally uninterrupted act of his own
generation'. In the same act whereby he receives himself he receives the
whole of the Father's will, including his will for the world, and he assents to
it as his own. Balthasar accepts St Thomas's thesis that Jesus Christ's mission
in this world is simply the prolongation under created conditions of his
eternal generation. His human self-awareness is the expression under the
conditions of this world of his eternal consciousness as the Father's Son. That
is why Jesus' statements about himself, in all the Gospels and not just St
John's, are meant to serve precisely his *mission*. The mind of the Word is the
archetype of the human mind when the human being is considered as made
to God's image and likeness which for Balthasar, as for the majority of the
Fathers, means in the first instance *made in the image of the Word*. So the union
of the natures in the God-man does not abolish or absorb the human self-
consciousness of Jesus, but leaves it intact with, however, an enhancement of
an incomparable kind.

These remarks are by way of a preamble to asking the question, What
does all this imply for Jesus' temporality, his way of being in time, when he is
considered as a creature? It implies that nothing could be more natural for
that divine person who is constituted by receptivity to the Father – namely,
the eternal Son – to live, once creaturely, in time. Time is a medium that is
perfectly suited to the expression of receptivity. In eternity the Son 'makes
nothing his own in any way that contradicts its being given to him, continually, ceaselessly, by the Father'. So now in time, as the man Jesus:

> his possession and experience in this world of that which is his own is
> going to be, not all in one flash, but something received from the
> Father, possessed only in him and through him, and hence continually
> offered up to him, given back to him, and again received as yet another
> new gift of love.[15]

There is then no contradiction between the Son's eternal being and the Son's
temporal being. Rather is there harmonious congruity between them. Indeed,
Christ's being in time is the manifestation of his eternal being, just as his
mission is the manifestation of his generation. So for Balthasar, the Transfiguration episode, for instance, should not be preached about as eternity
breaking through momentarily into time in Christ's public ministry. Rather,
in the mystery of Thabor, the entire structure of Christ's temporality shows
itself transfigured – appropriately, since it is the expression of the Son's
eternal receptivity vis-à-vis the Father and the Father's will. It may seem odd
to speak of 'temporality' as itself 'transfigured'. Here Balthasar is influenced
by his early reading of Martin Heidegger's *Sein und Zeit*: for Heidegger, time
is ontological, indeed it is (on his non-theistic view of things) being itself.[16]

14 *A Theology of History, op. cit.,* p. 26.
15 *Ibid.,* p. 29.
16 See A. Nichols, OP, *Scattering the Seed, op. cit.,* p. 206.

Balthasar accepts St Irenaeus's analysis of sin and notably of the Fall. What transpired in the Garden was a premature attempted anticipation of the outcome of God's dealings with us. Jesus did not emulate that folly. He waited on the Father, not trying to rush the 'hour' of the decisive break-through of the Kingdom. The Son's restoration of true order between God and man included what Balthasar calls the 'annulment of that premature snatching at knowledge, the beating down of the hand outstretched towards eternity'. This is why, he says, the virtue of patience is so praised in the apostolic letters. By 1959 when he wrote this work, Balthasar himself rated patience even more central to the Christian life than humility. But maybe that was because patience is a unique expression of humility, the meekness of a lamb that is – precisely – *led*.

Of course, as God, the Son could, if he wished, 'know' the hour to which his whole life as man was moving and take its measure. But if he chose so to know it he would not behave filially. As Balthasar puts it, the Son

> wants rather to receive it so fresh, so immediately born out of the eternal source of all love, that there will be no trace, no fingerprint, of anything on it except the Father's will.[17]

And in this way his knowledge or non-knowledge of the hour is typical of his knowledge generally. He allows it to be measured by his mission with its peculiar demands.

> To regard Christ's knowledge as though he carried out his actions in time from some vantage-point of eternity – rather like a chess-player of genius who quickly foresees the whole course of the game and simply moves his men through a game which for him is already over – [this] would be to do away entirely with his temporality and so with his obedience, his patience, the merit of his redemptive existence. He would no longer be qualified to narrate the parables of expectation and waiting which describe the life of his followers.[18]

This refusal to anticipate, in itself a negative quality, can also be put positively. Positively, it is the God-man's allowing the Holy Spirit to mediate to him moment by moment the Father's will.

And the upshot is that the 'whole basis of time for the Son is his receptivity to the Father's will'. Here we return to our starting-point. He receives time from the Father *as the Father's will*, time in its form and time in its content. What Balthasar means in the first place by saying time *in its form* is that there is for Jesus no such thing as empty time, time to kill. He never simply had 'time on his hands'. For him to have time means to have time for God, and indeed the Son who in the world has time for God is the point at which God has time for the world.

The varieties of time

Here Balthasar takes a further step. If we say that the time the Son inhabits is the medium of God's time for the world, then we are closely connecting it

17 *A Theology of History, op. cit.*, p. 31.
18 *Ibid.*, p. 32.

with the concept of grace – which is precisely the concept of access to God granted by God himself. A further step comes when Balthasar introduces the idea of 'real' time. By that he means time in which man encounters God and accepts his will, as contrasted with 'unreal' time in which man ignores or rejects God and so falls into pointlessness, for such time is duration leading nowhere. Naturally, theologically unreal time is just as real when measured by the clock or the movement of the earth as is theologically real time. But when we consider them in and of themselves – consider them theologically, that is – these modes of time are at the antipodes from each other.

Actually, Balthasar wants to distinguish more modes of temporality, theologically speaking, than just these two diametrically opposed ones. He speaks not only of *sinful* time (that is, time moving to disaster), but also of *paradisal* time (the original time when God was open to man at his creation and conversed with him in the Spirit – Balthasar's interpretation of the Genesis author's 'in the evening breeze' or 'cool of the evening'[19]). Naturally enough for a Christian author there is also *redeemed* time, which is the time when God once again takes time to himself for the sake of the world. The latter is of course centred in Christ's time, but Christ's time in itself cannot be identified with any of the modes thus described simply as such. Modes, like categories, are subordinated to Christ's uniqueness. If that were not the case, it would be the modes – in our context, the modes of time – that would be the standard, and Christ would cease to be the norm. His time must be different from all of them just because it has to become *the universal norm for time*.

Balthasar gives us an idea of how that will work out. First, so far as paradisal time is concerned, Christ's time fulfils Adam's since it gives access to God over and above Adamic grace. Going beyond what Adam knew, it opens the world to participation in the inner relations of communion of Father, Son and Holy Spirit. Again, Christ's time is necessarily related to sinful time, because he came to be the Saviour of humankind. His time is focused, accordingly, on the hour when the Father opens himself supremely to the God-man in the seemingly contrary conditions of the Son's abandonment – his own supreme sacrifice – on the Cross. Christ's time is a time that

> as it grows toward fulfilment assumes into itself the growing emptiness and desolation of the unreal time of sin...

It is a time that

> in its truth and validity contains within itself the modality of untrue, non-valid time; not only in order to know it and having known it to overcome it, but in order to fill it with valid meaning.[20]

From the moment of the Atonement – the Paschal mystery – onwards all human time has been determined by Christ's time. Unusually, this is the perspective in which Balthasar would like to see presented the famous three theological virtues. It is by faith, hope and love that human time reaches through Christ's time its intended perfection in God. Balthasar holds that, while in one sense only love remains in the participation of eternity which is

19 Genesis 3.8.
20 *A Theology of History, op. cit.*, p. 36.

heaven, in another sense, to cite St Paul who after all was the one who brought these three virtues together in the first place, all three abide.[21] In heaven, faith and hope do not disappear. Instead, they become internal modalities of love. As Balthasar writes:

> In its perfection, hope is simply the readiness of love to say yes to everything, to be available for everything, always open to the infinite in the knowledge that God is always its greater good, while faith for its part is simply that disposition in the creature by which it makes an offering and a surrender of itself, and thus of all its own truth and all its own evidence, in a love which prefers God's invariably greater truth to its own.[22]

(Incidentally, this explains why Balthasar can speak of Jesus as having faith – something impossible on, for example, the Thomistic notion of the faith virtue.) For Balthasar, faith, so understood, is *Hingabe*, self-surrender, and notably of one's own creaturely truth to (as we read) the greater truth of God. Thus owing to this emphasis on truth, the Balthasarian concept of faith retains a cognitive dimension from its Thomistic beginnings – unlike (it might be thought) the Lutheran version, fiducial faith, which is essentially trust and therefore equivalent to the virtue of hope in Thomas (and in Balthasar too for that matter). So understood, faith and hope, though transformed, can endure in the beatific vision. In, respectively, the vision of God and the possession of God they become what we might call adverbial qualifiers to the charity which for Balthasar, as for Paul, is the greatest of these three, and the central virtue of the redeemed in heaven. Balthasar can appeal in all this to St Irenaeus who remarks that faith and hope abide in eternal life as well as love.[23] In heaven – and here Balthasar could have invoked other favourites among the Greek Fathers likewise (notably, Nyssa) – we can always hope to receive more of God's bounty and keep on learning from him for, says Irenaeus, 'he is the Good One and possesses riches inexhaustible and a kingdom without end and unbounded wisdom'.

> To believe, to hope, to love means, in fact, to imitate the faithful obedience, the self-denying patience of Jesus, by which he brings the eternal into time.[24]

The inclusion of history within the time of Christ

What then of the next of Balthasar's themes – the inclusion of history within the time of Christ? In the first instance, this for Balthasar means something retrospective or, better, retroactive. In obeying the Father, the Son obeys the promises and prophecies of the Father, laid out as these were in past time, the time of ancient Israel (hence, promises), and concerning as they did time that was future from the standpoint of their speakers (and so, prophecies). If Jesus' obedience is vertical, to the Father, it must also be horizontal, to the

21 1 Corinthians 13.13.
22 *A Theology of History, op. cit.*, pp. 37–38.
23 Irenaeus, *Adversus Haereses* II. 28, 3.
24 *A Theology of History, op. cit.*, p. 42.

Father's plan laid out through Israel in time. First of all, the Old Testament lays down 'certain points', remarks Balthasar, from which Jesus cannot depart. There are certain spiritual situations he must make his own if he is to be the one awaited by Israel. His life must be the fulfilment of the Law and the prophets in their entirety. The Father's will, which is the content of his existence, does not present itself to him independently of the historic form it has already assumed. The will of God for the world which prepares the way for the Incarnation was already in Israel Christological in form. That said, Balthasar can also add – and this is more than just a footnote – that exactly as the fulfilment Christ must be called the foundation of the promise – the archetype to which all the Hebrew types are drawn. That is a profoundly Barthian point, even more than an Alexandrian one. And the upshot is that Christ's acceptance of tradition, which means primarily but not exclusively Jewish tradition, is his responsibility for the truth and work of the Father – and yet none of it is in the slightest degree alien to him, for from all eternity he *is* that truth and that work.

Compared with the Israel of old, what is new in the human performance of Christ? Balthasar replies:

> The scope of it, the precision, the motivation: no man has ever yet fulfilled the Law like *this*: no man has even been *this* just before. No one has ever before grasped the ultimate, mysterious intention of the Spirit in the letter to this degree.[25]

For Balthasar, while the Son sees the Father in Torah, the Father sees the Son in it. The Law and the prophets were all for this – that, by the love with which he obeys, the Son should make the Law the servant of love. That finds concrete expression in the relation between Jesus and Mary. In obeying his mother as the bearer of the tradition of Judaism, Jesus obeys the Father. But on the Cross, which is the overflowing fulfilment of every obedience the Law enjoins, their situations are inverted. Mary is now integrated into the total all-embracing obedience of the Son.

However, Christ's fulfilment of what preceded him is not limited to Israel. Indeed, the Gentile Job, says Balthasar, is the 'most profound and direct prophecy of the Cross' – a position already articulated in the sixth century by Gregory the Great. The natural law, which Paul in Romans regards as the equivalent for pagans to the dispensation of Torah for Jews, is also related to the life of Christ as promise to fulfilment. *Israel as such cannot fulfil paganism; only Christ can do this.* Until his coming, as the Writer to the Ephesians saw, the 'dividing wall of separation' (between Gentiles and Jews) must stand.[26] Naturally, all this opens up the widest perspectives of world history since the creation, or at least the creation of man. Echoing Barth, and anticipating his own theological dramatics, Balthasar insists that

> The Son's action is what history is for, his uniqueness sets it free to attain its proper character ... God the Father set it in motion with the expression intention of leading it up to the Son ... the parts and scenes

---

25 *Ibid.*, pp. 54–55.
26 Ephesians 2.11.

in it are recapitulated by the Son, summed up and realised to their highest level of truth and reality.[27]

It is the Holy Spirit who, for Balthasar, orients history towards the Son and makes it specifically *salvation* history. As he writes:

It is the Spirit who makes history into the history of salvation, which is to say prophetically oriented towards the Son, and it is he who places the Son in those situations which fulfil the Promise. Because he is the Spirit of the Father and the Son in personal unity, he can at the same time be the heart of the Father's command and the heart of the Son's obedience, of the Father's promise in history pointing towards the Son and of the Son's fulfilment of history pointing towards the Father.[28]

So history has a Trinitarian structure: it is from the Father, towards the Son, and thanks to the Holy Spirit.

The New Covenant sealed on the Cross fulfils or surpasses both Torah and the natural law. This is one obvious exemplification of the truth that the world was framed in Christ incarnate, which is how Balthasar interprets the various references in the Pauline corpus to Christ's cosmic significance. It is *in view of Christ* that the venture of having a world and therefore a world history was undertaken by the Father at all. Anticipating his discussion of the purpose of the Incarnation in his 'Theology of the Three Days', later dubbed *Mysterium Paschale*, Balthasar writes:

Just as there is a true sense in which sin caused the Cross and Christ would not have come as Redeemer if the guilt of mankind had not called on him to make good in this way the pledge given at creation, so in another and deeper sense the Cross is the condition for the possibility not only of sin but of existence and predestination itself.[29]

Through his Passion Christ merited our being and our God-intended destiny.

Situations and missions

Balthasar backs up this claim with a substantial citation not – as might be expected – from any member of the Franciscan school but from the commentary on Thomas's *Summa theologiae* by the seventeenth-century Spanish Dominican theologian Pedro de Godoy, the first holder of the chair of theology in the University of Salamanca. We register a position more distinctively his own as he unravels implications of the way Christ's fulfilment of creation took the form of kenosis, self-emptying. As he puts it, Christ experienced not just the human situation as such, but all those diverse sorts of situation which lie in between fulfilment and utter non-fulfilment of the creative project: the abyss between God and creature, the situation of man under the commandment of God as Adam knew it, the widened gulf brought by sin, the dark land of temptation, and above all the 'mounting disproportion' between divine demand and human powers, as that is shown in the Agony in the Garden of Gethsemane. Balthasar comments:

27 *A Theology of History, op. cit.*, p. 59.
28 *Ibid.*
29 *Ibid.*, p. 62.

The measure of man had been shrunk by the sinner, and the Lord had to wrench it violently open again in the extreme of suffering; in the racking of his limbs on the Cross, to which corresponds a yet deeper straining apart of all the powers of his soul, he reaches the furthest dimension of that guilt of which creation has concrete knowledge: the abyss between the flaming, raging justice of God and man 'abandoned' and rejected by him. He attains this point as substitute, i.e. no longer distinguishing, subjectively or objectively, between his own innocence and the guilt of others.[30]

He can do all this because he is the God-man, though proper weight must be given to both parts of that title, God and man. This is the sort of Balthasarian passage that makes some Catholic theologians nervous that he is coming too close to an Atonement-theology of penal substitution. Balthasar does not, however, speak of substitution as penal, though it is for him certainly real.[31]

Given Balthasar's view that the creation is from the beginning Christo-centric, he quite appropriately calls the 'space' humanity has in which to make history happen a space that belongs to Christ. It is already in a certain way pre-shaped, being as it is, in the last analysis, a space made possible by the freedom of God. And Balthasar explains that the framework of this space is constructed from out of the situations – he means the inner meaning of the situations – found in the life of Christ towards whom all world history is meant to move. Like Aquinas and in a later century the French Oratorian cardinal Pierre de Bérulle (and building on such as these, the Christological section of the present *Catechism of the Catholic Church*), Balthasar's favoured Christological approach is through *explorations of the mysteries of the life of Christ*. It is of course the approach of the Liturgy and indeed on a lower level of the Rosary. What is more unusual is the way Balthasar sees the various interior situations comprised within the mysteries of the life of Christ as generating an indefinite number of further 'situations' in the lives of disciples, of Christians. He writes:

> Each situation in the divine-human life is so infinitely rich, capable of such unlimited application, so full of meaning, that it generates an inexhaustible abundance of Christian situations, just as any number of essences can be subordinated to an idea without its being exhausted or restricted by them. For like the Idea [he is making a comparison with Plato's ontology of the Idea or Form, *eidos*, in relation to the particulars it informs], the situation of Christ is of a different order from that which it rules. Its elevation above all things makes it proof against depletion; it is the wellspring of history, of unfathomable depth and abundance.[32]

30 *Ibid.*, p. 64.
31 We can note that, after *A Theology of History* was written, he would give more emphasis, in *Man in History*, to the way Christ's death – which must always be seen in union with (his descent and) the Resurrection, triumphantly achieves mastery of time. Thus he writes in that later work, 'This Word does not poetically transfigure death, playing around it, he bores right through it to the bottom, to the chaotic formlessness of the death cry (Matthew 27.50), and the wordless silence of death on Holy Saturday. Hence, he has death in his grasp: he dominates it, limits it, and takes from it all its sting. Thus, he has passing time also in his grip, not through a poetic, legislative, transcendence of time, but by dominating the inner time structure', *Man in History*, p. 242.
32 *A Theology of History, op. cit.*, p. 67.

In other words, a situation in the life of Jesus is not to be regarded in the same way as a situation in the life of some other historical figure, however major – a Gautama, a Bonaparte. In the case of Jesus, each life situation manifests in this world the eternal life of God. This further dimension entails that the number of its possible applications is indefinitely extensible. This is why saints have been able to spend years or even their entire lives contemplating some one single mystery in the life of Christ.

Consequently, it belongs to the essence of the grace of Christ to place the individual in particular Christologically defined situations. (Adrienne von Speyr's case, located in the mystery of the Descent into Hell, is only one extreme example.) To call grace Christological is more than to say it is caused by the merit of Christ. More than that, Christian grace creates situations which replicate in a thousand different ways the situation of Christ himself. One important corollary is that grace, so Balthasar puts it, is not just a philosophical sun, like the Form of the Good in Platonism, constantly, at all times, universally affecting or at least available to affect the world. On the contrary, grace prompts personal decisions to re-situate ourselves on the model (in some way) of Christ himself. Hence its summons is not at any and every moment but in specific moments, and our encounter with it is at various times in our lives unrepeatable. There is more than a little in this of Barth's actualism, but Balthasar bases it on the twelfth chapter of St John's Gospel: 'The light is among you still, but only for a short time ... While you still have the light, have faith in the light ... '. (John 12.35-36).

What Balthasar is talking about of course is *acts of choice in history*, and arising from this what he terms 'Christian missions' – the missions we take on as Christians to live this or that kind of life, to pursue this or that type of vocation, to perform this or that task in the Church, in the world. This is the key notion of Balthasar's hagiology, his theology of the lives of the saints, but in the present context of a theology of history he is more interested in noting the temporal links which bind such missions together. Precisely because they all originate in indefinitely novel replications or applications of situations in the life of Christ, they are essentially internally connected one with another, or can be. Every mission, if fulfilled, provides a basis for new missions in the future, just as some Church Father or mediaeval doctor might have mentioned in passing some truth which a later generation will pick up, place in a proper perspective and interpret fruitfully for the good of the whole Church. All our destinies are interwoven and until the last of us has lived, the significance of the first of us cannot be fully clear. However, all such mutual influencing of destinies is subordinate to the destiny of the Son, who will be our judge, and can be our judge because he measures with at once the transcendent divine standard and the human standard of One who knows *from within* what is humanly possible. And Balthasar adds, tying in this thought more completely to the mini-theology of the missions which has preceded it: in the Last Judgment the saints too will be involved.

In the measure in which his saints have been a force that has shaped history, they will join with him in being the measure of judgment.[33]

33 *Ibid.*, p. 74.

Christ as the norm of history

Christ is the norm of history, first and foremost in relation to the Church. Balthasar has already said that by recapitulating history Christ becomes its norm. He now wants to show how that norm is applied in the concrete, first in relation to the being of Christ as that develops or is shown forth in a variety of human situations in the Church, and then secondly to the rest of history, which will be Balthasar's final theme. Thanks to the economy of the Spirit, a segment of history – the slice that joins Christ to the Church, and Christ and the Church to the missions of Christians – is rendered pertinent to the whole of history, and becomes the key to the historical process in its entirety.

How, then, is Christ the norm of history in relation *to the Church*? For Balthasar, the Holy Spirit, working in and upon the incarnate Son, actively relates Jesus, now transformed in the 'hiatus', to the historic Church in each succeeding age, with her life expressed, as it is, in the sacraments. And the same Holy Spirit creates the missions of people in history as the life of Christ and the Church are applied in a widening arena. This is privileged history from which the rest of world history is finally to take its bearings.

Sacramental time

Balthasar's theology of the interrelation of Christ, the Church with her sacraments, and Christian mission gives especial prominence to the 'Forty Days' between Easter and the Ascension, a period whose unity and distinctiveness was more manifest liturgically in the 1950s when in Latin-rite churches the Ascension provided the limit day for the lighting of the Paschal candle, symbol (in that particular liturgical epoch) of the risen Christ enjoying bodily fellowship with his own. We shall defer consideration of that topic until the next chapter, which presents his account of the Paschal mystery. But we must note here the metaphysical significance Balthasar detects in the period of the risen Christ's fraternizing with his own, and the importance he ascribes to the time of the Resurrection appearances for the sacramental time which is proper to ecclesial living.

Before speaking in this connexion of the sacramental time of the Church, Balthasar enters a metaphysical flourish. It was because the Son was already, in the Incarnation, the eternal made temporal that he can be, in the Resurrection, a temporal being made eternal. As such, he 'solves' theologically the problem of universals – how a particular thing can share in some wider significance. Because he is the supra-temporal in time he can be called *universale in re*, the universally significant – the eternal, then – *in* the temporal, *in* the particular. As such he can supply meaning *after* the event for the whole time of promise, and meaning *before* the event for the life of the future – both for the Church, and for disciples as persons. So we should not have any great difficulty in making the transition to sacramental time, the time when his personal intentions in our regard are mediated in signs, signs creative of personal, historical situations.

For Balthasar the Forty Days are crucial to sacramental time. First of all, so far as concerns himself, the mode of existence which Christ enjoys in the sacraments, supremely in the Eucharist, is no different from what the Forty

Days reveal. He is in the sacraments as the risen Lord inhabiting the eternity of the Father, and accompanying his own through the time of earth. What changes after the Ascension (and, we may add, Pentecost) is that whereas during the Forty Days he let this companionship appear openly, now in the sacraments it appears only as concealment. St Thomas's celebrated Eucharistic hymn, the 'Adoro te', makes a similar point in poetic guise. In Hopkins' translation, while 'on the Cross his Godhead gave no sign to men', in the Holy Eucharist even his manhood 'steals from human ken'. The senses are not to be trusted here, save in one regard, the sense of hearing, which gives access to the *auditus*, the hearing of faith, which, by contradistinction, *is* to be believed. Before his Passion, anyone occupying the same space-time with him could see Jesus. For this very reason, says Balthasar, he was veiled to spiritual sight. After the sealing of the tomb, by contrast, he is visible in principle only to believers. And the explanation for that for Balthasar is that 'his appearance now always implies the revelation of divinity in his humanity'.[34]

That this is so is owed ultimately to the Cross. The Cross ensures that from now on the covenant of God with man lies beyond all human vacillation, and therefore all possible modification of divine response. From now on it is in the medium of faith in him, the unfailing presence of which is assured in the Church by the Holy Spirit, that the Son will be present to people, in sacramental mode.

To say that Christ's sacramental mode of existence, above all in the Holy Eucharist, does not differ essentially from that of the Forty Days, is among other things to say that in the sacraments Christ is still revealing, bestowing, interpreting, the mysteries of his earthly life for us. In this sense, Balthasar accepted the *Mysterientheologie* of the German Benedictine theologian of the Liturgy, Odo Casel. In all the sacraments – indeed, in the entire Liturgy conceived as in the widest sense a sacramental sign-system – there is a 'mystery-presence'. Only, Balthasar wanted the disciples of Casel (Casel himself had died at the end of the 1940s) to emphasize more vigorously how Christ's presence in the sacraments is 'qualitatively determined by himself personally, and ... rooted in his earthly life'.[35] This leads Balthasar to depart from – or at any rate, to treat as only a secondary range of consideration – the Thomist theology of the sacraments which sees them as the application of the grace of the Christ to a variety of human needs, thus constituting a supernatural parallel to the natural order in its basic shaping. (Thus Baptism corresponds to birth, the Eucharist to nourishment, and so forth.) Balthasar did not reject that completely, but he did not think it the first thing to be said about the so-called sacramental 'system'. He writes:

> We are not allowing the archetypal, formative power of the life of the God-man its full validity if we regard the sacraments as defined and differentiated not from within themselves but by various basic situations in human life and the life of the Church (with Christ's grace applying and adapting itself to them but with *them* acting as the specifying principle).[36]

34 *Ibid.*, p. 91.
35 *Ibid.*, p. 92.
36 *Ibid.*

Thus for Balthasar the sacrament of Marriage is the drawing of natural marriage into the relation between Jesus and the bridal Church on the Cross; the sacrament of Penance (pure von Speyrism this!) is the drawing of the confession of guilt into the Son's confession of the world's sin on the Cross and its absolution by the Father in the Resurrection. These examples suggest that Balthasar would have wanted to maintain one theme of Thomasian sacramentology, which is the necessary relation of all the sacraments to the Cross.

Presence in mystery

Of course Christ's existence in the sacraments is not exactly what it was in history, in Galilee or Judaea. That existence is a mystery-presence in the phrase popularized by the liturgical theologian Dom Odo Casel: it is a presence *in mysterio*.[37] However, the continuing exemplary causality of the mysteries of the life of Christ appealed to in the sacraments is not just a matter of the continued survival and action of the person, Jesus, now the exalted Lord, with his historical *acta et passa* – the things he did and underwent – being now, however, fully past in absolutely every sense of that word. For Balthasar, the redemptive deeds of the Saviour in history are, rather, universalized and on that basis made historically concrete again in the time of the Church. He expresses this by the metaphor or extended comparison of two features of the Thomistic theory of knowing: 'abstraction' which corresponds to the universalization of the Lord's saving deeds, and *conversio ad phantasma*, the 'turning to sensuous realities', to which there corresponds the new mode of historical concreteness enjoyed by the events of Christ's life in the Church's liturgical time.

Naturally, given the Catholic view of the Eucharistic Sacrifice and Eucharistic Presence, the Mass has to be a special case of the outworking of these principles in the sacraments – and even more the Liturgy – at large. Balthasar writes:

> It is not, as in the other sacraments, some one special aspect of Christ's earthly existence which is here turned upon the Church and the individual, but his whole bodily reality in its supreme fulfilment on the Cross.[38]

When speaking of the Mass, Balthasar from as early a date as the 1950s wants to find some way of saying that at the Cross the Church was already there, co-offering with Christ by offering through him. Adrienne von Speyr's mystically generated intuitions – on the Cross the Son was 'no hermit' – surely suggested this to him. Eventually, partly provoked by her, he will find the right way to express this through Mariology. But for the moment, he does not find so elegant a solution. Instead, he puts forward an argument with two prongs. First, there is something of the sort suggested by the mere fact of a Chalcedonian understanding of the identity of the One who died. He says:

---

37 For an account of Casel's work and its significance, see A. Nichols, OP, 'Odo Casel Revisited', in *idem*, *Beyond the Blue Glass. Catholic Essays on Faith and Culture* (London, 2002), pp. 151–70.
38 *A Theology of History, op. cit.*, p. 94.

In so far as the new and eternal marriage between Godhead and manhood was sealed in blood on the Cross by the loving sacrifice of that one individual whose dual nature [divine and human] was itself the centre and source of the Covenant, to that extent his one sacrifice to the Father contains, from the very start, a duality within itself: it is the sacrifice of the Head and of the Body, of the Bridegroom and of the Bride.[39]

Moreover, there is the question of the implications of what took place before Calvary, in the Upper Room. The Lord had 'already drawn [the Church] into his liturgy of the Cross by the liturgical con-celebration of the Last Supper'. So when in the Mass the Church is granted a 'true bodily contemporaneity with her Head in his sacrifice', this is perhaps new but it is not unexpected. Later, Balthasar will say that owing to the role of the Mother of God at Golgotha, it is neither unexpected nor is it new.

The time that comes into existence from the communion between the Saviour and the Church can be called not only sacramental but more especially *Eucharistic* time.

Its peculiar character is that the eternal Lord is constantly coming afresh into contemporaneity with his Bride, but without becoming subject to or measured by passing time.[40]

The fact that sacramental time is rooted in the Forty Days is what for Balthasar gives the sacraments their eschatological orientation. The Forty Days show the Son of Man drawing his disciples into his own glorious present and future. So it is with the sacramental signs thanks to the work of the Holy Spirit who, so Balthasar declares, 'charges the waiting form [the liturgical sign employed in the sacrament] with infinite content'.

Such sacramental time needs to find expression in the time of ordinary living. The Church and the Christian have a mission to pursue, a tradition to express, outside of the celebration of the rites. So how does this work? For Balthasar it is the task of the Holy Spirit to bring into accord (a favourite Balthasarian term) situations in the life of Christ on the one hand and situations in the life of the believer on the other. As he puts it, it is the Holy Spirit who

determines the manner and degree to which the current moment is required to enter into this or that aspect of the life of Christ: at what moment we are to act with the Lord or pray with him, to hide with him or to confront our enemies with him, to preach with him or to be silent with him, to feast with him or fast with him, to rejoice with the Lord or to suffer with him in his forsakenness.[41]

Christ the norm of history at large

Balthasar makes it clear that, if we wish to talk about the relation of the entire process of world history to Jesus Christ as norm we have to keep in mind at

39 *Ibid.*
40 *Ibid.*, p. 95.
41 *Ibid.*, p. 98.

all points the distinction – but not separation – of natural and supernatural which so exercised him in his evaluation of Barth, and which he tried to resolve in adjudicating the issues raised by the career of de Lubac. We have to think through what is involved in transposing the terms in which he resolved those issues into terms of history and its purpose. When we do so, we get the following result. On the one hand, as he writes:

> the whole history of the human race, which is transformed in its whole nature by the Hypostatic Union, cannot ultimately stand over against Christ as independent of him; it will attain its final justification, its ultimate meaning, solely because it comes within the realm of the life and lordship of him to whom is given 'all authority in heaven and on earth' (Matthew 28: 18) and who is now waiting 'until all his enemies are made a footstool under his feet' (Hebrews 10:13).[42]

In other words, we should recognize only one concrete supernatural end and ultimate meaning for history in Jesus Christ. On the other hand:

> This completion of the meaning of history in Christ is not to be understood as though created nature had in it no immanent meaning, no intelligibility, *eidos*, of its own, but only in Christ. Unless the Incarnation involves the acceptance of an immanent essence conferred by the act of creation and not able to be lost, there could be no true Incarnation, no possibility of God's becoming man and becoming history. It is not a definition of the essence of man that he is a member of Christ, nor of world history that it is co-extensive (invisibly) with the history of the Kingdom of God.[43]

In other words, affirming the single concrete supernatural order must be done without prejudice to the reality of a natural and primordial meaning for history on the basis of its created unfolding.

As Balthasar presents things, history has both a supernatural pattern of meaning and a natural pattern of meaning. The task is to hold them together. Curiously, he sees the supernatural pattern of meaning, in its relation to the natural, exemplified above all in the Religious life, and the natural pattern of meaning, in its relation to the supernatural, chiefly illustrated in the lay state – 'curiously', because this seems a strangely ecclesiocentric way to write a *general* theology of history. What he is trying to get at is the complementarity, for a theologically historical viewpoint, of two angles on time. For the first angle, the one symbolized in the Religious life where people are chosen, so as to 'subordinate the form of their existence to that of Christ', man knows that:

> fundamentally, the only context within which any meaning arises and becomes event is that of man's being broken open towards God: faith and prayer. It is only to such an attitude as this that a mission is entrusted, and it is always the grace of mission which provides the full and overflowing content of meaning for each successive historical 'now'.[44]

---

42 *Ibid.*, p. 112.
43 *Ibid.*
44 *Ibid.*, p. 118.

However, the 'eschatological longing' which is the heart of this attitude, a longing for the definitive End when God will consummate his creation, has to 'enlist the active powers in the service of passive surrender'.[45] It has somehow to subordinate to itself 'all man's working energy', all his 'plans and designs'. The law of the Incarnation 'requires that the meaning of history should not be imposed from above, from outside'. Though in the Kingdom of Christ the summit of history 'rises above all human situations', it is 'necessarily continuous with its foundations'. And those foundations

> cover the full extent of all those situations, with all the historical, sociological and psychological factors on which they are based.[46]

So the *eidos* – the form of man in history, when seen in its transcendence, its relation to the supernatural – must now be scanned in its complementary immanence, its continuing relation, despite its ordering to an End above history, to our human nature.[47] And this we see shown to us in the lay state, which is quintessential life 'in the world'. God 'uses the vehicle of historical progress', its ambiguities not excluded, so as to arrive at his own 'wholly different and unambiguous goal'.

So what is this goal? Describing it will require Balthasar to put together the *eidos* of man in history in its transcendent form (symbolized by the Religious state) and that same *eidos* in its immanent form (symbolized by the lay state in the Church). His aim is to reproduce how the Fathers and the mediaevals would have synthesized the two aspects – call them vertical eschatology on the one hand, and horizontal historical progress on the other. His key statement runs:

> Christ, who is fullness, has come at the end of the ages ... shortly before the transition to eternal life, and so of course everything that has gone before appears as one single progression towards him.[48]

For his part, Balthasar wants both to affirm this picture and yet to nuance it. First, it is quite true that salvation in Christ, humanity's true freedom, is now present to history, and this is itself the definitive criterion for all 'progress'. It, or rather he, is the Eschaton in history (Balthasar also uses the formula 'The Absolute in history' or 'the historical Absolute'). As such, in the fullness that is his, he represents henceforth a 'challenge to all secular and cultural history'.[49]

But were the Fathers and mediaevals sufficiently conscious of how the entry into history of the Absolute meant confronting the historical process *from that point on* with a clear either/or (the term is Kierkegaard's), so that what we find, ever since Christ appeared in the fullness of time, is *ever sharper alternatives or options for or against*? A simple developmental model is not appropriate for time after Christ. Balthasar will emphasize this with particular vigour in his use of the Johannine Apocalypse in the second volume of

45 *Ibid.*, p. 123.
46 *Ibid.*
47 This is something Balthasar had learned from, among others, the philosopher of culture Herder: see *Apokalypse der deutschen Seele I. Der deutsche Idealismus*, reprinted as *Prometheus. Studien zur Geschichte des deutschen Idealismus*, op. cit., pp. 62–70.
48 *A Theology of History*, op. cit.
49 *Ibid.*, p. 135.

the theological dramatics. The kernel of this approach is already there, however, twenty years earlier in *A Theology of History*. The time after Christ is supremely the time when godless beasts raise their heads and howl – though, as the Apocalypse's Letters to the Seven Churches show, this battle between the 'pro-God- and 'anti-God' powers also runs through the Church where the Son of Man holds perpetual judgment on his Bride.

But the ever sharper divisions the entry of the Absolute into history provokes does not mean that henceforth human nature in its quasi-progressive unfolding in history should be written off as irrelevant to salvation. On the contrary:

> It is precisely in the sunshine of the Absolute (which is the concept and reality of Christian love) that everything thrives in man's historical development of his potentialities.[50]

The decisive question is whether man will turn the future development of this potential in the direction of the Absolute, an Absolute now found as a gift in history, in the Church of Christ, and not simply beyond history's limits.

> The Church, transcending history but acting as its content and nucleus, is the ultimate gift of the creator to human history, given it to bring it to its own realization from within.[51]

Despite – or is it because of? – the conflictual element intensifying in history after Christ's incarnation, death and resurrection, there is now 'only one history, and its fulfillment, both immanent and transcendent [is] in the Kyrios'.[52] And the explanation for *that* runs:

> History does indeed have its own immanent *eidos*, but in descending into hell and then ascending into heaven and sitting on the right hand of the Father, Christ has taken it all aloft with him, and ultimately it is only there that history can seek and recover it.[53]

Which brings us rather neatly to Balthasar's theology of the Paschal mystery.

50 *Ibid.*, p. 137.
51 *Ibid.*
52 *Ibid.*, p. 139.
53 *Ibid.*, p. 140.

8

❀

Divine Climax: the Paschal Mystery

For Balthasar, as – one hopes – for any Christian theologian, the climax of the divine self-involvement in historical time as disclosed to us in revelation is the Paschal Mystery. The Paschal Mystery is the definitive revelation of the Holy Trinity.

The Trinity and the Incarnation

Of course, such a statement already presupposes a high view of the Incarnation, and indeed Balthasar always presents the Incarnation as a Trinitarian event. In his book on the mysteries of the Rosary, *The Threefold Garland*, Balthasar describes the Incarnation in these words:

> The Son of the Father allows himself to be born into a human womb, and so the heavens open in a new way and reveal a threefold life in God.[1]

In the Incarnation, human nature was united exclusively to the *second* Trinitarian Person. And yet it is an established principle of Catholic theology – clear for example in Albert, Thomas, Bonaventure – that the works of the three Trinitarian Persons are common though without derogation from the specific role of each.[2] And so, as Balthasar underlines, the entire Trinity was at work in the union achieved at the Annunciation. 'The Father sends the Son; the Son lets himself be sent, and the overshadowing Spirit fashions a body for him from the flesh of the consenting Virgin.'[3]

The Annunciation, then, and the manifestation of what happened there at Christmas and in the Epiphany, is the opening act of the Trinitarian revelation. But that revelation's climax comes with the mystery of Easter: the Son's Cross, Descent into Hell, Resurrection and Sending of the Spirit from the Father. First and foremost, indeed, the Holy Trinity is disclosed on the Cross.

---

1 *Der dreifache Kranz. Das Heil der Welt im Mariengebet* (Einsiedeln, 1977); ET *The Threefold Garland* (San Francisco, 1982), p. 27.
2 See G. Emery, *La Trinité créatrice: Trinité et création dans les commentaires aux 'Sentences' de Thomas d'Aquin et de ses précurseurs Albert le Grand et Bonaventure* (Paris, 1995).
3 J. Saward, *The Mysteries of March. Hans Urs von Balthasar on the Incarnation and Easter* (London, 1990), p. 7. On the topic of the present chapter I have learnt a great deal from this work.

Balthasar's theology is perhaps the most perfectly Johannine the history of Christian thought has known, and it has as its centre the essential paradox rehearsed in the Fourth Gospel. The glory of God's triune Love finds its supreme manifestation in the human form of the Son precisely as we see that humanity broken on the Cross, obedient unto death. 'I when I be lifted up' – with all the ironic ambivalence of that phrase: at once lifted up on the gibbet and exalted to the Father – 'shall draw all men to myself'.[4] Now for Balthasar, as for Barth, there is both unity and distinction between the economic and the immanent Trinity. In the event of reconciliation on the Cross (which is certainly 'economic' if anything is!) the true character of God – and so the divine immanence, God's 'in-himself-ness' – is seen. In this sense, Karl Rahner's celebrated axiom in the theology of the triune God is right: the economic Trinity *is* the immanent Trinity. But Rahner adds, and here neither Balthasar nor Barth, would follow him, 'and vice versa'. But we *cannot* say without more ado that the immanent Trinity *is* the economic Trinity. To do so would be, however unintentionally, to underplay the gracious condescension of God in what he did on the Cross. On the Cross, God did something which, in terms of the divine immanence, was amazing, utterly unexpected.[5]

The Resurrection too must be seen as a Trinitarian event likewise. That is how Balthasar presents it in the same profound set of Rosary meditations:

> The Father awakens the Son from the dead so that the Son, as one freshly united with the Father, can send forth God's Spirit into the Church.[6]

We shall return to this later but meanwhile we can just note that in these words Balthasar indicates how the Resurrection leads into Pentecost.

In all this Balthasar is presupposing the teaching of the Fifth Ecumenical Council (Constantinople II, 553) to the effect that the 'one hypostasis' (or 'person') in Christ, spoken of by the key formula of the Fourth Council, the better known Chalcedonian Council of 451, is in fact not some composite person brought about by the Incarnation, but really, strictly, the second Trinitarian Person, the pre-existent, uncreated hypostasis of God the Son. This is he who in Mary's womb takes on our nature and in that nature suffers, died and rises again. That is why the entire mystery of Christ has to be seen in terms of the Trinitarian relationships. Or as Balthasar himself puts it, the one Lord Jesus Christ:

> as God *as well as* man ... exists only in his relation to the Father in the unity of the divine Holy Spirit.[7]

The Son, then, in his own personal existence as deployed on earth, *is* the revelation of the Trinity. In vocabulary borrowed from Barth, Christ is the 'concretion' of the triune God, the whole divine Trinity. From this it follows that the drama of our redemption – Christ's costly self-engagement for our

---

4 John 12.32.
5 J. Saward, *The Mysteries of March, op. cit.*, p. 10, with reference to Balthasar's discussion of Rahner's axiom in the theological dramatics.
6 *The Threefold Garland, op. cit.*, p. 110.
7 *Der anti-römische Affekt. Wie lässt sich das Papsttum in der Gesamtkirche integrieren?* (Freiburg, 1974); ET *The Office of Peter and the Structure of the Church* (San Francisco, 1989), p. 136. Italics are original.

salvation – must also be a Trinitarian revelation. Whatever he does or suffers can only be carried out or undergone in a 'filial' way that corresponds to his Trinitarian position, by obedience to the Father in the Holy Spirit – the way, in other words, proper to the Son of God.

For Balthasar it ought to be regarded as axiomatic that just as there can be no Trinitarian doctrine without Christology (something that no doubt all theologians could agree on), so likewise (and this is less often heard), there can be no Christology without Trinitarian doctrine. First: no Trinitarian doctrine without Christology. This tells us that the doctrine of the Trinity is not the result of reason working through the materials of general experience. It has been disclosed to us only in and by the Word made flesh. But then to recall the other side of the coin: there is no Christology – no adequate Christology anyhow – without Trinitarian doctrine. Only if God, eternally, from everlasting, and internally, in his own interior life, is Father, Son and Holy Spirit, can we get the hang of the drama played out in the life of Jesus. That drama cannot be explained without reference to the primordial inter-play of God's inner life, the mutual love of Father and Son in the Holy Spirit. So if we are to understand Jesus Christ God has to be acknowledged as Trinity, not just in revelation – as addressing himself to us in the economy of salvation (as Sabellian modalists and their modern successors held and hold) – but in himself, in his innermost being, in what the Greek fathers call 'the theology': God in his own divine life.

Incarnation and Passion

These preliminaries may help us to grasp the way Balthasar opens his 1969 study *Theologie der Drei Tage*, 'Theology of the Three Days', later published as *Mysterium Paschale*, a title retained in the English translation.[8] This study was itself a contribution to the great multi-authored German-language immediately post-Conciliar dogmatics *Mysterium Salutis* – which, had it been translated into English as it was into Italian and French, might well have exerted a – to coin a word – 'salutary' influence on the very thin not to say reductionist theology too often produced by English-speaking Catholics in the Council's wake. Balthasar begins by considering the rationale of the saving Incarnation which, he argues, after the fashion not only of Thomas but of the great majority of the Fathers likewise, is always looking towards the Cross: that Cross which the Resurrection shows to be our salvation. What binds together the Old Testament promise and the New Testament fulfilment is that one shall come who will set the Covenant to rights. When we hear the Greek Fathers saying that the Incarnation itself, at the Annunciation or at the Nativity or at the Baptism of the Lord – long before the Passion, Death and Resurrection, then – 'changed' human nature, we have to bear in mind, says Balthasar, that the affecting of human nature by the Incarnation is expounded in the East only in relation to the 'entire economy of the divine

8 'Theologie der drei Tagen', in J. Feiner and M. Löhrer (eds), *Mysterium Salutis III/2. Grundriss heilsgeschichtlicher Dogmatik* (Einsiedeln-Cologne, 1970), pp. 133–326. Published as *Mysterium Paschale* (Leipzig, 1983, 2nd edition), and in English translation as *Mysterium Paschale. The Mystery of Easter* (Edinburgh, 1990). References below to 'Mysterium Paschale' will be to that translation.

redemptive work'.[9] The Incarnation looks to the Cross, to Calvary. Are we to say, then, that the Scotist school, and the authors on whom it drew, was simply mistaken in arguing that the Incarnation would have happened anyway even had there been no sin? Not really, says Balthasar, for that school is correct to say, first, that the purpose of the Incarnation was to show God's glory, and secondly that the manifestation of that glory cannot be made into a mere instrument of some other purpose, however salvifically important. As Balthasar puts it in *Mysterium Paschale*:

> Is not God's glorifying of himself in this world here made dependent on man's sin, so that God becomes a means to promote the purposes of the creation?[10]

Implicitly, Balthasar argues that insofar as the later Franciscan school was mistaken, its mistake was not to see that *precisely by becoming savingly incarnate in a world of sin God was able to realize even better the showing of his glory which is the Incarnation's principal end.*

In his sympathetic account of the highly original Thomistic theologian Matthias Joseph Scheeben in the theological aesthetics, Balthasar had already worked out his view on the question of the Incarnation's rationale some years before *Mysterium Paschale* was composed. He took from Scheeben's study of nature and grace, *Natur und Gnade*, the proposal that, while one cannot in so many words defend the Scotist position that the Word would have taken flesh even without the Fall, one can nevertheless admit that the 'nuptial union' of God and the world was not undertaken as a mere means to our redemption.[11] Rather, that union is the supernatural order's 'highest idea', and in that sense both its 'point of departure', and its 'norm'. Balthasar himself tries to resolve the Thomist–Scotist disaccord here by offering a formula which contains an important element of each of the two views. He writes:

> Inasmuch as God serves, washes the feet of his creatures, he discloses himself in what is most properly divine, and makes known his final glory.[12]

The theologian's task, therefore, is to offer an account of the orientation of the Incarnation to the Passion which does not devalue the Incarnation by making it a mere means to the repair of a defective world. In the single *de facto* order of the world, man is to be taken beyond his own limits to a life of sharing in God's glory – not simply a sanation of his own being, a purification and healing. Appealing to the hymn embedded in the text of Paul's Letter to the Ephesians, Balthasar points out that the human creature is predestined to a fullness of more than earthly blessing even before the 'foundation of the world' (Ephesians 1.4). He is elected to stand 'holy and spotless' before his Creator, in the beloved Son, indeed in the beloved Son's *blood*. The significance of Balthasar's stress on the single *de facto* order of the

---

9 *Mysterium Paschale, op. cit.,* p. 20.
10 *Ibid.,* p. 11.
11 *The Glory of the Lord. A Theological Aesthetics. I. Seeing the Form, op. cit.,* pp. 104–17, and especially p. 110.
12 *Mysterium Paschale, op. cit.,* p. 11.

world here can be gauged from the controversy aroused by de Lubac's writing on natural and supernatural – and especially by his book *Surnaturel* at its first appearance. The inference Balthasar drew was that, if there is only a single *de facto* order, the order of salvation, such that 'pure nature' exists only as a 'moment' within this analysable by thought, then the very idea of the human creature – not in itself, admittedly, and yet as it is *in that concrete order of salvation* cannot be determined except by reference to the Trinitarian economy in its fullness. The First Adam is causally linked, in the order of finality, to the Second.

As we know, the Fall, and the advent of sin, massively ruptured the scheme of things. When death came into the world the human essence as it is in God's sight was shattered. Only God can make the fragment which is our present existence, lived as this is towards death, into a meaningful whole. Here Balthasar refers to his earlier collection of essays on man in history, *Das Ganze im Fragment*. Analysing different but complementary modes in which the human creature needs to find wholeness, Balthasar had plotted convergent paths of development whereby the human being (as, at the same time, inhabitant of the cosmos, mind open to the generosity of being in all its breadth, and person capable of addressing a unique 'other') could envisage some ultimate fulfilment or completion. But Balthasar had brought his own beautiful construction tumbling down like a pack of cards by introducing the topic of death, which he called there 'the great rock thrown across the path of all thinking that might lead to completeness'.[13] Only by some kind of resurrection, through the hiatus of death, to a new life in a world-environment that is itself 'in' God, can we reach the fullness of being God wills for us. If the 'whole' is to emerge from the 'fragment', it will only be by way of a point of total breakdown: death, Hades, lostness in distance from God. The decisive act of man's salvation cannot be situated, then, in the Incarnation alone, nor in the earthly ministry of Jesus. Its place is the 'hiatus' of death and nowhere else. If God wanted to experience our human being from within so as to re-align it and raise it to himself he had to act at the point where man is, so to say, at the end of his tether. To bind together the torn ends of man, he did so act. The reality of this 'binding' is seen in the self-identity of the humiliated Jesus and the risen Christ.

Balthasar's scanning of the biblical sources produces the conviction that

> The New Testament is wholly oriented towards the Cross and Resurrection, just as it proceeds from them also.[14]

And Balthasar adds for good measure:

> In this perspective the Old Testament can be considered a first approach to the *Triduum*, itself at once the mind-point and the end of the ways of God.[15]

He brings forward, moreover, a chain of patristic references to show the consensus on this point of the Fathers of East and West. These can be

---

13 *Man in History, op. cit.*, p. 48.
14 *Mysterium Paschale, op. cit.*, p. 20.
15 *Ibid.*

summed up by a statement from the mediaeval Byzantine theologian Nicholas Cabasilas:

> As men were triply sundered from God – by their nature, by their sin, and by their death – the Saviour so worked that they might meet him unhindered and come to be with him directly. This he did by removing successively all obstacles: the first, in that he shared in human nature; the second, in undergoing the death of the Cross; and finally, the third wall of division when he rose from the dead and banished wholly from our nature the tyranny of death.[16]

Balthasar finds in all this divine action to repair the world from within a fundamental change in the God–world relationship. With the Incarnation and Atonement, God subsists as the humanly incarnate one who has known experientially the furthest reaches of this world, down to the abyss of Hell. But if this is not merely rhetoric, says Balthasar, then its claim must be worked out in terms of some kind of kenotic Christology, with the particular set of possibilities for construing a Christian doctrine of God which the theme of kenosis allows. Incarnation means first of all God stooping down, 'descent', before it means man being raised up, 'ascent'. As Balthasar has been insisting ever since 'The Fathers, the Scholastics and Ourselves', the *Abstiegsbewegung* is more primordial than the *Aufstiegsbewegung*. Balthasar begins, as all kenotic theologians do, from the Christological hymn included within the Letter to the Philippians, chapter 2. Christ Jesus:

> though he was in the form of God, did not count equality with God a thing to be grasped, but emptied himself, taking the form of a servant, being born in the likeness of men. And being found in human form, he humbled himself and became obedient unto death, even death on a cross.[17]

That is why, explains the text, 'God has highly exalted him and bestowed on him the name which is above every other name'.[18]

If we look back at Philippians 2 from the standpoint of the ecumenical Councils, notably Ephesus and Chalcedon, we detect in its 'archaic language', says Balthasar, a 'plus factor' to which the established formulae of the unconditional divine changelessness cannot, he thinks, do full justice.[19] The question is, how might we affirm this 'plus' without intolerable paradox, given that the same practice of reading Philippians within the ecclesially determined tradition, also leads us to affirm the unchangeability of the divine nature.

The Kenosis of Christ and the impassibility of God

Basically, Balthasar believes that the precedent set by the fourth-century Church Father, St Hilary of Poitiers, the 'Athanasius of the West', enables us to have our cake and eat it: to accept at any rate a moderate kenotic

16 Nicholas Cabasilas, *On Life in Christ*, 3, cited *ibid.*, p. 22.
17 Philippians 2.6-8.
18 *Ibid.*, 2.9.
19 *Mysterium Paschale, op. cit.*, p. 26.

Christology and a doctrine of God compatible with that Christology while at the same time not abandoning what the biblical and later ecclesial Tradition has to say about the divine changelessness. For Hilary, God whilst abiding in himself (for everything in the Incarnation and Atonement happens according to his sovereign power) can yet leave himself in his 'form of glory'.[20] Hilary avoids the mistakes of modern – in particular nineteenth- and twentieth-century-kenoticists. He realizes that the Incarnation and Cross are not a negation or an abandonment of the divine power. Rather, the divine power is so ordered that it can make room for surprising developments in the God–world relationship, or what Balthasar for his part terms a 'possible self-exteriorisation' of God such as that which is found in the Incarnation and the Cross.[21] In Balthasar's gloss, it is as absolute Love that God's sovereignty manifests itself in these mysteries which do not, therefore, signify a denial of divine power but rather the transcending of the opposition all too familiar to us on earth between power on the one hand and impotence on the other.

As is obvious, Balthasar wants to modify the received picture of the divine unchangeability without altering it out of all recognition. The Church Fathers, when they presented the doctrine of the Incarnation in the context of ancient Graeco–Roman culture, were anxious to distinguish the Church's message from the idea, common in classical mythology, of gods that can change and suffer just as mortals do. The Incarnation, they insisted, is not the changing of God into a human being, an idea totally repugnant to rationality, but rather the assumption, or taking up, of manhood into God. It is a becoming to which no change is attached for God, for the Uncreated, since the change is entirely in the created, in man. For Cyril of Alexandria the divine Word, in becoming incarnate, remained immutable as God – remained what he always was, is and shall be. Applying this to the Redemption, as distinct from the Incarnation, we get the idea that, though the Son assumed and also suffered in a passible human nature for our sake, in his divine nature he remained by contrast absolutely impassible. A century before Cyril Athanasius had declared that the same person suffers as man but not as God. The opinion of such Fathers of the Conciliar faith has to be of considerable weight.

Balthasar's approach to the immutability and impassibility of God – already signalled in *Mysterium Paschale* but not fully worked out until the last volumes of the theological dramatics twenty years later, is one of the more original, and therefore controversial, aspects of his thought. In theology, as in marriage annulment, the burden of proof lies with those who would question the reality in possession. However, Balthasar does not depart in any flagrant way from the witness on this point of the majority of the Fathers, strongly continued as it is in Christian Scholasticism.[22] Unlike the character Thibault in Helen Waddell's novel about Peter Abelard, Balthasar rejects 'Patripassianism' – the notion that the Father suffers in the same way as the Son does. He is, moreover, impatient with the view of some modern biblical theologians that the impassibility of the divine nature in Scripture is just another way of referring to God's faithfulness to his Covenant, the attitude of

20 Cited, from Hilary's *De Trinitate*, at *ibid.*, p. 27.
21 *Ibid.*, p. 29.
22 Cf. J. K. Mosley, *The Impassibility of God. A Survey of Christian Thought* (Cambridge, 1926).

fidelity by which he promises he will remain unchangeably faithful to his word. For Balthasar, through that 'economic' attitude of the biblical God – unflinching faithfulness – Scripture glimpses an attribute of God as he is in himself – unchangeableness, and so a strictly *theological* divine attribute. The reason why God is unshakeably faithful to his Covenant is that in his divine nature he actually is essentially unmoveable.

However, and this is the point where Balthasar diverges from a more 'standard' position, he also thinks that in the period after the patristic age theologians came to treat the impassibility of God more narrowly than had the Fathers themselves. When Scripture speaks of the divine pity, the divine wrath, the divine tenderness and so forth, these are not simply anthropomorphic accommodations to a human way of talking. Rather, these terms typically used by and of human subjects have an objective correlate in God himself. These objective correlates Balthasar will come to call, by the end of the writing of the theological dramatics, forms of the divine vitality, the divine ultra-livingness. They are to be understood by analogy with emotions, even though they could not be regarded *as* emotions without drawing God into 'passibility' in some quite univocal sense.

So though Balthasar is at one with the Scholastics in maintaining that there cannot be change or suffering in God in any straightforward, univocal sense, he considers nonetheless that the way the Scholastics presented divine immutability often failed to express the dynamism, the sheer 'event-quality', or eventfulness, of God's own inner life. (Barth had seen in the description of the divine being as *Actus purus*, sheer act, a way of saying how God is maximally *Ereignis*, 'event'.) And his conclusion is that, in the light of the externalization of that life in the Incarnation and Passion, we should be willing to admit that there is in God that which makes his sharing human pain as man conceivable. That is, of course, an onward reference to Balthasar's theology of the Atonement. It is true that the Son suffers as man, not as God. Yet there is something about the Godhead that makes it possible for a divine person to suffer humanly.

Balthasar was aided in these reflections by the book *Dieu, souffre-t-il?* from the hand of the Gregorianum Jesuit Jean Galot.[23] For Galot all the negative experiences ('les renonciations') incarnate crucified Love accepted in the work of our salvation have their source and archetype in the mutual out-goingness of the Trinitarian persons – what he called the 'intra-Trinitarian ecstasy', from the Greek word *ekstasis*, a 'standing outside oneself'. In other words, as between Father, Son and Holy Spirit in eternity there is already a constant renunciation of self – and precisely this is the condition of possibility for a suffering *divine*–human Saviour. Balthasar wrote this idea into the foreword for the second edition of *Mysterium Paschale*, which was published in the German Democratic Republic (surprisingly), at Leipzig, in 1983. It became increasingly important to him, as the later volumes of the theological dramatics show. In that 1983 foreword, Balthasar expresses his conviction that a kenotic teaching acceptable to Catholic doctrine would begin from what he called the eternal 'event' of the divine processions, supra-temporal yet ever actual. If he had spoken of the divine nature itself as full of eventful

---

23 J. Galot, SJ, *Dieu, souffre-t-il?* (Rome, 1976).

vitality, that, he now implied, has to do with the way it is possessed by the Trinitarian persons – the way the divine essence is, as he put it:

'given' in the self-gift of the Father, 'rendered' in the thanksgiving of the Son, and 'represented' in its character as absolute love by the Holy Spirit.[24]

Speaking of an 'eternal "super-kenosis"' in God, Balthasar declared that:

Everything that can be thought and imagined where God is concerned is, in advance, included and transcended in this self-destitution which constitutes the person of the Father, and, at the same time, those of the Son and the Spirit.[25]

In effect Balthasar expanded the high mediaeval Scholastic teaching about the manner the creation of the world is shaped by the Trinitarian relationships within the Creator God – expanded it by making the shaping power of the Trinitarian relationships encompass the events of the Atonement likewise. As he put it:

God as the 'gulf' [or 'abyss'] ... of absolute Love contains in advance, eternally, all the modalities of love, of compassion, and even of a 'separation' motivated by love and founded on the infinite distinction between the hypostases – modalities which may manifest themselves in the course of a history of salvation involving sinful humankind.[26]

And so Balthasar could conclude:

God, then, has no need to 'change' when he makes a reality of the wonders of his charity, wonders which include the Incarnation and, more particularly, the Passion of Christ, and, before him, the dramatic history of God with Israel and, no doubt, with humanity as a whole. All the contingent 'abasements' of God [compare Galot's 'les renonciations'] are forever included and outstripped in the eternal event of Love.[27]

By the time he came to write his theological dramatics, Balthasar had also found perhaps unexpected independent confirmation of his large interpretation of divine changelessness in the Neo-Thomist philosopher and lay theologian Jacques Maritain. Writing in the *Revue Thomiste* for 1969, the year when the first edition of *Mysterium Paschale* appeared under its original German title *Theologie der Drei Tagen* Maritain, who would die four years later, had a proposal to make about what could be considered a neglected divine attribute.[28] As with all creaturely perfections, there must be something in God corresponding to that wonderful quality of some human beings whereby they accept pain in a really generous and even triumphant spirit – as distinct from a spirit that could be called either resigned or resentful or masochistic – and are ennobled by that victorious acceptance. Maritain found

24 *Mysterium Paschale, op. cit.*, p. viii.
25 *Ibid.*
26 *Ibid.*, pp. viii–ix.
27 *Ibid.*, p. ix.
28 J. Maritain, 'Quelques réflexions sur le savoir théologique', *Revue thomiste* 77 (1969), pp. 5–27.

here an essential attribute of God, though it is one for which, as he conceded, we have at least in the best-known European languages no obvious single word. Insisting that, unlike our suffering, this quality involves no imperfection in God, he treated it as an integral aspect of the divine beatitude, the divine bliss.[29]

Balthasar took this intuition of Maritain's and incorporated it into his concept of God's specifically Trinitarian 'livingness', his vitality – a term already used in *Mysterium Paschale*.[30] The 'selflessness' and even 'recklessness' with which Father and Son surrender themselves to each other in the Holy Spirit from everlasting to everlasting enables in time the atoning suffering of Christ. In the final volume of the dramatics, he presented the mutual surrender of the Persons as without safeguards of any kind. The Trinitarian Persons are at one and the same time utterly impassible and yet absolutely defenceless. Or, as John Saward has expressed matters:

> In their transparency to each other as subsistent relations, they are selves without self-protection.[31]

In her meditations 'At the Heart of the Redemptive Mystery', Adrienne von Speyr had spoken of this as the 'ever-open wound' in the Holy Trinity, a 'wound' that is neither more nor less than the Trinitarian processions themselves.[32] And this for Balthasar is the ultimate explanation of the manger of Bethlehem, the *via crucis* to Golgotha. The incarnate Word loves with an 'extravagance' which mirrors the unrestrained 'recklessness' in the Trinity, as each person finds himself only in constantly giving himself away to the others.[33] Jesus' life is therefore oriented to that 'hour' he speaks of in the Fourth Gospel when this unguarded love can demonstrate its mettle fully for the first time. And this happens when it comes into collision with the all-resistant brick wall that is the selfishness of sinful humanity. Divine recklessness meets human selfishness head-on. Nor is the prodigality of God's self-giving, shown on the Cross brought to an end by the resurrection. In Christ's heavenly intercession, the Lamb stands for ever 'as slain' beside the Father, just as, in the expression of that intercession which is the Eucharistic Sacrifice and the Real Presence in the Tabernacle, Christ continues to pour himself out for the redeemed in the Holy Eucharist.

Balthasar's general conclusion, then, is that God is not mutable in the way ancient mythology maintains but nor is he immutable in the way some philosophy would have it. Certainly he is not subject to the imperfections that creaturely change and notably suffering imply. Nonetheless in his triune Love he is more surprising than the words 'immutable' and 'impassible' might lead us to suppose.

Influenced as he was by the Russian Orthodox theologian Sergei Bulgakov and the English Congregationalist Peter Taylor Forsyth, Balthasar would surely have agreed with a modern Anglican theologian who, recognizing

---

29 Also against a Thomist background the English Dominican Gerald Vann spoke about an eternal 'will to share' – a 'mystery in which compassion and triumph are one', *The Pain of Christ and the Sorrow of God* (London, 1947; 1954, 4th edition), p. 70.
30 *Mysterium Paschale, op. cit.*, p. 35.
31 J. Saward, *The Mysteries of March, op. cit.*, p. 14.
32 A. von Speyr, *Au coeur du Mystère rédempteur* (Paris, 1980), p. 40.
33 J. Saward, *The Mysteries of March, op. cit.*, p. 14.

what he terms the 'metaphysical naivety' of much nineteenth-century kenotic Christology, nevertheless sums up:

> Some element of kenotic theory must undoubtedly be called upon to give an account, as far as human language permits, of this paradoxical fact of a genuinely human life lived out from a centre in deity.[34]

Unlike, however, those Incarnation-centred Anglicans, chiefly of the Liberal Catholic school, who seem content to leave the doctrine of the Atonement to Evangelicals, Balthasar worked closely with the axiom, Whoever says Incarnation says Cross. Balthasar went out of his way to commend those theologians who, like the New Testament Letters, had kept together a soteriology of abstract concepts – redemption, justification – with sustained reference to the person of the Saviour, the *concretissimum*, the God-man. He singles out for praise in this connexion the late mediaeval German Dominican John Tauler and two very different figures of the sixteenth century: Ignatius Loyola and Martin Luther. But his strongest approval goes to three relatively obscure writers in French who wrote what he considers the kind of theology of the Passion of the Word incarnate we need by holding together conceptual or Scholastic and affective or spiritual theology: Jean de la Ceppède, who was broadly Ignatian in his approach, the Oratorian Jean-Jacques Duguet, and the Dominican Louis Chardon whose 1647 *La Croix de Jésus où les plus belles vérités de la théologie mystique et de la grâce sanctifiante sont établies* was reprinted by the Dominican publishing house Editions du Cerf in 1937.[35] But indeed it is time now to turn to the death of Christ.

The bridge over the hiatus

In *Mysterium Paschale* Balthasar refers to the death of Christ as 'the hiatus'. In one sense, he explains, every death is a hiatus. Christians must not obscure this truth by too easily drawing in the hope of resurrection. He wrote:

> Between the death of a human being, which is by definition the end from which he cannot return, and what we term 'resurrection' there is no common measure.[36]

But there is also something absolutely unique about the death of Jesus which itself is 'a hiatus' in no common sense. Balthasar invokes the profound liturgical poetry of the Byzantine hymnographer St Romanos the Melodist. Christ's death is the realization of all Godlessness, as expressed in the sin of the world. One who is God in human kind assumes what is radically contrary to the divine and in the moment of his fullest self-concealment discloses himself most effulgently. The glory of God is shown forth in the death of Jesus under, through, in and by means of its contrary, since all this was endured for love: love for us. He became poor, St Paul tells the Corinthians, so that you might become rich (2 Corinthians 8.9). From now on, any

---

34 B. Hebblethwaite, *The Incarnation. Collected Essays in Christology* (Cambridge, 1987), p. 67.
35 See the excellent introductory analysis by F. Florand, OP, in *La Croix de Jésus où les plus belles vérités de la théologie mystique et de la grâce sanctifiante sont établies, par le P. Louis Chardon, O. P.* (Paris, 1937), pp. XI–CLXI.
36 *Mysterium Paschale, op. cit.*, p. 50.

theology worthy of the name must take its intrinsic character and structure from what Paul calls the 'word of the Cross'. Balthasar writes:

> ... the death, and the dying away into the silence, of the Logos so became the centre of what he has to say for himself that we have to understand precisely his non-speaking as his final revelation, his utmost word.[37]

The Paschal Mystery is the true centre not only of Balthasarian theology but of any theology worth considering. We must not, warns Balthasar, be fobbed off with any counterfeits: theologies that in effect reduce revelation to a human philosophy by treating the Crucifixion as essentially symbolic. But the Crucifixion is not a general symbolic idea, which could be expressed analogically in various world-views – featuring as, for example, a law of history or a law of existence. The Cross of Christ is not to be made into an example of some general truth about the essentially tragic nature of the human struggle towards perfection. Philosophy, when it attempts a takeover of the Cross, always betrays itself by claiming to know either too much or too little. Too much, because it makes bold with words and concepts at a point when the Word of God is silent, suffers and dies so as to reveal what no philosophy can know except through faith: namely: God's ever greater Trinitarian love. Too little, because philosophy does not measure that abyss into which the Word sinks down, having no inkling of the true dimensions of the hiatus concerned. Here only theology, tutored by the sources of revelation, can serve our turn. So Balthasar is strongly opposed to what he calls the 'turning of the Cross into philosophy'.[38]

The 'bridge over the hiatus' is not accessible to human reason, it is found only in the destiny of God made man, and in human destiny through him alone. As Balthasar explains, Christian preaching consists in the proclamation of the Risen Crucified One, and that is the continuation of Jesus' self-proclamation. Only he can bridge over the hiatus since he took it up into his own continuity in the Resurrection. Balthasar cites St Paul's Second Letter to the Corinthians again:

> He died for all that those who live might live no longer for themselves but for him who for their sake died and was raised (5: 15).

Balthasar comments:

> The descent of One alone into the abyss became the ascent of all from the same depths, and the condition of possibility for dialectical change-about lies on the one hand in the 'for all' of the descent (and so not just in the 'dying' but in becoming a holocaust outside the camp of God [cf Hebrews 13. 11ff.]), and on the other in the prototypical Resurrection with which this passage deals. Without that Resurrection, Christ would sink into the abyss, but 'all' would not be raised. He must be, then, the 'first-fruits of those who have fallen asleep' (I Corinthians 15: 20), the 'first-born from the dead' (Colossians 1: 18).[39]

---

37 *Ibid.*, p. 79.
38 *Ibid.*, p. 63.
39 *Ibid.*, p. 53.

A theology of Good Friday

Not only the Scriptures but also the Creed, indeed, assert that the divine Son became incarnate, died and rose again not for himself but 'for us', *pro nobis, huper hêmôn*. In his Rosary book, *The Threefold Garland*, Balthasar calls these simple words of the 'pro nobis' the 'first and most fundamental word of the Christian faith'.[40] 'Pro nobis' does not mean simply 'for our benefit' or 'in solidarity with us'. Neither of these descriptions of the death is wrong, but both are inadequate. When the Church affirms that the incarnate Son suffered and died 'for' us what she intends first and foremost to say, according to Balthasar, is that *he changed places with us*. His atoning work was above all a work of vicarious substitution: in German, *Stellvertretung*. Paul wrote in Second Corinthians, 'For us God made him to be sin who knew no sin, so that in him we might become the righteousness of God'.[41] He became what we were so that we might become what he is. The sinless Son put himself in the situation of sinners so that they could be re-situated as sons in the Son, and so in the bosom of the Father – which is where the Johannine Prologue declares the Son's place to be. He took on himself, for St Paul, the weight of our guilt so that we might enjoy the glorious freedom of the sons of God.

Already in the Incarnation, by what the Roman Liturgy calls an 'admirable exchange', he had taken on himself the poverty of our humanity, so that we might become rich with his divinity.[42] Now in the Atonement, he confirms that exchange by a climactic dramatic gesture that constitutes the turning-point of the whole history of God with man and man with God. Drawing on Karl Barth, Balthasar declares that in the Atonement God makes his own the being of the humanity opposed to him through sin, but without in any way collaborating in our opposition.

Despite homing in on the word *Stellvertretung*, Balthasar does not want to be confined to just one perspective in his 'staurology', his theology of the Cross. He has no inclination to reduce the mystery of the Cross to a single formula. Like St Thomas, he is insistent that no one concept can subsume that mystery under itself.[43] As the theological dramatics will make plain, Balthasar regards the New Testament writers as unfolding four other aspects of the Atonement, but he still regards these as held together – coherently united – by the *Stellvertretung* idea. The redemptive act was, firstly, *in its essence* the Father's giving-up of the Son, which can also be described as the Son's letting himself be given up by the Father. Secondly, the *purpose* of the atoning act was, put *negatively*, our liberation from sin, death and the powers of evil at large, while looking at the same issue of *purpose* from a *positive* angle, the goal of the Atonement was, thirdly, our entry into the divine life of the Holy Trinity. The final aspect of the Cross identified by Balthasar from the evidence of the New Testament witnesses identifies the *source* from which the purposive essential acting, at once negative and positive, proceeds. And this is the love which the Holy Trinity is.[44] As with the Incarnation, the entire

40 *The Threefold Garland, op. cit.*, p. 91.
41 2 Corinthians 5.21.
42 Cf. 2 Corinthians 8.9.
43 See A. Nichols, OP, 'St Thomas Aquinas on the Passion of Christ. A Reading of *Summa theologiae* IIIa., q. 46', *Scottish Journal of Theology* 43 (1990), pp. 447–59.
44 J. Saward, *The Mysteries of March, op. cit.*, p. 40.

Trinity was involved in the Passion of Christ where Balthasar gives the Holy Spirit a larger role than do many theologians. As he writes:

[Jesus'] inspiration by the Father... is not simply the inner *élan* of his love, but submission to the rule and leading of the Holy Spirit of mission who 'impels' him. In the time of the Son's abasement, the Spirit (proceeding eternally from Father and from Son) receives a primacy over the Son who obeys him (and by him obeys the Father): this constitutes the expression of the fact that all of his existence is ordered, functionally and kenotically, to the Cross.[45]

No staurology can begin to be adequate to Catholic faith unless it grasps simultaneously something like all these dimensions. This emphasis on the multidimensional nature of what was done on the Cross, and, especially the stress on its proceeding from the unconditional triune love, already distinguishes Balthasar's account somewhat from those of the Continental Reformers, notably Luther and Calvin.

But then in addition, and this too cuts him off from much of Protestant Evangelicalism, Balthasar also rejects the notion of specifically *penal* substitution. In his collected sermons on the liturgical year, *You Crown the Year with Your Goodness*, we read:

There is no sense in which we can say that God the Father 'punishes' the suffering Son in our place. There can be no question of punishment, for the work accomplished here between Father and Son with the co-operation of the Holy Spirit is pure love, love most undefiled, and therefore a supremely voluntary work, on the part of the Son as much as on the part of the Father and the Spirit. The love of God is so rich that it can assume even this form of darkness out of love for our dark world.[46]

I shall come back in a moment to Balthasar's emphatic statement that nonetheless we must continue to speak in this context of the burning *wrath* of God.

Because Christ is God – because he is infinitely all-embracing – his human sufferings have an inclusiveness that enables them to affect the condition of the world at large. His uniqueness as the God-man, the man who is God, is the ground of his relationship to all human beings as their Head, the Second Adam. Only because he is both man and God is Christ able to substitute himself, to take upon himself the otherwise unsustainable weight of the guilt of the whole world. The unique way Jesus Christ *is* also explains the way that once he has carried out his substitutionary act, once he has put it in place, he can also take us up into it. In *Mysterium Paschale* Balthasar has this to say:

This absolutely unique man ... is unique precisely because he is God. And for this and for no other reason he can give a share in his once-for-all Cross to his fellow human beings, with whom he is in deeper solidarity than any man could ever be with another. He can give them

45 *Mysterium Paschale, op. cit.*, p. 91.
46 *Du krönst das Jahr mit deiner Huld. Radiopredigten* (Einsiedeln, 1982); ET *You Crown the Year with Your Goodness. Radio Sermons* (San Francisco, 1989), p. 85.

in other words, a share in his death, where every man otherwise is absolutely alone.[47]

Only Christ can reconcile the world to God, which is then in one sense a solitary task. Yet he wants others to participate in it. Writing of the agony in the Garden Balthasar describes the sleeping disciples as the 'absent presence of the Church at the side of the suffering Head'.[48] So they were a failure. That does not mean that Christ's intention was frustrated. It was efficaciously expressed earlier that same day in the institution of the Eucharist. In instituting that sacramental sacrifice, Christ actively incorporates the participants into the power of his death, where the offering to the Father of his body and blood is spirit and life.[49] Balthasar calls the 'hour' that is the Passion of Christ the 'quite decisively unique suffering of substituted Abandonment'.[50] Insofar as it is unique, we are, he admits, inevitably distanced from it. Yet to some degree we can approach it and gain an understanding of it. That happens notably in two ways. First, through the study of the Old Testament, where various representative figures such as Job or the unnamed Suffering Servant in the Book of Isaiah experience abandonment by God as something worse even then death, since this is the loss of the grace of the covenant – not just life in general, but *life with God*. Secondly, through the Church that originated in the New Testament, for the Holy Spirit has initiated Christians through the centuries into what Balthasar terms the 'inexpressible depths of the Cross and the Descent into Hell'.[51] He calls for example St John of the Cross's experience of spiritual 'dark nights' experience of the 'inner condition' of Hell as the loss of God.[52]

Looking at the Passion more widely, we can say that while only one who is God, One of the Trinity, can as man die 'for all', there is a peculiar congruence about the fact that the Trinitarian person who actually died for all was also the *Word* through whom, as the Johannine Prologue and various New Testament hymns put it, all things were made. The Trinitarian One who died was the second Trinitarian person, the Logos, the universal Word through whom, with whom and for whom all things were made. His being that Word and no other explains how he can communicate to the human nature united to his own person something of his divine universality without, however, robbing that human nature of its particularity. And this prepares us for the discovery that his vicarious reconciling action on Calvary is not only something exclusive. It is also something inclusive – inclusive of ourselves, of the entire human race. This is the deepest reason why Balthasar can call Christ the true 'concrete universal' sought in vain by Hegel. As the Balthasar scholar Medard Kehl has commented:

---

47 *Mysterium Paschale, op. cit.*, p. 138.
48 *Ibid.*, p. 101.
49 For Balthasar's account of the Sacrifice-meal, see *ibid.*, pp. 95–100.
50 *Ibid.*, p. 72.
51 *Ibid.*, p. 76.
52 *Ibid.*, pp. 78–79.

Perfect 'exclusivity' (i.e. to be incomparably unique) and perfect 'inclusivity' (i.e. to be infinitely integrative and perfecting) are not excluded in Christ but require and promote one another.[53]

The sinless God-man acts exclusively in doing what only he can do, but he acts inclusively in standing in for us as our Head.

For Balthasar, Christ's divinely absolute innocence and quintessentially Trinitarian vulnerability are the keys to his capacity to be in this way our representative substitute. Modern commentators on religion and human affairs sometimes give the impression that, as perhaps in the novels of Graham Greene, the *non*-innocent – sinners – are the essentially sympathetic characters. But the word 'sympathetic' can hardly be more misplaced than when linked to sinfulness. As Balthasar points out, the more a person is attached to sin, the less in fact he or she is capable of placing themselves – whether mentally or really – in someone else's position, to see things from their standpoint. Sin is essentially self-enclosure, in one respect or another. It is a hindrance and often a crippling one to self-outpouring love. And so a sinful self-substituting Redeemer would be a contradiction in terms. But in any case, not even the greatest saint could bear and could carry away the guilt of all his or her brethren, all the world. This is why once again we have to say, No Christology – and in this case no theology of the Redeemer – without Trinitarian doctrine. Whereas the sinful human being is always able to shield himself or herself by growing a protective shell, a carapace, the divine Son, even in his human condition, is for the reasons connected with triune personhood we have looked at, essentially incapable of following this example. He is and can only be absolutely vulnerable. Through hypostatic union with his literally selfless divine person – for the Trinitarian persons *are*, as Thomas Aquinas says, their relationships, the human heart of Christ is vulnerable to the total limit. It is absolutely incapable of non-compassion.

Balthasar's account of the Lord's sin-bearing is graphic and could well furnish materials for a rich devotion to the Passion of Christ as well as numerous sermons and meditations for Passiontide. The Lamb of God, who as the truly Innocent One, alone sees freely enacted evil for what it is, wants to bear away this hideous insult to the Father's goodness which is at the same time the source of human woes. In his Rosary book, *The Threefold Garland*, Balthasar writes of the Atonement:

> Christ gathers up into himself ... the world's sin, which offends the goodness of the Father, in order to burn it utterly in the fire of his suffering. The Father is henceforth to perceive this sin as being only fuel for the Son's love: 'Behold the Lamb of God, [the scapegoat,] who takes away the sin of the world [into the desert, into a place which is out of sight and unreachable]'.[54]

The suffering of Christ, is, then, primarily spiritual. But Balthasar sees his physical torments as the perverse sacrament of this spiritual agony. In the

53 M. Kehl, SJ, 'Einführung: Hans Urs von Balthasar: ein Porträt', in *idem* and W. Löser (eds), *In der Fülle des Glaubens: Hans Urs von Balthasar-Lesebuch* (Freiburg, 1980); ET M. Kehl, SJ and W. Löser (eds), *The Von Balthasar Reader* (New York and Edinburgh, 1982), p. 30.

54 *The Threefold Garland*, *op. cit.*, p. 71.

same Rosary book – which in its doctrinal thoroughness is in many ways a throwback to seventeenth-century treatises on the Rosary mysteries, aimed to justify the adage *Rosarium est magis praedicandi quam orandi* – Balthasar calls the Lord's scourging, his crowning with thorns, and the driving of the nails into his body the 'obscene sacrament' of the world's sins which were at that moment being so to speak forcibly knocked into his total divine and human person.[55]

Yet, consonant with the fundamental Balthasarian soteriology, for which the saving substitution on the Cross manifests not the Father's will to punish the guilty but the triune Love, all the events of the Passion serve only to display this intra-Trinitarian mutual commitment of the Father and the Son in the Holy Spirit. How so? In his eternal divine love for the Father the Son wants to do all he can to renew the Father's fallen world, while the Father, by sending the Son into a world that was made through him, wants all things to be reconciled and integrated in the person of his Son. And just because divine love is committed in the Passion so is divine wrath. The wrath of God is the form God's love takes when it meets the resistance of sin. The Father could not be angry with his beloved Son. Nor could he ever cease to love his creatures. But he *is* angry – in the non-univocal sense in which emotions can be ascribed to the divine – when he sees the self-destructive folly of his creatures' wickedness: the sin of the world that the Son is ready to bear. The Son, allowing himself to be given up, abandons himself to the impact of the Father's negation of sin – that is, to the fire of the Father's ultra-positive love as of its nature that burns and must burn whatever is love-less. 'In that cross-fire, the Trinity is revealed as an eternal communion of love.'[56]

The ultimate paradox, or mystery, of the Cross is that the Father's economic abandonment of the Son is what reveals the *homoousion*, the unity of substance of the triune life, the union of persons in the divine being. In his love for his consubstantial Son, the Father makes for all eternity an infinite space in which the Son can respond to him. In his abandonment on the Cross, the Son presses this distance to the uttermost so as to enter the sinner's condition of Godlessness from the inside. But precisely because this is the fullest correspondence there can be with the Father's will, the seeming abandonment proves that highest unity reigns between them. The distance in question is itself both sustained and overcome by the third Trinitarian person, the Holy Spirit – the hypostasis who proceeds from the Father, the Giver, and from the Son, the Receiver. It is the task of the Holy Spirit to bring about, within the absolute distinction and in that sense distance between Father and Son their highest possible unity, their supreme intimacy. It is through his being led by the Holy Spirit that the incarnate and crucified Son lets the Father's love for the world once made in the Word burn up the dross of human evil which is spoiling the world, and which he now carries in concentrated form in his own humanized person.

And the telltale result of that redeeming work will be the creation of the Church as itself a communion of love.[57] In the life of the redeemed,

55 *Ibid.*, p. 79. The Latin tag may be translated, 'The Rosary is more to be preached than prayed'.
56 J. Saward, *The Mysteries of March, op. cit.*, p. 52.
57 *Mysterium Paschale, op. cit.*, p. 134.

estrangement from others, where we are different from each other in an evil way that produces spite and conflict, gives way to 'good' otherness, the otherness of love where I can rejoice in the difference of others and enter communion with them without any possibility of either my identity or theirs being placed at risk. The Church is thus to be a communion in the likeness of the divine life. Thanks to the 'pro nobis', Christ's blood seals a new and everlasting covenant by which the Trinitarian life flows over into the world – not, however, before it has in Christ descended into Hell.

Holy Saturday

Balthasar's theology of Holy Saturday may be said to begin with the dying Lord's experience of Godlessness on the Cross. In his account of the last hours of Jesus, Balthasar, aided and abetted by Adrienne von Speyr, departs from the Scholastic tradition, including St Thomas, and the more common teaching in the Church. He does so by the *total* way in which he understands Christ's dereliction. Although Balthasar does not understand Jesus' 'cry' as reported by St Matthew (27.46) as one of despair or even protest but as a cry of *obedience*, he does interpret it as an entry into Godforsakenness (if not only that). In obedience to the Father's plan, out of love for humanity in its spiritual misery, the Son renounces all perceptible contact with the Father so as to experience in himself the sinner's distance from God. Since no one knows and loves the Father as the Son does, none can be more abandoned. All that is left is hard obedience. But even when forsaken by the Father, he remains Father-centred. In a spiritual darkness deeper than that known by any mystic (though for Balthasar the dark nights reported by the mystics are some kind of participation in it), he dies surrendering himself into the Father's hands. For Balthasar this is the essential sacrifice that makes our peace with God. The hour when the Son glorifies the Father is the hour of darkness when the Son identifies with the sinner in the estrangement from God produced by the sinner's 'No!'. In the way he does this, the Saviour enters into solidarity with all those who feel abandoned or forgotten by God experiencing with them and for them God's absence. We should not fail to note how this ultra-negative is also, for the Christian doctrine of salvation, the most ultra-positive thing imaginable.

> In the same sense in which the cry is the end of the articulated Logos on earth, it is, as the cry of redemption, the new beginning of true speech on earth.[58]

Nonetheless, Balthasar does go beyond the common teaching, which has been more concerned to exclude any notion that the Atonement entails some kind of inner disintegration of the triune life or imperils the continuing conscious communion of Jesus with the Father. For the Scholastics, even during his Passion Jesus did not cease to enjoy the beatific vision of his Father – though he felt, they considered, a sorrow surpassing all the suffering endured or endurable by human beings. For St Thomas this is to be explained by the different levels or ranges of experience open to Christ's human soul. At the apex of his soul Jesus always looks on the face of his

---

58 *Man in History, op. cit.*, pp. 282–83.

Father, even on the Cross; it is just that his human will to suffer for us prevented this bliss from flowing down to the lower slopes of the soul where, on the contrary, he is in agony. In this region, as Pope John Paul II commented in his letter *Salvifici doloris*, Jesus' soul is a wasteland. In the sphere of the feelings and affections, he no longer registers the presence of the Father. This lack of interior consolation is the greatest of his agonies. This goes some way towards Balthasar's position but without abandoning that of St Thomas whom, we can note, understands the Father's 'abandonment' of the Son in a very low-key way, as, rather, the Father's non-protection of the Son against his enemies. At the same time, Balthasar's denial that the apex or 'peak' of Jesus' created spirit continued to enjoy, on the Cross, the beatific vision does not amount to a complete reversal of the dogmatic intention of Aquinas's teaching to the contrary, since Balthasar considers the dereliction to be the most radical form of the mutual love of Father and Son in the Holy Spirit. But, as John Saward has written:

> It is at least arguable that the greatest possible spiritual suffering is not so much the Godforsakenness of One who *hitherto* has enjoyed the vision of the Father but rather the feeling of God's absence in a soul that still, at some level, rests in his presence.[59]

Louis de Chardon, Balthasar's admiration for whom we have noted, argued that the same fullness of grace in Jesus' soul was the principle *both* of its 'unconquerable joy' *and* of its 'inconceivably immense sorrow'.[60]

Be this as it may, Balthasar continues the extremely strong stress on the negativities of the Atonement when he follows the Lord's journey into the pit. The descent of the Logos in the Incarnation, giving as it does powerful expression to the divine initiative in human redemption – the Father's prevenient love and mercy in sending his Son to pick us up when we were fallen – already stands in sharp contrast to all schemes of human ascent to the divine by what we might term a surge of self-transcendence. Such schemes are legion, not only in ancient religious traditions like that of India but also in the fine literature and philosophy of nineteenth- and twentieth-century Germany. But being found in human form, the Word humbled himself further, not only to the death on the Cross but even lower still, to Sheol, to the realm of the dead, the epitome of human wretchedness. Among other things, Balthasar is very much a theologian of the most neglected clause of the Apostles' Creed: he descended into Hell.

Balthasar's theological understanding of this clause was shaped by his spiritual direction of Adrienne von Speyr who, as we have seen, enjoyed – if that is the right word – a mystical experience of the mysteries of Holy Saturday beginning at 3 o'clock on the afternoon of Good Friday and lasting till the early hours of Easter Sunday morning. As she herself put it in *Kreuz und Hölle*, 'The Lord does not rise from the Cross but from the Hell of Holy Saturday'.[61] As we say in the Roman Canon in the prayer beginning *Unde et memores* 'we call to mind the blessed Passion of Christ thy Son our Lord, and also his Resurrection

---

59 J. Saward, *The Mysteries of March, op. cit.*, pp. 57–58.
60 *Ibid.*, with a reference to L. de Chardon, OP, *La Croix de Jésus, op. cit.*, p. 48, but also *passim*.
61 A. von Speyr, *Kreuz und Hölle* I, *op. cit.*, p. 275.

from Hell, *ab inferis resurrectione'*. Von Speyr and Balthasar conclude from credal, mystical and liturgical sources that the Descent into Hell is not a peripheral article of our faith but marks the centre of the Paschal Mystery and accordingly the centre of revelation as a whole. It is the true terminus of the Crucifixion as well as the starting-point of the Resurrection.

But what is this 'Hell'? It is what an older theology called *limbus patrum*, the 'Limbo of the fathers' – our ancestors. According to both St Peter's Pentecost sermon in the second chapter of the Acts of the Apostles and the First Letter of Peter, between the Crucifixion and Easter morning the soul of Jesus sojourned in Sheol, sometimes translated 'the underworld' – using there the imagery of descent common in evoking the post-mortem state in poetry as well as the Scriptures.

Balthasar argues that until the Cross and Resurrection there could only be the more or less undifferentiated Sheol of the ancestors.[62] Here he goes beyond writers like St Thomas for whom before Christ there was no heaven, no enjoyment of the beatific vision (except for the good angels), but there was Hell and the inter-mediate state, already becoming known in his day as Purgatory.[63] For Balthasar, however, there was before Christ neither Hell (in the ordinary theological sense of that word) nor Purgatory either. All three – Heaven, Hell, Purgatory – are effects of Christ's descent among the dead on Holy Saturday. It is by the differentiated response of the dead, the ancestors, to the Christ of what the Byzantine tradition calls 'Great Saturday' that these conditions of life for the separated soul are finally established.

But why *did* Christ go down into Hell, the *limbus patrum*, Sheol, thus understood? The primary reason given by von Speyr is that our compassionate High Priest wished to have first-hand experience not only of our dying but also of our being dead. This, for what it is worth, agrees with the Scholastics. Hell is where the search for the lost sheep ended. Though, like von Speyr and Balthasar, Thomas Aquinas too maintains that strictly speaking Christ did go down to Sheol as the Risen One but rather as a dead man united to the Word, what we find in these twentieth-century Swiss commentators is a reiterated emphasis on the sheer powerlessness of Christ's separated human spirit in this engulfing experience of death, and not just death in general but the sinner's death apart from God. As portrayed in the Hebrew Bible, Sheol is a place of helplessness, isolation, inaction, remoteness from God and man. All these motifs are painted in the darkest colours by our authors. In *Science, Religion and Christianity* Balthasar opined:

> It is a shortcoming of Western theology that it does not consider seriously enough from what God has redeemed us ... In the Old Covenant death means having to leave the region of light and life, which are taken in an indivisibly natural-supernatural sense ... Faith, hope and love have their home in heaven; they cannot dwell where heaven is closed and the ruling reality is ... exclusion from the vision of God. Death is the same reality as seen by the apocalyptic seer: the Fourth Horseman of the secret revelation is 'death, followed by hell', the gate of hell that introduces man into the lost region of Hades.[64]

62 *Mysterium Paschale, op. cit.*, p. 177.
63 Thomas Aquinas, *Summa theologiae* IIIa., q. 49, a. 5; *ibid.*, q. 52, a. 5.
64 *Science, Religion and Christianity, op. cit.*, pp. 132–33.

And in *Kreuz und Hölle* von Speyr claims:

> Christ did not (as in the icons of Eastern church) descend as the victorious Risen One – Holy Saturday is not Easter – but as the Dead One, who no longer speaks as the Word of God, or rather 'has become the silent Word of the Father'. And so we have to learn to share this silence between Death and Resurrection.[65]

Balthasar too in *Theologie der Drei Tage* insists that the Word enters a state of total speechlessness. And yet the silence into which he falls in his humanly ensouled hypostasis is the most eloquent proclamation of the Father's love for us there could possibly be. It speaks volumes about the extent of the divine loving-kindness.

The effect of Christ's presence in this silent, lonely world of the departed is electric. Taken in conjunction with his Resurrection and Ascension which, as already mentioned, begin from here, the transformation he works turns Sheol into its opposite: the indestructible communion of the Holy Souls in Purgatory and the blessed in Heaven.

Consonant with the strongly marked Trinitarian character of his theology in general and his Christology in particular, Balthasar – with whom here, given her key role, I bracket Adrienne von Speyr, both as influence and author – regards Christ's descent into Hell as an event in which the entire Trinity is involved. First, and most obviously, the descent is a Christological event, and so a Filial event: one that concerns the divine Son. It is the last consequence of that obedience to the Father which expresses in time the Son's own eternal relationship to his divine Source. Now in Hell, the Son confronts the mystery that is the Father's permission of sin, of evil.

And so, secondly, the descent has a Paterological aspect: the Father too is intimately concerned with it. Hell belongs to the Father inasmuch as the Father has created freedom, and Hell is the resting-place of perverted freedom. It is what Adam and all those who in some way ratified Adam's sin – all the human dead (I leave to one side here, though, the question of infants) – have made of the promise of immortality. In creating the world, so von Speyr suggests in *Kreuz und Hölle*, the Father foresaw that in an important sense his world would revert to the chaos whence it was drawn in the course of the creative act. Hell mirrors the chaos at the beginning of creation. And just as at the beginning through his Word and his Spirit God brought the world out of chaos, so now in his re-creative relation to the world as the Redeemer–God – and no longer simply, then, the Creator God – the Father sends the Word, filled as man with his Spirit, into the 'second chaos' of the descent into Hell so as to re-focus human freedom on God and in this way re-establish the ordered beauty which ought to typify human life in God's world.

And thirdly, the descent is a Pneumatological event, unthinkable without the Holy Spirit. When considering the death of Christ, we saw how on the Cross, the Holy Spirit brings about the maximal possible intimacy of Father and Son in the moment of their greatest conceivable distance. And so here likewise, where the Son seems most abandoned by the Father that

---

65 A. von Speyr, *Kreuz und Hölle, op. cit.*, II., pp. 208; 337, cited J. Saward, *The Mysteries of March*, pp. 113–14.

abandonment is used by the Holy Spirit to burst open the prison-house and bring the Son, along with the redeemed dead, into the Heaven of the Father.

The result is the coming to be of Hell as we now understand that term, Purgatory, as defined in Catholic doctrine, and Heaven. First, then, Hell. At the Resurrection, the Sheol in which the fathers waited, is left behind. It ceases to exist. In its place, Hell arises. For Balthasar Hell is a Christologically determined concept. It is unthinkable except in relation to Christ. Hell is the torment of those who have rejected the divine Love that descended into Godlessness for their sake. Though Christ did not experience damnation, he saw the second Death. He grasped what was involved in the despairing or contemptuous rejection of his own presence as the sacrificed Lamb. Christ's vision of Hell is more complete than that of any damned person (should such exist), and this is owed to three factors: his divinity, his human innocence, and the redemptive mission which marries these two. For Balthasar and von Speyr that vision constitutes the most important sense in which Christ's suffering in the Paschal Mystery was the greatest conceivable, embracing the world's own agonies and yet going beyond even them. As became notorious in conservative Catholic circles at the end of Balthasar's life, Balthasar was inclined to hope that Hell might be empty: since only man can condemn himself to this condition, may not the patience of God with human blindness be everlasting and so, eventually, have its reward? Contrary to what is sometimes alleged, Balthasar was not, however, an out-and-out universalist. He expressly rejected apocatastasis on the model of Origen's or Nyssa's teaching. 'We are intrinsically beneath the judgment and have neither the right nor the possibility of seeing in advance the cards the Judge holds.'[66] St Paul, he noted, had forbidden all anticipating of judgment (Romans 14.7) since the believer throws himself into the hands of God – that is, for Balthasar, a crucial aspect of the movement of faith, the *credere in Deum*. The Saviour himself in his teaching left us enough light that we may hope in God, yet also warnings sufficient that we cannot exclude the real possibility of losing our salvation. Balthasar considered his attitude well aligned with that of St Ignatius who in the final meditation on Hell in the *Spiritual Exercises*, invites us to consider the state of the damned with the 'most extreme gravity' – it is that condition which awaits me personally not by hypothesis but 'in full right'. Yet, having learned this lesson, I must live in thanksgiving to him who sustained me 'through the ice of his God-abandonment'.[67]

But the descent does not only create Hell, in the sense in which we now use that word doctrinally. It also brings Purgatory into being as well. Purgatory is a gift from the Conqueror of Hell, and von Speyr, followed by Balthasar, links it with the sacrament of Confession. She sees Purgatory as a kind of total act of confession, made possible for us by Christ's bearing the sin of the world on Good Friday and as it were burying them on Holy Saturday. In her own words in 'Objective Mysticism':

---

66 *Kleiner Diskurs über die Hölle* (Ostfildern, 1987, 2nd edition), cited according to the French translation, *L'Enfer, une question* (Paris, 1988), and here at pp. 8–9.

67 *Ibid.*, p. 27. This, we may think is Ignatius seen through the eyes of Adrienne. But then Balthasar could remind us of Pope John Paul II's message seemingly favouring her inspirations at the Castelgandolfo colloquium on her work: thus H. U. von Balthasar, G. Chantraine, A. Scola (eds), *La mission ecclésiale d'Adrienne von Speyr* (Paris-Namur, 1986).

The possibility of instituting both Confession and Purgatory is something the Lord receives from the Cross. He bears all our sin, experiences it in a way he had never known before. He now sees at first hand how deeply rooted it is in us and how radical the measures he takes must be, measures which are, of course, measures of love, though inevitably rigorous. He redeems us, and yet not in such a way that we can stand by indifferently, but by letting us share in his love for eternal life.[68]

And then in the third place Heaven is the perfect fruit of the descent of the Crucified and his Resurrection. In all sound eschatology the final reality is God. And where such eschatology is Christian through and through it will mean by this phrase that in the end there is God in Jesus Christ. As Balthasar wrote in his essay collection *Sponsa Verbi*:

> God is the 'last thing' of the creature. Gained, he is heaven; lost, he is hell; examining, he is judgment; purifying, he is purgatory. To him finite being dies, and through and to and in him it rises. But this is God as he presents himself to the world, that is, in his Son, Jesus Christ, who is the revelation of God and therefore the whole essence of the last things.[69]

And here our future eschatological experience will only be our present potential Christian experience realized and writ large. At any rate for certain souls in the Church there is a vocation – a mission – to share in the Lord's experience in Sheol, not as an end in itself but rather to

> assist their brethren in the Church, to aid those who find themselves plunged into the black hole of depression, doubt, confusion, despair.[70]

For Adrienne, the dark nights of St John – and their analogues in other mystical testimonies – are much more a share in the descent than they are in the Cross. Her explanation of St John of the Cross's failure to interpret it in those terms was that, fixing his eyes as he did so much on the crucified Lord, he sees the latter's 'non-vision' but not what is revealed to the dead Lord in this non-seeing. More straightforward at least is St Teresa of Avila's declaration in her autobiography that the Lord plunged her into Hell so that she could see that from which his mercy had delivered her. Perhaps there is something too that is highly pertinent to the last hundred years in the emergence or re-emergence of this theme – through Balthasar and behind him Adrienne. So many great writers, both Christian and non-Christian, have testified in that period to the apparent absence of God on earth.[71]

> However deep we may feel we have descended, God made man has descended more deeply, so even [in the words of the Psalmist] 'If I descend into hell, thou art there also'.[72]

68 *Idem, Das Wort und die Mystik. I. Objektive Mystik, op. cit.*, p. 356.
69 'Some Points of Eschatology', in *The World Made Flesh. Explorations in Theology* I, *op. cit*, pp. 260–1.
70 J. Saward, *The Mysteries of March, op. cit.*, p. 127.
71 It is interesting to note the appearance in a twentieth-century Russian Orthodox spiritual father of the theme of divine forsakenness – linked, however, to the Christ of Gethsemane and Golgotha more than of the Descent: see N. V. Sakharov, *I Love, Therefore I Am. The Theological Legacy of Archimandrite Sophrony* (Crestwood, NY, 2002), ch. 7.
72 J. Saward, *The Mysteries of March, op. cit.*, p. 132, citing Psalm 138.8.

Easter

In his atoning work, Jesus does not only undergo to the end the *Abstiegsbe-wegung* of his kenosis. Through that kenosis he enters, as Forsyth put it, into plerosis – a state of unsurpassable fullness. Through the Paschal Mystery Jesus is exalted: a process comprising two moments, his Resurrection and that other mysteric event, formally distinct yet integrated therewith, the Ascension.

Balthasar is extremely clear about the essentially bodily nature of the Resurrection. It was in his Virgin-born body, scourged, nailed, pierced and laid in the tomb that the Lord rose – a body changed in state but not in nature. Unless this be true, one cannot even state the fundamental principle of all theology of the Resurrection worth the name: the principle, namely, that the Risen One is the Crucified, a proposition to be found countless times in Balthasar's work. Thus for example, in *Man in History*, he finds this the significance of the risen Lord's stigmata:

> The stigmata are more than an external sign, a kind of honourable distinction for having suffered; they are, beyond the gulf between death and Resurrection which reaches to the bottom of hell, the identity of the subject in the identity of consciousness.[73]

To suppose that he rose in his soul alone, or in the faith of his disciples only, or by some sort of 'replacement' body, would be Gnosticism, indicative of disdain for the material order – first God's and then ours! – and the rejection of its capacity for transfiguration. And yet – and this helps to explain the difficulty felt by many Christians labouring under misapprehensions of a Gnosticizing kind – the Resurrection is an event without analogy. Balthasar calls it 'the Event of events', meaning by that the event against which all others are to be measured and evaluated – and therefore not to be judged in terms of what is not itself.[74]

> In what words are we to describe the logic of the Resurrection, whose nature is to burst open the graves of our ideas, to surpass our conceptions of time and space, to pass through in sovereign manner the closed doors of our minds. It is so spiritual that all the laws of matter are suspended, and yet so physical that the Son of God not only appears, not only speaks, but also lets himself be touched and felt, and he eats and drinks in community with his own.[75]

It should not surprise us to learn, given the pervasively Trinitarian character of all Balthasar's theologizing, that this incomparable event too is Triune from start to finish. First, the Resurrection is a Paterological event: it is the Father's acceptance of the Son's sacrifice. The Resurrection of the Son is the culmination of the Father's work as the Creator, for here the Father shows himself as faithful to the covenant of the creation and all its renewals in the history of Israel. Moreover, by means of the Resurrection the Father displays the Son to the world as its *Pantokrator* or all-ruler, thus answering the prayer

73 *Man in History, op. cit.*, p. 285.
74 Cf. *Mysterium Paschale*, pp. 193–95.
75 *Man in History, op. cit.*, p. 285.

made by Jesus on the eve of the Passion that the Father might glorify him with the glory he had before the world was made. Secondly, the Resurrection is a Pneumatological happening. It is in the Spirit that the Father raises the Son, as Paul attests in chapter eight of the Letter to the Romans. The Spirit then overflows from Jesus' glorified manhood onto his corporate body, the disciples of the Church. As Balthasar puts it succinctly in *Mysterium Paschale*:

> The reunion of the Father with the Son (in his human nature) in a single (economic) principle of spiration is the precondition for the (economic) sending forth of the Spirit into the Church and the redeemed world.[76]

And finally, of course, the Resurrection is a Christological event. As we have seen from his *A Theology of History*, Balthasar emphasizes the importance of the Forty Days between Easter and Ascension, viewed as the archetype of the time of the Church, for here the risen Christ shows himself to his friends in a very human fashion. This is genuine earthly time, as will be the time of the Church after Pentecost, and yet it is time filled with bliss, with the serenity and confidence that follow from the victory over sin and death. Every celebration of the sacraments, for Balthasar, is an entry into the distinctive time of this unique period in those two combined respects – earthliness yet sovereign graciousness. The Resurrection makes possible for the Church in the power of the Spirit our salvific sharing in Christ's sufferings and the power of his resurrection.[77]

In our preaching about the Resurrection, so Balthasar maintains, we must not concentrate on what he calls the 'symptoms' – the empty tomb or even the Resurrection appearances, important as these are. We must stress rather *the event itself* in its central constitutive meaning which is the closing of the 'hiatus'.

> The content of preaching must be the closing of the hiatus itself, the salvific healing by God of man who in the death of sin lay irremediably torn open and apart.[78]

In his essay 'Who celebrates Easter?', Balthasar remarks that only they can celebrate the Resurrection triumph who have 'lived through Good Friday with faith', 'have not refused to stand under the Cross, ... the sign of God's judgment on sin'. 'How should someone participate in the feast of the redemption from sin, the feast of absolution, who was not convinced that he had been guilty of fault for which he is pardoned?'[79] Pagans and Jews cannot celebrate Easter, not because the Lord did not die for them too but because to share consciously in the grace that was lavished they must in some way confess their 'co-guilt [with Christian sinners] in the death of the humanized God'.[80]

---

76 *Mysterium Paschale, op. cit.*, p. 276.
77 Cf. Philippians 3.10.
78 *Mysterium Paschale, op. cit.*, p. 68.
79 'Wer feiert Ostern?', *Pfarrblatt des Dekanates Basel-Stadt* 35. 14 (26 March 1948), p. 105.
80 *Ibid*. This essay is an early example of Balthasar's debt to Adrienne von Speyr's theology of the death and resurrection of Christ as understood by reference to sacramental confession and absolution respectively.

Ascension and Pentecost

The importance, in Balthasar's eyes, of the forty days from Easter to Ascension is the way they show the risen Lord existing contemporaneously with his witnesses while at the same time inhabiting eternal time – only a contradiction if we suppose time and eternity can never be united. Balthasar's exegesis of the Lucan episode of the encounter of the Lord with the disciples walking to Emmaus shows 'the eternal allowing itself to be drawn into time and going along with it in genuine companionship'. When Jesus vanishes from their sight that is, not, in Balthasar's view, to resume a sheerly eternal mode of existence but because he is

> Going on, in fact, along the road of which the forty days are the beginning, on into that time which is the Church's time, and drawing his disciples after him along that road.[81]

The time of the Forty Days is 'resurrection time', the characteristic of which is to be a 'time of sovereignty' as opposed to servitude: a time, namely, when the Son enjoys sovereignty over time as something received from the Father. Though his previous life must strike the disciples as past time, to him it is not such. Rather, in Balthasar's words:

> The whole of it is transformed into his resurrection, taken up into it, eternalized, and thus made a living possession that he can share, the thing of which he is going to build his Church.[82]

Balthasar will not agree that the Ascension makes much significant difference to this state of affairs. Indeed, at the time of writing *A Theology of History* he treats it as simply a 'signing off gesture, purely for our benefit', a somewhat enigmatic phrase. The mode of time revealed during the Forty Days – a mode when Christ radiates eternity into time – remains the foundation for every other mode of his presence in time, whether in the Church or in the world. Indeed, his manner of being as demonstrated by those days is the 'ultimate form of his reality'. When to the disciples on their way to Emmaus he opens the Scriptures and shows them how the experience of Israel pointed to himself, he the personal eschaton, who in himself is the end of history, was present at one particular significant moment in the midst of history instructing them on the meaning of every past significant moment that can biblically be thought.

As the accounts of the Resurrection appearances show, however, the past when fulfilled points to the future that is the Church. The instructions to the apostles in Luke, the commissioning of apostles in Matthew and Mark, the scenes between Peter and the beloved disciple in John which convey an entire ecclesiology in embryo, all bear this out. These are the days, for Balthasar, of the Church's founding. They are the anticipation of Pentecost, and they reinforce the theme that the work of the Holy Spirit who is then to come proceeds from that of the Son incarnate.

81 *A Theology of History, op. cit.*, p. 83.
82 *Ibid.*, p. 84.

By the Ascension the Jesus who, as the Father's Word, eternally points back to him, now performs the same movement in human flesh. Like the Resurrection, with which it is intimately connected, the Ascension brings the Son's incarnate work to term.[83]

> Here God's might is perfected. Now as an immeasurably great power (Ephesians 1: 19–20), God not only finishes speaking his own word of creation, but also take as well the *no* of man and fashions out of it his own and man's *yes*. The dialogue between God and creation, YHWH and Zion, becomes, in the incarnation of the Word, a single word which resumes everything in itself. It reveals the internal dialogue of God, it represents the world's affirmation of God, and in that affirmation it wipes out every contradictory *no*, not only symbolically, but also really (in the truly vicarious suffering for sinners on the Cross).[84]

In particular, the Ascension is the 'final "divinization" of the completed mission', its 'passage into the eternity of the Father', the 'lifting up of the whole cycle of actions and suffering into the potency of God'.[85] It does not darken Easter, but, on the contrary, leaves behind, as the evangelist Luke testifies, 'great joy'.[86] And the reason is:

> it promises the pouring out of the Holy Spirit, which can only take place when the Word, returned to the Father, transforms, through his human nature which had entered into the one Breath of the Father and the Son, the outpouring of the Spirit within the divine nature into world history for salvation.

Now the Holy Spirit can become the 'perfecting representative of the Word'.[87]

The Holy Spirit is the Spirit of the Son, sent by him (cf. John 16.7), and this may lead us, in preparation for the coming of the Holy Spirit, to call the Son the revealer, the Spirit the revealed. Yet in the post-Pentecost economy of the Church the roles are reversed: the Holy Spirit is the revealer, the Son the revealed. And furthermore, because the Holy Spirit proceeds from the Father, and is simultaneously, then, the Spirit of the Father and the Son, the Spirit reveals the Father too. Revealing the Son, how can he not reveal the Father since the Father is what – or rather the One whom – the Son himself discloses? The Son sketched for us the image of the Father: the Holy Spirit so illuminates that image that it appears to us as intelligible and splendid. At Pentecost, then, the Holy Spirit 'will bring the entire revelation to its complete end', since, as the Spirit of the Father and the Son, he brings to light the 'final, innermost mystery of God': the mystery that God is Love, through the eternal love that joins the Father and the Son.[88] In so doing, the Holy Spirit

---

83 *Man in History, op. cit.*, p. 231.
84 *Ibid.*, p. 240.
85 *Ibid.*, p. 292.
86 Luke 24.52.
87 *Man in History, op. cit.*, p. 293.
88 'Die Offenbarung des Heiligen Geistes', *Pfarrblatt des Dekanates Basel-Stadt* 35. 24 (11 May 1948), pp. 1–2.

brings it about that we may understand the objective revelation of the Word of God in the Son – in the Gospel and the Church. His mission it is so to let us appropriate this revelation that it becomes subjectively received by us not only as grasped, believed, and turned into concepts, but also as filling us, satisfying us, and making us blessed.

In Balthasar's pneumatology, the Holy Spirit's 'place' in the divine Trinity, to conjoin Father and Word incarnate in 'heavenly and earthly love', is not to be separated from his role as 'soul' of the Church – the link between the two being the flesh of Christ, which 'in Jesus Christ can be a true vessel for the divine Spirit of Love, who then can really be "outpoured" into our hearts'.[89] Here, crediting de Lubac's dictum that every true rebirth of the Catholic ethos is an 'Augustine-Renaissance', he appealed to St Augustine who had declared in his sermons that

> The Christian man is catholic, so long as he lives in the [church-] body, whereas the alienated member does not follow the Spirit. If you want to live from the Holy Spirit, hold fast to love, cherish truth, long for unity.[90]

'The entire Augustinian doctrine of the Church', declared Balthasar, 'rests on the inseparability of catholic love in the Holy Spirit and the Church structure in the same Spirit'. From which two consequences follow: outside the *Catholica* one may have Church structures yet lack the 'living catholic spirit'; inside it, one may lose love and be a Christian but in seeming, *ein Scheinchrist*.

At Pentecost, as the Church and her members become Spirit-filled, infinite Subject and finite subject do not simply co-exist but live by a 'flowing into one another', *eine Flüssigkeitineinander*, for which there is no earthly parallel.[91] The Church participates in Christ's own fullness as the *Geistmensch*, the 'spiritual man' (cf. Galatians 6.1), or the *Geistgemässer*, the One who lives 'according to the Spirit' (cf. Romans 8.5). By virtue of the Pentecostal Gift, the narrow confines of spatio-temporal facticity are taken up into the 'medium of a comprehensive and interiorizing understanding'. But at the same time the Holy Spirit shows himself to be in no way an 'abstract medium', since he is the *Conkretissimum*, the most concrete Reality, and also the *Personalissimum*, the most personal Reality, and not at all 'mere objective spirit'. The Spirit's gifts to people in the community of the Son reflect this twofold character – at once drawing the individual out of his limitations into the broadest and highest divine-human life, and yet distributing special personal graces to elevate and complete what is unique about the image of God in each created self, whether man, woman or child. For Balthasar, 'general *charis* is necessarily special *charisma*'.[92]

It is typical of Balthasar's Christian humanism that he illustrates this claim about a real distinction – but also real continuity – between grace and charism by the case of *Shakespeare* who 'expressed the general spirit of his

89 'Augustinus und der Heilige Geist', *Vaterland* 123 (28 May 1977), p. 1.
90 Augustine, *Sermo* 267, 4, cited *ibid.*
91 'Charis und Charisma', *Liturgie und Mönchtum* 20 (1957), pp. 57–67 and here at p. 57.
92 *Ibid.*

people in what was most supremely personal, most his own'.[93] The re-making of humanity in the all-representative New Adam is the aim of the Paschal Mystery. But this must express both the highest solidarity of the redeemed and their greatest differentiation. Here we have already began to trespass on the topic of the Church (with which, for Balthasar, that of the Mother of the Lord is inseparably united) and of the saints.

93 *Ibid.*, p. 58.

9

༺ꕤ༻

Divine Society: the Church

Balthasar did not write a systematic ecclesiology. But he had much to say on the mystery of the Church.[1] What, after all, he was trying to do, outside the trilogy as well as in it, was to salvage enough of the best theology, spirituality, literature, of past and present to transmit to posterity a Catholic culture wide and rich enough to serve as a basis for Christian life and mission as it ought to be rather than often is. Not surprisingly, then, one can turn up major ecclesiological discussions in all sorts of places in Balthasar's highly diverse *oeuvre*.

Four themes stand out in Balthasar's ecclesiology: the origin of the Church in the kenosis of Christ, the manifestation of the Church at Pentecost, the operation in the Church of what Balthasar terms 'Petrine', 'Marian' and 'Johannine' – and sometimes further eponymously New Testament – 'principles', and finally, and most elaborately developed, a highly original theology of the 'states of life' in the Church, the chief ways of being a Christian.

The origin of the Church in the kenosis of Christ

The place to look for the theme of the Church's origin in Christ's kenosis is likely to be anywhere Balthasar gives an account of the Incarnation in its relation to the Atonement. So his theology of the Easter Triduum makes for especially fruitful investigation. In *Mysterium Paschale* Balthasar accepts the patristic theologoumenon that the Church is born from the opened side of Christ on the Cross.[2] In his own elucidation: at the Crucifixion the people of the Covenant were completely reconstituted from the being of the one and only fully valid representative of that Covenant on earth, Jesus Christ, the

---

1 For the trilogy this was especially so in the first volume of the aesthetics where he considers the Church as the community that perceives the beauty of Christ, responds to it, and becomes in turn its mediating form (see in this 'Introduction to Hans Urs von Balthasar', A. Nichols, OP, *The Word has been Abroad, op. cit.*, pp. 32–33 and 51–53), and the last volume of the logic where in looking at the truth of the Holy Spirit Balthasar considers how the Spirit makes his truth known in the Church both in subjective ways through personal experience, especially in the charismatic missions of the saints and mystics but also in objective ways, through Scripture, Tradition, especially the Liturgy, and Church office, the magisterium (thus *idem, Say it is Pentecost, op. cit.*, pp. 167–85).
2 *Mysterium Paschale, op. cit.*, pp. 132–34.

new Adam, as he lay asleep in death. The Church is consequently 'the second Eve, created from the "wound" in the side of the new Adam to complement him'.[3] Or, in a more theologically complex formulation:

> As man, he [Christ] allowed himself to fall into the sleep of death so that, as God, he might derive from this death the mystery of fruitfulness by which he would create for himself his Bride, the Church.[4]

It is when the Son undergoes Incarnation to the uttermost, in the final sufferings on the Tree of the Cross, that the Spirit most completely penetrates his manhood and thus enables that manhood to become the principle of a new, engraced humanity in the Church. Given that Christocentric – not ecclesiocentric – emphasis, this 'womanly' Church is not, then:

> a self-sufficient entity, interposing herself as an 'intermediary' between the believer and Christ [but]… she is primarily an open womb and teaches mankind, in her and with her, to be similarly open.[5]

Balthasar's theology of how the Church originates from the self-offered body of the Lord at the point of his maximal Incarnation on Calvary which saw Jesus at his most humanly vulnerable makes him deeply opposed to any counterposing of the word 'spiritual' with the word 'incarnational'. The flesh that is the hinge, the crucial factor, in our salvation (a favourite Balthasarian phrase taken from Tertullian) is not to be set over against the spiritual life, the pneumatic life, the life that the Holy Spirit gives. Quite the contrary, in fact. Just as the Holy Spirit never renders the Word discarnate – not even when Jesus is exalted to the Father at his Ascension, so in Christian living 'pneumaticization' always increases in direct proportion to 'incarnation'. For Balthasar – and this position was already signalled in his pre-war 'The Fathers, the Scholastics and Ourselves' – the more spiritual you are the more incarnate you must be.

This has obvious consequences for ecclesiology. No Church that would be exclusively spiritual and subjective and not at all corporeal and objective in its manner of proceeding could possibly be the continuing Spirit-borne presence of Jesus Christ in the world. It also has implications for individuals within the Church. In an intervention in the ecclesiastical controversies of the period after the Second Vatican Council when many people came to say 'Jesus and his Gospel, Yes', 'The Church, No' or at least 'The Church as it has been hitherto, No', Balthasar had this to say:

> Those who are not saints prefer to distinguish between the 'sinful structures' against which revolt is permitted or even commanded, and the substance which, they presume, can be directly derived from the Gospels, bypassing any ecclesial structure. Here, however, they are already part of the ideological process that aims to discarnate the existential Church as the flesh and body of Christ by splitting the 'for me now' subjectively valid *logos* from the 'superfluous' structure, the *sarx*, which must be discarded. Yet what the New Testament calls *pneuma* does not blow exclusively in a *logos* stripped from its *sarx*. It is

3 *The Office of Peter and the Structure of the Church*, op. cit., p. 184.
4 *The Christian State of Life*, op. cit., p. 233.
5 *The Office of Peter and the Structure of the Church*, op. cit., p. 185.

for this reason that we must question – from the standpoint of the New Testament – the discrediting of ecclesiastical structures or the intention radically and fundamentally to 'change' them. The New Testament shows us a Church which, in a hard shell – hardened through suffering – shelters the tender and sweet fruit of the Spirit exhaled on the Cross . . .[6]

That does not mean, he explained, that everything connected with the Church's 'visible contours' is absolutely sacrosanct, never to be tampered with. We can carry out occasional 'modifications', provided – and the proviso carries a heavy theological charge – we do so

while obediently contemplating the mystery underlying the system, [and] only to bring out in bold relief the form that from the very beginning has been a stumbling-block.[7]

Not surprisingly, given the criticisms by liberal Catholics of those 'visible contours', what Balthasar has in mind there is first and foremost the Petrine office, the exercise of the Roman primacy.

Less controversial but equally central for his theology of the Church born from the side of the crucified Christ was his conviction that the mediatrix of that birth was Mary, the Mother of the Lord. In 'Who is the Church?', Balthasar asks whether there is 'some kind of second agent cooperating in this founding and outpouring of the Church' on Golgotha.[8] Is there some sense in which the Church pre-existed the Cross as the 'bride' for whom Christ died there – an entity that is the continuation of Israel, the Bride of YHWH? That, after all, is the plain sense of the Writer to the Ephesians: 'Christ loved the Church and gave himself up for her.'[9] In the writings of the Fathers, reports Balthasar:

The Church as bride, difficult to grasp in herself as a person, appears as it were polarized in the person of Mary, and Mary herself as crystalizing round herself the whole community of the faithful.[10]

Balthasar's own view is that it is impossible to understand how the Church already existed at the Cross as the 'bridal Church' *without* referring to the Blessed Virgin who embodies the 'adequate response awaited by God from the created sphere and produced in it by his grace through the Word'.[11]

6 *Ibid.*, pp. 20–21.
7 *Ibid.*, p. 24.
8 'Who is the Church?', in *Spouse of the Word, op. cit.*, pp. 143–91, and here at p. 147.
9 Ephesians 5.25.
10 *Ibid.*, p. 153 where Balthasar remarks: 'If we go on to examine the theology of the Fathers, we find it difficult not to speak of an extension and amplification of the bride motive that is not certainly authorised by Scripture: the Church (even though come forth from Christ, or purified and exalted by him) is made a subject on her own, with a womanly beauty, whose form and adornment, feelings and sentiments, destinies, humiliations and exaltations can be described. A powerful contribution to endowing the Church with a personality and life of her own was made from the earliest times (of Justin and Irenaeus) by the parallel drawn between Mary and the Church, which, in the twelfth century, came to pervade the commentaries on the Song [of Songs]. . .'.
11 *Ibid.*, p. 161. Hence the Mother of the Lord is key to Balthasar's mature theology of the Eucharistic Sacrifice: see his 'The Mass, A Sacrifice of the Church?' in *idem., Creator Spirit. Explorations in Theology* III (San Francisco, 1993), pp. 185–244.

He begins from the presupposition that *der Mensch*, 'the human being', is not *eingeschlechtlich*, 'of one gender'. Rather is 'he' man and woman. If, then, we acknowledge Christ as the 'New Adam', from whom a new God-pleasing race is to spring, the question must immediately arise of a 'New Eve', the 'helper' of the new Man. As Balthasar puts it:

> If it is in the woman that the fruitfulness of the man first attains visibility (in that she carries and gives birth to a child), so it is in the woman formed for Christ that Christ's supernatural fruitfulness will become visible, and indeed no longer in the incomplete way of the Old Covenant when the Word had not yet been made flesh, but in that perfection which corresponds to the New.[12]

The Letter to the Ephesians testifies that Christ has a bride 'without spot or wrinkle'.[13] But this immaculate Church is unlikely to be simply an idea or an ideal, possibly to be embodied on the Last Day. That would ill suit the reality of the Incarnation which was there and then and therefore here and now. No, the sponsal Church is formed initially in Mary who, when at the Cross her role reaches its fullness, becomes by the same token the 'most ecclesial of beings'.

> Mary our mother becomes the Church our mother, for the Church has in Mary her wellspring (*Quellpunkt*) and abiding centre.[14]

'*Abiding* centre' not least because, for Balthasar, the Church will continue into the Kingdom, that is, into eternity. The hierarchy and sacraments will disappear, yes. But the Church *as bride* will endure for ever. As Balthasar puts it, 'What never falls away is the nuptial encounter between God and the creature' to which the hierarchy and sacramental structure of the Church are ordered.[15]

The manifestation of the Church at Pentecost

But the Church born on the Cross is manifested at Pentecost. The Church brought to birth on Calvary is shown for the first time as what it is in Jerusalem, where the apostles receive the Holy Spirit of the Father and the Son, while they are gathered with Mary in the Cenacle, the Upper Room. In Balthasar's pneumatology, the Holy Spirit is not only the personal love of Father and Son, the expression of their inter-subjectivity. He is also supremely objective, the fruit of their love. This duality has ecclesiological consequences if is it by the Holy Spirit that the Church born on Good Friday is manifested at Whitsun. In the Church the Spirit shows himself as both totally subjective and totally objective.

First, he shows himself as totally subjective. That means: he is the Person who inspires sanctity in human subjects, initiating prayer, stimulating

12 'Marienverehrung heute', *Titlisgrüsse. Zeitschrift für Freunde und Schüler der Stiftschule Engelberg* 55. 1 (1968/9), pp. 2–6 and here at p. 3.
13 Ephesians 5.26.
14 'Marienverehrung heute', *art. cit.*, p. 5.
15 'The office and the sacrament are forms of communicating the seed; they belong to the male aspect, but their end is to lead the bride to her womanly function and fortify her in it.' Thus 'Who is the Church?', *art. cit.*, p. 158.

repentance and reconciliation, granting people mystical and charismatic gifts, some of them outstanding or extraordinary, as well as giving individuals the capacity to bear witness to Christ. All of that – 'subjective Spirit' Balthasar calls it, in a play of words (and concepts) drawn from Hegel's phenomenology (and more specifically Hegel's account of the development of freedom in civil society) – the Holy Spirit most certainly is.

But the Spirit also shows himself in the Church as totally objective. That is to say, he inspires such outer forms and institutional mediations of the saving revelation as Tradition, Scripture, Church office, preaching, the Liturgy and sacraments, and even canon law and theology. All of this – 'objective Spirit' – is also he. What, on the basis of Christ's founding activity, the Spirit constructs in the Church institution is as much the expression of the divine love as is the subjective holiness that the pattern of the Church's life makes possible. So Balthasar writes a pro-mystical ecclesiology which is also, and equally, an anti-Gnostic one.

In his study of Bernanos, for example, which in the German original carries the title 'The Church as Lived', and in the American translation the subtitle 'An Ecclesial Existence', he praises the novelist for realizing that:

> The saint – ... the subjective following of Christ and the realisation of [Christ's] holiness within the sphere of the human person – is simply unthinkable without the objective holiness of the Church, of her official ministry and of her sacraments ... This is the exact point where Bernanos' saintly heroes begin to emerge.

To continue the quotation will exhibit an important entailment:

> The whole of the hierarchical and sacramental order in the end is there for the saint, that is, for the subjective sanctification of Christians in general, for those who *au fond* have already been made holy through baptism.[16]

This emphasis on the way objective holiness or objective 'Spirit' is there for the sake of subjective holiness or subjective 'Spirit' which itself requires its objective counterpart for its realization, enables Balthasar to give a very well-rounded portrait of the Church, omitting no major element.[17] Everything, from mystical grace to canon law, is provided with a theological interpretation within a comprehensive and coherent view of the place of the Church in the economy of the Holy Spirit. But above all, the two poles of holiness, objective and subjective, are summed up in two contrasting yet interrelated figures, the priest and the saint. The portrayal of that is what he admires in this regard in Bernanos' Catholic novels. There 'the ecclesial drama is played out between the priest and the saint'.[18] There will be more to say about this subjective/objective difference when we consider Balthasar's theology of the saints.

16 *Bernanos. An Ecclesial Existence, op. cit.,* p. 260.
17 The word 'Spirit' is thus placed between inverted commas to show its deliberate ambivalence: we are speaking of the economy of the Holy Spirit bearing fruit in the spirit of man.
18 *Ibid.,* p. 263.

The Petrine, Marian and Johannine principles in the Church's structure

In his book on the structure of the Apostles' Creed, Balthasar's French Jesuit mentor Henri de Lubac explained that the best way to avoid either exaggerating or minimizing the place of the Church in the corpus of Christian theology as a whole is to consider her as the true subject of the word *Credo*. The 'I' of 'I believe' is the 'I' of the Church. She is the corporate subject who carries out the activity of believing to which the Creed attests. As individual Christians we believe by *participating* in the Church's primordial act of faith. And the more we grow in the life of faith, the more we deepen our appropriation of her – the Church's – faith. As we mature as Christians we become more, not less, dependent on our Mother.

Balthasar takes this idea further. He agrees with de Lubac that the Church is the primordial subject of believing. But he asks a further question, which is about how the fundamental (he calls it the 'archetypal') Christian experience comes to be constituted in the apostolic generation, thence to be transmitted by participation in all the generations that come after, right down to our own. In sharing the faith of the Church we participate in the Church's archetypal experience of salvation through Jesus Christ. How does that happen? Balthasar argues that the Church receives from the apostolic generation a fourfold tradition of archetypal experience – fourfold because it is Petrine, Pauline, Johannine and Marian. Peter, Paul, John and Mary together contributed to the Church an experience of grace, and this, continually made available, goes on nourishing the Church's members over time. Their archetypal experience of the Gospel shapes our experience of the Church – when, that is, we allow our experience to be maximally full, or, as Balthasar would say, maximally 'catholic': a word he uses not just to denote the claim to catholicity made in the Creed but also to denote, as it more commonly does in everyday speech, what is distinctive about that Church that is in communion with Rome.

What Balthasar says about these co-constituting inputs into archetypal apostolic experience is relatively plain. The *Petrine* contribution consists of the apostolic preaching and the sacraments which are its follow-up. Through the hierarchy, that is, the apostolic succession of teachers who are also celebrants of sacraments, this will continue in the later Church. The *Pauline* contribution consists of charismatic and visionary graces which, however, are not simply for the enjoyment (if that is the word) of individuals. Such graces, as Paul's Damascus Road experience could demonstrate, generate missions (in the plural) that serve the overall mission (in the singular) of the Church. The *Johannine* contribution consists of contemplative love, so notable in the Fourth Gospel and the Letters, and the impetus to move forward to the heavenly Jerusalem, typical of the Johannine Apocalypse. The *Marian* element is whatever enables us to experience the bodily, visible life of the Church with its sacraments and institutions (the Petrine contribution) as a means for the spiritual experience of Christ and of God. Just so the virginal body of Mary was the means for the incarnation of the uncreated Word. All these are archetypal experiences, originally enjoyed by Peter, Paul, John and Mary. They are called 'archetypal', notice, not simply because they happened in the first days of Christianity. Balthasar is not *just* staking out the historical claim that suchlike factors early influenced the Church. That, though true, would be a commonplace. He is saying more than this, namely: these experiences found the life-form of all subsequent Christians considered precisely as believers. They found the life-form of believing humankind.

This was an idea Balthasar had hit on as early as the 1944 essay on the Mother of the Lord, 'Die Erscheinung der Mutter'.[19] He then spent thirty years developing it and thinking it through. In the upshot, best inspected in *The Office of Peter and the Structure of the Church*, Balthasar treats of the above mentioned constituent features of Christian *subjectivity* in the Church as similarly constitutive principles of the Christian *objectivity* of the Church, principles that give the Church her *basic structure*.

In the mature form of this thesis, the Pauline element typically drops out. This is not because Balthasar was uncertain as to whether to regard the Pauline element as all that important. Unusual charisms and extraordinary mystical graces are certainly important to him. Not only did Adrienne von Speyr, during her lifetime, constantly present him with a dramatic living example of them. More than this, he also saw unusual charisms and extra-ordinary mystical graces as the driving force behind many of the missions of the saints. For while some saints became saints simply through living in heroic fashion the ordinary Christian life, others were raised up by God so as to launch new missions in the Church, new forms of spirituality, new kinds of service, for which such charisms and graces are prerequisite. But precisely because it is a matter of extraordinary vocations, the Pauline element does not enter into a description of the most basic structure of the Church.

For Balthasar, then, the Church is essentially – but not exhaustively – constituted by the interplay of the Petrine, Marian and Johannine factors, now seen not so much as contributions to archetypal experience (that is the subjective perspective on ecclesiology) but as structuring principles in the Church's objective make-up. The Petrine and Marian factors are familiar enough from Catholic theology at large. We can begin with the Marian because for Balthasar it is the most comprehensive of the three.

(i) The Marian factor

The Marian principle is pretty straightforward, but Balthasar builds a lot on it. The Virgin Mother realizes in advance, in her own person, what the Church is to be. The quality, under grace, of her obedient faith and loving consent to the Word and the efficacy these have for salvation make her not only the model of the Church but its matrix, its nurturing source.

> Mary is the womb and archetype of the Church, she is the fruitfulness of the Church herself, she is the internal form of the Church, since she is the Bride of Christ ... Mary is the virginal-nuptial vessel of all obedi-ence, out of which flows not only the Christian's obedience but Peter's demands as well.[20]

For Balthasar, while the Church, originating in the kenosis of the Son, is born on the Cross, the new Covenant made in Christ's Blood is not sealed until Mary, the Daughter of Zion, waiting with the Beloved Disciple St John

---

19 'Die Erscheinung der Mutter', *Schweizer Rundschau* 44 (1944), pp. 73–82.
20 *Razing the Bastions, op. cit.*, p. 40.

at the foot of the Cross, has given her 'Yes' to it, thus renewing the *fiat* she made to the entire saving economy at the Annunciation. The scenario of revelation requires us to keep together the doctrines about the Woman who responded and the Church that lives forever from her response. The Marian *fiat*, originally made at the Annunciation and, says Balthasar:

> unequalled in its perfection, is the all-inclusive, protective and directive form of all ecclesial life . . ., the interior form of *communio* [communion in the Church].

With the approach of the Paschal mystery,

> As sin closes in on [Mary] – actually on her Son, and through his suffering, on her – she knows all that she needs to know about sin, and she has no other remedy than her own availability, *Verfügbarkeit*. Thus her attitude becomes foundational for the Church of the faithful, the Church that is pure *communio*, the Church of the 'priestly people' who suffer with Jesus Christ.[21]

Obedience, explained Balthasar in *Razing the Bastions*, is 'not an attribute of the "people of the Church" alone'. Rather is it 'the attribute of Ecclesia as a whole', before ever the distinction between the 'teaching Church' and the 'listening Church' comes into view.[22]

That is a genuinely liberating thought. However, the ecclesiological implications of Balthasar's Mariology are not restricted to the significance of Mary's continuing Annunciation attitude at the Cross. Balthasar's entire ecclesiology and Mariology do not so much stand side by side as intimately interweave. Just as there is a *perichôrêsis* or 'coinherence' of Father, Son and Spirit in the Trinity where each person lives through the others, so there is for Balthasar a *perichôrêsis* or coinherence of Mary and the Church. Mary and the Church do not exist separately from each other; they exist *in* each other. Of course, that can only be because this unique position was 'given to [Mary] for her motherly task by the grace of the Father and the merits of the Son'. Just so, Mary's task itself is

> focused wholly beyond herself and subordinated by his trinitarian work of salvation, i.e. to make human beings be children of the Father by the gift of the Holy Spirit and thus gather them into a community founded on trinitarian life.[23]

As the Irish Balthasarian scholar Brendan Leahy explains, the Marian dimension in Balthasar's ecclesiology lays bare the heart of the Church, on earth and in heaven.

> The Marian element in the Church is Mary's spousal-maternal presence providing a Marian unity at the core of the earthly-heavenly Church, where the order of nature is fulfilled in grace, *erôs* in *agápê*, the created cosmos in ecclesial love.[24]

---

21 *The Office of Peter and the Structure of the Church, op. cit.*, p. 208.
22 *Razing the Bastions, op. cit.*, p. 94.
23 *The Office of Peter and the Structure of the Church, op. cit.*, p. 204.
24 B. Leahy, *The Marian Element in the Church according to Hans Urs von Balthasar* (Frankfurt am Main, 1996), p. 36.

Balthasar considers the Marian principle to be more fundamental than the Petrine because it is a principle which renders the Church in an all-embracing way holy and immaculate. That can only be done in a Marian way since only in the Mother of God is the Church already, in the words of Paul, 'without stain or wrinkle or any such thing'[25] – already that *now*, rather than prospectively at the eschaton. As Balthasar writes:

> In Mary ... the Church is not only infallible in the official sacramental sphere (though always fallible subjectively and existentially, always defective and hopelessly falling short of the ideal inherent and proclaimed). In her the Church is also personally immaculate and beyond the tension between reality and ideal.[26]

The holiness of the Church is concretely constituted in Mary – that is how, in earthed reality, she (the Church) comes to have what the lay theologian Jacques Maritain termed an indefectibly holy *personnalité* which is distinct from her all too defectible 'personnel'. It is because the Church originally exists as Mary that the Church is the *sancta Ecclesia* of the Creed. Even if, *per improbabile*, all her members on earth at any one time in her history were sunk in mortal sin, she – the earthly Church – would still be the 'holy Church' by virtue of the continued matrix of her life that is the Mother of the Lord.

All this helps to explain of course why Balthasar (and many other writers of past and present) so likes to refer to the Church by the feminine personal pronoun – *she*. The Church is more primordially feminine than she is masculine because she is more fundamentally Marian than she is Petrine. Peter has to follow the Marian way, the way of the *fiat*.[27] In the twenty-first chapter of St John's Gospel, the risen Christ three times asks Peter, 'Do you love me?'. For Balthasar, what this brings out is that

> Peter's subjective spirit is not equal to the objective spirit of office and sacrament, not only because Peter is a sinner and his sinfulness was never more terribly revealed than when he was confronted with the demands inherent in the spirit of the office but even more so because Christ alone can bring unison into the two sides in the uniqueness and singularity of his mission as Redeemer and Sacrifice ...

And yet, he continues, this identity of subjective and objective must somehow be reproduced in the Church since the Lord

> wills to see his Church standing before him, not as a singular, palpable failure but as a glorious bride worthy of him.

And Balthasar concludes, 'Here the Marian principle in the Church necessarily comes into play'.[28]

> It is Christ, not Mary, who brought the Church into being by his Passion. All the same, she took part, as an intermediary, in this creation by the universality and unrestrictedness of her *Fiat*, which the Son is able

---

25 Ephesians 5.27.
26 'Who is the Church?', *art. cit.*, p. 162.
27 *The Office of Peter and the Structure of the Church*, p. 211.
28 'Who is the Church?', *art. cit.*, pp. 160–61.

to use as an infinitely plastic medium to bring forth from it new believers, those born again.[29]

All this exemplifies Balthasar's insistence that a Catholic ecclesiology should be full-bloodedly *Catholic*. He does not apologize for proposing theologically a way to limit appropriately one ultra-Catholic element in his picture of the Church, the Petrine principle, by invoking another equally ultra-Catholic, the Marian principle – even if, as he remarks, the ecclesial communities that spring from the Reformation will probably regard this as casting out the Devil by means of Beelzebul, prince of demons!

For Balthasar, the paternal or masculine ordained ministry is anchored in the sphere of a maternity or femininity which characterizes the Church as a whole, and not any one group or 'estate', *Stand*, within it. Balthasar calls the Marian dimension of the Church a 'protective mantle' encompassing all the other principles in the Church's make-up.[30] The very centrality of the Marian relativizes hierarchy, and draws attention to the fact that, at the deepest core of the Church, there is only the faithful reception of grace. Forget this, Balthasar warns, and we hand over the Church to huffing and puffing hierarchs, organization freaks and busy little committees. The Church is not primarily bureaucratic, nor is it chiefly to be investigated by sociologists. Here conservative authoritarianism and radical *chic* (if for diametrically opposed reasons) go up the same cul-de-sac towards a dead end. The fading of the image of Mother Church from Catholic consciousness was for Balthasar, writing in the early 1970s, an ecclesiological disaster waiting to happen. He thought that, unless halted and reversed, it would lead to an increasingly soulless image of the Church in the minds of her people, a counter-traditional demand for the ordination of women, the subverting of Christological symbolism for priesthood and an ever more impersonal Church of administrators – *ecclesia photocopians* he called it, from which both women and men would flee in droves. (We shall come across a deservedly classic citation along those lines when looking at his Mariology in its own right.)

(ii) The Petrine factor

However, Mary does not stand alone as a figure of, and for, the Church *simpliciter* – though she is unique as the figure of its matrix, its foundation in and from Jesus Christ. A pattern of figures is involved, for Balthasar's is a *constellational ecclesiology*. As he puts it, introducing this fruitful concept:

> Jesus ... stands ... within a constellation of his fellow men. This constellation is an inner determinant; it has relevance for his divine humanity. It is essential, not accidental, to his being and acting. He cannot be detached from his constitutive human group, though this fact in no way infringes upon his sovereign person. If one attempts to detach Jesus and the doctrine about him (Christology) from this constitutive group, his figure – even when kept in the Trinitarian context – becomes hopelessly *abstract*. Clearly this holds not only for Protestant Christology but implicitly also for Catholic Christology, insofar as the

---

29 *Ibid.*, p. 165.
30 *Ibid.*, p. 177.

persons essentially associated with Christ are assigned to separate theological treatises, if a place is found for them at all in dogmatics.[31]

So the Church is based on a constellation of figures whose relations with Jesus are formative for the human prolongation of his divine mission, and in the way we think about them these figures – such as Mary, Peter, John – should not be separated one from another any more than they should from Christ himself.

The principle that takes its name from Peter is another fairly obvious one. In three out of the four Gospels, Peter is given a share in the divine–human authority of Christ in the Church. His office of pastoral rule – a pre-eminent example of the 'judging' for which Jesus commissions the Twelve as a whole – is going to serve as the underlying rock for the Church's stability and unity. Humiliated by his own failures and also by hard words from Jesus, the office laid on him (to 'pasture the flock of the incomparable Shepherd')[32] is an excessive demand, but what seems impossible can be granted by the grace of Christ. According to tradition, Peter will be crucified upside down, which Balthasar finds appropriate since in this manner Peter preserves the shape of Christ's destiny, though in reversed fashion as befits sinful man. The actual office of Peter is continued in the Church by the pope, though the Petrine principle is wider than simply the Petrine office. It is in fact the entire element of office-holding, official authority, in the Church. To see how Balthasar understands 'Peter' requires prior attention to his account of 'John'.

(iii) The Johannine factor

What, then, of the Johannine principle, which is less familiar to us? Balthasar stresses how this is indeed a distinct principle. When in the last chapter of the Fourth Gospel Jesus comments to Peter about the Beloved Disciple, 'If it is my will that he remain until I come, what is that to you?'[33], this for Balthasar is a prediction that, in his words:

> the Beloved Disciple will really remain, for all time, in the Church, his presence not ceasing with his death, and that this presence, sealed by the will of the Lord of the Church, is exempt from Peter's control.[34]

The Johannine principle in the continuing life of the Church is the principle of what Balthasar terms 'holy love', a love that accepts Peter's pre-eminence but also knows that only itself, responding love, and not authoritative office, is, in the words of the fourth evangelist, 'the Beloved'. The Johannine and Petrine factors are, however, interrelated, just as both of them are intrinsically related to the Marian. John, as 'apostle-priest yet adoptive son of Mary', bonds the Petrine and the Marian together.[35] For Balthasar, the words from the Cross linking Mary and the beloved disciple in St John's Gospel – 'Woman, behold your son! ... Behold, your mother!'[36] – are 'the Church's

---

31 *The Office of Peter and the Structure of the Church, op. cit.*, p. 136.
32 *Ibid.*, p. 153.
33 John 21.22.
34 *The Office of Peter and the Structure of the* Church, *op. cit.*, p. 153.
35 J. Saward, *The Mysteries of March, op. cit.*, p. 78.
36 John 19.26b-27b.

foundation document',[37] issuing from that suffering which gave the Church birth. For in binding Mary to John, they also bond her to Peter, since, as the closing chapter of that Gospel will indicate, John has some sort of representative role vis-à-vis Peter and the Twelve. Holy love – John – remains, that is, at Peter's side, at the side of the Church of office, so as to draw attention to the presence of the Lord. In this way John mediates between the Lord and Peter. In their interrelation, love and office constitute, says Balthasar, a 'huge, subtly complex figure in the Church'.[38] The visibly organized pilgrim Church on earth, with all its imperfections as well as strengths, is entrusted by Christ with the task of caring for the primordial Church created in Mary in perfect purity and holiness. In this way, John is to be the connexion between

> the whole Church, which, even as distinct from Christ, is greater than its members and surrounds them as a motherly presence, and that sacramentally consecrated portion, which is masculine and fatherly, the office of unity in the truth.[39]

The nature of this linkage means that Balthasar considers the distinction between the Petrine and Johannine principles subordinate to their complementary operation. The Church in its unity is a (Marian) communion not only in (Petrine) faith but also in (Johannine) love. But this union is manifested in the unbreakable unity of the faithful with their bishop – a Peter-figure, as the late- first-century Letters of Ignatius of Antioch show. It is also manifested – and here it is the writings of the third-century Cyprian of Carthage that are pertinent – in the unity of the bishops with each other, a unity embodied in the bishop of Rome – another Peter and an even more crucial one. The unity of the bishops around the pope 'brings about and demonstrates', writes Balthasar, 'the loving communion of all the churches'.[40] The distinction between the Johannine and the Petrine, then, cannot be taken to mean that office-holders in the Church are entitled to leave 'love' to someone else. Precisely as vicars of Christ the Shepherd, Peter-figures such as pope and bishops are required to internalize the love John represents. Peter, we note, is asked in John 21 whether he loves Christ 'more than these [others do]'.[41] Peter needs Johannine love if he is to give the Lord the response that is worthy of his supreme office.

Balthasar reminds his readers, if reminder be needed, that Protestants and the Orthodox are sceptical about the claims of the Roman bishop. This should not surprise us. Though Peter is bound together with John – meaning, his task is lovingly to shepherd the flock, the *communion*, and strengthen his brethren, the *collegium* of bishops – there is always going to be a certain controversial isolation about this figure.

> Peter *has to* step forward as an individual, over against the others, be they the people with whom he is in *communio*, or the bishops with whom he forms a *collegium*, not by 'domineering' (I Peter 5:3), but as a servant who does not detach himself from *communio* or *collegium* but

37 *The Threefold Garland, op. cit.,* p. 103.
38 *The Office of Peter and the Structure of the Church, op. cit.,* p. 160.
39 J. Saward, *The Mysteries of March, op. cit.,* p. 78.
40 *The Office of Peter and the Structure of the Church, op. cit.,* p. 164.
41 John 21.15.

rather 'strengthens' them (Luke 22: 32), frees them to be themselves in true liberty.[42]

The pope must be in some sense alone if he is to be at the service of what Balthasar calls 'Marian liberation', which is precisely liberation from all the negative spiritual bonds that the closeness of Christians to their own earth, place, time, culture may unwittingly entail, just as Mary was unconditionally free for whatever the Lord wanted in her Annunciation consent.

> To do this, Peter really needs the freedom that has had to be fought for down the centuries in the face of Conciliarism, Protestantism, Galli- canism, Jansenism, Josephism, Febronianism etc. All these place his office in shackles in order to claim for themselves, by stipulating con- ditions for 'consent' or 'reception', the authority to 'set free'; in reality their aim was to give authoritative freedom to themselves. Whereas, if the primacy was taken seriously, there seemed to be a danger of inviting the bearer of this office to use his authority irrespective of *communio* and *collegium*, the conditions demanded by these movements actually *accomplished* a break in *communio* and *collegium* by restricting the exercise of the primatial ministry and denying the primate his liberty to perform his – Marian – liberation.[43]

Still, Peter must also act in a Johannine way – which means, in the first instance, with loving respect for the Twelve. Thus, when acting as judge and teacher, the pope should use all appropriate means to ascertain the truth and express it suitably, must make an enquiry into the mind of the episcopal College – and indeed of the entire *communio* of the Church. Likewise, his mode of exercise of the primacy should be Johannine in its sensitivity to the dimension of loving contemplation that John represents. Contemplative love must shape authority's exercise. For Balthasar, what this latter imperative means in practice is an obligatory openness of the universal pastor to the missions of the saints – whether of his own time, or another. John's place is 'filled primarily by the saints', themselves living links between the Marian and the Petrine in the Church, as John was, archetypally, at the beginning.[44]

(iv) Other factors

Not even this complex interplay of Marian and Johannine with Petrine exhausts the fecundity of Balthasar's ecclesial vision where the structure of the Church is concerned. He speaks of a continuing Pauline principle – not in this context a 'subjective' matter of unusual charisms and extraordinary mystical graces in Christian experience but an 'objective' one, a principle of appropriate adaptation and creativity in preaching to Gentile (that is, pagan) culture. At the same time and conversely, there is also a Jacobine principle, named for James, the Lord's 'brother', whose defence of Torah gives him the right to stand for all that traditional continuity with the faith and practice of Israel would indicate. Balthasar has John the Baptist representing hope-filled witness and Joseph fatherhood and labour. He evokes Mary Magdalene and the spice-bearing women so as to represent the role of females in bringing

---

42 *The Office of Peter and the Structure of the Church, op. cit.*, p. 211.
43 *Ibid.*
44 *Ibid.*, p. 225.

forth Resurrection faith. He uses Martha and Mary of Bethany to stand for
the tasks and dignity of the domestic church – and the list could go on. Just as
the Petrine principle cannot function well without these others, so the pope
as chief pastor of the Church must in his policies and outlook take into
account what all of them represent. In fact it would not be hard to show that
a number of the magisterial documents of the last pope of Balthasar's lifetime, John Paul II, aim to do just that.

Behind all these 'many dimensions' is the conviction that the Church must
be at least as comprehensive as the world. Commenting on the belief of the
Fathers that Christ came to earth to bring home his bride, Balthasar says: 'The
Church represents mankind, stands to it in a necessary dynamic relationship,
even if this cannot be clearly elucidated'.[45]

> Knowing that mankind is envisaged in God's plan, she can know
> herself (in the humble consciousness of her election) as representative
> of mankind before God, in faith, prayer, and sacrifice, in hope for all,
> and still more in love for all.[46]

Balthasar's best explanation for that is found in the words: 'Bride as [the
Church] is, she is also [Christ's] body, informed by the consciousness of the
Head'.[47]

The states of life in the Church

Balthasar's theology of the states of life possible for a Christian at large is
complex, but it is also satisfying. Its originality – and difficulty – mean we
must give it space.

(i) Multiple criteria

The complexity involved is owed chiefly to Balthasar's defining the kinds of
life open to a follower of Jesus in terms of three distinct, though related,
criteria. The choice of states of life offered to us by the Church turns, that is,
on three things.

The first such criterion is twofold: the life of the Word incarnate who chose
as his state of life the mission ordained for him by the Father, and, alongside
this, the life of the Blessed Virgin Mary, prototype of the Church. In these two
persons the basic differentiation of types of life in the Church emerges fully
for the first time. It is also the case, for Balthasar, that in the Saviour and his
Mother this variety of lives finds its supreme reconciliation – shows itself, in
other words, to be not just a diversity but also a unity, since those who
occupy different Christian states of life – for instance, Religious and those
living in the world as priests and laity – do not for all that belong to different
churches. We can call this Balthasar's 'Christo-Mariological criterion' for
judging the Church's different 'estates'.

Secondly, Balthasar explains the main alternatives set before us – the life
of the commandments lived in the world or the life of the counsels lived in
Religious life – in terms of that criterion which is the fundamental situation of

---

45 'Who is the Church?', *art. cit.*, p. 182.
46 *Ibid.*, p. 183.
47 *Ibid.*

man before God. Man who was originally created in integrity or 'justice', who by abuse of freedom fell, is called by grace to resume in a new, Christ-centred way, the life of righteousness. We can call this Balthasar's 'soteriological criterion' for evaluating different life-ways in the Church.

And thirdly, Balthasar presents the choice of lives in the Church as a function of the way the Jesus of the Galilaean ministry called to himself twelve special disciples[48], where the 'primary election' was to share in a definitive and intimate fashion Jesus' own life and only secondarily and later, to form these men into the nucleus of the ecclesiastical hierarchy, the ministerial priesthood. On the basis of the Lord's public ministry Balthasar feels able to hold that the 'state of evangelical perfection' enjoys a pre-eminence vis-à-vis the 'ecclesiastical ministry' though he by no means denies the origins of the latter in the Jesus of history's words and will. He writes:

> The *duae vitae* [the two ways of life], neither of which excludes the other, existed in the Church from the beginning, as did the priestly office, which throughout history has sought in often dramatic ways to define its relationship to [them].[49]

We can call this Balthasar's 'Jesuological criterion'. Its perspective is more simply human, and less explicitly Trinitarian than the first. Perhaps because it is the easiest to grasp, Balthasar will begin with it. But in point of fact all three criteria, in keeping with the general caste of Balthasar's theology, are at root Christocentric in character. (Even the soteriological criterion is really Christological through and through since for Balthasar, 'all chronology to the contrary notwithstanding, ... Christ comes before Adam: as the true omega, he is also the true alpha'.[50])

One might ask why Balthasar employed these three different criteria – Christo-Mariological, soteriological, 'Jesuological' – simultaneously when any one, taken by itself, could have sufficed for drawing up a nice little theology of the states of life. Why does he make his account so complicated and risk, therefore, cluttering it up? Quite apart from the synthetic quality of his own theological mind, which naturally wanted to draw into the picture as many elements of the faith as possible, we can say that the reason has to do with the subtlety of the conclusion at which he aims. He wants to show that the states of life in the Church 'refer' (as he puts it) to each other. They depend on each other not only for our understanding of them but also for their intrinsic value. Accordingly, each can be seen as primary, depending on our perspective. At the same time, however, he wants to marry to this thesis of the 'fruitful complementarity' of the states of life the doctrine of the Council of Trent that, as between these states of life, there is a definite ranking of lower and higher which it would be seriously wrong (he actually says 'anathema') to deny. Having both these aims in view simultaneously,

---

48 Balthasar draws here on H. Schürmann, 'Der Jüngerkreis Jesu als Zeichen für Israel und als Urbild des kirchlichen Rätestandes', reprinted in *idem, Ursprung und Gestalt. Erörterungen und Besinnungen zum Neuen Testament* (Düsseldorf, 1970), pp. 46–60; and M. Hengel, *Nachfolge und Charisma* (Berlin, 1958) which attacks the idea that the historical Jesus merely accepted temporary disciples, whereas only after Easter was this relation understood as binding for life.

49 *The Christian State of Life, op. cit.*, pp. 15–16.

50 *Ibid.*, p. 18.

Balthasar can hardly escape making his account more complicated than we might like.

(ii) Commandments or counsels?

Balthasar's study *Christlicher Stand* begins with St Ignatius, and more specifically, with his *Spiritual Exercises*. In those 'Exercises' Ignatius points out that Christ has given us an example of both the life of the commandments and the life of the counsels. Jesus exemplified the first in his own obedience to his parents, Mary and Joseph. He exemplified the second by leaving his family so as, in Ignatius's words, to 'devote himself exclusively to the service of his eternal Father'. Ignatius draws from this duality of Christ's example to us the conclusion that we can love God perfectly in either way of life – that of the commandments or that of the counsels. Balthasar juxtaposes with this broad statement, reassuring to the ordinary laity and the secular clergy in the Church, Ignatius's other statement in his so-called *Directory*, dictated a few months before his death, that nevertheless clearer signs are needed to show someone that they are called to the life of the commandments when compared with those signs which indicate that someone should enter Religious life, the life of the counsels. This reversal of what we might reasonably expect (surely Religious life is something exceptional, for the comparative few?) reflects Ignatius's commitment to the teaching of the Gospel and the Church that the life of the counsels is in some sense a better way. What Balthasar aims to do with these interestingly contrasting texts is to show that there is no dichotomy in the Church between the evangelical state and the secular state – the state of being in the world as a layperson or, where this exists, as a married priest (the case of *celibate* secular clerics is, evidently, less clear-cut) and also at the same time to demonstrate that nonetheless these states are indeed meant to be different. They are not interchangeable and should not be merged or confused. From the standpoint of the early twenty-first century we can add that, if to exaggerate the distinction between the states was a weakness of Catholicism before the Second Vatican Council, to minimize their difference was a typical failure of Catholicism after that mid-twentieth-century watershed.

One simple principle cuts through the complexity of Balthasar's project: love, as command and as calling. Charity – love – defined by Jesus in the conversation with the scribe close to the Kingdom in Matthew 22.36-40, and declared by reference to his own practice a 'new commandment' at the Last Supper in John 13.34-35 – is the objective norm for every kind of call to discipleship, just as it is also the subjective norm for every answer to those calls. Balthasar – instructed, surely, by Gregory of Nyssa – sings a paean to love's indefinite capacity for growth. Analysing the *structura amoris* he finds that love delights not only in giving self but also in accepting gifts: '[f]or love, even receiving is a form of self-giving'.[51] If we truly love, says Balthasar, anticipating his discussion of the evangelical counsels:

> We will regard it as our greatest *freedom* to do, not our own will, but the will of the beloved. We will treasure it as our greatest *riches* to possess nothing but what the beloved bestows upon us. We will esteem it our

---

51 *Ibid.*, p. 29.

greatest *fecundity to be but a vessel held in readiness for every fructifying seed of the beloved.*[52]

Love, notes Balthasar, following the lead of Maximus the Confessor in a way clearly pertinent to the vows:

> is so steadfast that it never reverts to the point of indifference that precedes choice. It rejects 'freedom of choice' [what Maximus had termed 'gnomic will'] in favour of freedom of love.[53]

In this context, the commandments are positive inasmuch as they point to love. They are negative in that, by their veiling the unity of freedom and inevitability typical of love, they can never be indices of perfection. Love fulfils the law, certainly. But it is more than the sum of the individual commandments. 'The very structure of our ethics changes as we draw near to or away from love.'[54]

For Balthasar 'ethical time' *tout court* is that time when we live simply by reference to particular obligations. Only when love becomes the animating principle of life do the commands find their unity, whereupon ethical time is transfigured by the light of the eternal. This turnabout reflects the transition from the Torah, central to the Old Testament as that is, to the Paschal Mystery, key to the New.

> It is the path from slavery under many commandments to the freedom of 'sons of the house' which they enjoy who have received the Holy Spirit of love poured into their hearts by the loving action of God in the Incarnation and Cross of his Son.[55]

More specifically, the Son made man shows us how the dichotomy of command and counsel, obligation and choice, may be overcome:

> Since the Son has no other wish than to fulfil every wish and will of the Father, he has bridged the gap between ethical time and loving eternity.[56]

Balthasar piles up citations from the Fathers (Cyril of Alexandria and Ambrose), the mediaevals (Anselm) and modern – well, nineteenth-century – theologians (Johann Baptist Franzelin) to show how in the Son obedience and freedom coincide. The commands he obeys are counsels of the Father given him not by way of precept but by his generation – as who he is, the Father's beloved Son. Balthasar adds that this enables us to see how the Holy Spirit can be the 'epitome of the most free, and yet the most demanding, love'.[57] These considerations throw light on the somewhat mystifying claims to peculiar turpitude sometimes made for themselves by the saints. 'The disobedience of one who loves to even the least wishes of love is much more serious than that of one who is far from love...'[58] No progress in love ever

52 *Ibid.*
53 *Ibid.*, p. 30.
54 *Ibid.*, p. 33.
55 *Ibid.*, p. 34.
56 *Ibid.*, p. 35.
57 *Ibid.*, p. 37.
58 *Ibid.*, p. 38.

takes place, asserts Balthasar, without a modicum of *Hingabe*, self-surrender, and this always implies a will to lay one's freedom 'once and for all at the feet of love'. When love is awakened, time is transformed into a form of eternity in which love seeks to outlast time and 'for this purpose, to rid itself of its most dangerous enemy, freedom of choice'. This is why 'every true love has *the inner form of a vow*'.[59] In the first instance, Balthasar has in mind the Baptismal vows. But – following St Thomas who makes the same connexion – the vows of the Religious life are already in view.[60]

Balthasar now needs to show how the distinction between a life of love based on the evangelical counsels and a life of love based simply on the precept to love can best be sustained. He looks first to St Thomas. In the *De perfectione spiritualis vitae* Thomas speaks initially of the three counsels represented by the vows of poverty, chastity and obedience as chiefly means to an end that is common to all the faithful: the perfection of charity. The counsels dispose us to the perfect love of God. But soon enough Thomas changes his tack. The counsels also embody higher degrees of love since they proceed from greater renunciation of self. Balthasar's description of Thomas's condensed account of the vows in the *Secunda Pars* of the *Summa theologiae* is not unfair. Thomas depicts them:

> now as a means to a goal that transcends them, now as participation and repose in that goal, now again as a representation and exemplification of the goal.[61]

But as Balthasar points out *pace* Aquinas, the Church has never taught that the two states of life – according to counsel, according to precept – can properly be distinguished as a state of perfect love and a state of imperfect love respectively. So if the differentiation of the states is not to be explained in terms of our love for God it is incumbent on us to find some other way of understanding it.

This is where he turns to St Ignatius who places so much emphasis, as is well known, on the idea of *election*. How can we choose to be what God himself elects us to be? Reference to Ignatian principles adds a new dimension. 'True love', says Balthasar:

> is ready to follow any path, whether rough or smooth. It is as ready to follow the way of the commandments as the way of the counsels. Such a love is perfect even when the ultimate gift is not required of it. [Those who possess it] ... are content even if more is not demanded of them as it is of other, more privileged, souls. They accept it as a sacrifice not to have been called upon to sacrifice all they were willing to sacrifice.[62]

In this case, to choose the life of the commandments would imply no inferiority vis-à-vis a choice of the life of the counsels *if one were perfectly indifferent as to which one chose and simply followed in this respect the will of God*. And yet – shades of the problem we encountered in Thomas – Ignatius *also* presents the

59 *Ibid.*, p. 39. Italics are original.
60 Thomas Aquinas, *De perfectione vitae spiritualis*, 12.
61 *The Christian State of Life*, op. cit., p. 53, with reference to Thomas Aquinas, *Summa theologiae* IIa. IIae., q. 186, a. 7.
62 *Ibid.*, p. 55.

way of the counsels as 'unambiguously better than the way of the commandments'.[63] (Ignatian) appeal to the elective love of God for man, it would
seem, is no more helpful in our quest than is (Thomasian) appeal to man's
love for God.

So Balthasar must try yet another tack. *In via*, he suggests, on our pilgrimage, the counsels are best seen as a means to an end that can be achieved
without them. But *in patria*, in our homeland, or when we contemplate love
in its unconditional perfection, the picture looks different. Since such love

> is essentially the gift of self, it ... contains in itself both the content and
> the form of the vows, to which it gives a constantly new expression.[64]

Here we have the key we need. Thus, speaking *formaliter*:

> every objective differentiation of the individual states of life will be
> based on the extent to which the totality of this vow to love is realized
> in each of them...

and speaking *materialiter* there is here a material totality which – ever since
the twelfth century – has been divided into three segments covering together
all that perfect love can offer, namely: all the goods of this world one has or
might have (compare poverty), the goods of one's own body (compare
chastity), and all one's spiritual goods, one's powers of memory, understanding and will (compare obedience). The solution is the intrinsic relation
of the views *eschatologically*, to what the love-command represents.

(iii) From primal image to final likeness

Balthasar will endeavour to show later how the *spirit* of what Thomas called
these *tria principalia vota* – the 'three chief vows' – may be incorporated into
every Christian state of life. Meanwhile he wants to move out from this
'immanent analysis of the structure of love' to a more 'substantial and concrete consideration of man as God conceived him', in humanity's *Ur-stand* or
primordial condition, the 'state' of original righteousness. For the Book of
Genesis, man is created in the image of God and if he is to grow into the
likeness of his archetype this will be, following Balthasar's version of the
analogia entis doctrine, not through any identification where the Mirrored and
the mirror become one, but on the contrary by maintaining that difference
which is a prerequisite of love. Humankind's love for God, then, must 'have
the inner form of dependence and submission'.[65] To love God is for the
human creature a privileged service – in which sense Balthasar feels able to
reinstate the language of duty and obligation he had earlier – in a consideration of love grown cold – deemed unworthy of this subject.

> If, by reason of the distance from God that is inherent in man's crea-
> tureliness, the concept of 'duty' must after all come to be associated
> with love, it is only because, for the creature, a love that is whole and
> undivided cannot be separated from that *glorification of God in service*
> that is the natural concomitant of its creaturehood.[66]

63 *Ibid.*, p. 57.
64 *Ibid.*, p. 64.
65 *Ibid.*, p. 68.
66 *Ibid.*, p. 70.

As will readily be seen, when considering man's original state, Balthasar deems it necessary to look forward to the future condition in whose direction that state moves us: we are to be not only in God's image but to his likeness. From the start our nature – though in itself not grace, not love – is enwrapped in a gracious calling. Human nature was first established in a 'state of grace'. But straightaway Balthasar adds – and this is in keeping with his presentation of the doctrine of man in his theological dramatics – that how each person is to draw on and utilize his or her gifts by virtue of human nature under grace turns entirely on their personal mission, and this 'proceeds directly from God'.[67]

In the beginning, holds Balthasar, there were no 'lines of division' between states of life. The 'lines' we see today in the Church are linked to the epoch of redemption and consequently presuppose the Fall. Those lines presume human sin. Still, the order of redemption is precisely that of a redeemed creation. Accordingly, Balthasar argues:

> The later states must, each in its own way, reflect something of the one idea that God intended from the beginning to realize in the creation of man.[68]

Looking back, we should be able to see the present states as pointing convergently to that primordial condition.

Actually that is not Balthasar's method – at any rate not immediately – in what follows. Rather, he reviews a great deal of patristic and mediaeval commentary on the original condition of man (before the arrival of the Latin Aristotle, note well!) and comes to the conclusion expressed in the following citation whose importance for his thesis justifies its length. What was man like in paradise?

> He was the wholeness of what was later split into opposites: the perfect, seamless and unassailable unity of obedient faith as insight and freedom; of virginal purity as fecundity; and of poverty as fullness and riches without distinction of mine and thine. Because Adam was obedient, he was the sovereign ruler of all creation. Because Eve and he were virgins, they were destined for the highest fecundity of purity. Because they were totally poor, they lived in the superabundance of God's gifts and knew neither need nor want. *Man's original state, then, was the perfect synthesis of the Christian state of life whether in the world or in the way of the evangelical counsels, in which the state of the counsels expressed the inner attitude and disposition, the worldly state the outer counterpart and fulfillment.*[69]

---

67 *Ibid.*, p. 75. By contrast to the account in *Theodrama* Balthasar here introduces the theme of mission as a way of avoiding the ascetic strain which the difference between nature and grace otherwise entails. Any danger of split personality or resentment against God for the new, non-natural nobility of the order of grace would be withdrawn if 'grace is perceived as the inner form of man's personal mission rather than as a beautiful garment that clothes him without removing the underlying poverty of his nature and origin', *ibid.*, p. 74.
68 *Ibid.*, p. 84.
69 *Ibid.*, p. 121. Italics are original.

So: *interiorly* paradisal man had the substance of the counsels to perfection. But *exteriorly* he had all riches, blessings, fullness. And that was because in his unfallen condition the counsels entailed no renunciation of any created gift.

The Fall would have led man to certain destruction had it not been accompanied by the promise of salvation – through the Mother and Child envisaged in the Proto-evangelium of Genesis 3.15. Holy Mary is the turning point in a drama whose outcome is the fulfilment of what the original paradise inaugurated on earth.

> In the full obedience of her assent, she would extinguish what Eve's greedy obedience had kindled. In the flawless purity of her perfect virginity, she would realize – and more than realize – the fecundity of paradise by bearing God himself, who would redeem the world from its guilt. In the perfect poverty that put her whole being, body and soul, at the disposal of God's design, she would replace with the riches of man's original self-giving the poverty of need he was compelled to endure in his fallen state.[70]

The heaven to which the Incarnation of the Word thus points through Mary is the 'perfect union of what, in this fallen world, is now found disunited in the two states of life'.[71] Heaven, humanity's eschatological goal, is the perfect identity of obedience and freedom, of virginity and fruitfulness, of poverty and riches shared, Balthasar's account of the latter being most original (and controversial), since under 'poverty' he includes the hard lesson that those who have been

> preoccupied with right and justice in this world will have to struggle to accept, [namely,]... that there is no distinction of mine and thine even in matters of guilt; that they must see in every sin, by whomsoever it has been committed, an offence against the eternal love of God; ... and must be disposed, therefore, to do penance, as long as may be deemed necessary by God, for every sin no matter who is its perpetrator.[72]

But, as history records, the unity which, so revelation teaches, existed in the paradisal state and was meant to continue into the heavenly, disintegrated on man's Fall. To this two equally undesirable reactions have proved possible: sullen resignation and defiant titanism. Only one possibility, however, can serve man's turn: divinely initiated reconciliation. Balthasar presents a little theology of sin and redemption which climaxes in a teaching on *klêsis*, election – God's choosing people, and *eklogê*, vocation – the manifestation of God's choice. He identifies these undoubtedly Petrine terms (compare Second Peter 1.10) by placing an Ignatian lens over the New Testament's pages. Election and vocation form the basis of the Christian state of life which subsists, therefore, in a divine act of engracement that places one 'outside the "world"', by life in a new and separated community – a life *in the Church*. Indeed,

70 *Ibid.*, pp. 122–23.
71 *Ibid.*, p. 123.
72 *Ibid.*, p. 127.

in its substance, the Church is none other than the objectification of God's choice and the formalization of his call manifested in the world as the state in which man finds himself when election and vocation have touched an individual or community.[73]

One might suppose, then, that all Christians would share the same state of life. The Gospel makes it plain, however, that this is not so. A further division appears and of a twofold kind: between the life of the counsels and the secular state, and between the priestly state and the lay. We saw at the outset of this exposition how for Balthasar the calling of the people – disciples generally – must be distinguished from the calling of the Twelve, a calling ordered first to a more intimate sharing of life with the Saviour and only secondly to the constitution of the ministerial priesthood. The calling of the Twelve is not only from the world that lies outside the Church, but even 'from the world within the Church' and for such, accordingly:

> Every attempt to cling to the world one has renounced threatens not just a part but the totality of one's apostleship.[74]

To the future apostles all the hard sayings of the Gospel tradition apply with full force, including those on which the evangelical counsels find their foundation. At the same time, the Lord proposes for the needs of those who answer this more radical call by following him in poverty, chastity and obedience, a 'supernatural sociology' whereby – albeit 'in the midst of persecutions' (Mark 10.30) – they shall have goods, including relations and spouses, a hundredfold.

Poverty comes first. It is the entrance gate to the rest, the most visible version of 'leaving all things'. At first, virginity will seem a subset of poverty (abandoning one's partner is part and parcel of becoming poor). Eventually, it will acquire a primacy but, to begin with, the Redeemer made his choice from the faithful of the House of Israel for whom marriage was itself a 'state of promise'.[75] The core of the apostolic life, however, is obedience, which allows

> Christ's perfect obedience to the Father ... to become actually incarnate in the relationship of superior and subject within the supernatural sociology of the evangelical state.[76]

The call to go to Christ, *pros auton* (Matthew 10.1); to be at his side, *met' autou* (Mark 3.14); to be near him, *peri auton* (Mark 4.10); to be with him, *syn auto* (Luke 8.38) is a call to join him in a

> love that revealed itself in radical renunciation, by a sacrifice no longer [as retrospectively in paradise or prospectively in heaven] joined to fulfillment and joy, but accomplished in the night and abandonment of the Cross.[77]

---

73 *Ibid.*, p. 140.
74 *Ibid.*, p. 150.
75 *Ibid.*, p. 155.
76 *Ibid.*, p. 157.
77 *Ibid.*, p. 159.

In such a life, however, there is 'rest' for the soul (Matthew 11.29), and a peace 'which passes all understanding' (Philippians 4.7), since there is here – despite what has just been said – a foretaste of the heavenly homeland. How so? Balthasar explains that

> The new state created by the Lord and possible only on the basis of his own way of life, of the unity of the two natures in his divine person, is, in its turn, a synthesis of earthly and paradisal life. It means taking one's stand by the Cross, which is the gateway to paradise, or taking one's stand in the paradise that has been restored to mankind in the form of the Cross. It is fullness despite renunciation.

This cannot be the final form of life, since in the Age to Come suffering will be no more. But it is 'a principal access by which man can attain to this final state'.[78]

(iv) Monasticism and Christian secularity

Now Balthasar has to relate *to each other* the two states of life in the Church: the life of the counsels, and the 'secular' life, redeemed life lived in the *saeculum*, the still-to-be-redeemed world. Basically, whereas there is a universal vocation to perfect Christian love, the calling to express this in a 'state of perfection' – the life of the counsels – turns entirely on God's elective will. A moment's reflection will show that a call to renunciation of the kind required by the counsels could not be universal in this world. Were it to be so, it would endanger the continuance of the natural order. The universalization of the evangelical state within the Church would revive Marcionism. It would disjoin redemption from creation, nullifying the Creator's initial demands, 'Be fruitful and multiply; fill the earth and subdue it' (Genesis 1.28). That would never do. Thus Balthasar concludes that:

> the dividing of the states of life was the most meaningful way of establishing within the fallen world an order of redemption.[79]

Those called to the monastic or Religious life are always going to be a minority among the people of God. However, its iconic value to the Church *is* universal. As Balthasar puts it:

> The state of election ... is ... the representation of what was once *form-giving* in man's lost state of innocence and will be *form-giving* again in his hoped-for final state ...

In the upshot, then, the anathemas of the Council of Trent are vindicated. The 'secular' state in the Church is not of equal significance with the monastic. It 'can be described only as a not-having-been-called to a qualitatively higher state'.[80] What compensates positively for this negative formulation is that Christians living in the world, unlike Religious, have the privilege of cultural responsibility ('subduing the earth') which depends on the initial creation calling. That is so even though the call to perfect love carries such 'secular' Christians beyond the order of creation – which is why St Paul could regret

78 *Ibid.*, p. 161.
79 *Ibid.*, p. 166.
80 *Ibid.*, p. 168.

they were 'divided' (1 Corinthians 7.33). They are in this world, but not really of it. Putting all this together, then:

> While the state of election, by reason of God's special call, allows one to anticipate the world to come even in this world, but always on the foundation of the Cross, the secular state embodies life in transition from this world to the world to come.[81]

When Christians carry out their cultural task, accordingly, they perform 'works of longing' rather than 'works of fulfilment'.

In what sense, then, can the secular Christian make the counsels his or her own? Balthasar's reply is that they can and should make the *spirit* of those counsels their own. 'In the last analysis, the common denominator of the two states consists in their readiness for the renunciation that makes one free for love.'[82]

So far we have been thinking of the states of life principally on the basis of the 'Jesuological criterion': Jesus' differentiated call to discipleship in his ministry, though, to be sure, the 'soteriological criterion' has also come into play, thanks to Balthasar's 'tensing' of the states between Paradise and Heaven through redemption in Christ. But now we need some reference to the 'Christo-Mariological criterion' which is surely the profoundest of the three. The primacy of Christ is such that he does not, by his own 'state of life', simply overcome the disparity between the paradisal state or state of innocence and that of fallen nature. (Here a perspective of a quasi-Scotist sort enters Balthasar's vision – compare the account of Incarnation and Passion in the last chapter.) Rather, even the former, original, state of man must be understood in terms of Christ's state – and not vice versa. Any state of life worth having must be 'in' the 'personal divine–human reality that is Christ'.[83] Indeed, the created world can turn away from the Father by sin only because it was first incorporated into the Word's orientation towards the Father!

In a Trinitarian excursus, Balthasar tells us that:

> Just as all the words Christ spoke on earth are but facets and aspects of the one eternal Word that he is, so all the states that he experienced in the course of his life, death and Resurrection are outward manifestations of his unique eternal state in the Father.[84]

As students of Balthasar's theology of the Paschal Mystery will be aware, he holds that, in the 'economy', the relation of the Son and Spirit in the 'theology' – the Triune life in and of itself – is temporarily reversed – and this is pertinent now. That 'inversion' alone explains (in Balthasarian thought) how the Son can become the model of filial obedience for man.

> [B]y the self-emptying of the Incarnation, he has placed himself in a position where, *even within the Godhead*, he must first *receive* from the Father the possibility of breathing out the Spirit together with him – that is, *in the position proper to created man*, who has no other way of

81 *Ibid.*, pp. 170–71.
82 *Ibid.*, p. 172.
83 *Ibid.*, p. 185.
84 *Ibid.*, p. 189.

receiving the Spirit (or of bestowing him on others) than by obeying him as the missioning Spirit (that is, as the Spirit who conveys God's will).[85]

Yet throughout the Son made man is 'in his own person, the realization of the comprehensive and unified idea of the world that the triune God had in the beginning'.[86] As the 'measure' of the analogy between God and the world – something he remains in all his incarnate conditions, there is no dichotomy between his state in the world and his state in the Father, he is the 'concrete analogy of being', a familiar *topos* in Balthasar's Barthianized Thomism. For creation 'there is ultimately no other relationship to God than that established in Christ the Lord'.[87] That being so, we must be able to find in him the key to the duality yet unity of the states of life in the Church. He must be 'the source of both possible states of life without himself having to take a double stand'.[88]

Any reader of the Gospel can see at once how this can be. In the first thirty years of his earthly life, the Lord exemplified the 'secular' state of family, work, society, and so 'the possibility of taking one's stand as child, youth and adult in the Father and in his will and mission'.[89] But then with the start of his public ministry he distanced himself from all of this, seeking to found a new supernatural community around the disciples he called. In both, however, the incarnate Word obediently does the Father's willing, thereby furnishing the foundation for their subsequent unity in the life of his holy people. At the wedding feast of Cana we see the Saviour distancing himself from the first state, represented by his Mother, while also looking ahead to the 'hour' of the Cross when their states will again be identical. Reference to the Cross is key since there the Son freely offered to the Father all the resources of his humanity to dispose of as the Father chose. This carries implications for the future 'state of election' in the Church.

> The radicalization of the secular state is not in itself sufficient to give form to the state of election; for that, there is needed a new and qualitative act of God who, in an ecstatic transcendence of all secular possibilities, establishes a new state of life through his acceptance of the Son's sacrifice on the Cross.[90]

Both states are rooted, however, in Christ's unique state – which is why Balthasar is optimistic they can share the same 'spirit'.

Balthasar's allusion to the mystery enacted at Cana, the first – so St John would see it – of Jesus' 'signs', already hints that he will not here leave out of account the Mother of the Lord. (I called his primary criterion for distinguishing the states of life not simply 'Christological' but 'Christo-Mariological'.) So, having argued that in his all-embracing state of life the Word incarnate founds in himself both the unity of the states of life in the Church and their distinction, Balthasar now wants to say something similar

85 *Ibid.*, p. 190. Italics are original.
86 *Ibid.*, p. 192.
87 *Ibid.*, p. 193.
88 *Ibid.*, p. 194.
89 *Ibid.*, p. 195.
90 *Ibid.*, p. 199.

of Mary who *is* the Church at her beginnings. Blessed Mary passed through both states – the secular state, and the state of election – and can claim to be patron of both (after all, she is both mother, in a natural community with her husband Joseph, and virgin, in a post-Calvary 'community of virgins' with John). But like her Son she stands above both, and *by virtue of this very transcendence can share with him in their actual founding.*

How does she 'stand above both'? Owing to her Immaculate Conception, the post-lapsarian break-up of the integrated state of original righteousness does not affect her. At the same time, as a human creature she has to grow into, or towards, the will of God. Not all was light for her all the time. As Balthasar attractively puts it:

> Until her meeting with the angel, she was indeed at God's disposal, but only in the mode of a waiting that did not yet know its true mission.[91]

Her 'indifference', however, was always 'the indifference of the most perfect love'.[92] But because Mary became a mother *thanks to her virginity* – her bodily fecundity followed from the spiritual fecundity of her *Fiat* – she is not virgin and mother 'by an equal title'. Rather, the 'pre-eminence' of the state of election over the secular state is manifest in her. At the same time, however, the purpose of her entire existence *lies in her motherhood*. And this shows that the state of election is only 'superior' because it is subordinated to the good of the secular state in the Church, placing itself at its service. In evangelical hierarchicalism, nothing can be higher unless it serves more. Balthasar's account of Mary's 'service' consists in a theology of her role at the Cross and in her heavenly intercession.

> Mary does not have to leave the contemplation of her Son to dispense her love, her assistance and her mediation on all the paths of earth. She does so because her Son has done so before her in Eucharistic pro-digality, and it is no more necessary for her than for him to alter her stand in God's will in order to bend pityingly and efficaciously over all the world's suffering and guilt.[93]

But this disposition was shaped by her standing at the Cross.

> Only by embracing the extremity of this suffering does Mary become the mother of all Christendom. For the mystery of her virginity and exclusive dedication of herself to God must extend to that final emp-tying of herself of all things that is possible only in God if it is to attain beyond all worldly fecundity to the new fecundity that is likewise possible only in God.[94]

Both states of life in the Church, Balthasar insists, are called to represent the 'Christo-Mariological criterion' – of which, evidently, the 'Christic' component is primary – in different ways. The Christian 'stand', not least in the secular state, is 'in' Christ – which means (here Balthasar combats the secular*ized* theology of the 1960s and 70s) that no stand outside Christ can for

91 *Ibid.*, p. 202.
92 *Ibid.*, p. 203.
93 *Ibid.*, p. 206.
94 *Ibid.*, p. 209.

a Christian create a bond between Christ and the world. And to guard against misunderstandings of the very concept of a secular state, and one, moreover, once inhabited by Christ, Balthasar adds:

> By using nature for his own ends, which are always divine and supernatural, he enables it to fulfil the purpose for which it was created. It would have been pointless for him to appear personally in the world as the Word of God if his purpose was merely to confirm the laws of nature rather than to reveal a totally new being who surpassed and transcended them. What he came to demonstrate was *God's freedom with respect to his own creation* even when he was within that creation.[95]

And this same freedom he calls 'even' Christians in the world to share. 'Secular' Christians are in the world but free of it since free for Christ. Every Christian is one of those 'whom God, by his loving choice, has allowed to participate in the redemptive work and suffering of his Son'.[96] His or her life and state are likewise a sharing in the Resurrection of the Lord, since the Head of the body is already in glory. The order of the day can hardly be, then, for the natural man, 'business as usual', though Balthasar insists this does not call into question the normal earthly framework of existence, which is taken up, not destroyed. Balthasar finds the case of marriage a good example – if also one it is incumbent on him to treat since a theology of the Christian state of life can hardly prescind from mention of the life of the married.

> By filling all things with his grace ..., *he* [Christ] *also filled marriage*, but he filled it *with a grace that had its source more deeply in the mystery of God than did the marriage of paradise*. That is why marriage, as a Christian sacrament, must henceforth issue from this higher source. Having its model and measure in Christ, it must also adopt his mind and spirit if it is to be a Christian marriage.[97]

Of course, a like transformation happens to celibacy too – which in principle *could* be undertaken naturalistically, so as to secure this – worldly goals – in the service of art, say, or one of the caring professions. But 'Christian virginity stands or falls with the mystery of the Cross'.[98] It belongs with the wound in Christ's side from which the Church is born. Incidentally, Balthasar will recognize no third state alongside marriage and virginity. There are countless exceptions but they prove the rule. 'Until one chooses a state of life [i.e. one of these two], one must continue in a state of waiting ...',[99] which may, for reasons beyond one's control, last until death. Holy widowhood, recognized as a distinct condition since the Pauline Letters, is no true example of a third way: the widow, for Paul, is free to choose re-marriage or spiritual virginity. Balthasar is no Jerome. He has an exceptionally high doctrine of marriage which, he says, cannot be regarded simply as a natural reality subsequently raised to sacramental status.

95 *Ibid.*, p. 214. Italics here, and in all other citations from this work, are in the original.
96 *Ibid.*, p. 219.
97 *Ibid.*, p. 233.
98 *Ibid.*, p. 235.
99 *Ibid.*, p. 242.

Marriage could only be made a sacrament by sharing in the spirit of Christ on the Cross, and in this spirit it could not share unless it had retained 'something of the spirit of paradise as it was before the division of the states of life'.[100] The self-surrender and fruitfulness of the Cross is re-found in marriage's two conjoined meanings: the giving of the spouses to each other unto death and their glad acceptance of fruit in children. Here – following Balthasar's analogy between the Holy Trinity and the family, and his thesis that the Cross is itself a disclosure of the Trinity, the 'law of Trinitarian love is itself revealed'.[101]

(v) Priestly or lay?

So far Balthasar has not discussed the distinction between ministerial priesthood and lay Christian existence, which constitutes the 'second division' ('distinction' would be a better term) among the states of life envisaged by the Lord for his Church. He does not regret this delay, since the state of the counsels pre-existed the priestly state, and the Twelve (or, following St Luke, the *apostles*) were led from the one to the other only at the time of the Saviour's death. On the other hand, as he admits – indeed emphasizes – there is a special affinity between them.

> To the extent ... that *poverty, chastity and obedience are the inner modalities of the Son's perfect love, which becomes, through them, a sacrificial offering,* these modalities cannot fail to signify *the establishment of his priesthood.*[102]

And this because Christ becomes priest when he offers himself as victim. Christ contains in his own divine–human being the unity of priestly office and love – and this unity he realizes precisely because his is a *victimal* priesthood. For Balthasar it is crucial that Christ's 'objective' high priesthood be not seen as extrinsically added to his 'subjective' being as the One who is the Son given to, and accepted by, the Father. In his atoning work, there is for Jesus no 'bare *opus operatum*', and from this standpoint, where 'the objective act of offering is absorbed by the subjective passivity of being offered':

> the state of the counsels – the state of the total offering of oneself (the holo-caust) – would seem to be the authentic Christian continuation of the priestly state of the Old Testament.[103]

To this extent, then, the virginal life formed at the foot of the Cross is sacerdotal – and Mary and John are its primal embodiments.

But this cannot be the whole story. There must also be a sense in which the Lord's priesthood exists in its sheer objectivity – and as such is mediated to others in the later Church. We have here, then, a bipartite claim about the incompleteness of subjective absorption.

Balthasar's reason for making the first assertion entailed by this claim is entirely dependent on his personal staurology, his somewhat idiosyncratic theology of the Cross. The Redeemer, in taking upon himself the sins of the world:

100 *Ibid.*, p. 244.
101 *Ibid.*, p. 247.
102 *Ibid.*, p. 252.
103 *Ibid.*, pp. 255, 254.

must divest himself so completely, in his sacrifice, of all conscious and sensible love that *his act of sacrifice acquires in the night of the Cross the character of pure objectivity, of an official priesthood.*[104]

In the second assertion, by contrast, Balthasar reflects the tradition. The Lord of the Church did not choose to bestow his grace invisibly but through the 'visible signs that are meaningful for man's corporeal and sense-bound nature'.[105] To meet the needs of the faithful, there had to be for the whole Church a priesthood whose authority is comparable to that of a superior for a Religious community (let us call it, then, a pastoral priesthood), and furthermore, such a priesthood, so as to fulfil its mandate, *'mediates the entire fullness of the concrete presence of the Lord within the Church and dispenses his grace through the sacraments'* (which must mean it is also a sanctifying priesthood).[106] Nor could such a priesthood be empowered for its work unless it also communicated Christ's perfect representation of the Father's truth (and so, finally, it has to be a teaching priesthood). Thus we get to the 'threefold office' which, for many, if not all, Catholic theologians in Balthasar's lifetime, was considered the best way to lay out the tasks of the ordained. We do not have to prove, states Balthasar blithely – though certainly not incorrectly – that the Lord instituted such an apostolic priesthood since the Gospels show him doing so. More vital for us is to reflect on how no subjective love could ever warrant acceptance of so awesome an office. Even though these office-bearers must strive to reproduce such love to the degree possible (*fully* would be impossible), the 'mark of absolute imparity between person and office is the beginning and end of the Church's authority'.[107] Here is Augustinian anti-Donatism and no mistake!

How shall we see, then, the relation of such priestly office to the state of the counsels? The question is of no mere theoretical interest since it cannot but raise the issue of the celibacy of the (secular) priesthood in the patriarchate of the West. Though the priesthood is first and foremost an objective function it is also, secondly, a way of life congruent with that function though for Balthasar the congruence is of a paradoxical order.

The priestly existence ... is definitively rooted in the gaping discrepancy between office and person and thus in an ethos that stems radically from humility and is kept alive by the constantly renewed humiliations that manifest and actualize the lasting imparity between [official] dignity and [personal] accomplishment.[108]

The Religious seeks to represent the Lord subjectively in his life, while the priest by office can by the power accorded him make Christ objectively present in his ministerial acts – which Balthasar summarizes as 'sermons, Mass, sacraments and pastoral ministry'.[109] The priest is an instrument

---

104 *Ibid.*, p. 255. For Balthasar, as the last chapter showed, Christ suffers on the Cross in an absolute or blind obedience, no longer seeing the Father or understanding the meaning of his own action.
105 *Ibid.*, p. 260.
106 *Ibid.*
107 *Ibid.*, p. 264.
108 *Ibid.*, pp. 268–69.
109 *Ibid.*, p. 270.

through which God can work even when the man resists. But the gift given a Religious is a reciprocal love which will not move forward unless the human recipient is willing. It might seem, then, that the subjective call made on a priest is rather slight. Balthasar denies this not in spite of the fact that for him a priest is merely an instrument but, rather, because of that fact.

> No priestly ethic can have any other basic content than the total expropriation of one's own private interests and inclinations so that one may be a pure instrument for the accomplishment of Christ's designs for the Church .... Consequently, [the priest] will seek his 'perfection', that is, the proper conduct of his service, only where one called to the state of the counsels seeks his, namely, in poverty, chastity and obedience, although, in his case, the manner of self-emptying, of renunciation of what has hitherto constituted his life and work, will have points of resemblance to the special anonymity inherent in the functional aspect of his office.[110]

The ever-ready preparedness of a serviceable instrument, the keynote of a good secular priest, means that, however distinctively coloured by the sacerdotal office, the ethos of the counsels must be his.

In the closing chapters of the Fourth Gospel, Balthasar sees a dialectic in play between objective and subjective priesthood – or, better, between the primarily functional secular priesthood, typified in Peter, and the primarily participatory state of the counsels (which may of course be united with the priesthood), typified in John.

> Peter received an office and love was then bestowed upon him for the sake of office – that he might accomplish it more perfectly. John was, from the beginning, the epitome of love: It was he who followed the Lord to Golgotha and was there initiated into the ultimate mysteries of sacrifice. He received the office of priest by reason of his personal dedication.[111]

It is key to Balthasar's account of the interrelation of priesthood and Religious life that John stood at the Cross with the Mother of the Lord. There Mary inaugurated that life by letting her own way of life become the life-way of Religious, just as her Son was engaged in transferring his Sacrifice functionally to priests. John unifies the two, thereby mediating between Mary and Peter. We are returned to the quintessentially Balthasarian theme of the 'constellation' around Christ. As he puts it, compendiously:

> The community of the apostles with Jesus represents *in nuce* all the essential ecclesial relationships and structures of the later Church. It is at once the representation of the whole Church (as that which was chosen from among men), of the whole state of election (as opposed to the 'people of the Church'), of the priestly state (as opposed to the 'laity'), and finally of the state of the counsels per se (as opposed to a broader circle of the elect that is perhaps best represented by the seventy-two disciples).[112]

---

110 *Ibid.*, p. 275.
111 *Ibid.*, p. 287.
112 *Ibid.*, p. 290.

St Thomas, recalls Balthasar, held that the apostles took vows implicitly,[113] and the sixteenth-century Jesuit theologian Francisco Suárez goes further, saying they lived the 'mixed life', carrying out an active ministry on the basis of the fullness of contemplation.[114]

There are, then, *two* states of election: the priesthood as such, called to share the ethos of the counsels (as with Peter), and the Religious life which may (as John) or may not (as Mary) be conjoined with priesthood. The unity of the two is attested, Balthasar shows, in dependence on the work of the historian of asceticism Ludwig von Hertling, in the sameness of the vocabulary frequently applied to virgins, monks and clergy indifferently. Those who belonged to each of these categories were said to make a – 'sacra' or 'deifica' – 'professio'. All were consecrated, accepting in irrevocable fashion sacred obligations, and their various promises may be regarded as implicit vows.[115] Only in the eleventh century, claims Hertling, did the concept of secular clergy arise as a denomination of those clerics who refused incorporation among the canons regular. At roughly the same period, the concept of vows underwent clarification in Religious orders, eventually by the emergence of the trio of poverty, chastity and obedience. Even so, the secular clergy retain the obligation of celibacy as an 'implicit vow' and that of obedience as, at any rate, a promise. We see in Thomas, however, that among the hierarchical degrees only the episcopate is considered as a state of perfection, an office with an intrinsic call to personal holiness, and not the presbyterate, the priesthood of the second rank. That is reflected in the Eastern churches, in the restriction of the episcopacy to ascetics.

> The religious strives for his own perfection; the bishop, as the perfector of the Church, has by reason of his office the obligation of requiring and inducing the perfection of others. But to do this, he must himself be perfect.[116]

As might be expected, there was often invoked in this context the symbolism of the bishop's 'marriage' to the Church, a vowed lifelong service whether to the local church or to the Church as a whole. But by the Baroque period this theology of the episcopal state had largely collapsed, while for their part 'discerning' priests sought to revive the link between holiness and priesthood at large found in a number of the Fathers.

We thus come to the modern period whose tendency it is, starting in the late nineteenth century, to go beyond a common opinion that priests (and even bishops) are only bound to a certain 'virtue and propriety'. Twentieth-century Popes proposed distinguished models for these orders of minister: Charles Borromeo for bishops, John Vianney for secular priests. As with Pius X in his 1908 exhortation *Haerent animo*, they urge ministerial priests to practise union with Christ in prayer, meditation and spiritual reading. Or with Pius XI in the 1935 encyclical *Ad catholici sacerdotii*, they bid them seek a more wide-ranging holiness of life which includes not only the counsels of

113 Thomas Aquinas, *Summa theologiae* IIa. IIae., q. 88, a. 4, ad iii.
114 F. Suárez, *De statu perfectionis* III, 2, 10.
115 L. von Hertling, 'Die Professio der Kleriker und die Entstehung der drei Gelübde', *Zeitschrift für katholische Theologie* 56 (1932), pp. 148–74.
116 *The Christian State of Life, op. cit.*, p. 308.

virginity and obedience but the spirit of the counsel of poverty and, interestingly, dedication to learning. All subsequent magisterial documents echo these appeals. The influential twentieth-century primate of Belgium, Cardinal Désiré Mercier of Malines, sought indeed to suppress the term 'secular' in favour of 'diocesan'. By their sacramental participation in the high priesthood of the bishops, he argued, presbyters were obliged to live out the same perfection to which the bishops were traditionally called. In fact, he told diocesan priests their office obligated them to a higher degree of perfection than Religious, for the service of souls is more noble than is contemplation. The regular clergy Mercier deemed 'but embellishments and adjuncts'.[117] Balthasar considered some of Mercier's theology of priesthood way off target. (He chides him especially for his neglect of women Religious who are 'under the patronage of the Lord's own mother' and his curious notion that the specific charisms of Religious orders are only limited selections from the universal charism of the diocesan clergy.) But beneath Mercier's 'aberrations' may be heard a very necessary call to 'reclaim the primitive evangelical unity of the ecclesial state of life from the divisions that obscure it'.[118]

The natural counterpart to 'priest' is 'layperson'. So an account of the 'second division of the states of life' must end there. The sheer variety of the charismata given the laity, and the transitoriness of some, strongly suggest that charism by itself does not found a state of life. Rather, charisms are given as the Holy Spirit wills in his distribution of personal missions on the occasion, normally, of the sacraments of initiation, notably Baptism and (especially) Confirmation. Their very variability draws attention to what is common – the lay state as such, which is the fundamental state in the Church. As Balthasar writes:

> Since this is so, and since the two other states are formed by specific differentiations of this first state, they may be regarded as classifications, emphases and *concretizations* of this state, to which they stand in a relationship of service.[119]

The spiritual 'wealth' that seems to belong to priests and Religious 'belongs to them only for the sake of the whole Church'.[120] The priesthood shows the whole Church the divine gifts that belong to it by right; the Religious show the Church the possibilities of Christian development. The layperson must allow the priestly ministry of Word and sacrament not only to be fruitful in him or her, but must translate them into the truth of their own state if they are to achieve their ends. Likewise, the layperson must translate into terms of his or her own life the example furnished in the state of the evangelical counsels.

> The Gospel [actually, Balthasar depends here chiefly on St Paul] engages in no casuistry about the extent to which the laity must strive for perfection or to which they may consider themselves dispensed therefrom. Its only concern is with perfection itself: the perfection of

117 Cited in *ibid.*, p. 325.
118 *Ibid.*, p. 327.
119 *Ibid.*, p. 333.
120 *Ibid.*, p. 334.

what the Christian *is* by reason of his participation in God by grace, and the perfection of what he *ought* to be by reason of that same grace.[121]

The ministerial priesthood and the Religious in the Church are there to draw the whole Church, the body and the Bride, into a ceaseless outpouring of love and praise, all directed to the Father.

(vi) The Church's mission

But what of the relation of the Church in her differentiated unity to the world – the name of which is *mission*? In answering this final question we must note a distinctive feature of Balthasar's soteriology, most clearly apparent in the theological dramatics. 'Nowhere does the Church meet a natural world, but always and everywhere one that is polarized for or against God's work of redemption.'[122] Balthasar's basic *prises de position* are: there can be no light without a luminary, and, it is pointless for the Church to offer the world something the world can acquire on its own. In practice, the movement that joins Church with world can be seen as a breathing-in and breathing-out: breathing in the world by transformingly assimilating it in a Christian fashion; breathing out by a self-transcending movement of the Church into the world outside its limits – outside, even when breathing in has taken place. Balthasar sums up the purpose of the first movement – 'breathing in' – as 'the formation of the Church as luminary of the world'.[123] Priests and Religious are both called to this; (Benedictine) monks have been especially good at the creation of a Christian culture by penetrating the leaven natural structures with the yeast of the Gospel. How are those in the states of election now to be creators of such a culture? If I interpret him correctly, Balthasar – writing in 1977, towards the end of a deeply unsuccessful pontificate – is inclined to say that they should re-learn to pray and suffer first.

> The 'holy heart of the nations' may need to retreat at times into its own interior, into the idea of the world as it is found in Christ Jesus, in order to prepare itself there in contemplation and passion (as opposed to action) for an eventual renewal of its cultural activity.[124]

Balthasar seemed more confident of the success of the role of the laity whose task in this regard he now defines. It is

> to demonstrate visibly and practically in the body of the Church how the spiritual and material goods of a fallen world order can be placed at the service of a selfless Christian love.[125]

As he sees it, this takes three forms: liberating economic wealth from an antithetical relation to Christ; clarifying the relation of erotic love to Christian charity; showing people that the 'most complete freedom' is not merely compatible with but actually achieved by obedience to God in Christ.

What, then, of 'breathing out'? All the 'great and qualitatively higher missions' bear a close relation to the counsels: it is the state of the counsels

121 *Ibid.*, p. 343.
122 *Ibid.*, p. 347.
123 *Ibid.*, p. 349.
124 *Ibid.*, pp. 350–51.
125 *Ibid.*, p. 353.

that the Lord commends in the Gospels as salt for the earth, a city set on a hilltop that cannot be hid. But the then novel (1977) experiences of Western Catholicism with 'political theology' lend Balthasar's remarks a cautionary tone. He writes:

> Just as it would have been dilettantism in the Middle Ages for con-templative monks to turn their hands to compass and plumb-lines when their true mission was to lend inspiration to the master builders of the cathedrals, so it would be dilettantism today for religious and priests to believe themselves capable of solving economic and socio-logical questions instead of expending their efforts to open the eyes of and hearts of capable lay persons and encouraging them to lay the foundations of a Christian social order.[126]

We can expect, he thought, if this continues, fiascos comparable to the mediaeval Crusades: the comparison with Liberation Theology would be drawn in more favourable terms somewhat later by the Dixie Professor of Ecclesiastical History at Cambridge, the historian of the Crusades Jonathan Riley-Smith.[127] Balthasar looked instead to the coming of age of a competent laity imbued with the 'full spirit of the Church' – which for him meant tutored by those in the states of election in such a fashion as to allow the laity to 'transfer the fruits of contemplation to their work'.[128] And here Balthasar invested hope especially in the Secular Institutes, of which his own *Johan-nesgemeinschaft* was an example. It is interesting to note a shift of emphasis from *Razing the Bastions*. In the post-Conciliar period Balthasar is far more alert to a worldly instrumentalization of the Church which will deprive her of transcendence and Gospel substance.

> The more deeply the higher, formative law of the Church impresses itself upon the world, the more the world will strive to overcome this formative power and to extract its whole content by worldly means until the Church becomes but an empty shell – an 'institution', an 'establishment'.... For the sake of the Church's mission to the world, then, the states of life within the Church have no other recourse than to distinguish themselves more and more consciously from this world/ body by a decisive movement toward him who, as the source and head of the Church is, at the same time, the beginning and end, alpha and omega, of all creation.[129]

---

126 *Ibid.*, p. 357.
127 J. Riley-Smith, 'Revival and Survival', in *idem* (ed.), *The Oxford Illustrated History of the Crusades* (Oxford, 1995), pp. 386–91.
128 *The Christian State of Life,* op. cit., p. 358.
129 *Ibid.*, pp. 363–64.

10

❧

Divine Handmaid: the Mother of the Lord

One is ashamed for a Christianity that today is ashamed of its own mother.[1]

This statement, made by Balthasar a few years into the post-Conciliar crisis in the Western Catholic Church (it appeared in an article in the journal of his old *alma mater*, the Benedictine school at Engelberg), announces what will be an increasingly accentuated theme in his later theology: Mary, the Mother of God. Not that it is by any means absent from his earlier writing. Chiefly, though, Marian themes exercised him through the theological help he gave his dirigée and collaboratrix, the mystic Adrienne von Speyr: help to express her own intuitive inspirations in the fuller form which a priest with a profoundly rooted and widely ranging ecclesial culture could provide. It will probably never be possible to ascertain with certainty what he gave Adrienne von Speyr, and what she gave him. But we can at least say that a surprising number of the leitmotifs of his mature Mariology are already announced by way of overture in her 1948 study 'The Handmaid of the Lord'.

The substance of his Marian doctrine

Balthasar's Mariology has at its heart the question, What of the human consent to all God has done for us in the saving drama found in the Trinitarian revelation, and climaxing in the Paschal Triduum, with the victorious humiliation of the Death and Descent into Hell? That consent, *Zustimmung*, cannot be described without reference to the Blessed Virgin Mary. If any one motif can be called crucial to Balthasarian Mariology this would seem to be it. At the Annunciation, Mary gave her consent to the Incarnation of the Logos in her womb. On Calvary, she likewise consented to the sacrifice her Son offered for the sins of the world. With Christ's rising in glory, this *fiat* (or act of saying Yes) was transformed into a ceaseless alleluia. Undivided – that is, single-minded and single-hearted – assent to the unique mission of Christ:

---

1 'Marienverehrung heute', *art. cit.*, p. 2. The reasons, he thought, were: human respect (people might laugh) and a false ecumenism (false not least because it ignored the Orthodox, many Anglicans and not a few [other] Protestants).

229

such is the focus of Balthasar's Mariology. It is also the focus of Adrienne's, who wrote:

> As a sheaf of grain is tied together in the middle and spreads out at either end, so Mary's life is bound together by her consent. From this consent her life receives its meaning and form and unfolds towards past and future. This single, all-encompassing act accompanies her at every moment of her existence, illuminates every turning point of her life, bestows upon every situation its own particular meaning and in all situations gives Mary herself the grace of renewed understanding.[2]

There can be no Christology without Mariology. As Adrienne von Speyr remarked to Balthasar a short while after her conversion:

> If Mary is taken away, all you are left with is an abstract Redeemer.[3]

Or again, more thoughtfully, in her own Mariological study, *Das Magd des Herren*:

> Though the Mother does not utter her Yes without the grace of the Son, neither does the Son become man without the grace of the Mother.[4]

And in any case only a defective anthropology would think of the Word becoming man *as an isolated individual*. Here we must bring into play the insights gained from our investigation of Balthasar's ecclesiology. When he writes in his book on the office of Peter that certain figures, such as Peter and Mary, belong essentially and irreplaceably with the foundation of the Church, he bases the claim in part on the anthropological dictum that each and every human being belongs with others in *eine mitmenschliche Konstellation*, a constellation of his (or her) fellow humans.[5] If, in the words of the Genesis creation narrative, it is not good for man to be alone, then presumably it is not good for the Son of Man, the new Adam, to be alone either. Moreover, since the eternal being of the Son in the Holy Trinity is itself relational being, we should expect that, with the Incarnation, when he enters the world of human relationships it is these relationships above all he will sanctify and raise to a new dignity by the way he inhabits them.

Balthasar considered that neglecting the figure of the Mother and Handmaid damages not Christology alone but the Church herself. He warned his fellow-Catholics that, where people cease to think quasi-instinctively of the Church as personified in Mary, the Mother of God, they will soon neuter the Church, reducing her from a 'she' to an 'it', and come to experience her not as encompassing motherly presence but only as an oppressive or at least interfering clerical institution.

> Without Mariology, Christianity threatens imperceptibly to become inhuman. The Church becomes functionalistic, soulless, a hectic enterprise without any point of rest, estranged from its true nature by

---

2 A. von Speyr, *Handmaid of the Lord, op. cit.*, p. 7. For reasons of consistency I have altered the translation of *Zustimmung* in this text from 'assent' to 'consent'.

3 *Idem, Erde und Himmel. Ein Tagebuch* (Einsiedeln, 1975), I., p. 271, cited J. Saward, *The Mysteries of March op. cit.*, p. 61.

4 A. von Speyr, *Handmaid of the Lord, op. cit.*, p. 12.

5 *The Office of Peter and the Structure of the Church, op. cit.*, p. 136.

the planners. And because, in this manly-masculine world, all that we have is one ideology replacing another, everything becomes polemical, critical, bitter, humourless, and ultimately boring, and people in their masses run away from such a Church.[6]

Balthasar gives fuller intelligibility to Adrienne's conviction that 'consent' is Mariologically crucial by thinking through the implications of the claim that Mary's relation to the Logos could not have been sheerly biological. Simply at the human level (to start with that), it is unthinkable that a mother could regard herself as just a biological space where a child is gestating – though at the end of Balthasar's life an abusive medical technology was making possible the practice of womb-renting by surrogate mothers. The question of the 'naturalness' or congruence with human nature of such technologically enabled practices can hardly fail to arise. For Balthasar, the natural relation of mother and child is no less than the key to general metaphysics. Whereas for Balthasar's old sparring partner, Karl Rahner, it is in the knowing of anything at all that the human mind locates itself vis-à-vis the horizon of infinite being, for Balthasar himself that horizon only really opens up as a baby is awakened to self-consciousness by the loving smile of its mother. On the basis of that meeting of mother and child, it can be stated that the child is one in love with his mother and yet is not his mother – and so the being that undergirds our existence is one; that this love is good – and so such being in its totality is good; that the love in question is true – and so being is true; and that love is a cause of joy – and so being is beautiful. These are, for Balthasar, primordial intuitions which our subsequent experience of life may and will lead us to test and question, but which remain foundations of consciousness, bases of spiritual experience.[7]

And if the idea that a mother *could* simply relate biologically, and not at all spiritually – with her whole mind, heart and feelings – to her child is humanly questionable, the objection to the notion that Mary of Nazareth was simply a way for the Word to become incarnate multiply when we start thinking theologically. (Here we return from general metaphysics and anthropology to specifically dogmatic theology.) St Augustine, followed by St Leo, insists that Mary conceived Jesus in her mind by faith before ever she conceived him physically in her womb.[8] Balthasar provides three reasons why these two Latin fathers of the fifth century were correct. First, in becoming incarnate God must not violate his creature, for this would be a transgression of the basic Creator–creature relationship. God could not use force on his free creation, nor does the Father 'inflict' salvation, imposing the Son on those who would not have him. And so in the Annunciation he turns to Mary, appealing to her will, waiting (though not for long) for her reply. Secondly, this particular mother had to be capable of introducing her child as man into the fullness of Israel's religion, which was the already existing divine revelation to mankind and as such would form the indispensable presupposition and background for Jesus' mission. This is an important emphasis in Balthasar's discussion of our Lady in *Herrlichkeit*, a very anti-Marcionite work concerned to do full justice to what we owe Jewry. Thirdly,

---

6 *Klarstellungen* (Freiburg, 1971); *Elucidations* (ET London, 1975), p. 72.
7 'A Résumé of my Thought', *Communio* 15 (1988), pp. 468–73.
8 Augustine, *Sermo* 215, 4; Leo the Great, *In nativitate Domini* I, 1.

the Incarnation of the Word requires what Balthasar calls 'a flesh that welcomes him perfectly'.[9] In other words, the matrix into which the Logos entered when he stepped into the created, material realm had to be perfectly disposed to union with himself.[10]

Virgin, Mother, Bride

The consent Mary gives is in the first place a virginal assent which subsequently becomes maternal and bridal. (Handmaid to Mother to Bride had been Adrienne von Speyr's Marian sequence in *Das Magd des Herren*.) First of all, the Mother of God is the *Virgin*. The virginity of Mary's body constitutes the outward and visible sign of her poverty of spirit: her looking to God alone for fruitfulness, her readiness to receive whatever God can give her. By the quality of this virignal receptivity, Mary fulfils, for Balthasar, the faith of Israel.

> Israel's faith was constantly falling, regularly flawed by hesitation, doubt, even flagrant infidelity. Here at last, by the grace of the Immaculate Conception, is the all-pure Daughter of Zion, unreservedly ready to give herself to God.[11]

In a second moment, then, the Virgin becomes the 'Blessed Mother'. It is of course the motherhood of Mary that brings her into the circle of the Church's dogmas where she appears at Ephesus as *Theotokos*. In this context, Balthasar makes the thought-provoking remark that the prayer of Mary is identical with her *Hinsein zum Kind*, her being towards her Child.[12] Her prayer is indistinguishable from the totality of attitudes – contemplation, love, worship, petition and so forth – her Son arouses.

Finally, Balthasar speaks of our Lady as a Bride. When thinking of Mary's bridal life, he shifts from thinking about her relation with Israel (the focus of his theology of her virginity) or her relation with Christ (the focus of his theology of her motherhood) to thinking about her relation with the whole of humanity and indeed the cosmos. The hypostatic union is a marriage between divine nature and human nature for which Mary is *not* just the 'venue of the nuptials'. The marriage of divinity and humanity in the single person of the Word Incarnate does not take its matrimonial character exclusively from the side of God. Mary had to give a bridal consent on behalf of all creation. For Balthasar it is because she is a woman that she *can* represent humanity vis-à-vis God. A male human being would be unable to do this. There is, he thinks, something archetypally feminine about creaturehood, creatureliness, as such.[13] His reason for saying so is this. Since

---

9 A. von Speyr, *Au coeur du Mystère rédempteur, op. cit.*, p. 55.
10 Once again, an excellent guide is John Saward in *The Mysteries of March, op. cit.*, pp. 61–81.
11 J. Saward, *The Mysteries of March, op. cit.*, p. 65.
12 *Christlich meditieren, op. cit.*, p. 60.
13 For further reflections, and a comparison with a Russian Orthodox on the same theme, see C. Giuliodori, *Intelligenza teologica del maschile e femminile: Problemi e prospettive nella rilettura di H. U. von Balthasar e P. Evdokimov* (Rome, 1991). Also, R. Zwank, *Geschlechtanthropologie in theologischer Perspektive? Zur Phänomenologie des Geschlechtlichen in Hans Urs von Balthasars 'Theodramatik'* (Frankfurt am Main, 1996).

humankind is not made in the image of the Father but in that of the Word, the human creation is more primordially receptive than it is creative – just as in the eternal Trinity the Son is primarily receptivity, sheer obedient reception of the Father's life, and only on that basis can he be creative (whether metaphorically so when the Father spirates the Spirit, or literally so when the world is made through him). Humankind is creative only on the basis of being receptive (a statement of enormous importance for the Christian critique of contemporary thought and culture), and of its two genders, it is the female which the better represents the substance of creaturehood in this respect. Though physiologically speaking, the female contribution to generation is as important as the male, at the level of the human totalities involved it is the woman who receives and the man who gives. And if in the Incarnation the part of man is taken by God as giver, this does not render the human recipient of the divine gift passive. This assent is the most fruitful human activity there has ever been.

The phases of consent

Balthasar considers Marian consent in terms of three great events or phases: the Annunciation, the public ministry, the Cross. First comes the Annunciation, the moment of the consent's paradigm expression. Only as the Immaculately Conceived could Mary be at the moment of the Incarnation 'infinitely at the disposal of the Infinite'.[14] As he wrote in a book co-authored with Cardinal Ratzinger, someone affected by original sin would never have realized such direct openness.[15] Through the pre-redemptive grace of her conception, Mary's assent is freed from internal encumbrances. No sinful self gets in its way. Unconditional self-surrender to God, sheer *Hingabe* to him, this is for Balthasar the highest achievement of grace. Here the prevenience of God's grace is crucial. This is truly Mary's action, yet it is made possible by God's action first. It is typical of Balthasar's theology of Mary's Annunciation consent to stress its Christological character. Strange as it may sound, it was the Yes of the Son ('I come to do thy will') which made possible the Yes of the Mother. Mary's faith can only be unbounded if it is pre-redeemed by the grace of the Cross. Mary's obedience is an anticipated participation in the obedience of Christ.

Next, Balthasar considers how Marian consent manifests itself in the public ministry of Jesus. Here the keynote is the 'infinite flexibility' of her consent. She does not insist on understanding in advance everything there is to know about her mysterious Son. In 1948 Adrienne had written:

> She gave her assent in full readiness without wanting to survey that to which she gave her consent ... Her task is to let the mystery happen.[16]

In his short study *Mary for Today* Balthasar wrote nearly thirty years later, in 1987:

14 *First Glance at Adrienne von Speyr, op. cit.*, p. 51.
15 *Marie, Première Eglise* (FT Paris-Montreal, 1981; 1987), p. 49. German original, Joseph Kardinal Ratzinger-Hans Urs von Balthasar, *Maria-Kirche im Ursprung* (Freiburg, Basle, Vienna, 1980; 1983, 3rd edition).
16 A. von Speyr, *Handmaid of the Lord, op. cit.*, pp. 35, 34.

Just as Jesus little anticipated the fate that lay in store for him but let it be revealed to him from day to day by his Father, so too would his mother have anticipated little of what was to come: part of her faith (the fulfilment of the faith of Abraham) was always to accept God's dispositions.[17]

The similarity is striking. Even more striking is Balthasar's recourse in this context to the idea of the nights of the soul. The Mother of the Lord is called to enter the night of the senses – the rupture of physical contact with her Son, and also the night of the spirit, the breakdown of understanding of him. Here we see Balthasar's indebtedness to the Carmelite school, for this is the vocabulary of St John of the Cross, one of the dozen writers whom Balthasar chose in *Herrlichkeit* to illustrate the unexpected aesthetics of the divine glory.

The most original aspect of Balthasar' theology of Mary's consent during the public ministry is his interpretation of the 'distancings' between Jesus and Mary: moments like the losing in the Temple; the rebuke at Cana; the declaration that the true mother is whoever does the will of the heavenly Father. Much Protestant exegesis has seen these as indicative of a low Mariology on the part of the evangelists. Catholic exegesis has often felt a consequent obligation to vindicate the Gospels from such a charge. Like typically Protestant exegesis, Balthasar interprets these moments as definite turnings away of the Son from the Mother. But unlike such exegesis, he regards these self-removals of Jesus from Mary as invitations to the Mother by the Son. Jesus is calling her to enter with him the experience of abandonment which will come to its climax on the Cross, where the abandonment of Christ revealed – paradoxically – the perfect loving union of Abandoner and Abandoned, Father and Son, in the Holy Spirit. Here too in seemingly negative actions Jesus is engaged in superlatively positive activity. He is transforming his mother's faith. Once the faith of Israel, it is to become a cruciform faith of a kind that will typify the Church. Precisely by turning away from her, he teaches her the demands of his mission and what is going to be her share in the mission of the Church which she will personally embody. Implicitly, he teaches her the new mode of her faith, the way her *fiat* will have to persevere through darkness and incomprehension. And this lays the foundation for the Mother's future collaboration with the Son, her role as what some would call 'co-redemptrix' (though in strict dependence on Christ). In turn, this establishes the basis for the Church's co-operation in redemption.

Adrienne had already proposed that when Jesus says in Mary's hearing that whoever does the will of his heavenly Father is his mother, he was asking Mary to surrender her maternal prerogatives in favour of what von Speyr calls, discreetly, 'a certain universality'.[18] Mary – so Balthasar interprets this – must become the most ecclesial being, the least individual being, if one day she is to be for the Church 'her fountainhead and abiding centre'. We must relate this suggestion to Balthasar's judgment that the faith of Mary does not precede in a simply chronological way that of the rest of the Church. Mary is not just the exemplar of a faith which the rest of us have to try and

---

17 *Maria für heute* (Freiburg, 1987); ET *Mary for Today* (Middlegreen, Slough, 1987), p. 16.
18 A. von Speyr, *Handmaid of the Lord, op. cit.*, p. 111.

reproduce after her as best we may. More than that, Mary's faith includes or englobes the faith of the Church of all succeeding generations. It constitutes not just a moral exemplar for the attitude of believing but a theological a priori for all the content the later Church believes. Mary's faith pre-contains the faith of the Church, so that when the Church explores the foundations or the structure or the chief internal relationships found within her faith, what she is doing is always sustained by the faith of the Mother of God. This is Balthasar's contribution, really, to the theme of the 'development of doctrine'. The unitary identity of the faith throughout all such development and continuing theological exploration is only made possible by the faith of the Virgin and Bride.

Finally, there is the consent of Mary at the Cross – something we have looked at in the context of the birth of the Church on Calvary. This too is a 'let it be done'. On the Cross, the Head and Bridegroom gives himself up Eucharistically – that is, in a sacrifice of petition and praise – for love of the Church. In Mary the Church accepts that gift. As Balthasar sees things, the God-man did not want the Church to consent to, and share in, his atoning sacrifice simply after the event. He wanted the Church to be contemporary with the event, so that from the very beginning the sacrifice of Calvary was inseparably that of Head and members. Even in the utter dereliction of Calvary he did not wish to act without the accompaniment of the Church. And this Mary provided.[19]

'Placing' Mariology

In Balthasar's lifetime, Catholic Mariology was frequently divided between a maximalist school which 'placed' her Christologically – by the side of Christ as Christ is by the side of God – and a (relatively) minimalist school which emphasized Mary's theological 'location' within ecclesiology, the doctrine of the Church. For the maximalists, if Mary is the New Eve then she is the helper of the New Adam through her consent to his Incarnation and her co-suffering in his Passion. This is why it pleased the Saviour to make her a channel of his grace. While she is saved by Christ alone the rest of redeemed humanity finds salvation through Christ and (by his disposition) the primordially engraced Mary. In reaction, the minimalists held Mary only has a mediatorial role inasmuch as she is the Mother of the Saviour (and hence a necessary condition for the coming of the Word incarnate). This is what gives her the place properly hers in the Church: its pre-eminent member. In Balthasar's view, this Christological/ecclesiological divide is unnecessary. Dramatically, Mary passed from the condition of Virgin and Bride to that of Mother of the Church. In the development of her role in the divine drama, she must be seen in both contexts, albeit with a shift of emphasis in the different 'acts' of the play.[20] Balthasar echoes the Marian eighth chapter of *Lumen gentium*, the Second Vatican Council's Dogmatic Constitution on the Church, in his desire to overcome a false dichotomy. But he also found that

---

19 *Au Coeur du mystère rédempteur, op. cit.*, p. 54.
20 This is well analysed by Hilda Steinhauser in her study, *Maria als dramatischer Person bei Hans Urs von Balthasar. Zum marianischen Prinzip seines Denkens* (Innsbruck-Vienna, 2001).

chapter somewhat disappointing: much more could have been said about the identity of Mary and Church in their origin in Christ and through Christ the Holy Trinity itself, and more too about the historically concrete realization of this relation as well as its eschatological fulfilment.

Balthasar was deeply formed by the Marian piety of the Catholicism of his youth – including the messages of the various modern Marian 'apparitions' – in his account of Mary's role now. He has the audacity of the visionaries, but for a theologian of enormous erudition and intellectual range such audacity bespeaks great humility. In language of moving simplicity, he writes that she who once brought her Son into the world, introducing him as a stranger to his new home, still brings him by bringing others to him, 'putting the human into the God-man's hand'. This she can do because 'in heaven she thinks in an earthly way, on earth in a heavenly'.[21] She appears to visionaries on the earth's surface as the Mother of mercy, but since she understands what judgment is she rarely makes her appearance 'without grief and tears', though her smile is of surpassing beauty. In the Parisian Rue du Bac, at Lourdes, Pontmain, Fatima, she comes as her Son's ambassadress, and yet she follows her own goals. 'She has', wrote Balthasar, 'her plan'. And in that plan:

> what she says is so endlessly simple, that fundamentally everyone who is aware of the Lord and his love should know it. But we have all forgotten it and coming from the mouth of a mother it sounds like a new truth.[22]

He is careful to add that when she speaks of the future all is 'enveloped in a great "if" '.[23] This is not a *fata morgana* but the humble handmaid of the Lord.

21 'Die Erscheinung der Mutter', *art. cit.*, p. 77.
22 *Ibid.*, p. 79.
23 *Ibid.*, p. 80.

11

༺༻

Divine Missions: the Saints

A hagiology of mission

Balthasar's hagiology – his theology of the saints – is closely tied in with his pneumatology – his theology of the Holy Spirit. Naturally enough, that pneumatology can be found throughout his writings wherever he speaks of the Holy Trinity and the Trinitarian nature of the salvation wrought for man in the Incarnation and the Paschal mystery. Yet it is probably true to say that, in Balthasar's *oeuvre*, the greatest concentration of references to the Holy Spirit occurs when he has occasion to deal with the topic of holiness.

As we have seen, for Balthasar, holiness is either 'objective' – and by this he refers to the action of the Spirit in the dominically given structures of the Church in word, sacrament and pastoral authority – or it is 'subjective', by which he refers to the action of the Spirit in human hearts, and more particularly in the lives of the saints.

Why does Balthasar present the theology of, on the one hand, the *Amtskirche*, the Church of office, and, on the other, the *Kirche der Heiligen*, the Church of the saints, in terms of this contrast of objective and subjective Holy Spirit? As already mentioned when looking at the theme of the Church's manifestation at Pentecost, it is meant to be something of a theological equivalent – whether by parody or transformation – of an important aspect of the thinking of the most comprehensive and systematic of all German philosophers, Hegel. Hegel had spoken of spirit as present in, so to say, solidified form in human institutions, and in, as it were, liquid form in human subjectivity – in the use we make of our powers of emotion, of mind, of will. He had regarded objective and subjective spirit as dialectically related, each helping the other. In civil society, good institutions assist the emergence of rightly ordered human freedom, just as rightly ordered human freedom helps institutions to be good. So likewise, Balthasar considered, with the objective and subjective dimensions of the economy of the Holy Spirit. In the *Amtskirche*, the hierarchical office – which is objective sanctity in what Balthasar calls the Church's 'foundation and tradition, her sacraments and orders'[1] – has as its *raison d'être* the subjective, personal holiness of the Church's members in the *Kirche der Heiligen*, the Church of the saints. And correspondingly, those who really are aiming at the goal of subjective

---

1 *Thérèse of Lisieux. The Story of a Mission, op. cit.*, p. xi.

sanctity, can realize that aim consciously and fully only in the Church founded by Christ. As Balthasar put it in the extended preamble to his study of the mission of St Thérèse:

> As a member of the Church the individual is not left to choose the way in which he shall surrender his self for the sake of the whole community... The characteristic of love lies in its interior order, just as the Spirit of love which produces subjective sanctity within the Church's objective framework at the same time produces order within its offices and charismata.[2]

That term *charismata* – a reference to the 'different kinds of gifts' which the Spirit, according to Paul in First Corinthians (12.4) distributes in the Church – crops up regularly in Balthasar's writing. The offices of bishop, priest and deacon are to him just as much filled with charismata as are the many further kinds of graced existence God raises up in the Church. Office should not be counterposed to charismatic missions, whether frequent or unusual. All are gifts of the Spirit for the common good of the Church in service of the common Lord. It is just that some charismata fall under the heading of 'objective' charisms, those which find their outflow through Church office, while the rest of this golden shower of gifts God pours down on the Church in all ages take the form of 'subjective' charisms, those requiring no office for their manifestation, only Christian initiation in Baptism, Confirmation and the Holy Eucharist. In conversation with Angelo Scola Balthasar remarked:

> Every permanent office is a charism but not every charism is by any means a permanent office. We have mentioned before that St Paul was deeply aware of his official authority; under no circumstances would he have placed it on the same level as his gift of healing or glossolalia (which, by the way, he maintained he possessed to a greater degree than others).[3]

More helpfully for our subject, Balthasar had earlier called the (non-official) charisms those precise points to which the Holy Spirit wishes to draw attention at some definite epoch of the Church's life: grace through Augustine, the incarnate love of God through Bernard and Bonaventure, humility and poverty through Francis, and so forth.[4] They are 'new illuminations and expositions of the Gospel'.

The notion of charism is important for Balthasar's theology of the saints, then. But it is not absolutely foundational. The true keystone of the edifice is, rather, the idea of *mission*. As Balthasar writes:

> The mission which each individual receives contains within itself the form of sanctity which has been granted to him and is required of him.[5]

Theologically speaking, what for Balthasar renders someone a *person* (so the theological dramatics will have it) is precisely such a mission. Without that mission, they can be a person philosophically speaking – a conscious subject

---

2 *Ibid.*, p. xii.
3 *Test Everything. Hold Fast to What is Good, op. cit.*, p. 64, with a reference to *ibid.*, p. 63.
4 'Exerzitien und Theologie', *Orientering* 12 (1948), pp. 229–32.
5 *Thérèse of Lisieux, op. cit.*, p. xii.

– but they will not be a theological 'person in Christ', someone whose name appears among the *dramatis personae* of the divine drama. Our particular mission *is* the form of sanctity predestined for us. It is the way God wants us to dispose ourselves to his plan. Our temperament, the slant of our human nature, our particular set of aptitudes and inclinations, will of course be relevant to this. But, so Balthasar insists, our mission, and therefore our path to sanctity, cannot simply be 'read off' from these natural gifts and predispositions. Just assessing our nature cannot by itself lead to a just idea of God's gracious intention for us. That requires the sort of discernment of God's will through meditation and prayer which, for example, the Ignatian *Exercises* recommend. The *Spiritual Exercises* tell the user precisely to

> contemplate his life, to investigate and to ask in what kind of life or state his divine Majesty wishes to make use of us ... and how we ought to dispose ourselves in order to arrive at perfection in whatever state or kind of life God our Lord shall propose for our election.

Does this mean, then, that there are as many kinds of sanctity as there are shadings of personality on the one side, possible contributions to the Church on the other? Given his concept of mission as what defines uniqueness of personality in the theological context, Balthasar has to answer – in one sense – yes. But in another sense, he thinks it possible to as it were carve up the saints into broad categories.

Thus for instance we can draw a clear line between what Balthasar terms (in not especially perspicuous vocabulary) 'customary' and 'representative' sanctity. 'Customary holiness' flows from the fulfilling of vocation by the 'normal, unspectacular round of the Church's life'. By contrast, 'representative' sanctity entails God's singling out of individuals for some unusual mission in the Church, a mission which may well act as the catalyst for others to follow in their steps. So it was with the founders of the great Religious Orders. The representative saints suggest new types of holiness in the Church, whereas the customary saints live out a holiness of which any well-instructed Christian is conscious – though not every such Christian lives in the sacrificial fashion that would enable him or her to be a 'customary saint'. In terms of this distinction, then, personal mission is always deployed as a unique variant of either customary or representative holiness.

Linked to this distinction is a second main cleavage among the saints. And this lies between those who have been made holy by the way they respond to impulses – missions – coming to the Church from Jesus Christ as Head of the mystical Body, and those who have arrived at sanctity by they way they live out impulses – missions – offered by the mystical Body for the service of the Church's Head. This notion of a two-way traffic in sanctity, from Christ to the Church, from Church to the Christ, seems at first sight very odd as a piece of putatively Catholic theology. For, while it is true that both Christ and the Church draw on the holiness of God the Holy Trinity, the Church does not do so except by means of Christ. What on earth is Balthasar talking about? What he is getting at is a distinction between, on the one hand, missions – and therefore versions of sanctity – which *come as a surprise* to the Church, so that she treats them as gifts of the Lord of the Church *from without*, and, on the other hand, missions – and therefore versions of sanctity – which *come as no surprise* to the Church (except in the sense that they are singularly pure and fruitful expressions of her common life), leading her to treat *these* saints as gifts of the Lord of the Church *from within*.

Though Balthasar has no single term for saints from without or saints from within, we might call them examples of, respectively, 'exoteric' and 'esoteric' sanctity since the words 'exoteric' and 'esoteric' mean literally 'from without' and 'from within' respectively. The esoteric saints embody, in Balthasar's words, 'an intensification of customary virtues' (there is a link then between the concepts of customary and esoteric sanctity). They are held up to the faithful as shining examples of their own kind, 'examples of the Christian virtues brought to perfection'. For layfolk, one might suggest St Margaret of Scotland as such an example; for clerics St Hugh of Lincoln. By contrast, the exoteric saints constitute

> a new type of conformity to Christ inspired by the Holy Spirit, and therefore a new illustration of how the Gospel is to be lived.[6]

St Francis of Assisi is the almost inevitable example of these.

Balthasar writes about such exoteric saints in a way that bursts all bounds of theological decorum. Quite why we shall see in a moment. He writes for instance:

> These direct missions from God all share the divine quality of being perfectly concrete, yet beyond all comprehension. Comparable in this respect to God's nature, they are absolutely determinate and unchangeable whilst yet harbouring boundless interior riches which ultimately transcend adequate definition or determination.[7]

In this exalted statement, Balthasar claims to be reflecting the sense of the faithful, who venerate precisely those saints (an Anthony of Padua, a Thérèse of Lisieux) whose way of life is least directly imitable by them. The explanation for this (undoubted) phenomenon, Balthasar holds, is that such saints are instinctively recognized as 'great warm centres of light and consolation sunk into the heart of the Church by God'.

This comment takes Balthasar halfway to making good his claim that the exoteric saints share in the divine mystery, combining the determinate and the indeterminate, the conceptualizable and that which is beyond concepts, in an analogous fashion to God himself, of whom we speak both cataphatically and apophatically, by affirmation and negation. The principal reason why Balthasar makes this second claim about the exoteric saints is to do with the fact that they constitute a fresh interpretation of divine revelation – something that cannot be said of the esoteric saints, those who express in 'customary' fashion the 'normal' sacramental and moral life of the Church. As Balthasar puts it:

> For theologians [the exoteric saints] are ... a new interpretation of revelation; they bring out the scarcely suspected treasures in the deposit of faith ... Their sheer existence proves to be a theological manifestation, which contains most fruitful and opportune doctrine,

6 *Ibid.*, p. xvi.
7 *Ibid.*

the directions of the Holy Spirit addressed to the whole Church and not to be neglected by any of its members.[8]

This is strong stuff, and Balthasar must consider various objections to it.

In the first place, no Catholic is obliged to entertain a special devotion to any particular saint. Nor is he required to accept their words as the authoritative interpretation of the Word of God. But Balthasar would regard such statements as *regulative* (only) in force. They are designed to protect the uniqueness of the revelation in Jesus Christ. In other words, they are statements about the basic rules of the Christian community and its discourse, for which the Word Incarnate can never be in the same category as any other human speaker. Accordingly, such statements are not directly cognitive: they are not immediately illuminating about the reality of the saints in and of themselves. And if we ask after that reality Balthasar tells us:

> In the saints we are faced with a living and essential expression of the Church's tradition ... the saints ... are the 'living Gospel'.[9]

But how then would Balthasar respond to an Evangelical Christian who would no doubt maintain that such a position impugns the sufficiency of Scripture? *En passant*, we can note it is also a perfectly orthodox Catholic view that all divine revelation is contained in Scripture *in some fashion* (that latter phrase entering an important qualification). To this Balthasar replies, the Holy Spirit has set the exoteric saints before us *precisely as guides to the meaning of the Bible*. Familiarity with such saints is a necessary condition of all sound exegesis of Scripture. 'Only they can understand and interpret God's Word who themselves live in the world of the saints.'[10]

This answer leads us back to Balthasar's fundamental theology – or at any rate to his fundamental account of what theology is. Just as doctrine and life must fertilize each other, since each is barren by itself alone, so theology must be intimately penetrated by sanctity, by the 'theology of the saints'. (Here, it is probably fair to say, Balthasar has chiefly in mind Scholastic theology of a speculative kind, the sort of theology which, from its roots in Christian Hellenism, has furnished the Church with her basic language for the articulation of doctrine.)

This is one of Balthasar's signature tunes. As we saw when looking at Balthasar's basic concept of revelation and its expression in theology, theology and the quest for holiness have become divorced, to the great damage of both. Theologians have pooh-poohed hagiography as 'mere' spirituality, beneath their intellectual notice. At best, they have created, for the interpretation of the lives and testimonies of the saints a subdivision of theology called 'spiritual theology'. But this was sufficiently far removed from the dogmatic heartlands of theological science to be safely forgotten.

And here we need to revisit Balthasar's essay on theology and holiness, this time from the standpoint not of the question, What is theology?, but from that of the spiritual life.[11] Historically, Balthasar's chief contention is that, after the age of the great scholastics, theology became overloaded with

---

8 *Ibid.*, pp. xvi–xvii.
9 *Ibid.*, p. xvii.
10 *Ibid.*
11 'Theology and Sanctity', *art. cit.*

secular philosophy in such wise that spiritually minded people turned away from the theological heartlands, and began – quite self-consciously – to produce that very different literature we call spirituality. Really, Catholic thinkers should have been content to use philosophical concepts as 'pointers to the final truth which is supernatural and divine'. Had such concepts been regarded Christologically – as included within that human nature which in Christ was taken up into union with the Word, they would have undergone appropriate 'transfiguration' without losing any valid content. They would thus have become, like the humanity of Christ, 'wholly a function and expression of his divine person and truth'.[12] Albert, Bonaventure, Thomas managed to do this. Afterwards, though, it required a superhuman effort for the student of theology to treat the concepts of philosophy as other than fixed containers into which the substance of revelation had to be drawn off. As a consequence, the spirituals took flight.

Nor, in the modern period, have hagiographers done much to narrow this gap. Their approach to their own subject-matter – the saints – has been overwhelmingly historical and, especially, psychological. In Henri Bremond's great 'literary history of religious feeling', the work of spiritual writers in the Catholicism of the early modern period is comprehensively described without the author ever needing to mention the contemporary state of theology or doctrine. Balthasar calls this 'one of the most alarming facts of recent Church history'.[13] This was not entirely Bremond's fault. Balthasar ascribes some of the responsibility to the saints themselves. St Ignatius recommended study of the Fathers and mediaevals, but he evidently had taken little advice from them on how to overcome the estrangement of spirituality from dogmatics in his own work! Only in the middle decades of the twentieth century did such Jesuits as Erich Przywara and Karl Rahner in Germany, Gaston Fessard in France, synthesize the *Exercises* and dogma. Others, like St Francis de Sales, made only a half-hearted attempt to integrate theology with spirituality, or, as with St John of the Cross, fitted out their mysticism rather clumsily with sometimes inappropriate Scholastic armour. Above all, the mystical saints of the post-mediaeval period did not appreciate sufficiently that even the most strictly mystical charismata are given so as to serve what Balthasar calls the 'single act of revelation' in the Church.[14] Too much concentration on spiritual autobiography precluded a close attention to doctrinal teaching as God and his creative and redemptive work. The penalty such saints paid was that dogmatic theologians largely ignored their work. If the saints, disenchanted by the excessive conceptual entanglements of theology, felt unable to collaborate in the exposition of theological doctrine, the thinking of the theologians became by the same token, less fruitful for salvation in the Church. And all of this, so 'Theology and Sanctity' adds, was aided and abetted by a growing dualism in Western culture and philosophy – a dualism between idea and existence, theoretical reason and practical, Apollo and Dionysus. These are thoughts from *Apokalypse der deutschen Seele*.

---

12 *Ibid.*, p. 185.

13 *Ibid.*, p. 187. Bremond's eleven volume work, *Histoire littéraire du sentiment religieux en France* was published at Paris between 1916 and 1933 (with a volume of indices in 1936). The title of the chief English study is not entirely encouraging: H. Hogarth, *Henri Bremond. The Life and Work of a Devout Humanist* (London, 1950).

14 'Theology and Sanctity', *art. cit.*, p. 191.

Analysing this schism in sensibility is not enough. We must overcome it. Balthasar proposed a two-pronged attack. One prong consists in making dogmatics once again the 'theology of the saints'. Philosophy itself, Balthasar thought, needs to become more religious. Even outside Christianity, he considered:

> All true philosophy is at bottom theology, since it lives and is kept alive by a point, a gravitational pull, external to itself, that mysterious Absolute that lies beyond the purview of merely human reason and alone makes thought worthwhile.[15]

And as to philosophers who are Christians, they must philosophize *qua* Christians, so that all their thought is a function of faith. Here we see Balthasar supporting the Neo-Augustinians over against the Neo-Thomists in a debate over the nature of Christian philosophy – or was it just 'philosophy as practised by Christians?' – lively in the 1930s, 40s and 50s. No doubt this *would* make the philosophical component in Catholic theology less offputting to, say, enclosed Carmelite nuns, but in point of fact this prescription is ancillary to another whereby Balthasar bids the theologian to keep her eye always on revelation's *centre*. In a way clearly indebted to the theological aesthetics, he says that the proportions of theology should always be those of revelation itself. This entails centring theology on the Trinitarian epiphany in Christ. Everything the Christian thinker has to say about being and history should be related to the Church's doctrine about Father, Son and Spirit. And the point of mentioning this here is because it will mean that the saints – of past or present – can contribute to the work.

For instance, the theology of the Passion of Christ can only profit enormously from integrating what the saints have experienced in their dark nights – nights which Balthasar interprets (shades of *Mysterium Paschale*) as 'graces of participation in the Passion, given to the Church'.[16] And if that be true of Christology, the doctrine of the second Trinitarian person, how could a Pneumatology, a theology of the third, be composed without continual reference to the way the holiness the Spirit sheds abroad is lived out in the saints? A theology which does not learn from the saints is de-natured, self-disqualified, because theology, quite as much as mysticism, takes the form of a dialogue between the Bridegroom, God in Christ, and the Church, the Bride. Accordingly, theology, to be authentic, requires the action of the Holy Spirit: purifying, illuminating, and uniting the theologian to her subject matter in a fashion analogous to the whole Church's bridal union with God. Not for nothing is sanctity one of the criteria, along with competence and orthodoxy, used in declaring certain theologians doctors of the Church. The theological life of the Church requires all the graces of vision and knowledge that the Church's members can receive – not only those 'Gifts of the Holy Spirit' which render our faculties more receptive to the theological virtues of faith, hope and charity, but also the strictly mystical charismata poured out in such abundance on the mystical saints.

In the context of this strategy for putting theology and sanctity together again, Balthasar proposed a new (or at least rejuvenated) sort of self-

15 *Ibid.*, p. 195.
16 *Ibid.*, p. 199.

consciously *theological* hagiology – what he termed in the introduction to his study of Thérèse of Lisieux a supernatural phenomenology of the mission of the saints.

He explained. It involves identifying the unique mission of a saint and exploring the concrete way the human individual concerned realized that mission to a greater or lesser degree. The psychology of the saints (the alternative kind of focus) enters in only as the 'matter' which the 'form' of the saint's mission must take up and shape.

> All the saints – they especially – realize how inadequately they fulfil their mission, and they are to be taken seriously when they insist on their inadequacy. What matters about them is not their heroic 'personal achievement' but the resolute obedience with which they have utterly surrendered themselves to serving a mission and have come to see their very existence in the light of it. We must bring to light what they wished to bring to light, what they were bound to: their representation of Christ and the Scriptures. We should leave in obscurity what they wished to leave in obscurity: their poor personalities.[17]

We must find what is intelligible – the divine 'idea' of their mission – in the sensuous manifold of their personalities, but that means, then, discerning an essence in its concrete manifestations. This is indeed *phenomenology*: it is not mere empirical description for its own sake. And of course, if it is to be *supernatural* phenomenology that we are to practise then a mind equipped to identify the intelligibility in question will be a mind which enjoys the light of faith and, if possible, some share in the life of holiness with the 'connaturality' with the supernatural that brings.

Balthasar stresses that the main thing that is 'perfect' about a saint is not his or her empirical personality but the mission which with all the strengths and frailties of that personality the saint tries to live. And this enables him to give a subtle explanation of how not all the saints practise all the virtues. Some saints seem in some aspects of their lives far from saintly. (St Jerome's sarcasm comes readily to mind.) Some saints have allowed the 'concrete demands' of their mission to 'lay hold on every fibre of their persons'. Others, by contrast, have been 'content to accept the essential demands, leaving many corners of their selves untouched and empty'. Anyway, it is an established principle in Catholic eschatology that in Heaven the saints enjoy different degrees of glory.

> The kingdom of the saints knows many degrees from the lowest limit, where the integrity of a mission is just preserved, to the highest level of all, where the mission and the person become indistinguishable. The Mother of God alone has reached that level.[18]

Balthasar's assault on a psychologizing school of hagiology is not intended to deflect our attention from the actual saints to – simply – the theological *idea* of their mission. As he puts it, the 'truth that their missions are so different' enables us to see the drama of their lives more sharply than would otherwise be the case. And the same is true of the light and shadow in their

---

17 *Thérèse of Lisieux, op. cit.*, p. xviii.
18 *Ibid.*, p. xix.

characters. To this too we can do far more justice by supernatural phenomenology than would be the case by applying psychological criteria that in this context are not quite the right tool.

Balthasar also noted the possible beneficial effects for dogmatics. 'Few things', he wrote, 'are so likely to vitalize and rejuvenate theology, and therefore the whole of Christian life, as a blood transfusion from hagiography'.[19] Balthasar exemplified this in his theology of the communion of saints in its relation to the principal Trinitarian and Christological clauses of the Creed. The theological personality and mission of every saint is founded in the sending of the Son while the interrelation of those personalities and missions in the communion of saints is founded in the unity of the divine life in the Holy Trinity. To take the second point first, as Gerhard Ludwig Müller puts it:

> The communion of saints, seen as the community of redeemed, called and beatified persons, is the comprehensive goal of the triune God insofar as the *communio sanctorum* has its archetypal root in the *communio Trinitatis* which puts forth a creaturely reflection of itself through creature, grace and glorification.[20]

Triadologically – in terms of Trinitarian theology, that is: in the communion of saints there is a 'rhythm' relating individual and community which reminds us of the reciprocal relations between the uniqueness of the divine Persons and the uniqueness of their self-gift to the communion of their common life. The first rhythm, which is hagiological or ecclesial, is a 'real parable' of the second, Trinitarian rhythm which originates it. Christologically – in terms of a theology of the person of Christ: if Jesus Christ is the centre of what is representative and universal in the mission of the saints, their response of discipleship can be called the 'centre of gravity of Christ's effective influence in history', inviting us to consider Christ in the Church as the norm of historical time, as Balthasar did in his own theology of history.[21] There are good reasons, Balthasar thought, for introducing not only hagiology but also Church history into the dogmatic heartlands of theology proper.[22]

Two exemplars

The best place to see Balthasar's approach at work is in his studies of the two Carmelite women saints Thérèse of Lisieux (1873–1897) and Elizabeth of Dijon (1880–1906).

(i) *Thérèse of Lisieux*
The mission – and message – of Thérèse may be simply put. It was at once to exemplify and to teach how the way to glory is the hard, relentless truth of a

---

19 *Ibid.*, p. xxvi. For Balthasar the trail-blazer here was the Dominican M. Philipon's *Saint Thérèse de Lisieux, une voie toute nouvelle* (Paris, 1946).
20 G. L. Müller, *Gemeinschaft und Verehrung der Heiligen. Geschichtlich-systematische Grundlegungen der Hagiologie* (Freiburg-Basle-Vienna, 1986), p. 288.
21 *Ibid.*, p. 305.
22 'Die Heiligen in der Kirchengeschichte', *Internationale Katholische Zeitschrift* 8 (1979), pp. 488–95.

'little' way of childlike self-surrender to God at every moment, in every detail of existence. Only a life of that extraordinary intensity, thinks Balthasar, could have

> modestly and skillfully dissolved traditional notions of spirituality and mysticism, submerging them in the original life of the Gospel, whence they might be born again.[23]

Given the innovatory character of this 'mission', the authenticity of her teaching needed, he considered, subjecting to 'particularly rigorous tests'. His study attempts this, and declares her 'existential theology' to emerge triumphantly. Her inspiration displays all the qualities that the presence and operation of the Holy Spirit typically manifests, summed up as: 'freedom, mastery, penetration, fullness and joy'.[24] As Balthasar explains the essence of the Theresian way:

> In its negative aspect the little way means demolishing the structure of 'great deeds'. If this were its only result it might just as well be described as the way of mediocrity or fecklessness. But in fact it is the way of New Testament love, a way therefore which leads 'unto the end' (John 13: 1) ... Love is brought to a state of weakness in which it learns the power of divine love, of littleness and darkness in which the greatness and glory of divine love are displayed.[25]

It is not difficult to see what attracted Balthasar to this 'sister in the Spirit'. Here again, in the little Carmelite doctor, the Balthasarian *Abstiegsbewegung* or 'movement of descent' is verified one more time.

Thérèse confirmed in Balthasar his devotion to the infancy of Christ, which he had long expressed in Claudelian terms – the utterly novel, distinctively Christian theme of the youthfulness of God. When God himself becomes a child he rehabilitates this aspect of creation which now becomes a fully valid expression of the divine life – indeed, the preferred and especially eloquent symbol of his heart and reign. Balthasar interprets this extraordinary 'novelty' of the youth of God in terms of the eternally youthful vigour of the triune love. Habituation, 'accustomedness', is a product of time, not eternity – which is why in the theological dramatics he will present 'wonder' as a feature of the relations of communion of the Trinity. This miracle of the 'childhood of God' is the source in us of the theological virtues of faith, hope and charity – which Balthasar was always keen to show as a unity, a single albeit differentiated gift. That gift can only live in us in propitious circumstances: namely, when we ourselves persevere in our rebirth as children of God.[26] Thérèse's spirituality appealed to him in just this context.

Though he notes some of her predecessors as theologians of spiritual childhood, Balthasar points out the overwhelming evidence she read none of them. For a doctor of the Church her insouciance towards works of Christian literature was astounding. She relied on Holy Scripture, on the

23 *Thérèse of Lisieux, op. cit.*, p. 35.
24 *Ibid.*, p. 16.
25 *Ibid.*, pp. 198–99.
26 *Anbetung des Kindes* (Freiburg, 1990), pp. 37–44.

unwritten tradition of the Church and on her interior master, Jesus, prompting her by his grace. She breezily admitted that books on spiritual theology gave her a headache and expressed pleasure she had not lionized the convent library, losing thereby precious time better spent in loving God.[27] 'All her attention is fixed upon her task: to embody the Word of Love in her life.'[28] That was the point of her autobiography, written under obedience as it was. With a devastating candour, she enacts, writes Balthasar, her own self-canonization. Her objective mission is to display *herself*. In an extraordinary comparison Balthasar describes her as a mannequin, who shows herself off to an audience so that they can see not herself but the clothes she is wearing – which in Thérèse's case means 'the clothes of grace'.[29] So far from being vanity there is here the supreme humility of treating oneself as the instrument, merely, of the Gospel. What she offered as doctrine was what she discovered accounted for the stream of graces she experienced. Then quite directly she 'expropriates herself and places her doctrine at the disposal of the Church, to serve as the common good of the faithful'.[30]

> Instead of devoting herself to idle speculations about the next world she infers its laws from the eternal love dwelling in her at the moment. Nor do these inferences lead her to abstract generalizations about 'grace', for she expresses them in terms of the concrete, personal love binding her soul to God, and of the personal mission bestowed on her by God. She knows that her love and her mission are essentially beyond time, in eternity; only in the next world will they come to full fruition – even her mission, which she feels stirring within her as death comes closer.[31]

She rediscovers the patristic eschatology for which even heaven, before the general resurrection, is in some way a state of transience since the saints are typified by an eager desire lovingly to help their brethren still struggling on earth. Her eschatological longing is not for happiness, though she will accept all the joy God may give her with childlike gratitude. Still, that longing is actually for love – not only to receive love but above all to return it.

What we know about Balthasar's debt to Barth, and consequent revulsion against anything that might smack of a subjective re-writing of revelation, be it Modernist, be it pious, might make us wonder at his *attrait* to this particular saint. He takes the wind out of our sails by saying:

> Thérèse's existential method should not lead one to assume that she sets herself up as the measure of the Word of God. The fact is that she only dares to make her achievement a standard of divine truth because she herself has received her measure from God.[32]

But he also acknowledges that she cannot easily be claimed as a representative of 'strict contemplation', the contemplation that means 'losing

27 *Thérèse of Lisieux*, p. 13. This was not altogether true, however: she did not hide her indebtedness to St John of the Cross and the author of the *Imitation of Christ*.
28 *Ibid.*, p. 17.
29 *Ibid.*, p. 18.
30 *Ibid.*, p. 20.
31 *Ibid.*, p. 29.
32 *Ibid.*, p. 37.

oneself in the objectivity of God's revealed Word'[33] – with which we can compare the 'objective mysticism' dear to Adrienne von Speyr. Her prayer consisted essentially in meditative *lectio divina* punctuated by 'lights' which 'are all centred upon her mission'.[34] This would be highly dangerous were it not for the fact that she reads Scripture obediently, in a context of self-denial and self-conquest. Balthasar finds 'shadows' in her personality: she foolishly spoke to others of a childhood vision of the smile of the Virgin, and she accepted at face value her confessor's 'indiscreet' remark to her that she had never been guilty of grave sin. She hovered on the edge of a 'deviation' in which her principal concern would have been (her own) sanctity. But by the time of her death she had overcome this: her

> primary motive is no longer sanctity but the love of God, the glory of the Church, the salvation of souls and the fulfillment of the divine will.[35]

Moreover, in her period as novice-mistress, she became detached from herself in a quite new way. 'I prefer to admit quite simply that "He that is mighty hath done great things to me" [Luke 1.49]; and the greatest of all is to have shown me my littleness, my inability to do any good.'[36] Actually, Balthasar criticizes an element here in the Carmelite tradition, the concern with self-analysis which came in with the sixteenth-century Spanish reformers, and which he thinks does not fit entirely with the Order's dominant trait, 'hidden obligation before God'. More telling is her conviction that in the exercise of her office she was simply 'an instrument in the service of love'.[37] She believed that her vocation 'made her quite literally a mother of souls, an office no less dignified than that of the priest'.[38] Though Balthasar cannot quite bring himself to say so, she reverses the Ignatian formula 'contemplative in action', so that it becomes 'active in contemplation'. And of course it fits with this that she sees heaven as the launching pad of her most intense missionary action. Balthasar altogether approves of this approach which treats the excellence of contemplation as inhering in its fruitfulness – Adrienne von Speyr was teaching exactly the same doctrine. Other versions found in the tradition, like Thomas's, allow too much to the (philosophical) 'prejudices of the ancient world'.

Balthasar shows Thérèse surprising us time and again. She firmly negates the (common-sense) opinion of a sister that a long life of fidelity is better than a short one. It seems to her that 'love can substitute for a long life'.[39] Devotion to the Sacred Heart of Jesus fails to move her (a traditional nineteenth-century French Catholic!). Her own heart is drawn to the Holy Face, the 'face' at once of the Transfiguration and the Passion. 'Yes, I recognize You, even through tears, Face of the Eternal, I recognize your beauty.'[40] Though at the time of her father's tragic incarceration in an asylum she was allowed to add

33 *Ibid.*, p. 47.
34 *Ibid.*, p. 48.
35 *Ibid.*, p. 62.
36 Cited *ibid.*, p. 116.
37 *Ibid.*, p. 123.
38 *Ibid.*, pp. 135–36.
39 Cited *ibid.*, p. 155.
40 Cited *ibid.*, p. 158.

this 'title of devotion' to the earlier form of her religious name – Thérèse 'of the Child Jesus', Balthasar holds this was not mere happenstance. A real synthesis of these terms – and realities – came to characterize her spiritual outlook. The childlikeness which drew her to adopt the first 'title' is fully expressed in artless candour of the 'game of veiling and unveiling' she plays with the countenance of Christ.

Balthasar states it as a dictum that 'every saint lives theological truths' (as does, for that matter, at their own level, every Christian).[41] Thérèse lived the radicality of the Gospel seen as the prodigal love of God, bestowed on the humble of heart. She goes all the way with this amazing evangelical concentration. In *The History of a Soul* she hit upon an especially telling metaphor.

> So long as our actions, no matter how trivial, remain within the focus of love, the Blessed Trinity ... gives them a wonderful brilliance and beauty. When Jesus looks at us through the little lens, which is to say Himself, He finds all our doings beautiful. But if we abandon the ineffable centre of love, what does He see? A few straws ... besmirched and worthless deeds.[42]

Hence her distaste for the 'great way' of 'extraordinary' penances and 'heroic' deeds. The 'way of weakness' is actually *more* meritorious.

In any case, she recasts the doctrine of merit. For the Gospels, she insists, God distributes rewards *by virtue of his grace*. She recovers, without being aware of it, St Thomas's teaching that the free disposition of divine love establishes the correspondence of merit and recompense – and that supernatural charity in us is the only principle of merit.[43] After the manner of the evangelist John, she comes to be beyond fear, since she had made room enough in her mind and heart for love's fullness to dwell. But what is this fullness? Having de-constructed the 'great way', the construction of the 'little way' will tell us. It is when

> love is brought to a state of weakness in which it learns the power of divine love, of littleness and darkness in which the greatness and glory of divine love are displayed.[44]

This could be misunderstood. Balthasar explains that Thérèse 'does not love weakness for its own sake'.

> But she prefers to be in a condition where she is naked to the grace of God. Weakness, not only physical but moral weakness, also brings with it a marked sensitivity to grace which she would not have apart from her failures. Thérèse's Christian view of time as a constant encounter with eternity demands this refinement of her soul if her whole being is to be bared to the stress of God's love.[45]

41 *Ibid.*, p. 167.
42 Cited *ibid.*, p. 183.
43 Thomas Aquinas, *Summa theologiae* Ia.IIae., q. 114, a. 4, corpus.
44 *Thérèse of Lisieux, op. cit.*, p. 199.
45 *Ibid.*, p. 208.

This is not Luther's 'sin boldly!', but a manner of bringing even one's faults into the movement towards evangelical perfection. Balthasar terms it a 'bold, irrefutable answer to Protestant spirituality'.[46]

The little way of spiritual childhood is one of trust and surrender (which must be carefully distinguished from mere resignation). It means 'expecting everything from the good God'.[47] It is little but not easy: '[H]er basic presupposition is that of a saint: that life has no meaning unless it is at the service of God'.[48] Stressing the parallel between the Theresian 'way' and Ignatian 'indifference', Balthasar writes: 'suffering and joy are equally acceptable so long as they come from the hand of God'.[49] By not only teaching the little way but also embodying it, Thérèse fulfilled her mission – which is not to say that Balthasar lacks all criticism of her. Her rejection of the schemes of mystical development proposed by the Carmelite doctors of the sixteenth century was not entirely to her credit. Significantly, she never knew, claims Balthasar, the Sanjuanist 'dark nights'. Nor, he thinks, could she since, until the last month of her life, misled by a foolish confessor, she believed herself to have been, since her Baptism, sinless if not wholly without blemish. This moralizing interpretation of what the 'nights' involve is surprising – and out of keeping with Balthasar's doctrine of prayer, the subject of the next chapter.

We have seen that Balthasar wished to replace a psychologistic hagiology with one that functioned as a sort of phenomenology of mission. A saint like Thérèse can only be understood if we grasp in what way she continues the mission of Christ. Now there cannot, for Balthasar, be a *psychology* of Christ. His 'I' – his personal hypostasis – is divine and as a consequence, in his human nature, 'all Christ's words, deeds and conditions have only one meaning: to reveal God'.[50] And every responsible thinker would agree there is no such thing as a psychology of God. To seek Jesus' ultimate identity and mission by making an inventory of the features of his human mind would be rather like inspecting the manuals of J. S. Bach's organ at Leipzig for an explanation of a great fugue, or monitoring an artist's palette to predict the emergence of a masterpiece. The case of the saints is not of course the same as that of the Word incarnate. But there is an analogy. The saint's psyche, and his personal 'I', thanks to their

> incorporation in Christ [are] relativised to be an expressive field for the life of Christ in that saint, which henceforth is the only meaning-furnishing principle for his life and the law of his thinking and acting.[51]

This incorporation takes concrete form in the Church and the Christian receives his mission – the precisely tailored form of grace for him – by reference to the 'organism of the community of salvation'. This mission, with its charisms, is

46 *Ibid.*, p. 209.
47 Cited *ibid.*, p. 220.
48 *Ibid.*, p. 222.
49 *Ibid.*, p. 242.
50 'Psychologie der Heiligen?', *Schweizer Rundschau* 48 (1948), pp. 644–53, and here at p. 645.
51 *Ibid.*

the most utterly personal reality in his person, and the most utterly impersonal and functional reality in his being-an-instrument for the Church.

And the significance of *that* is:

Everything in the soul of the Christian is relativised in relation to this mission which is not abstract but the most concrete thing imaginable – the life of Christ through the Holy Spirit in [the saint's] soul whereby it is wholly placed at the service of the glorification of the Father.[52]

Every attempt to understand a saint by prescinding from faith leads to no less distortion than the chimaera of trying to write a study of the 'psychology of Christ'. Paul Sabatier's life of Francis of Assisi is worth no more than Ernest Renan's life of Jesus of Nazareth, which is as good as to say, it is worth nothing at all.

By the 1970s, Balthasar was more preoccupied with the activist assault on monasticism, asceticism and contemplation than he was by the need for a new methodology in writing saints' lives. As he explained in the preface he wrote in 1970 for a new edition of the two books on Elizabeth and Thérèse, now conflated as *Schwestern im Geist*,[53] the meaning of the contemplative life was not in dispute in the Catholic Church in the 1950s. By the early 70s , even among Carmelites, it was.

For most people [he wrote] 'openness to the world'; makes sense only in the form of dialogue and directed experienced 'sociability' accompanied by practical goals and measurable successes. Yet did not even the great contemplative tradition, when it was fully Christian and evangelical, live out of a much deeper insight? – the insight that all social actions smash into the same barrier Jesus encountered in his active life, the insight that this world's mounting resistance can only be overcome when one gathers one's entire existence together into a unitive yielding to God so that God can ceaselessly marshal them on behalf of all men and women in the service of his cosmic plan of salvation?

Balthasar argued not only that the Passion of Christ and contemplation are intrinsically interlinked. Not only are they the 'inward continuation of action'. They are also the 'goal' of all the activity God planned from the beginning and Jesus freely affirmed.

God does not give himself in Christ merely for the sake of a bit of dialogue and action among men and women; rather, God eucharistically pours himself out endlessly in absolute love.[54]

So, the life of Carmel, and all purely contemplative life-forms in the Church must be situated here. Far from being a 'flight from the world', they extrapolate the encounter between the world and the living God of Jesus Christ to its most radical point.

52 *Ibid.*, p. 646.
53 *Schwestern im Geist. Thérèse von Lisieux und Elisabeth von Dijon* (Einsiedeln, 1970); ET *Two Sisters in the Spirit. Thérèse von Lisieux und Elisabeth of the Trinity* (San Francisco, 1992).
54 *Ibid.*, p. 9.

The closer one comes to modernity, thought Balthasar, and the more the Church recognizes the crucial importance of apostolic action and, even for Religious Orders, the fusion of contemplation with action, the more clearly the biblical basis for a sheerly contemplative life and effort stands out. In this process he believed, the final step was taken at the end of the nineteenth century: its name is Elizabeth-and-Thérèse. What they have in common is that they:

> understood the act of total surrender to the triune God as the highest possible form of engagement on behalf of the world's salvation.[55]

Furthermore, in retrospect Balthasar finds their 'theological existences' to be conveniently complementary. Missions that 'emanate from the centre' should not be 'weighed against each other'. But they can, though, be 'fruitfully opposed'. And he explains how:

> Thérèse wants Scripture and dogma to take on flesh and blood in her existence, and this brings the accompanying risk that objective truth might disappear into existential truth, thereby reducing the framework of the Church's great doctrine to the framework of an experienced 'little way'. In contrast, Elizabeth permits her entire existence to disappear into the truth of the Gospel to the extent that the overpowering objectivity of divine truth threatens to destroy her subjectivity ... Each points to the other; they construct hemispheres that, fitted together, make Carmel's spiritual world round.[56]

Three years later, at the celebrations for the centenary of her birth (1973), he was more acerbic. Canonization, he suggested, is often a means for relegating the calls of the Spirit to the archives. In a democratic age, the spiritual 'aristocracy' of the saints is suspect. Is not their elevated example divisive, if the goal is solidarity with everyone, sceptics and atheists included? But 'God only gives them this singularity so as to illuminate a multitude without number'.[57]

(ii) Elizabeth of Dijon

Of these two Carmelite saints, Elizabeth is by far the less well known, and in putting her forward Balthasar offers, as the subtitle of the English translation tells us, 'An Interpretation of her Spiritual Mission'.[58] She was born at Bourges in 1880 and as early as the age of seventeen expressed the intention of entering Carmel. Her mother's initial refusal of permission delayed that event for two years. She took her final vows at the beginning of 1901, after which she made a study of the chief writings of the Carmelite doctor, John of the Cross. In 1904 she was deeply impressed by Pius X's encyclical letter 'To Renew All Things in Christ', and later that year wrote her much copied prayer 'O mon Dieu, Trinité que j'adore'. In the spring of 1905 her health began dramatically to decline and she was allowed some mitigation of the

---

55 *Ibid.*, p. 11.
56 *Ibid.*
57 'Actualité de Lisieux', in *Thérèse de Lisieux. Conférences du Centenaire 1873–1973* (Paris, 1973), pp. 107–23, and here at p. 109.
58 *Elizabeth of Dijon. An Interpretation of her Spiritual Mission* (ET London, 1956).

austere Carmelite rule. In the summer she devoted herself to the study of St John's Apocalypse. Elizabeth of the Trinity died on 9 November 1905, at the age of twenty-five.

Balthasar believed that both these young Carmelite nuns – and indeed, the whole of Carmel – had a mission in the modern age to attest the primacy of God and contemplating God in human life. But Elizabeth's mission was more specific. She had a call to testify to her vision of divine revelation – a vision Balthasar praises for its lucidity and theological compactness. It amounts to a personal synthesis of two great Pauline texts (Ephesians 1.4-6 and Romans 8.29-30) on the mystery of divine predestination as giving us the meaning of creation, redemption, the Church.

> They went straight to her heart, bringing a sense of peace and joy – how different from the terror experienced by all who have tried to probe the mystery, from Augustine to the Protestants and Jansenists! To them a dark and terrible abyss, to her a mystery full of light, compelling love and adoration.[59]

Or in her own reworking of the apostle's words:

> Whom God foreknew, them he also predestined to be made conformable to the image of his divine Son, crucified through love. Once I am perfectly conformed to this divine image, completely absorbed in him and he in me, then I will have fulfilled my eternal vocation, that which God chose for me *in principio*. I will continue to fulfil it *in aeternum*, in the bosom of the Trinity, a continuous song of praise to his glory, *in laudem gloriae ejus*.[60]

Balthasar emphasizes the great objectivity of Elizabeth's doctrine when compared with that of her older contemporary of whose life, teachings and holy death she was well aware. The danger with Thérèse, as Balthasar sees her, is that her mission had so many 'personal' traits that its 'revealed content' was in danger of being obscured. Elizabeth passed the Teresian message through the sieve of the Letters of St Paul. The slightly exhibitionist personality traits slip through, leaving what is truly precious – the 'objective message and its universal application – safely caught in the silver grid'.

> It is as though Elizabeth had exerted herself to reset the individual 'lessons' of Teresa one by one in their framework of revealed doctrine, and so deprive them, it may be, of the gloss of an interesting novelty.[61]

She relocates the message of the saint of Lisieux no longer autobiographically but in terms of her (Elizabeth's) favoured biblical themes.

On Balthasar's analysis, those themes are essentially five: predestination, 'infinity', adoration, praise, and (very briefly) service. Her versions are rendered by him in ways which pick up motifs already sounded in his own theological work – though one cannot rule out their more constructive role in confirming and extending perceptions he had reached by other routes. Thus, on predestination he emphasizes how Elizabeth has no doctrine of

---

59 *Ibid.*, pp. 23–24.
60 Cited *ibid.*, p. 26.
61 *Ibid.*, p. 47.

individual predestination save as a participation in the predestining of Christ and the Church. Who can say which predominates – the influence of Barth, of de Lubac's patristic and later sources, or simply a careful reading of St Paul – when Balthasar brackets the apostle with Elizabeth in the following passage:

> In making known God's universal plan from the foundation of the world, both are far from admitting the thought of an 'enumeration' of particular individuals to the exclusion of others. On the contrary, God's plan of universal salvation, beginning with the election of the saints in Christ, issues finally in the *instaurare omnia in Christo*, in the binding together of all things in heaven and earth to the Head which is Christ, the Saviour and Redeemer of the world.[62]

Only to a 'profane' thinker does the thought of the reprobation of some follow necessarily from that of the election of others. In Balthasar's gloss on Elizabeth's teaching:

> No one is redeemed for himself alone, but his brethren are included with him, for he of necessity co-operates for their salvation in working out his own.[63]

Here predestination becomes a term for high responsibilities of function, though with Elizabeth this is ancillary to the doxological purpose all election in Christ has in view: an existence suffused by the praise of God's glory. Balthasar, however, uses the opportunity to present his own case that we can hope for the salvation of all human beings while nonetheless working out our own in fear and trembling. *Qua* exegete of Elizabeth's texts, Balthasar is on firmer ground when he stresses the way the doctrine of predestination serves her as an entrée to eschatology. To live from the 'standpoint' of eternal election is to tend toward the goal of that election: namely, 'living in holiness in the presence of God'.[64] Faith animated by charity also implies *hope*: it is faith in the love God has in store for us. And, thanks to God's indwelling by grace in the elect soul, this is already a sharing in the life everlasting. Conscious of her inadequacy, by her own resources, to live up to this calling, Elizabeth invoked Christology, casting herself on him whom St John called the faithful and true (cf. Apocalypse 19.11). Or as Balthasar puts it: '*Pistis*, faith, implies the presence of *Pistos*, the one who is always true'.[65] Elizabeth defines Christ's 'truth' as the 'truth of love' whereby the incarnate Word loved us (and therefore her) and gave himself for us (and so for Elizabeth).[66] Our response must be to 'abide' in him – a highly Johannine concept which she interprets in Trinitarian terms. As in her celebrated and much-used prayer, 'O Trinité que j'adore', she asks the triune God so to fascinate her and 'ensnare' her that she may never stray from him, never desire to leave his 'fortress' or 'temple'. She wants to fall altogether under his spell. Balthasar assures his readers that:

62 *Ibid.*, p. 38.
63 *Ibid.*, pp. 38–39.
64 *Ibid.*, p. 27.
65 *Ibid.*, p. 30.
66 Cited in *ibid.*

This idea of captivity is far from implying restriction or constraint. On the contrary, Elizabeth looks on eternity as a boundless expanse, and abiding with God as a continuous process.[67]

If so she is at one with Gregory of Nyssa, one of Balthasar's chief patristic sources.

That brings us to 'infinity' which – Balthasar is at some pains to insist – does not form part of Elizabeth's rhetoric by appeal to philosophical discussion. Rather is it, at her hands, a way of expressing an evangelical confession. If predestination is her root doctrinal idea, she applied it to herself in a distinctively Carmelite manner. 'Her mission was to approach, by way of contemplation, the source of all grace, and so to a conduit of its flow in the Church.'[68] The Carmelite approach to this source was a ready, alert but silent waiting on the Infinite, to which she felt a call from childhood. She had sensed the barriers of the finite crumbling and, while aware that this experience was not itself God, also knew that it pointed to the One beyond. Her attraction to the Infinite, the unsoundable abyss, was to an Infinite who embraced the finite, detached it from earth and (in her word) 'infinitized' it so it could become itself a heaven for his dwelling. Balthasar notes her passionate language as she desires to be engulfed, invaded, inundated, buried, by God. He also approves her lack of the language of negative theology. 'What she seeks in the infinite is not the God of philosophy, distant and unapproachable, but the God of Jesus Christ, perfectly present and intimate.'[69] Her mysticism:

> though a mysticism of infinity, is unquestionably Christological, since the infinite irrupts into the finite only through the Incarnation, the Passion and the Eucharist, the fruit of God's love in Christ.[70]

Living in communion with Christ is to occupy a transitional state between the finite and the Infinite. This is the key to Elizabeth's understanding of Eucharistic reception. It suggests how this sacrament, received far more rarely, even by enclosed nuns, in Elizabeth's day than later, should send out vibrations during the rest of the week. In her last weeks on earth, she altered the inflexion of this Christological approach to the Infinite. Previously, that approach signified for her the 'excess of love' poured out from the human nature of God the Son. Now she came to see it as meaning above all the Passion of the Lord as 'gate of the infinite'. Through the passion, 'the world was enabled to see the abyss of God's love'.[71]

> Elizabeth, in her last months, came to see the mysterious unity of Mount Calvary and that mountain in the Apocalypse where the heavenly Lamb stands with his companions. The mountain of the night of suffering and abandonment is the same as that of election to the community of heaven, the *civitas Dei*, the *civitas Sanctorum*.[72]

---

67 *Ibid.*, p. 33.
68 *Ibid.*, p. 53.
69 *Ibid.*, pp. 63–64.
70 *Ibid.*, pp. 64–65.
71 *Ibid.*, p. 66.
72 *Ibid.*, p. 68.

Evidently, Elizabeth's third theme, on Balthasar's analysis, *adoration*, fits naturally here. Like Balthasar himself, Elizabeth made much of the Book of the Apocalypse, seeking to share the 'hymn of praise, this uninterrupted adoration' of the blessed as depicted in its pages.[73] Of course it was adoration of the Christian Infinite as made known in the Gospel of predestining grace. For her, adoration is a response to God's 'excess of love', a paraphrase of the Vulgate text of Ephesians 2.4, *nimia caritas*. Balthasar says he likes the word 'excessive' here since, even more than 'infinite', it 'excludes, by surpassing, every kind of comparison'.[74] The essence of Carmel is perpetual awareness of this excessive Love, in a presence which renders the soul unified in a simple gaze. The saints are 'lost in their Beloved', and it is in the hope of emulating them on earth that Elizabeth interprets her own Carmelite 'title of devotion' – 'of the Trinity' to mean she is 'Elizabeth of the disappearance'.[75] This is where, above all, Teresian trust and abandonment must enter the process of growth toward evangelical perfection. For faith, which is the medium of our presence to God, is exercised in the 'night'.[76] This is why Elizabeth describes the divine presence as that of God's *will*, though she is theologian enough to understand this is not something other than his very being. To relate to his will in every situation makes each situation a 'sacrament of faith', the obedience entailed bringing its sacrificial reward in the renewed bestowal of his nearness. Elizabeth makes her own St John of the Cross's teaching that faith is *possession in a state of obscurity*. It makes the future, eschatological gifts subsist in our souls prior to our capacity to enjoy them. Except that there is *some* capacity to enjoy them even now, as Elizabeth in her last months, huddled in a corner of choir, knew with joy. Christ dwelling in the soul teaches it how to adore the Father in the Holy Spirit.

Only one thing was lacking, thought Balthasar, to Elizabeth's doctrine of adoration: a linkage between this Trinitarian foundation to her life and her awareness of the (present and future) communion of saints. In an important text for his own dogmatics Balthasar explains:

> [I]n the degree to which the inmost self is 'inhabited' by the yet more interior Trinity – *Deus trinus interior intimo meo* – it is laid open to the Church and to the communion of saints at the deepest level; in fact, this communion can only be conceived as a dwelling together of all persons in the Trinity who, in turn, dwells in them all.[77]

Thus is the Plotinian 'flight of the alone to the Alone' rendered a civil mystery.

That leaves Balthasar, on Elizabeth's behalf, with the themes of praise and service. Her doctrine of praise follows from all that has been said so far. 'Only that soul which does not seek to shine itself, but lets God mirror itself in it, is a song of praise to his glory.'[78] What is given back to God is what he first gave. It is on this principle that, in the final volume of the theological dramatics, Balthasar will construct his (relatively) controversial account of

73 Cited in *ibid.*, p. 71.
74 *Ibid.*, p. 72.
75 *Ibid.*, p. 81.
76 *Ibid.*
77 *Ibid.*, p. 95.
78 *Ibid.*, pp. 98–99.

how the redeemed will 'enrich' – increase the glory of – the Trinity. When Elizabeth seeks to 'cover [Christ] with glory', the means she uses is to ask him to make of her life, by suffering and obedience, a 'reflexion' of his, an 'added humanity' – *un humanité de surcroît* – in which he can 'renew [his] mystery'.[79] And if we enquire what is the role of the Holy Spirit in all this, her answer is it is to 'kindle the fire of union with the Son', since by his office the Spirit carries out all that the Father's will for the Son implies.[80] 'Heaven is in ourselves, and the Holy Ghost wills to renew it with the heat of His flame.'[81] Balthasar regards Elizabeth's existence as proof of the Lord's promise about the Spirit that he would accomplish in the world the glorification of the Father through the Son (John 16.11). Balthasar fuses his own Trinitarian theology with her Christological thought when he says of Elizabeth's sense of the 'twofold abyss' – the abyss of God's infinity, the abyss of the soul's nothingness – that the Son 'clothes himself with it, divinizes it, *makes it the expression of the internal distinction of the divine Persons in their unity of nature'*.[82]

The love of God present to the soul so penetrates it as to place it at the apostolic service of others – in that mode alone possible to the enclosed nun which is prayer. Writing to a diocesan priest Elizabeth tells him that priest and Carmelite are equally John the Baptist figures, 'precursor-lives' that 'prepare the way for him the apostle calls a "consuming fire"'.[83] Like Balthasar she rejects the antinomy of Mary of Bethany, contemplative, and Martha, active do-gooder. Her prayer is service of others and Balthasar even allows here the dangerous word 'co-redemption'. In a highly un-Lutheran statement he declares, 'Grace involves work, redemption involves co-redemption'.[84] In Elizabeth's eyes, indeed, this is an entailment of pre-destination – whose social character, in her teaching, we have noted. As Carmelite, she had a double mission: to be virgin, yes, but also to be mother. Not the least of her affinities with Thérèse, this expressed itself in an offer of help from beyond death, just as with the saint of Lisieux. She saw no contradiction between that expectation and the belief that she was called, with all the saints, to discharge the office of praise for ever in Heaven. Balthasar stresses how her *Last Retreat*, the final text to come from her hand, is filled with the imagery of the Apocalypse, drawn on in such a fashion that her thinking becomes a distant replica of a patristic forebear, Denys the Areopagite.

> The idea of a hierarchy in heaven and earth makes the whole created world, steeped in the light of redeeming grace, a single cosmos of service; it expresses the fact that the idea of service pertains primarily to the heavenly world, while the earthly reflects in transient fashion, the forms of eternal service.[85]

We gather from Balthasar that Elizabeth invoked the Mother of the Lord under the title *Janua caeli*: 'The Gate of Heaven'. Balthasar ends with a

79 Cited in *ibid.*, p. 104.
80 *Ibid.*, p. 106.
81 Cited in *ibid.*
82 *Ibid.*, p. 109. Italics added.
83 Cited in *ibid.*, p. 114.
84 *Ibid.*
85 *Ibid.*, p. 118.

citation from Elizabeth's writings which sums up, really, the entirety of his own Christology and Mariology. She had in her room an image of Holy Mary in her relation to the three divine Persons:

> In the solitude of our little cell ... I will often contemplate the precious image, uniting myself with the soul of the Blessed Virgin when the Father overshadowed her, the Son took flesh in her, and the Holy Ghost descended to work the great mystery. What would be living for in Carmel, if we were not likewise enveloped by the divine?[86]

---

86 Cited in *ibid.*, p. 126.

12

Divine Living: Prayer and Mysticism

Introduction

From here it is no great distance, evidently, to Balthasar himself on prayer. So what is Balthasar's doctrine of prayer? In his most sustained treatment of the subject, *Das betrachtende Gebet*, 'Contemplative Prayer', he notes both the widespread desire for some form of contemplative prayer, and the equally widespread feeling that going beyond the point of reading the spiritual meditations of others is simply too difficult – even though it means 'We observe someone else eating, but it does nothing to fill our stomachs'![1] And so he proposes in a way all his own to give his readers confidence in this activity. He will be speaking:

> of the depth and splendour of this form of prayer *within the whole context of Christian revelation* ...

the aim being:

> to help readers discover delight in it and to develop their sense of its indispensable necessity in the Christian life in general and in today's world in particular.[2]

He divides his material into two principal sections: the *act* of contemplation and the *object* of contemplation. (A coda concerns the 'tensions' of contemplative existence.) But first of all, then, the *act*.

Prayer as conversation

Balthasar describes the state of mind of many Christians when faced with this subject as one of embarrassment – embarrassment of the sort that comes our way when we find ourselves having to stammer out some expressions in a language whose grammar we do not really know. In some respects, indeed, prayer *is* like a conversation. Balthasar mentions two of these respects. First, the *model of conversation* helps to grasp what prayer involves inasmuch as prayer *does* involve speech, and speech can never be entirely solitary, since it

---

1 Et *Prayer* (ET San Francisco, 1986), p. 7.
2 *Ibid.*, p. 8. Italics added.

both presupposes and manifests an 'I' together with a 'Thou'. By its very nature:

> speech implies reciprocity, the exchange of thoughts and of souls, unity in a common possession and sharing of the truth.[3]

And secondly, and this is crucial to Balthasar's study, the language in which such speech proceeds is *God*'s language, the language of his self-revealing Word.

> It was God who spoke first, and it is only because God has expressed, 'exteriorised', himself in this way that man can 'interiorise' himself towards God ... Whatever could we say to God if he himself had not taken the first step in communicating and manifesting himself to us in his Word, so that we have access to him and fellowship with him?[4]

It follows that the first 'moment' in praying must always be one of *listening* – listening to the Word of God. (It is not so surprising after all that in 1961 Balthasar called *Prayer* his most Barthian work so far.) Since there is no complete truth in ourselves, we must learn how to find the truth in God. Balthasar speaks of this truth in threefold fashion: it is a God-given truth about the way to God; it is a God-given truth about existence, and it is the God-given truth of God himself, his only-begotten Son of whom he declared, 'This is my beloved Son: listen to him'.[5]

Maybe the reader will retort that this is stale news, just as G. K. Chesterton was faced with the objection that Christianity has been tried and found wanting. And somewhat in the fashion of the great apologist, with his insistence that, rather, faith has been found difficult and not tried, Balthasar maintains:

> we fail to see that it is ourselves who are used up and alienated, whereas the Word resounds with the same vitality and freshness as ever; it is just as near to us as it always was. 'The Word is near you, on your lips and in your heart' (Romans 10, 8).[6]

Once the eternal Word has been spoken forth, in the fullness of time, in the midst of the world, no distance of chronology or geography can separate me from it or, better, him. Since it is God who is speaking, distance is not a problem. Conversely, I may not take up a purely historicizing attitude to the Word when I find it in the Scriptures, seeking to ram it firmly back into the past history from which it came. Supremely, I may not do this in those situations where the Word made flesh enters into dialogue with human beings.

The contemplation-founding divine initiative

The divine initiative that founds contemplation is Christologically focused yet integrates both Israel and, behind Israel, the cosmos. The encounters with

---

3 *Ibid.*, p. 14.
4 *Ibid.*, pp. 14–15.
5 Matthew 17.5.
6 *Prayer, op. cit.*, p. 16.

the Lord Jesus of the men and women of the Gospels are what Balthasar first thinks of when he considers the biblical archetypes of prayer. I can put myself in the situation of, say, the Woman of Samaria in John 4, not only because, from the viewpoint of understanding the divine Word, that figure of first-century Palestine was no better placed, for all her physical proximity, than I am. Also, and more importantly, the doctrines of predestination and justification mean that in any case *I am where she was*, confronted by the saving Word. As Balthasar puts it, in terms which anticipate his theological dramatics, 'Not only may I play this part: I *must* play it'. I have been taken up into this dialogue long before I could be consulted.

> I am this dried-up soul, running after the earthly water every day because it has lost its grasp of the heavenly water it is really seeking. Like her I give the same obtuse, groping response to the offer of the eternal wellspring; in the end, like her, I have to be pierced by the Word as it wrings from me the confession of sin.[7]

And the necessary condition for this confession, if it is truly to place us in the right, is that it be not only borne but 'overborne' by the justifying grace of this same judging Word in his fathomless mercy. A rather nice wordplay to convey what is, in essentials, the Thomistic doctrine.

Not that the presence of the Word in Jesus' public ministry is the be-all and end-all of the divine utterance. If the Letter to the Hebrews can open with a reference to the multifarious ways in which God spoke to the fathers, Balthasar can speak similarly of Israel's prophetic traditions as the 'many already existing streams' which went to feed the single torrent of the Incarnation.

> Today [i.e. after the Incarnation], presented with a single river, we see in these streams nothing other than the river's tributaries, rushing headlong to meet it and merging completely, in the fulness of time, with the unique Word which says everything. It is impossible [since the Incarnation] to listen to any individual word of God without hearing the Son who is *the* Word.[8]

And the Incarnation likewise brings to a head the cosmic revelation of God as well: the words of nature, in macrocosm and microcosm,

> the words uttered by the flowers and the animals; words of over-powering beauty and of debilitating terror; the words of human existence in their confusing, myriad forms, laden with both promise and disappointment: all these belong to the one eternal, living Word who became man for our sakes. They are totally and utterly his possession, and so they are at his disposal, to be understood exclusively in his interpretation.[9]

With the epiphanizing of the Son, anyone who hears the words of God as manifold must re-learn how to hear them, from the standpoint of their unity.

7 *Ibid.*, p. 17.
8 *Ibid.*, p. 18.
9 *Ibid.*, p. 19.

Only at this centre – Jesus Christ – will the human being at last understand the truth.

The divine initiative's free and personal character

Balthasar stresses not only the cosmic character of the Word made flesh, and his unique integration of the tradition of Israel, but also – and above all – his supremely *free* (because personal) character. Response to that Word in contemplation must have the same free and personal quality. Since the gracious self-communication of the Word springs from his absolute, sovereign freedom, the fact that grace is engrafted on being, and found objectively in the mystical body of Christ (above all, in the sacraments), does not excuse us from the necessity of responding to it as free spirits, if it is really to be ours. Not as body-soul amalgams primarily but as *hearers of the Word* do we humans have the dignity our Creator meant for us. And Balthasar's typical comment thereon is that we cannot be ourselves until the Word, receiving our free response, sends us out into the world upon our *mission*.[10]

But to say this, with its implications for my exterior comportment, must not be made an excuse to evade the demands of the interior life. These derive from the fact that God, though a 'Thou', is not simply another Personality (however transcendent and thus capitalized), over against my own – like, say, the head of a family giving a task to one of that family's members. As the absolute 'I', the Creator, he is the deepest ground of my finite 'I', and is so as One who is the sovereign Lord. So the journey inward here is also a journey deeper. As a result of this state of affairs, to look into the soul is simultaneously to look beyond the soul. This leads to the – apparent – paradox that the more contemplation finds God, the more it at once loses itself and yet finds itself *in* him.

And this, thankfully, is something we can never get used to, for God is the *Je-grösser*, the 'Ever-greater' One. Owing to the unplumbable depths of the divine freedom, the creature has continually to receive afresh the fulfilment the Creator offers it. And so even in heaven we shall not be simply 'seeing through' God but rather hanging on his every word – just as here on earth we are not restricted to listening to him as from a distance but, as the theological aesthetics tell us, we can glimpse him as he is. The customary association of faith here and now with hearing, and vision in the hereafter with seeing, is something of a simplification.

Balthasar understands the Word that is thus already close to us not on the basis of creation alone – though belief in God's creative act must ground the fact that the divine Word is 'the truth of me and about me'.[11] But more than this: all the mysteries of redemption have to be brought in as well.

> The Word within has attained a new level since, in order to reach us, alienated and sunk in the flesh as we are, it has taken flesh of our flesh and now communicates itself to us in the twofold form of Word and Flesh, of Holy Scripture and Eucharist, of spiritual and substantial Truth.[12]

10 *Ibid.*, p. 22.
11 *Ibid.*, p. 26.
12 *Ibid.*, p. 28.

This statement constitutes a compressed reference to the mysteries of the Incarnation and Atonement and their presence to us through the Scriptures and sacramental life of the Church. In this context Balthasar stresses that the 'pray-er' *par excellence* is Blessed Mary, Mother of the Church. As virgin-hearer of the Word she becomes the mother-locus of the Word's embodiment. Possibly, Catholics need to learn from Protestantism the centrality of attentiveness to the Word of God (here the allusion to Barth is, this time, patent). But Protestants cannot genuinely contemplate the Word without that sense of its indwelling which depends on the Marian principle – and this they need to learn from the Catholic Church. As we have seen, Balthasar treats Mary and the Church as joined in an intimate coinherence or *perichôrêsis*: for Catholics the Word of Scripture is always a word *entrusted to the Church*.

> [It is] a word from the Holy Spirit concerning the Son, a divine and authentic presentation and making-present of the revelation of the Father in the Son-Word, and hence also the Spirit of the Word himself.[13]

Revelation in *being* certainly does need revelation in *word* for its interpretation. We must know our Bible. Contemplating through Scripture – in the time-honoured phrase, *lectio divina* – is our school for proper listening to God. But we are sent to this school *in the Church and nowhere else*.

If contemplation is necessary it must of course be possible: 'ought' implies 'can'. Balthasar argues that, first and last, contemplation is a possibility given with faith, and specifically Christian faith at that. In the context of Christian revelation – the only setting in which a *theologian* of contemplative prayer would find herself –

> contemplation is not a mere gazing upon the Absolute, excluding as far as possible all its relations to the world in order to focus upon it in the greatest possible purity and detachment. Instead, the encounter with the Absolute – which never takes place with such force and such intensity except in this context – is always an encounter with the God who reveals himself within the setting of the world and its history, a God who is on the lookout for man.[14]

There may be felt absences of God that are objectively grounded (prophetic experiences of woe, Christ's experience on Calvary, the 'dark nights' of St John of the Cross) but these are 'forms and modes of love' that have nothing to do with sinful deficiency of response to the Word.

All this must now be thought through more thoroughly in explicitly Trinitarian terms which Balthasar proceeds to do. Here it is a question of apportioning 'roles' to Father, Son and Spirit respectively. Such is the thoroughness of Balthasar's treatment, that these pages constitute not only a Trinitarian 'euchology' – a theology of prayer in the light of the Trinitarian Persons and missions. They also amount to a mini-treatise on the Holy Trinity – a triadology. Balthasar is nothing if not a theologian of the triune God, so to say that an exploration of his teaching on the Blessed Trinity might do worse than to start here could be considered impressive.

---

13 *Ibid.*, p. 30.
14 *Ibid.*, p. 37.

The role of the Father

Under the role of the divine *Father*, Balthasar discusses four motifs in soteriology, the doctrine of salvation. And these are: election, vocation, justification and the *parrhêsia* or confidence before God to which these lead. Gratuitously – that is, by grace – the Creator invites us into his divine life, or, in a metaphor taken from horticulture rather than hospitality:

> As a result of the miracle of his merciful election ... our finite existence ... has been taken from its native soil, with all its roots and the earth which clings to them, and 'transplanted' into the garden of his wholly other, eternal being.[15]

In another simile drawn from agriculture, Balthasar compares our created nature to countryside before the generative sun has shone on it. Under grace, things become capable of blossoming and bearing fruit of themselves – yet only in the sunlight could they have done this. The transformative gaze of God, falling on the creature, is 'a look of utterly sovereign pre-election', dependent on nothing but itself (once again, we hear the anti-Molinist note of the repentant former Jesuit!).

Predestining grace finds expression in two ways, justification and vocation. In vocation it becomes perceptible in time (ultimately, for Balthasar, in the mission which manifests the vocation to be this or that 'theological person' before God). But justification is the initial and quite foundational realization of God's gracious purpose in me and for me. Our nature is clay until the potter has moulded it by giving it final supernatural meaning. In my nature as spirit, *Geist*, I already seek to understand and evaluate myself. But this is not the last word. That rests with the divine judgment which may make of me something very different. As the opening volume of Balthasar's theological logic has it, *cogitor*: 'I am thought'. But also, as he has it here, *judicor*, 'I am [divinely] judged'. And *ergo sum*: 'Therefore, I am the personality that I am'. In the Son, the Father both judges and glorifies us, settling us through Christ in his eternity where we can glorify him. This theme – giving God glory – which Balthasar develops not only in the closing, New Testament volume of the theological aesthetics but also in his elucidation of the spiritual mission of Elizabeth of Dijon, leads him to a most original part of his study which centres on that biblical key-word *parrhêsia*.

Parrhêsia is more or less the secular Greek for free speech. But the New Testament uses the term for the confidence of the Christian, redemptively forgiven in the blood of the Lamb. For Balthasar, however, and this explains why he discusses this theme under the heading of the Father's role in prayer, the prime subject of *parrhêsia* is God himself. This is the God who comes out of his silence, crying aloud in self-revelation by divine Wisdom (compare the Book of Proverbs, 1.20-21). Any *parrhêsia* that we may have is the effect in us of the Father's *parrhêsia*, the divine freespokenness. At the same time, our *parrhêsia* is also the way we grasp his new accessibility. We can be unconstrained and childlike in the Father's presence because we know that 'the truth, the love and the whole life of God is open to us'.[16] For Balthasar, that is

15 *Ibid.*, p. 40.
16 *Ibid.*, p. 47.

simply the other side of the coin of election, vocation, justification. It is the gift of a good conscience thanks to the vicariously representative, substitutionary work of Christ in atoning for us. It forms, accordingly, a natural link to Balthasar's account of the role in contemplation of the divine *Son.*

The role of the Son

Under the role of the Son, Balthasar discusses the Son as he who interprets the Father to us, and, more than this, gives the Father to us in his Paschal Mystery which furnishes the Christian's form of life.

The Son is the 'manifest truth of the Father'. This is Balthasar's reformulation of St Irenaeus' famous description of the Son as *visibile Patris,* 'what is visible about the Father'. It is in the Son the Father *predestines* us – to be 'fellow children with the one eternal Child', he who from the world's beginning has ever intervened to 'sponsor' his estranged creatures. It is in the Son the Father *justifies* us, giving the Son's righteousness to us as our own. And it is in the Son the Father *glorifies* us, enabling us to share the Son's Resurrection and setting us in that place which belongs by right only to the Son: namely, the Father's right hand.

From these three affirmations about the concrete way in which the Father predestines, justifies, glorifies, Balthasar concludes, reasonably enough, that it is *in the Son* that heaven lies open to earth. The Son is heaven's living apocalypse. Balthasar intuits that, at least in the contemporary period, some people considering contemplative prayer will feel a hidden – or not so hidden – resentment at the doctrine of Scripture, continued in Tradition, to the effect that the Word incarnate is the Father's *only* Mediator. For the Church, as the Declaration of the Roman Congregation for the Doctrine of the Faith *Dominus Jesus* found reason to insist some fifteen years after Balthasar's death, Jesus Christ is the one 'gate' through which all roads to the Father must pass.[17] In the context of modern inter-religious dialogue, this teaching is an embarrassment. What? *All* roads? And Balthasar puts the following objection into the critic's mouth:

> However magnificent a figure [Christ] may be, he is still one among others; eventually his immense historical influence will be exhausted, according to the laws of historical existence, and he will give way to fresh new perspectives. Surely there is something unnatural, both in the way Christians cling to these historical events and make them absolute, and in the arbitrary spiritualizing which they then apply to them?[18]

Clearly, a Christologically determined account of contemplative prayer cannot survive if these objections are sustained. So how does Balthasar answer them? He does so, *first,* by an argument from the uniqueness of the God-man. Precisely because the uniqueness of the one Mediator has been established by God as the counterpart of God's own uniqueness, the unity of Father and Son stamps everything that radiates from him. Thus *ad supra*

17 Congregation for the Doctrine of the Faith, *Declaration* Dominus Jesus. *On the Unicity and Salvific Universality of Jesus Christ and his Church* (ET London, 2000).
18 *Prayer, op. cit.,* p. 66.

Christ always points to the Father, while *ad infra* his influence is 'universal and integrating, and hence catholic'.[19] The mark of divinity, in other words, is *unitive uniqueness*: this is how Father and Son exist and operate.

Secondly, Balthasar offers an argument in terms of Christ's translation of the divine into human terms. In his words:

> It was essential that Christ, in his Incarnation, should translate God's indivisible unity into the multiplicity of time/space aspects, into the eloquent language of human existence with its change, its growth, its strivings, undertakings, sufferings, its dying; essential also to preserve this unity in propositional and conceptual shape, in terms of images and judgments.

And why so essential? Essential because otherwise:

> the contemplation of God would only have been possible in the forms of negative, apophatic mysticism, which seeks to encounter God beyond all that is of the world, as the Wholly Other, who can be neither conceived, nor beheld, nor comprehended.

'Such a view', Balthasar contends, 'inevitably does a great injustice to the world and our fellow creatures'.[20]

Thirdly, Balthasar proposes – and this is another key concept of his theology of prayer – that Christ is himself the creative archetype of all authentic mysticism, and that in two senses. One of these two senses concerns Jesus' saving achievement. As he writes:

> Christ, having dwelt among the forms of the world which are perceived by sense and intellect, returns to the Father, and in doing so he opens the real path of contemplation; as a man among men he had created images and concepts which spoke of the Father, but he does not leave them behind on earth in this form; he elevates and translates them, lifting them beyond their earthly, literal and prophetic categories into the realm of heaven, of the Spirit, and of fulfilment. He takes us, as those who have died, risen and ascended with him, into his own movement from the world toward the Father and empowers us to join with him in transforming the old world into a new, divine world, a world of the Spirit.

That text could perfectly well be taken from Newman's Anglican writings. But Balthasar, unconscious of the family resemblance with another as yet unacknowledged doctor of the Church, prefers to think of it as capturing the 'thrust of Pauline theology'.[21] For Paul, the Christ who was once 'flesh' and is now 'spirit' has taken us up with him to dwell in the heavenly places, and brought us too from fleshly existence to life in the Spirit.

And the other sense Balthasar would give his claim for Christ as the very model for mysticism? Jesus Christ is the archetype of the mystic *through what he underwent*. For example, is it the mysticism of the negative way you are interested in?

19 *Ibid.*, p. 53.
20 *Ibid.*, p. 54.
21 *Ibid.*, pp. 54–55.

No mystic in the tradition of negative theology has undergone more profoundly than he the 'dark night of the senses and the soul' which signals the entrance into the Absolute; in the terrible ruin of the cross the dying Christ not only experienced the withdrawal of the world; he was also left in the lurch by God.

Or is perhaps it the mysticism of the affirmative way that takes your fancy?

No one has experienced the bliss of transcending the whole transitory world and attaining to what abides, of going from appearance to reality, in the same degree as he did in ascending from the world to his Father.[22]

And in a wonderful connecting of the Ascension with Pentecost, he remarks, 'Now that the Son's contemplation has come to fulfilment, the Spirit will infuse the fruit of this prayer into the hearts of believers'.[23] This prepares us for the transition from the role of the Son in the act of contemplation to the role of the Holy Spirit.

Before leaving the role of the Son in the act of contemplation, however, there are one or two final points Balthasar wishes to underline. The amazing thing about the orthodox theology of the incarnate Son is that it is the *same* Person who is God's way to man and man's way to God. The downward and upward movements Balthasar has so far described singly in point of fact coincide. And this tells us something of enormous value about the life of grace we are called to share. It is not in some faceless way a further manner of participating, over and above our mere existence as creatures, in the reality that springs ultimately from God. This grace is not 'some general, vague, "supernatural elevation"' but 'a participation in the personal existence of the eternal Word of God who became "flesh" like us so that we should be "spirit" in him'.[24] Though made, as it were, to human measure, it has a 'Son-like form'.[25] Balthasar calls it 'christoform'. And this 'form', then, which re-shapes our existence as members of Christ's mystical body, also gives us our *mission*. In obeying one's calling one fulfils one's personal essence far better than the most sophisticated methods of analysis – psychological therapy or whatever – could ever assist one to do. Here once again, as in his theology of sanctity, Balthasar announces a major theme of his theological dramatics. Mission is, in the last analysis, what constitutes identity. Reversing the perspective of much modern ethics: life is not a matter of wondering how we can turn 'values' into reality, but of turning *this* reality, given by grace in the Word, into values: values to be realized in the course of expressing mission in a fruitful way. Contemplation is a necessary part of this process, and echoes its structure. For here too a prior gift of hearing the Word, however silently, tacitly, comes before the effort to contemplate it with deliberate intelligence.

The Christian's contemplative gaze, then, rests focally on Christ. But this is not Christ as disevered from history and the cosmos but Christ as their climax and key. These too are included: contemplation should bring not only oneself but also 'other realities' to definitive truth.

22 *Ibid.*, p. 55.
23 *Ibid.*, pp. 55–56.
24 *Ibid.*, p. 58.
25 *Ibid.*, p. 59.

All the isolated truths of nature and supernature, of the cosmos, of history, of the Church, are drawn together in the wealth, the freedom and the mystery of a beloved Person, who, though human like ourselves, is not a finite Person, but divine Love itself.[26]

Balthasar constantly stresses that 'Christian mysticism' is *not* a subset or secondary category of [a] general concept'.[27] Rather it belongs with 'rightly receiving the objective mystery' –

The mystery of Christ that God the Father has predestined before the foundation of the world and kept hidden before the eons and is now made known ... at the end of the times, the era of the Church.[28]

The role of the Spirit

Finally, the act of contemplation is enabled by the Holy Spirit who implants the divine life in the soul and makes it our own.

The sending of the Son and the Spirit are two phases of the action by which the Father communicates his truth and life. We shall not be surprised to find that Balthasar approaches the Spirit's contribution to the contemplative act from the Paschal Mystery. When in St John's Gospel the risen Lord breathes out the Holy Spirit on his disciples, this is the sacramental sign of what took place on the Cross, when he gave up his Spirit and not only blood but the water of the Spirit flowed from his side. It is likewise the sacramental sign of what will take place at Pentecost, when that Spirit will enter the hearts of the members of the apostolic Church. Once again, Balthasar insists on the Ascension as necessary prelude to Pentecost. Caught up to the Father's right, the Son's transfigured humanity becomes party to the eternal spiration of the Spirit, and the consequence is the Spirit's outpouring onto Christ's mystical body, the Church, on earth. This draws us into the mystery of divine Sonship and, in the view of many theologians (and mystics) though Balthasar does not name them, gives us what he calls, daringly, a share in the eternal generation of the Son. Insofar as the Spirit makes this possible for us, we can speak not just, as hitherto, of an *antecedent role of the Son making possible our relation with the Spirit* but also an antecedent role of the Spirit enabling our relation with the Son. In this inverted perspective, there is a sense in which the Spirit is active in all pre-Incarnation history, preparing the way for Christ. This reaches its apogee in the Mother of God for it is in the Holy Spirit that she utters her *Fiat* or 'yes' of faith whereby she becomes pregnant with the Word. That for Balthasar is the 'origin of all Christian contemplation'.[29] The willing Marian element in faith is simultaneously faith's contemplative dimension. By it, we appropriate the truth of the Son through the Holy Spirit.

It follows that in the subsequent life of the Church, the Spirit's agency is included in all the continuing unfolding that occurs – corporately or

26 *Ibid.*, pp. 66–67.
27 'Understanding Christian Mysticism', in *Spirit and Institution. Explorations in Theology* IV (ET San Francisco, 1995), p. 309.
28 *Ibid.*, pp. 311, 310.
29 *Ibid.*, p. 71.

personally – of revelation in Jesus Christ. The Spirit 'speaks' to us when new depths are uncovered in the revelation given with Old Testament and New. He also 'knows' in us as we assimilate this prophetic element in our inmost hearts. From this Balthasar draws an interesting conclusion. We cannot set over against each other the charism of prophecy – which tends to be stressed by more biblically minded and activist Christians – and the mystically oriented gifts of the Holy Spirit, which tend to be emphasized by more classically doctrinally minded and quietist ones. The gifts have nothing to work on without the effects of the charism of prophecy, and they manifest in the Church the 'missions' for which prophecy calls. It is always in the context of the Holy Spirit's saving activity – installing the ascended Christ as vital principle of the Church and initiating Christian life in its entirety – that we must think of him when think of him we do in matters of prayer and contemplation.

As the absolute divine subjectivity, the Spirit can inhabit our created subjectivities without suppressing human uniqueness but, to the contrary, permitting it to blossom. Of course it makes a huge difference to contemplation if I (mistakenly) believe myself to be 'alone with the Alone' as I confront the abyss of the Father or whether, by contrast, I appreciate that

> My acts of worship, petition and thanskgiving are borne along and remodelled by the Spirit's infinite and eternal acts ...[30]

By acknowledging the 'predominance' of the Holy Spirit's work in me, there is a *passive* side to contemplation. But by letting my personal energies be affirmed and utilized within his all-embracing activity, there is also an equally important – and really, for Balthasar, more important – aspect of *agency*. Action on the basis of receptivity is a key Balthasarian formula, and so is its expected issue: *bearing fruit*.

In the way Balthasar describes the fructifying activity of the Holy Spirit in the one who prays he sets out something of an agenda for theological epistemology too. The person who prays does not simply stand before the truth to contemplate it objectively. As the John of the Gospel and the Letters is fond of saying, he or she is 'in' the truth, and Balthasar explains this in terms of an intimacy with the Holy Spirit, cancelling out any element of 'uninvolvedness' in objectivity and replacing it with the spirit of prayer. In a passage that might have come straight from St Bernard he describes such intimacy as

> the unspeakable 'mouth-to-mouth' interchange between the Spirit of God and man's spirit, a kind of kiss ... in which, in faith, the human spirit experiences the distinctive essence of the divine wisdom (which is one with love).[31]

And consonant with his view that, in the theological life of the individual, as in the public theological culture of the Church, spirituality must never be separated out into some distinct sphere, Balthasar goes on:

> while it is true that the believer, in 'thinking' about divine truth, is inspired to further prayer, and that acts of the will (of surrender, of

30 *Prayer, op. cit.*, p. 76.
31 *Ibid.*, p. 79.

love, of trust) normally follow upon the acts of rational insight, it is also true that the reason would never be concerned with divine truth at all if it were not somehow aware, in a rudimentary and inchoate 'experience', of truth's divine quality, of a kind of implicit attitude of prayer. This underlying prayer provides the only effective motivation for our own preoccupation with divine truth and with making it known to others.[32]

The mediating role of the Church

But the contemplative act requires for its understanding not only an appreciation of the contribution thereto of the Trinitarian Persons. That act is also dependent on the mediating role of the Church. Even when prayer is carried out in one's 'secret room' – an allusion to the teaching of Jesus in the Sermon on the Mount, it remains rooted in the communion of the Church. On the one hand, Balthasar stresses that the contemplative act is irreducibly individual: God speaks to *this* person and to no other. The individual must not shield behind 'ecclesiastical anonymity' for fear of what the encounter could hold. On the other hand, Balthasar's most fundamental understanding of contemplation – responsively hearing the divine Word – makes it inevitable that he will identify the ecclesial community as the 'medium' of this so personal meeting. The Word is uttered in the midst of the Church, and it is interpreted aright only within, and by, her communion. Just as, in Jesus' promise, the Son of Man will return on the clouds of heaven, surrounded by the holy ones, so even now he is known in prayer only as surrounded by the angels and saints in the total ecclesial communion.

As this daring speculation already hints, Balthasar does not propose to leave the two issues: personal contemplation, and the ecclesial preconditions for contact with the Word, simply juxtaposed. On the contrary, he strains his theological resources to argue they are inextricably fused. For him, 'The Church is the original contemplative, sitting at the Lord's feet and listening to him'.[33] The Church is the virginal Mother, opening her womb to receive the seed of the Word and bear it in fruitfulness in the individual lives of her members. The 'social aspect' of hearing the Word was taken for granted in the Old Testament where the prophets – hearers of the Word *par excellence* – were chosen as representing the House of Israel to God and God to the House of Israel. In the Church of the New Testament this 'aspect' is enhanced – at first haltingly so far as theological understanding goes, but one sees it confidently set forth in Athanasius's portrait of the fruitfulness of the hermit's solitary battle in the *Life of Anthony*, or the conviction of the 'Bride mysticism' of the Middle Ages that the contemplative was somehow carrying out an ecclesial function. It was Balthasar's judgment that not until the late nineteenth-century reflections of Thérèse of Lisieux did the full implications emerge. Thérèse regarded the prayer of Carmel – and other 'official contemplatives' in the Church – as empowering all Church life, including preaching and missionary activity. As Balthasar points out, this was not a

---

32 *Ibid.*, p. 80.
33 *Ibid.*, p. 84.

question of the 'merits of the confessors' (to use a term from ancient Christianity – the merits of those who suffered for the faith were often invested in petitions for other Christians less happily placed), nor, to put it in terms of a later Catholicism, of the petitionary prayer of contemplative nuns. Rather:

> the profound unity which exists between the act of contemplation, which lovingly takes the Word into its very being, and the act of the Virgin Mother, Mary, and of the Virgin Mother, the Church, implies far more than this: it means that the contemplative, mysteriously, *is* 'Church' ...

And Balthasar goes on to assert that the contemplative shares in the 'universality' of the Church, in her 'boundless vitality'.[34]

We need to be clear that Balthasar is making a very unusual statement, rather than a usual statement in unusual language. Owing to the bond established between Incarnation and Church in the Virgin Mary, we are not dealing here with just another version of the solidarity thinking of Israelite religion. Instead, the contemplative – the 'genuine hearer ... actually shares, at the level of being, in the Church's very nature as Bride and Womb of the Word'.[35] Of course, to the extent that all Christians receive a 'remote' call to contemplation in Baptism, this might be said of all of them indifferently. But to the extent that their receiving of the Word does not reach the breadth and depth of the engaged contemplative's, such description would be misplaced. Balthasar holds that whatever a contemplative, however unknown, understands of God's self-revelation in her prayer becomes in some way the Church's corporate cognitive possession. He also maintains that whatever she does *not* understand (yet is genuinely offered her by God), if it leads her to adore the Word by respect for its infinite mystery, also 'enters as a living reality into the Church's attitude of worship, bringing forth fruit in others'.[36]

Naturally enough, there is no way of verifying these assertions historically. We can at least say, however, that if mystical graces are given within and for the communion of saints, this kind of transmission of the fruits of contemplation cannot be ruled out.

But Balthasar would go further still – and here we must reckon with the hand, and the heart, of Adrienne von Speyr. The contemplative may be asked to bear some negative spiritual experience by substitution for another person who can thus find in it, its sting drawn, not penance but joy. In a similar manner, the contemplative may be given some positive experience, the fruit of which is not intended for them but for some third party to whom it will be communicated by 'the Church's process of spiritual osmosis'.[37] Assuming these notions are based, as seems likely, on what Balthasar learned as Adrienne von Speyr's spiritual director in the 1940s and 50s, they bear quite a likeness to cognate ideas of 'substitution' within the 'coinherence' of the

---

34 *Ibid.*, p. 88.
35 *Ibid.*, pp. 88–89.
36 *Ibid.*, p. 89. Balthasar's ideas here form a way of understanding the teaching of *Dei Verbum*, the Dogmatic Constitution of the Second Vatican Council on Divine Revelation, to the effect that the Church develops her doctrine by, among other things, contemplation – a notion frequently traced to Luke's account of the Blessed Virgin 'pondering' the deeds of her Son in her heart (Luke 2.51).
37 *Prayer, op. cit.*, p. 90.

communion of saints expressed around the same time in the novels and lay theological writings of the Anglo-Catholic Charles Williams.[38]

For most people, no doubt, the necessary attempt at contemplative prayer amounts to a kind of holy day-dreaming, through which something like the 'prayer of simple regard' – taken by the classic sixteenth- and seventeenth-century analysts of the life of prayer as the threshold of contemplation – occasionally makes its appearance. Balthasar's view of contemplation could hardly be further removed. The Church, he says, has precise expectations of the contemplative, and he puts this in terms of a patron specifying the work a craftsman, or even an artisan, will carry out. What the Church expects is 'a piece of work properly performed according to the Church's mind', even if, as he goes on to allow, this will consist 'primarily in an attentive following and clinging to the curves and folds of the Word and the inspirations of the Spirit'.[39] Contemplation does not mean 'groping' around in prayer for ideas that suit us, but sober alertness to slight indications, and a willingness to let them open panoramas. This, I must say, has the feel of reality about it.

Defining contemplation as praying according to the Church's mind reinforces Balthasar's conviction that the individual only prays 'in' the bridal Church – as well as awakening some queries about where half a billion people are going to find the spiritual directors Balthasar seems to think necessary to ensure one's prayer life does not become too narrow in focus!

He concludes his account of the Church's role in contemplation by a meditation on the relation – or lack of it – between solitude and isolation. The person who 'prays according to the Church's mind' must accept solitude as a necessary condition of prayer – not just physical solitude, though this is recommended (Balthasar does not seem to have had much time for the idea of group meditation), but even more importantly what he terms 'ecclesial solitude'. I can only receive God's summons and represent in prayer the 'persona' of the Church in my own poor person if I am ready to come face to face with God and not take refuge in feeling part of a crowd. What that means is described in a passage of Baroque prose which it is difficult to understand as other than – once again – an account of Adrienne's experiences:

> The sense of being thrust up to the very bosom of God; the cataract of graces poured out, seemingly senselessly, on the unprepared servant; the solitude, both terrible and blissful, which surrounds the person thus elevated and chosen as bride; the dizzy height without anything to hold on to, remote from analogy and comparison . . .[40]

Under the heading 'the reality of contemplation', Balthasar will nonetheless seek out analogies and comparisons under the four headings of 'totality', 'liturgy', 'freedom' and 'eschatology'.

38 For an interpretation of this figure, see A. Nichols, OP, *A Spirituality for the Twenty-first Century* (Huntington, Ind., 2003), pp. 95–112.
39 *Prayer, op. cit.*, p. 91.
40 *Ibid.*, p. 96.

Dynamics of the contemplative act

(i) Totality

The preconditions, divine and ecclesial, are in place. What we are now shown is the 'dynamics' that result. The first dimension is *totality*. Through contemplation we so make room for the eternal reality of the Kingdom that its energies can enter time.

> This vast, living kingdom of heaven [God, Christ and the saints] watches over transitory time, endeavouring to carry out a wealth of ideas, intentions and plans in the earthly Church.[41]

The totality in question is the one that results *as heaven takes over earth*. This totality dimension of the act of contemplation is for Balthasar Christologically founded. In a secularized culture it is good to remind ourselves of the one point where the world is ceaselessly in conversation with heaven. And this is the 'open heaven' of the Son who, once given to earth, now desires to bring all creation home to the Father. The contemplative always occupies that spot open to the infinite where earth becomes heaven and heaven earth.

All Catholic action worth the name springs from this source. No great ecclesial deed can come from any other origin than contemplation of it. Here Balthasar cites to good effect Bernanos's life of St Dominic where the novelist turned hagiographer remarked: 'The Order of Preachers is presented to us as the charity of St Dominic spread out in space and time, his contemplation become visible'.[42] Had Balthasar been invited to take part in a psychological word-association test on the subject, the first word he would have chosen to link with 'contemplation' would be not 'serene' but 'urgent' – with all the urgency of the apostolic mission of the Church. Clearly, then, Balthasar will not be operating with any too dichotomous distinction between the active and the contemplative 'lives'. In his 1942 essay 'Aktion und Kontemplation' he makes the point that the opposition of action and contemplation cannot be primary in the life of the Christian since it was not primary in the life of Christ.[43] Anthopologically, spirit (*Geist*) is *actio*. Theologically, the two poles of action and contemplation are integrated in the unity of Christ's mission. In redeeming action Christian contemplation is fulfilled. Balthasar offers his readers the classical Jesuit motto 'Contemplativus in actione'. But he admits that action often leads to activism. The true role of the Lucan episode of Jesus in the house of Martha and Mary where Mary's listening to the Word is praised above Martha's busy-ness belongs here. The two women are not representatives, however, of contemplation and action but of 'true and false Catholic acting'. True action 'draws all its strength from the Lord'; for false action, by contrast, a 'noisy "apostolate" leaves no time for the Lord of all mission'.[44] In his commentary on St Thomas's discussion of these matters in the *Summa theologiae*, Balthasar remarks that when Thomas describes the 'mixed life' – passing on the fruits of contemplation – as 'best', he should really have described it as, quite simply, the Christian life in which the two counterposed forms (exclusive action, exclusive contemplation) participate in

41 *Ibid.*, p. 102
42 Cited *ibid.*, p. 106.
43 'Aktion und Kontemplation', *Die katholische Schweizerin* 29 (1942), pp. 114–20.
44 *Ibid.*, p. 114.

their different ways.[45] There is too much aristocratic Aristotelianism in Thomas here for Balthasar's liking. Wiser are those Fathers who realize that contemplation is another – higher, more interior – form of the *fruitfulness* (ever-recurring Balthasarian metaphor!) that genuinely apostolic action displays.[46]

(ii) Liturgy

The second dimension of the act that issues when its preconditions are duly met is *liturgy*. Contemplation is the continuation of the Liturgy because, like the Liturgy, it is responsiveness to the Word. The obverse is also true: being as it is responsiveness to the Word, the Liturgy is necessarily contemplative. In the Mass, Balthasar regards the Liturgy of the Word not as didactic but as contemplative: it is communion with the Word by way of preparation for communion with the Word made flesh. In the Liturgy of the Eucharist proper, presented by Balthasar as an 'anamnesis' of not only the Lord's death and Resurrection but his whole being, the Church becomes what she most fundamentally is: the 'spiritual, receptive and hence fruiful womb'.[47] This happens through the Holy Spirit who commands the course of the Mass, notably between consecration and eucharistic communion. It is the Spirit who enables the Church to offer herself in offering the Son, and who creates the unity of hearts that 'obliterates the distinction' (not an especially happy phrase) between the Son's self-offering and that of the Church. But if the Mass is an 'act of remembrance, springing from a human decision whose freedom is guaranteed by grace', then it is supremely an act of contemplation in Balthasar's terms.[48]

From this, he expects us to draw two conclusions. First, for Christians who do not find the particular way the Mass is presented spiritually helpful, it is all the more important to unite themselves to 'the spirit of the Church's liturgy'.[49] Secondly, contemplation outside the Mass should have a liturgical dimension: as the prayer with which St Ignatius prefaces all the meditations in his *Exercises* suggests, the aim of contemplation is worship. Contrasting this approach with German Idealism's search for the 'transcendental "I"', Balthasar sums up: 'It is by making our deepest self as a listening and worshipping self that we can be sure of being involved in the transcendence that really matters'.[50]

For Balthasar, and this is an essential part of his personalism, it is more true to say that the Liturgy points to contemplation, than it is that contemplation points to the Liturgy. The Missal and the Liturgy of the Hours do not contain the Word of God – divine revelation – in its entirety. There need to be in the Church those who adore the Word as *over and above what the Liturgy comprises*. This conviction helps to explain Balthasar's disapproval – or at least lack of encouragement – of those of the faithful who, in emulation of the older Religious Orders, like to recite some if not all of the Divine

45 Thomas von Aquin, *Besondere Gnadengaben und die zwei Wege menschlichen Lebens [Summa theologiae IIa.IIae 171–182] op. cit.*, p. 435. Cited below as 'Besondere Gnadengaben'.
46 *Ibid.*, pp. 455–56.
47 *Prayer, op. cit.*, p. 111.
48 *Ibid.*, p. 113.
49 *Ibid.*
50 *Ibid.*, pp. 115–16.

Office in private. He expected to find not only greater spiritual freedom but greater understanding in those who prefer to invest their energies directly in contemplative prayer. He considered that the direct cultivation of contemplative prayer alone can bridge the gap between sacred and secular, the Church and the cosmos. He warned the Liturgical Movement that, if it remains isolated from the movement to reawaken contemplation, it would become sheer Romanticism, a flight from time. It would inadvertently conjure up a Frankenstein, a counter-Romanticism, a 'false sacralization of everyday things'.[51] This was tongue in cheek. He knew that such was already appearing in the theological school called 'the theology of earthly realities'. Largely a French phenomenon, sympathetic to a soft Marxism and often linked to the worker priest movement, *la théologie des réalités terrestres* would have its influence on the Pastoral Constitution of the Second Vatican Council on the Church in the Modern World. What does not seem to have occurred to Balthasar was that the two movements, the Liturgical Movement and the theology of earthly realities could one day be combined in a form of liturgical practice which would see consciousness-raising about everyday issues as the best outcome of liturgical participation. His own principles ruled this out in advance: the Liturgy must be contemplative if it is to assist authentic mission, for it instructs us how to live on earth in the spirit of heaven.

(iii) Freedom

The third of Balthasar's 'dimensions' of the contemplative act is *freedom*, already touched on, if glancingly, in what has just been said. In contemplation, 'the child of God is free to speak to his father as his heart dictates'.[52] What has happened then to the earlier emphasis on finding a spiritual director? Balthasar now compares directors to the mother and older women friends of a new bride. It is prudent to seek good advice, but eventually it is the bride's heart that is the best guide to the bridegroom's love. Realizing perhaps that the equivalent of these mothers and older women are not so easy to come by in the spiritual life, Balthasar then puts into a nutshell the 'precepts' they might pass on, as a prelude to leaving the bride properly free. Typically, such counsel concerns the primacy of loving God, the mere relativity of programmes or structures for meditation and prayer, and the need to practise humdrum virtues in contemplation since love asks it. Except in regard to the second of these sets of precepts (the one about the provisionality of all 'methods' of praying), it may not be obvious why Balthasar discusses them under the rubric of 'freedom'. The answer is, in his words: 'Nothing is as free as love; apart from love, all so-called freedom is no freedom at all'.[53] These pages include a good many practically helpful remarks about the challenges of prayer – on aridity, for example, as the 'normal, "everyday" face of all love', to be distinguished, in Balthasar's view, from the 'dark nights' that are the sign of special missions in the Church.[54]

---

51 *Ibid.*, p. 121.
52 *Ibid.*, p. 127.
53 *Ibid.*, p. 128.
54 *Ibid.*, p. 138.

Throughout one can see how Balthasar tries so to shape his counsel that it keeps as its centre the Son of God and as its basis the love-gift of the Holy Spirit.

(iv) Eschatology

The last intrinsic 'dimension' of contemplative prayer Balthasar recognizes is *eschatology*. Christian contemplation is not simply entertaining awareness of an eternal 'Now'. Rather is it of its essence future-directed, a vigilant waiting for the Parousia of the Lord. However, at the same time, such contemplation cannot deny its situation has changed vis-à-vis the Old Testament. The Day of the Lord still to come to its fulfilment has already in another sense arrived with the first advent of the Messiah. Thus an anti-mystical eschatologism is out of place. Though waiting on God may never be sheerly dissolved through over-blown anticipation of the delights of heaven, nevertheless:

> In his good pleasure, the Lord of the whole Church gives the waiting Church on earth intimations, assurances and previews of things which, from its perspective, are to come, although as far as heaven is concerned they are present realities.[55]

The object of contemplation

This brings us to the question of the *object* or *content* of contemplation to which topic Balthasar will devote the remaining pages of *Das betrachtende Gebet*. An act without a content, after all, is even worse off than a Kantian concept without a percept. It is the smile on the face of the Cheshire Cat.

It is when Balthasar gets going on content that one realizes most fully how right are those who say this book on prayer is an excellent place to find his Trinitarian theology – and especially, I would say, his Trinitarian *Christology*. For Balthasar Jesus is never less than the 'Trinitarian Son', defined by his relations not only with the Logos, self-identical with him in his personal depths, but with the Father and the Holy Spirit.

First and foremost, the object of Christian contemplation is God, and other realities only in their relation to God – a formula which echoes, probably consciously, Aquinas's definition of *sacra doctrina*, 'sacred science', the theological understanding of Scripture and hence of divine revelation, in his *Summa theologiae*. 'Whatever we pay attention to in salvation history ... we do so only because it is through these things that God's salvation is brought to us.'[56] God's manifestation is always along pathways that lead to him and reveal him to us. Though Balthasar does not use the term in this connexion, he accepts that there is a natural metaphysical way to God. In the manner of classical Christian ontology, he argues that 'the world's sages' have sought to contemplate finite, relative being precisely in its relation to subsistent, fontal Being. They grasped that: 'No relative being is Being, but none is apart from Being, and each only exists in relation and as a pointer to Being'.[57] But how far does that get them? Only far enough to recognize that communion with

55 *Ibid.*, p. 148.
56 *Ibid.*, p. 155.
57 *Ibid.*, pp. 156–57.

Being is impossible unless Being chooses to epiphanize, to 'utter its own self in the form of a relative being' and thus become actually present to offer its own self-interpretation.[58] This is what the Word incarnate is. In contemplation, we do not simply rehearse the Chalcedonian formula of one Trinitarian person in two natures, divine and human, true though that formula is. Rather,

> contemplation starts at the point where the believing mind begins to perceive a dawning light in the abyss of the mystery, where the mystery begins to reveal itself in all its vast proportions.[59]

Schooled by the Old Testament, the contemplative will come in awe and trembling to the One made human for us. Of course, the fact of Jesus' humanity creates an immediate opening to understanding. But here 'the incomprehensible begins as soon as we start to "understand"'.[60] As faith contemplates, it lives increasingly in an atmosphere of worship, coming to appreciate the life of Jesus as the revelation and Word of the eternal God. Each concrete event of the life of Christ – in a language familiar to Thomas Aquinas, Bossuet and, in the twentieth century, Dom Columba Marmion, 'each of Christ's *mysteries*' – furnishes an opening through which the contemplative will glimpse something of God's inner life and be taught. We catch the resonance of that Catholic tradition but also echoes of the voice of Barth when we hear Balthasar say:

> The sudden explosion of the event into what seems to be an abstraction (not *a* truth, but *truth*) is only a sign that, from the standpoint of the person at prayer, the divine *concretissimum* has stepped on to the stage in a historical, concrete form.[61]

And of course the reference to 'stage' there suggests the theological dramatics now beginning to form as a Balthasarian 'theological method'.

Contemplation of the incarnate Word takes place in discipleship, in the Church the Word brought to be. Balthasar stresses that its riches are made available only for the follower who is willing to accept impoverishment – to accept that her knowledge of the Lord is subsumed within *his* knowledge of her (Galatians 4.9: 'You have come to know God, or, rather, to be known by God'). When a contemplative saint is commissioned to say something, their words seem to come, remarks Balthasar, from far away, and in such a manner that they do not seem responsible for their effect. The latter Balthasar ascribes to the 'impoverishment' whereby the 'surplus' fruit of contemplation is typically passed on to others to be its beneficiaries.

Contemplation always returns to the sacred humanity in whom the Father is at once displayed and veiled. Jesus is uninventable and yet elusive, as though God had no desire to prompt a systematic theology of himself. But when the eyes of our mind, as well as our senses, are illumined by the Holy Spirit, the contemplative enters by faith in Christ into the triune life.

> Grace is our mode of sharing in this [triune] life; it therefore endows us with the appropriate subjective faculty so that, with the certainty of

58 *Ibid.*, p. 157.
59 *Ibid.*, p. 158.
60 *Ibid.*, p. 162.
61 *Ibid.*, p. 165.

faith, we can see the trinitarian side of the phenomenon of Christ as the object of our contemplation.[62]

The single most important purpose of Christian prayer, for Balthasar, is to 'unfold' this implicit faith-knowledge, so that we can experience with all our powers what it means to say that God is love. For Balthasar, the statements 'God is love' and 'God is the Holy Trinity' really express the same thing.

Transforming effects

In all this, the Word, so Balthasar stresses in three important verbal forms, transforms, judges and saves. Notably, the Word *transforms*. In becoming incarnate the Word has at his disposal in our space–time world three 'quantitative media' through which he can pour out his spirit so as qualitatively to transform us. The first of these is the dramatic 'field of energy' of human life itself, so easy to contemplate since those who pray are themselves human. In the flesh of the Word, the Eternal is sacramentalized for us in an utterly human way (and Balthasar is generous in the leeway he allows for imagination-powered pondering on the Saviour's human development and flowering even when the Gospels are silent). This 'translation' of God into the idiom of the human

> is *his* translation, bearing the hallmark of his personality and insepar-
> able from it. We can perceive it only by looking at him.[63]

And as each human life is unique, so each person who contemplates the Word's earthly course will find something slightly different: 'each person's gaze will illuminate the Lord's archetypal existence in a different way'. Considered as a human existence, the life of Jesus is of course in one sense finite. 'The instrument has a limited number of keys, just as the words of holy Scripture are limited.' And yet that is not all there is to be said.

> [T]here is an unlimited number of possible variations on the one theme
> which is the self-sacrifice of divine love and our initiation into the
> depths of divine meaning.[64]

The second 'medium' the Word has available to him entails a transformation of the structure and trajectory of the cosmos in him before it makes any change in us. And this is the transformation from death to Resurrection, which reveals to the contemplative the Son's Lordship, his fullness.

> The contemplative is free to ponder ever anew this transformation
> which is the foundation and prerequisite of all subsequent transfor-
> mation within the Church. He can compare the Word of God in his
> humble, fleshly form, as the Gospel portrays him, with his glorified
> form after the Resurrection and Ascension, as he appears in his self-
> testimony from heaven through the Holy Spirit, and as he appears in
> the Church's proclamation in word, theology, and in Christian life and
> *martyrium*.

62 *Ibid.*, p. 179.
63 *Ibid.*, p. 203.
64 *Ibid.*, p. 204.

And when the person praying does so, in each case the same extraordinary result is registered.

> Each time it is a very particular, clearly defined humility and humiliation which blossoms forth and yields fruit in glory in such an astounding way, making a shattering impression upon the gazing contemplative.[65]

The power of this perceived transformation is such that it can tide the contemplative over the hiatus of Christ's death and descent – on which, as we should expect, Balthasar has his own version of von Speyrian meditation to share. In one sense, the Church can pursue her contemplation of Holy Saturday (in itself an 'improbable' thing) owing to the objective realities of Christ's Paschal triumph and the sacrament of Baptism whose grace applies to us that victory. In this sense, the death and descent are past for us, and we can simply enjoy their fruits. But in another sense, since what the Church represents to herself in these mysteries is not only a substitutionary action (in our stead) but a vicarious one (on our behalf but in such a way as to include us into it), this same grace implies, as Balthasar puts it:

> an embryonic participation in death and the descent to Hades, not only at the sacramental level but also at the spiritual and contemplative level.[66]

The Church's faith, hope and love must enter darkness. This is true at any rate of individual Christians if not for the corporate Church (later, in the post-Conciliar crisis, Balthasar spoke also of the 'Passion of the Church' as a whole). There is not only, then, a contemplation of the Paschal Mystery in its objective unity of death and Resurrection. There is also – perhaps for other individuals, rather than the same individuals at different stages on life's way – a contemplative entering of the hiatuses that interrupted the Lord's inner experience at the original Easter events, or what Balthasar terms 'incomprehensible foretastes of heaven and hell'.[67]

This brings us to the third transformation that we both see and are affected by, thanks to the saving economy, in contemplative prayer. It takes its rise from Pentecost. Through the Holy Spirit, 'heaven causes Christ's fulness of transformation to be "distributed" and poured out into history in the immeasurable richness of the Church'.[68] Here the Church becomes for the contemplative the medium in which the truth of Jesus Christ is communicated. Balthasar emphasizes that the truth of Jesus Christ is always an *ecclesial* truth. We hear his, strong though not unmitigated, dislike of the historical-critical method or other analogous critical tools – at least when applied to the New Testament witness to the Incarnation – when he writes:

> There is no such thing as historical truth about Christ which is available not to the Church, but to those who do not recognize it to be binding and universal and simply regard it as the product of history.[69]

65 *Ibid.*, p. 206.
66 *Ibid.*, p. 207.
67 *Ibid.*, p. 210.
68 *Ibid.*, p. 200.
69 *Ibid.*, p. 211.

It is, he says, 'forbidden' to try and look behind the ecclesial forms in which the incarnate Word has been given to us for some putative truth that would contradict the Church's vision and proclamation of her Lord. Balthasar anticipates the criticism that if this be so no dialogue about Jesus is possible between believers and unbelievers: in which case apologetics flies out of the window. He replies that the non-believer can already be attracted by grace and begin to share, however inchoately, in the Church's mediation of the truth. Anyway, what matters for the topic of prayer is that to discredit the Church's proclamation of Christ is to make havoc of contemplation. Later in *Das betrachtende Gebet* he will modify his somewhat blanket condemnation of biblical criticism. We can risk the 'so-called exactitude of scholarship' if, like the great Origen of Alexandria, we do not lose sight of 'the most important exactitude, namely, the ordering of all thought towards prayer'.[70]

Judging and saving contemplated Word

This Word, Balthasar goes on to say, is a Word that *judges*. By reference to it we can tell if we have been true to our baptismal vows, for all sin is some kind of preference for my word over against the Word of God. For a baptized person, sin means self-contradiction. If we do not 'go in for' contemplative prayer, we can put the whole problem out of our mind, or postpone its resolution to a later and, as we imagine, more propitious time. But the direct submission to God's gaze rules this out. Balthasar thinks moral issues are one major reason people avoid the call of contemplation, and reminds his readers of the extra-biblical but possibly authentic *agraphon* or unwritten saying of Jesus, 'he who is near me is near the fire'. Like St John at the opening of the Apocalypse the contemplative must have the 'courage to face the Word's sharp sword and fiery appearance'.[71] Balthasar warns, we shall fall to the ground as though dead: to contemplate only the sweet Jesus is to have a merely imaginary Redeemer. Contemplation is an anticipation of the fire of the Last Judgment.

This fire is meant, however, not only to judge but to warm and enflame, which brings us to the way the Word in contemplation also *saves*. In the context of contemplative prayer, Balthasar describes the Word's saving action as bringing the person who prays into a world of love which seems in a way humdrum, 'little' (the figure of Thérèse of Lisieux hovers over his text here) – except in one crucial respect. The love is shot through with God's utter purity. Balthasar tends to think the three stages of growth in prayer on the classical scheme of both East and West – purification, illumination, union – is best seen by telescopic vision as quasi-simultaneous. Elsewhere Balthasar put this quasi-coincidence of judging and saving in a striking paradox.

> The nakedness of prayer has clothed the world from beyond; the complete poverty of renunciatory existence has enriched it, the strictest obedience to God has set it free.[72]

70 *Ibid.*, p. 227.
71 *Ibid.*, p. 224, with a reference to Apocalypse 1.14-16.
72 'Die Nacktheit des Gebetes', *Der Christliche Weg*, Kulturbeilage der Katholischen Solothurner Presse, 4. 6, (22 March 1958).

A provisional conclusion

Balthasar's book certainly makes it plain how 'complex is the interplay between dogma and contemplative prayer'.[73] In itself, however, the interplay is good, desirable. Balthasar writes in a very 'Dominican' manner when he says:

> A knowledge of theology's fundamental principles will promote such contemplation by shedding a clearer light on what the person is experiencing existentially; it will save him from entering on circuitous and erroneous paths in prayer. Conversely, the person who is accustomed to pray will gratefully accept all the central insights that come to him from theology as an enrichment of his prayer.[74]

Ultimately, though, for Balthasar there are only two basic principles – and the second of these is very Jesuit. The first is that, precisely owing to the greater ultimacy of the Resurrection compared with the Cross, the fundamental approach of the praying person is *gratitude*. The second is that

> there is in contemplation ... a certain indifference, from the divine point of view, as to whether we find God in prayer or not.

It is up to God whether he chooses to appear to us, like the Risen One, or to remained veiled, like the Crucified. In the last analysis:

> The contemplative leaves it to the Word to decide that particular state of the Word in which he is to make his earthly pilgrimage, no longer at home in the world and not yet having reached his home in heaven.[75]

Among the main profound judgments in Balthasar's book on prayer this is perhaps the deepest. And probably he realized so himself in giving it – literally – the last word.

Mysticism

It will be clear from the above account of contemplation that, despite – or because of – his desire to overcome the disjunction he saw among ordinary Catholics, and even not so ordinary ones, between action and contemplation, Balthasar's theology of religious existence – the Christian life at its highest if also most fundamental authenticity – gives great attention to the mystical dimension. As we saw in the previous chapter, he found great inspiration in the Carmelite mystics to whom he devoted theological monographs – Thérèse of Lisieux and Elizabeth of Dijon. Yet the greatest influence on him in this regard was Adrienne von Speyr. Its testimony is the major anthology of extracts Balthasar compiled on the basis of her works in order to give people an idea of what she might mean by – in the title of that anthology – 'The World of Prayer'.[76] So let us treat of her, in this connexion, for a last time.

---

73 *Prayer, op. cit.*, p. 307.
74 *Ibid.*
75 *Ibid.*, p. 311.
76 A. von Speyr, *The World of Prayer* (ET San Francisco, 1985).

(i) Its root in the Paschal Mystery

One of her readers, the Flemish Balthasar scholar Georges de Schrijver, has identified the heart of Adrienne's concept of the mystical as what he terms in a complex and, in part, deliberately antinomic formula ' "imparticipable participation" in suffering by substitution'.[77] ('Imparticipable participation', a phrase drawn from the Platonist tradition, means, evidently: 'in one sense we share this, but in another sense we could never share it'.) The upshot of her influence on Balthasar, says de Schrijver, was to give ever-increasing prominence in his work to the theme of *mystical communion in suffering with Christ*. For Adrienne – and so, in this realm, for Balthasar – such communion is made possible by the sponsal relation of the Church to Christ.

> By a wonderful exchange, the Church-Bride for whom Christ gave his life becomes capable in his purified love of conforming herself to the Bridegroom's kenotic love.[78]

The Christian mystic, identified with the Church, lives by perpetual acknowledgement, and adoration, of the Trinitarian Son's descent into hell. In the nuptial exchange whose locus is the 'abyss-like space of the gift of the dying Christ', she knows that she is to take part in this fathomless drama – that she will receive, at the time appropriate, a mission to enter through him into dereliction: not, however, for its own sake but so that the Trinitarian love that was crucified for her may be given glory. Like Origen, von Speyr has, then, a mysticism of the nuptial relation of the ecclesial soul with the Word, though in her case this takes on a markedly Marian character by reference to the self-abandonment and consent to mission of Mary's *fiat*. Christian mysticism is a sharing in Mary's 'Yes' which will become at the eschaton the 'Yes' of the whole people of God. Adrienne emphasized how its obedience must be total, if it is, like Mary's, to be the sort of obedience that can be crowned in the obedience of the Son.[79] Like the mystics of the mediaeval Rhineland School, she sees the entire mystical way in Trinitarian terms. But because she highlights the aspect of dialogue between the soul and the Lord based on the saving economy (rather than simply wonder at the inner-Trinitarian relationships or their 'Ground'), she places the essence of mysticism in what de Schrijver, again, terms an 'acquiescent contemplation of the redemptive work of the Trinitarian persons'.[80] In this she gives, as we noted in Chapter 5 of this book, a special place to the Atonement and within that mystery of reconciliation to the descent into hell. Rather as Maximus the Confessor had done (in the *Centuries on Charity* he says, 'The abandoned must be saved by dereliction'[81]), von Speyr stresses the weakness of Christ in Sheol, but she gives to this, so we have seen, a prominence and, in general, an interpretation quite her own, seeing in it the solitude – and even the separation – in which the Son divinely assumes the condition of the reprobate. It is also for her the birthplace of the Church and of all Christian mysticism.

77 G. de Schrijver, *Le merveilleux accord de l'homme et Dieu. Etude de l'analogie de l'être chez Hans Urs von Balthasar* (Leuven, 1983), p. 312.
78 *Ibid.*
79 A. von Speyr, *Das Buch von Gehorsam* (Einsiedeln, 1966), p. 36.
80 G. de Schrijver, *Le merveilleux accord de l'homme et Dieu, op. cit.*, p. 312.
81 Maximus, *Centuries on Charity*, IV. 96.

In her commentary on the Apocalypse, Adrienne von Speyr develops the theme that the ecclesial community is constructed on the basis of a diversity of 'missions'. Each Christian has a distinct task within that body of Christ for which the Trinitarian Son gave himself. The missions are complementary and mirror each other in different ways.[82] But they all have one thing in common. They all take their fruitfulness from the intimate connexion of each mission with Christ's freely entered abandonment, the night of dereliction he endured for the sake of his Church. In her commentary on the Song of Songs, Adrienne speaks of how the whole Church – the entire network of missions – is called to 'go down from Lebanon', to 'descend below herself', following the way of Jesus' sufferings. The invitation of the Bridegroom to share in the Cross is at the same time a declaration to the bridal soul of 'how much she is for him attractive and dispensable, since she alone can fulfil his desires'.[83] 'The heart of Christian mysticism', she wrote, lies in Jesus' 'handing himself over to the Father in death'.[84] Marriage in the night: this is the hallmark of von Speyrian mysticism.

> In the same way that the life of Christ for the redemption of the world had to lead him to the Cross, so the life of Christian mystics must bear the seal of death. This is a death in God through which, no longer living to themselves, they allow the divine project in their regard to go forward. As long as day lasts, work continues. But then night comes and plunges day into darkness, for from the moment of the Cross, passivity has become more important than activity, powerlessness than power, silence than speech.[85]

(ii) Beyond Thomas – though not against him

As Balthasar says, Thomas, the classic theologian of the Church, produced no full mystical theology. Four *topoi* in his writing were widely regarded in later times as building-blocks for a house that was always in search of an architect. They were: his theology of the missions of the divine Persons; his teaching on the Gifts of the Holy Spirit; his doctrine of contemplation; and his account of the charismata of prophecy, vision, rapture. (Inexplicably, Balthasar omits mention of the theological virtues of faith, hope and charity, which for Thomas are foundational.) No synthesis of these was forthcoming until later times when this was done with the help of the work of the Carmelite saints Teresa of Avila and John of the Cross: clearly, Balthasar has in mind the French Dominicans of the early twentieth century, notably Réginald Garrigou-Lagrange whom he praises for linking the missions of prophets far more securely to the order of charity (and criticizes for withdrawing the extraordinary charismata from consideration in his greatly influential work, *Perfection chrétienne et contemplation*[86]). This is why the greatest prophets –

82 A. von Speyr, *Apokalypse. Betrachtungen über die geheime Offenbarung* (Einsiedeln, 1950), commenting on Apocalypse 21.19.
83 *Idem*, *Das Hohelied* (Einsiedeln, 1972), p. 47.
84 *Idem*, *Das Wort und die Mystik. I. Subjektive Mystik* (Einsiedeln, 1970), p. 115.
85 *Ibid.*, pp. 117–18.
86 R. Garrigou-Lagrange, OP, *Perfection chrétienne et contemplation* (Saint-Maximin, 1923).

Moses, Elijah – become the 'founders, archetypes and fulfillers' in later
Christian mysticism.[87] Mystical contemplation is response to the prophetically mediated Word of God on the basis of that Word and so belongs
intrinsically – even in the Old Testament as the texts ascribed to David and
Solomon show – to the 'prophetic thing'. What was needed now was more of
such broadened contexts and deepened connexions.

The most important re-contextualization Balthasar offers is, predictably
enough, the 'vision of the [incarnate] Son and the life of his Church'.[88] New
Testament prophecy has to be related to unfolding faith in Christ Head and
body, and the service of this body in the community of love. The Gifts of the
Holy Spirit, in making that inner life of faith 'living and personal' have to do
not with an abstract truth but with the 'personal truth of God made flesh in
Jesus Christ', and this will include the acceptance of divine 'wishes, commands, illuminations of the most personal kind'. The *real* organic context that
Thomists should have given Aquinas's scattered treatment is, quite simply,
that of the 'bearers and receivers of revelation'. Those two categories of
person, Balthasar points out, are closely interrelated. No one can bear revelation unless he has already received it, and no one can receive the 'light of
the world' without to some degree becoming a bearer of that light for others
in the Church – without becoming, in an extended sense, a charismatic and
prophet. (In between the two stands another figure, to whom Thomas and
Thomists have paid great attention, the hagiograph, or inspired biblical
writer.) Where the purpose of visionary insight seems determined by its
further transmission in the Church Balthasar would speak of *prophecy*, and
where it is for the expansion and enrichment of the life of the receiver he
would speak of *contemplation*.

Balthasar sees no difficulty in including in all this some role for 'all kinds
of artistic, philosophical and mystical intuition, and even for most diverse
possibilities of cosmic religiosity' – 'inner-worldly factors' of the sort that
crop up in Thomas's account.[89] For Aquinas, prophetic knowledge equals
spiritual insight plus sensuous image, and in the *De veritate* 12, 8, Thomas
explains that while the illumination of the prophet's spirit is God's own act,
the formation of imaginative species in the prophet's mind may be considered angelic – through the angel's natural knowledge for natural prophecy, through his supernatural knowledge for its supernatural equivalent.
Balthasar places here a discussion of the possible role of the fallen angels, the
'darkest and most dangerous zones where the ecclesial discernment of spirits
sets the most difficult tasks' – not least because, occasionally, supernaturally
evil prophecy can be used by God to communicate truth.[90] The Holy Spirit
has to be allowed to work in souls as he freely wills. That he chooses conditions and missions according to the uniqueness of each person is why
Balthasar to a degree mistrusts the *developmental* accounts of mystical prayer
offered by the doctors of sixteenth-century Carmel (and their modern disciples like Garrigou-Lagrange).

---

87 *Besondere Gnadengaben, op. cit.*, p. 288. Thus the *Vita Moysis* of Gregory of Nyssa, the
   sermons of the other Cappadocians, and in the West the tradition of Carmel.
88 *Ibid.*, p. 289.
89 Balthasar considers especially important the treatment provided by Thomas in the
   Quaestiones disputatae de veritate 12, and in this regard notably a. 3, ad ii.
90 *Besondere Gnadengaben, op. cit.*, p. 331.

Relieved from the task of Thomas commentator, Balthasar may fly where he will. It turns out he greatly approved the approach to the subject of the German Benedictine Anselm Stolz whose theology of Christian mysticism broke decisively with the psychological – or para-psychological – interests of most early twentieth-century writers on the subject. As Balthasar summed up Stolz's view, which he shared:

> The mystic, if his mysticism is genuine, can only lead a mystical life within the vision of God of the one Mediator, sharing in his relation to the Father and his mission from the Father, the mysteries of his Incarnation in his representatively substitutionary suffering for humanity, his transfiguration and heavenly and Eucharistic existence.[91]

The Christian mystic, explained Balthasar, knows no other rule than revelation which means primarily Scripture. And as Scripture shows, personal election and engracing is always for the sake of the wider mission of the Son to the world through the Church. Whether the mystic's mission be visible to the world, whether its fruit be recognizable to the one sent on mission, this is virtually a matter of indifference. What is important is that it is a commission from God which must be carried out with the same objectivity as all God's commands. So Balthasar produces the following definition of (Christian) mysticism's essence:

> It is an immediate divine seizing of the human being in his powers of intelligence, sense, and body, that crosses the limit of the God-experience of faith, a direct initiation of the person into God's mysteries for the purpose of a special task within the Church.[92]

(iii) Mysticism in the world religions?

Balthasar's mature reflections on the distinctiveness of Christian mysticism – within a certain 'commonality' that joins it to its non-Christian analogues – took this further. The *mystikos* of Christian mysticism has to do with St Paul's *mystêrion*: the objective divine saving plan for the world. That is 'fundamentally distinct' from everything 'mysticism' might mean in the framework of a general theory of religion.[93] And yet, as a degree of shared vocabulary confirms, not only the physical 'accompanying phenomena' of mysticism (raptures, levitation, luminosity),[94] but even the inner experiences (expanded

91 'Seelenführung und Mystik', *art. cit.*, p. 340.
92 *Ibid.*, p. 342.
93 'Understanding Christian Mysticism', *art. cit.*, p. 312.
94 Balthasar had read and reviewed a German translation of the noted study *The Physical Phenomena of Mysticism* by the English Jesuit Herbert Thurston. Praising the book's 'authentically English sobriety' as well as the narrative flair that gave some sections the excitement of a detective story, Balthasar regretted that there was too much accumulation of factual material and not enough interpretation. However, Thurston had proved to Balthasar's satisfaction that parapsychology was a 'welcome helper of *Mystikforschung*', but he did not agree that the extraordinary phenomena Thurston investigated (stigmata, cessation of eating, knowledge of hearts, physical transfiguration) were both inessential and dangerous to authentic mysticism. As charismata, if unusual ones, they 'belong at least relatively to the public realm of the Church'. Thus '*Die körperlichen Begleiterscheinungen der Mystik. Zu Herbert Thurstons Werk, Luzern 1956*', *Schweizerische Rundschau* 57 (1957), pp. 153–59.

consciousness, the reading of hearts) do indicate there is *something* in common between the mysticism of the Christian and the non-Christian traditions.

Balthasar remained convinced that *analogy* is the best term for the combined similarity yet difference which unites – and separates – the two. First, then, similarity. Barthianism is wrong to dismiss *all* non-biblical religiosity – even or, rather, especially, mystical religiosity – as the corrupt fruit of pride. What is a Barthian to make of Paul's speech on the Areopagus in the Acts of the Apostles where he tells Athenians who erected an altar to the unknown God that they are in truth religious, and what they worship unknowingly he can proclaim to them?[95] And what sense can a Barthian give to the axiom that whatever has not been assumed has not been healed if the Incarnate Word did not, with our humanity, assume its religious striving? How can we deny the possibility that in this or that pagan soul in a way known only to God 'natural mysticism' has not been made the vehicle of supernatural grace? Furthermore, to eliminate the mystical from Scripture is an impossible undertaking – what of the visions and auditions of Isaiah, Elijah, Ezekiel and the proto-martyr Stephen? What of the Transfiguration itself? And yet there is, secondly, difference.

> The whole life-atmosphere of the Bible is quite different from that of other mystical worlds. For is it not the poor in spirit, the mourners and the persecuted, who are here called blessed and not the 'clever and wise' (from whom the heavenly Father has kept this hidden), who know all sorts of techniques to construct for themselves a spiritual ladder to heaven? Nowhere in the behaviour of Jesus is there to be found even the least trace of a technical instruction for meditation ..., still less any enticements for his hearers to long for, or to strive to attain, special religious 'experiences'.[96]

Indeed, as we read on, we discover that, despite his strictures on 'dialectical theology' (for which read 'Barth'), Balthasar is more worried that we shall over-estimate the affinities than underscore the dissimilarity. The borrowing of categories, terms and practical counsels from Greco-Roman paganism can easily mislead us. (Here Balthasar draws on a useful pair of distinctions between 'mysticism' *qua* original experience, 'mystology' or 'mystography' as categories and terms for describing that experience, and 'mystagogy' as practical counsels for mystical initiation – something he found in a study of the Spanish mystics from the 1950s.[97]) The borrowing of non-Christian 'mystography' can obscure the fact that although mystics everywhere rely on a tradition of pressing back the boundaries of experience, breaking out of the ordinary through following methodically some path, actively making oneself empty as a preparation for contemplation and ultimately union with the divine realm of a kind frequently imaged as 'spiritual marriage', all this looks utterly different when seen through the lens of the Gospel. There it is not man's search for God that is primary but God's initiative in seeking out man. Response to the divine Word – above all, to the

95 Acts 17.16-34.
96 *Prayer, op. cit.*, pp. 316–17.
97 I. Behn, *Spanische Mystik* (Dusseldorf, 1957).

Word made flesh – by that fundamental Marian attitude of *disponibilité, Verfügung,* is key. The 'method' followed now can only be Christ himself who summons the disciple to ready obedience, which may have in store experiences dreadful and seemingly Godless, as well as wonderful and God-filled, as the Jesus of the Paschal Mystery knows well. In the wake of the Incarnation and Atonement, as well as the teaching activity of God made man, not the intensity of religious experience but charity – the love of God and neighbour – is now the criterion of perfection. However, where the gracious will of God demands the following of the mystical way – for the glory of God's name and the good of his holy people, the Church, then a *readiness to take up that task is itself the expression of charity,* and so, for this or that person, an index of perfection.

Special tasks in the Church are not, however, restricted to the mystics. So much Balthasar's account of imaginative writers – our final port-of-call – should suggest.

13

⁂

Divine Telling: on Christian Literature

In England by the 1970s, people were speaking – somewhat prematurely – of the disappearance of the 'Catholic novel'. But in the Continental Europe of the 1950s, Balthasar was already reporting a general mood of disappointment that the writers of the Catholic literary renaissance in France – Bloy, Péguy, Claudel, Bernanos – had no obvious successors in the post-war world. Wringing one's hands does no good, he thought. Far better to make a fuller effort of appropriation of what had been so richly given. Personally, he had already translated a huge amount of Claudel (more was to come), as well as Péguy's *Le Porche du Mystère de la deuxième vertu* and Mauriac's *La Pierre d'échoppement*. And, especially in the early 1950s, a good deal of Georges Bernanos too.[1] Balthasar was convinced that Catholic novelists, historical essayists, dramatists and poets could express the *sensus fidei* of the Church – and this become appropriate source-material for the theological enterprise. We give one example of each: Bernanos for the novelists; Reinhold Schneider for the historical essayists, and, more briefly, Claudel for the dramatist-poets.

Bernanos

In his book on Bernanos – entitled in the German, by no means fortuitously, 'Lived Church' – Balthasar presents Bernanos not as a lay theologian (more tempting in the case of Claudel) but as a practising Catholic who thinks and, as polemicist, acts courageously. As we might put it in our tired 'post-Conciliar' tongue, he addressed contemporary problems on the basis of the signs of the times. In his foreword, Balthasar writes rather:

> There are Christian truths that cry out with full throat from the events of the time, and thus they manifest that they are timely, that their time has come; but one must have the courage to hear them cry out.[2]

These were the truths Bernanos sought to proclaim in a French that is always lively and sometimes livid. He did not spare certain incidental features of

---

1 Notably *Madame Dargent, Dialogues d'Ombres, Une Nuit*, portions of *Les grands Cimitières sous la lune*, and selected letters.
2 *Bernanos. An Ecclesial Existence, op. cit.*, p. 18.

Church life, where he found at times inflated official rhetoric, dubious politics, arrogant theologians, a shallow approach to monasticism, mysticism and education. Not that he was simply an angry young man, or indeed simply an angry man of any biological age. Bernanos held that the creative writer, if he is a Christian, has an ecclesial function – a notion he had taken from one of his masters, Léon Bloy, who spoke of the 'sacrament of literature'.[3] Balthasar the critic captures something entirely true of Bernanos, though in quintessentially Balthasarian style, when he says that

> everything [Bernanos] created is *ecclesial existence that has been given form*: existence derived ... from the specific faith of the Church, which is the communion of saints and whose wellsprings of grace – the sacraments – nourish the life of faith.[4]

Balthasar will in fact structure the lion's share of his study by reference to the sacraments, though equally central to Bernanos are the saints who, says Balthasar beautifully, show love as reality.[5] Balthasar's attitude is: any reader of the popular press can discover the weaknesses of the Church's members, including her ministerial members. Let us for once hear something of her marvellous mysteries.

Before sinking his teeth into the meat of his material – the Bernanosian *themes* – Balthasar pauses to consider Bernanos' spirit, life, rationality, imagination and mission. In a word, his qualities and also – for Balthasar, the real explanatory goal of any Christian description – his *task*.

(i) Qualities

Balthasar's evaluation of Bernanos' qualities shows us what Balthasar himself admired theologically in the writers of his time. On Bernanos' 'spirit', the first thing Balthasar wants to say is that Bernanos 'fought for man'.[6] That statement needs clarifying in the light of his subsequent remark that Bernanos' enmity was directed against all that 'in the modern world and Church' threatens man's true 'measure' – that crucial Balthasarian term. Faced with a discarnate Church and a materialist world, Bernanos tried to draw both back to the 'measuring centre'. And though Balthasar is far from presenting Bernanos as a figure born out of time, lost in nostalgia for the 'snows of yesteryear' (*où sont les neiges d'antan?*), he nevertheless accords him a place with Péguy and Claudel in the

> old France of king Louis and Joinville, of Joan of Arc and Corneille, of Rabelais and Francis de Sales.[7]

3 Cited 'Die Stellung von Georges Bernanos zur Kirche', *Schweizer Rundschau* 53 (1953), pp. 293–305, at p. 294.
4 *Bernanos, op. cit.*, p. 19.
5 'Bernanos the novelist derives his image of man from the saints of the Church, who are constellations looming high over the life of Christians and all men and pointing out the way but who are also human beings like ourselves', *ibid.*, p. 32.
6 *Ibid.*, p. 25.
7 *Ibid.*, pp. 26–27.

Actually, Bernanos held that only islands of Christendom were left in the modern world – and we must turn to them.[8] Incarnate Christianity, from the ecclesial centre – because humanity needs it: this slogan will do to sum up his spirit and singles out what in him appeals to Balthasar. Divine and human is Christ, mystical and institutional the Church. One should neither be too comfortable in Zion nor foreswear 'healthy tranquillity' in her. This is 'Catholic balance', and if Bernanos occasionally seems to lose it through excess of zeal, we need to remember that *missions* (Balthasar will return to this aspect) are always complementary, and it could be that, at some moment, excess is needed to counteract deficiency.

Bernanos saw in his own age the menace of a technological deformation of the human spirit, and, in consequence, a false definition of contemplation as escape from, or refusal of, a world whose rhythms were set by machines.[9] What a contrast with graced human nature, which in a magnificently mixed metaphor Balthasar describes as the 'calyx of a flower in bloom ... launched on extraordinary adventures with God'. If the novels describe the adventures, the remaining part of Bernanos' oeuvre, his cultural criticism, presupposes the flowering of nature through grace in honourable virtues and all good works. Balthasar deftly indicates the interrelation of the two kinds of prose.

> The cultural criticism shows that the novels are, and intend to be, much more than mere narratives: they are an interpretation of existence and of revelation in view of the present situation. For their part, the novels demonstrate that the critical works are nourished from much deeper sources than may at first appear.[10]

Balthasar calls Bernanos possibly the modern Christian who was most longingly oriented towards the eternal since Cardinal Newman. In his early work, the hellish seriousness with which he takes spiritual combat inclines Balthasar to compare him with the early Barth (he juxtaposes Barth's Romans commentaries with *Sous le soleil de Satan*). But like Barth, Bernanos was dissatisfied with what he had written. Just as the *Church Dogmatics* becomes a paean to the generosity of divine election, so Bernanos' later novels are filled with God's tender mercy, *la douce pitié de Dieu*, or in the dying words of the parish priest of Ambricourt in *Le Journal d'un curé de campagne*, 'Tout est grâce'. This should not be considered a transition from rapier to flannel. Bernanos' mature doctrine of grace is linked by Balthasar to the spiritual teaching of the seventeenth-century Jesuit Père Surin: only to the 'denuded' heart is the sweetness of divine love revealed. Probably Balthasar's best attempt to capture his spirit is when he calls Bernanos 'steady witness for grace'.[11]

---

8 'Die Stellung von Georges Bernanos zur Kirche', *art. cit.*, p. 296. Balthasar pertinently draws in here Bernanos' admiration for Péguy, not only in the latter's praise of childhood and hope but for his exaltation of freedom, knighthood, honour in which Balthasar sees him as a medieval Christian or man of the *ancien régime* born (to the secular historian's eye) out of time.

9 On Bernanos' civic outlook, see A. Nichols, OP, '"Lift up a Living Nation": the Political Theology of Georges Bernanos', *New Blackfriars* 79. 993 (1998), pp. 502–08.

10 *Bernanos, op. cit.*, p. 34.

11 *Ibid.*, p. 54.

The steadiness of Bernanos' Christian witness was shown in a life that, from an empirical viewpoint, was distinctly rocky. It began well enough. His father was a successful interior designer; the family had houses in Paris and the Pas-de-Calais. Admittedly, the young Georges loathed his Jesuit school, and Balthasar reports a positive aversion for the Society ever afterwards. The alternative clerical educational establishments run by the diocesan clergy were more to his liking. As a boy he was already a serious Catholic. As a youth he identified his specifically Christian vocation to be a writer. As a young man, studying law in Paris, he rallied to *Action française* with its call to France to rediscover social, political and cultural discipline through re-attachment to the *ancien régime* via the distinctly modern (and, at the hands of its author, atheistic) philosophy of 'organic positivism'. Its royalism was rowdy. In 1909 he spent a period in prison for riot. In 1914 through these connexions he had a lucky break, and became the editor of a small Rouen newspaper. His writing career, not just as essayist but also as imaginative writer, began forthwith. His marriage brought a large family. That, combined with the vagaries of earning a living by the pen, and a curious, seemingly irrational, desire to pull up roots and move house and home at frequent intervals, made for a stressful life. In the 1920s he was forced to accept employment as an insurance salesman: a livelihood that went right against the grain of the virtues he most lauded. His religion was painfully existentialist in its expression. Balthasar describes his Great War correspondence as a cry to God that was more of a spiritual howl than an act of contemplation. In the inter-war years and beyond, a favoured theme was criticism of any attempt to 'substitute supernatural virtues (such as humility, repentance, love of enemies, and so on) for non-existing civil virtues . . .', and notably for, in their absence, justice and honour – a point that notably qualified the pacifism to which his experience of trench warfare in 1914–1918 otherwise inclined him.[12] Though after the success of his first major novel he could risk living off authorial fees and royalties, life remained an economic struggle – and an intellectual and religious one. He took the papal condemnation of *Action française* hard; but he also fell out with its leaders on his own account. A motor cycle accident left him permanently dependent on crutches. Really, he was quite an anguished soul – though Balthasar sees in this a vocational aid, not a hindrance, for Bernanos' mission.

> *Anguish* was for our author a kind of medium for poetic knowledge, the prerequisite for his descents into the underground of souls, that utter interior nakedness and exposure by virtue of which he could capture the softest vibrations of a concealed and precious truth that remained hidden from others.[13]

In 1934, sick of the public path France seemed to be following, he settled on Mallorca – just in time for the outbreak of the Spanish Civil War. *Les grands Cimitières sous la lune* expresses his nausea at the shortcomings of Spanish political Catholicism. Returning briefly to France in 1938, the climb-down of the democracies at Munich completed his disillusion and he emigrated once more, this time via Paraguay to Brazil. The tenor of his

12 *Ibid.*, p. 65.
13 *Ibid.*, p. 72.

French-language broadcasting during World War Two made him something of a hero at home, and it was to a certain adulation that he went back to France (and French North Africa) in 1945, there to produce his last and possibly greatest work, the film scenario *Les dialogues des Carmélites*, later adapted for the stage by Albert Béguin. Georges Bernanos died of a failed operation on the liver in July 1948.

Before investigating the scope of Bernanos' mission, Balthasar considers the way he deployed the powers of reason and imagination. Balthasar calls the kind of rationality Bernanos espoused 'believing reason' or 'prophetic reason'. Why do scenes at death-beds play a large part in the novels? In his essay 'Satan et nous' Bernanos explained. Practitioners of bourgeois rationality, who domesticate life, restricting reason to the calculable and carefully avoiding adventure and risk, get a shock when faced with death. Bernanos addresses them.

> You will suddenly recognize – without ever having seen it – the invisible universe to which your body had no access and away from which you carefully turned your interior glance ... It was here, however, that, almost unbeknownst to you, your soul had long been cultivating its habits, its life, here that it moved secretly, silently, like those fish in the ocean depths that at times are hauled up to the daylight by the lead of a plumbline.[14]

He was particularly irritated by people who regard truth as always occupying the mid point between extremes. As he put it in a 1944 article for *La Croix*, truth is not to be found reposing between two lies, like a slice of ham in a sandwich. Truth is found by taking the risk of 'proceed[ing] unswervingly to the very end of what's true'.[15]

It is perhaps surprising that Balthasar does not dub Bernanosian rationality 'eschatological reason'. That at least is the adjective – favoured, of course, ever since *Apokalypse der deutschen Seele* – Balthasar uses for the 'passion' animating Bernanos' deployment of reason, in its attempt to uncover the 'bare and eternal depths of existence'. A rationality adequate to the human condition must be prepared to confront invisible depths, and not simply register entailments given with the visible order. This is why the novels move in two directions: not just along a narrative trajectory but down to the abiding roots of action. There is a divinatory aspect to rationality which renders it akin to prophecy. If existence tends to go beyond itself towards God, reason, to be adequate to existence, must do likewise.

Bernanos stressed the freedom of reason. In the shape of the rational agent, reason is called to trust in a divine foundation and goal to life, but also to engage, through personal commitment, with the world. His hostility to the cultural influence of modern technology was largely the result of anxiety that such a concept – and practice – of reason would become even less recuperable under such a reign than in the epoch of Cartesianism. As Balthasar sums up:

---

14 G. Bernanos, 'Satan et nous', *Bulletin trimestriel de la Société des Amis de Georges Bernanos* 12–13, p. 24, cited *Bernanos*, p. 81.
15 Cited in *ibid.*, p. 98.

Total trust in God, which makes the soul transparent to the spirit, is paid for in the world with the solitary commitment to God's unabridged truth.

This is what constitutes freedom as a feature of reason.[16]

Balthasar emphasizes how in Bernanos' conception liberal reason had nothing in common with an individualistic liberalism. The ground of this assertion is characteristically Balthasarian and Bernanosian at the same time. It lies in the *communion of saints*. Bernanos was simply too convinced of the way the 'commonality of destinies and responsibilities ... reaches into the most intimate regions of a person' ever to feel the attraction of liberal individualism. Freedom – freedom of spirit – is a duty, burden, honour, exercised amid and on behalf of the human solidarity in a nation, a civilization, or the race as a whole. Christianity – and thus, concretely, the Church – has the task of defending freedom so conceived, notably against the neo-pagan State, just as it has the task of defending reason as Bernanos presents it.

The Catholic Church is the 'true Church'. Very well then: she must proclaim truth. Not all clerics – or laypeople for that matter – seemed to Bernanos to do so in all relevant respects. He did not expect them always to get the details right. But he *did* expect them to get right the basic proportions. Their failures did not, however, take him aback. Interpreted in Balthasarian categories: the objective aspect of the Church – her institutional life, is only a medium for the transmission of her subjective aspect – the life of grace. Yes, the charism of infallibility covers certain moments in the life of the institution. Yes again, a dominical promise underlines the indefectibility of the entire Church, and within it in a special way the hierarchy, in the truth. But not everything in the 'field of realization' of the Church of office has its veraciousness thus guaranteed. The only person with a claim to effortless superiority here is, for Bernanos, the saint.

> The saint is the one who lives the truth of the Church and therefore the full form of Catholic reason and reveals reason's prophetic character in the original sense of the word [prophetic]: an utterance from God representing God.[17]

Bernanos' question was, how can saints come in an age that undermines the presuppositions of sanctity?[18] It may be hard to credit, but Balthasar was strongly criticized by the conservative clergy for making Bernanos, with his sometimes withering attitude to the Church's office-holders, a theological authority comparable (so it was suggested) to a Father of the Church. In an open letter to one such critic, Balthasar made a spirited rejoinder.

> You studied in the Eternal City, I in the temporal one between Vienna and Paris ... You had before all to find the ear of the clergy, I of the laity. Your task was to examine and interpret the prescriptions and declarations of Church office, mine was to accompany the Christian in his fellow-feeling with the everyday life of the world, and so to put before him images of ecclesial love and holiness, from which he could

---

16 *Ibid.*, p. 102.
17 *Ibid.*, p. 114.
18 'Die Stellung von Georges Bernanos zur Kirche', *art. cit.*, p. 304.

draw courage in his battle with those without, being by those images protected, illuminated, warmed.[19]

In no way did Bernanos call into question the legitimacy of office in the Church. But he did think that the principle of office can be exaggerated, especially when prelates concern themselves with civil matters falling outwith the sphere of ecclesial obedience. Moreover, office in the Church could be made a substitute for love. And obedience could become servility, rather than 'free and responsible subjection'. These dangers, Balthasar pointed out, were real menaces to ecclesial obedience – and critics of Bernanos should recognize true friends when they saw them. They should also beware lest they failed to 'take seriously the voice of laypeople in the Church' especially when such people as Claudel or Bernanos, Gertrud von der Fort or Reinhold Schneider, had gifts of insight about Christian existence, prayed through, struggled for, suffered in love, to bestow upon the rest of us. Of course they did not practise formal theology, *Fachtheologie*, and it would be absurd to ask it of them. That would merely 'stylize' their witness. Churchly theology itself, however, should listen to them – because otherwise it will fail to hear voices lifted up through charismata of the Holy Spirit. Here Balthasar draws his readers' attention to his own study of the role of the charisms, as occasioned by his commentary on texts thereon from the *Summa theologiae* of St Thomas. Can it be possible, asks Balthasar ironically, that no layperson can 'open their mouth in the Church until they have first been 'raised to the altars [by canonization]'? On the contrary, we must make sure that 'painters and poets' have space to make their mark.

Balthasar is speaking, not least, of the ecclesial role of the Christian imagination. What is its place? Imagination is already implied, he thinks, in the fundamental situation of man and his rationality, as indicated by the notion of 'eschatological' reason. We are living towards eternity, and what we are living is a temporal life only seen aright when seen in the perspective of the eternal. Inevitably, therefore: 'The manner in which eternity dawns through all his [man's] acts must appear like the opening up of the depths of a dream'.[20]

This may be either positive or negative. The dream reveals the world in its character as appearance. The task of the human person is to dream in the direction of the truth. The sinner dreams in the direction of nothingness. But whether the oneiric experience is good or evil (and Bernanos' novels contain as many false dreams as true ones), the final criterion for the imagination is – just as it was for reason – the criterion of the saint. In the supernatural charism of *cardiognosis*, the ability to read hearts often vouchsafed to the saints, the 'dream zone' is transcended and there takes its place 'the truly real vision of invisible spiritual reality as God *himself* sees it'.[21]

The dreaming from which literary creation takes its rise finds here its judge. It is not just that the imaginative writer must beware not to sow evil seeds in the world through the sinners he depicts. (That is already a difficult demand.) But even more, Bernanos understood literary creation to be – by

19 'Über Amt und Liebe in der Kirche. Ein offener Brief an Alois Schenker', *Neue Zürcher Nachrichten* 49. 164, Beilage *Christliche Kultur* 18. 29 (17 July 1953).
20 *Bernanos*, p. 122.
21 *Ibid.*, p. 142.

aspiration – a humble participation in the saint's charism of reading hearts. For the Christian novelist that is a possibility, even if the author is no saint himself but only an average Christian. Using his terminology of objective and subjective holiness Balthasar explains how.

> The invididual Christian existence of the average Catholic is subjected to the criterion of this vision of sanctity in a twofold manner. First, he is confronted with the criterion of sanctity in the sacramental and objective form that the Word of God ... has in the Church: seen and judged by God's Word, a Catholic's existence is laid bare to its very foundation. And, second, he is also confronted with the criterion of sanctity in the existential, subjective form of the holy person. This person, the saint, can walk through an average Catholic existence and polarize it – like a confused jumble of steel splinters – in the direction of the truth, a truth that such a Catholic could not otherwise have found.[22]

For Bernanos, the counter-saintly dream is most often a solipsistic one. Typically, the sinner 'populates the theatre of the world solely with the chimeras of his own fantasy'.[23] This can be worse than a waste of psychic energy. In Bernanos' oeuvre the dream can stand for

> the evacuation of all meaning, the dilution of being, a vacuum, a distorting mirror, and the dissolution ... of a person's substance ...[24]

Increasingly, so Balthasar believed from his analysis of the novels in their chronological sequence, Bernanos came to the conclusion that he was making a mistake in portraying nothingness or evil – the death of the spirit – with means that amounted to its contradiction, since those means were simply brimming over with poetic life. Gradually he ceased to portray the satanic as its own truth, and treated it as *par excellence* the kingdom of dream – that is, as 'absolute, intrinsic appearance'. In an extraordinary passage Balthasar comments on how this is achieved. The novelist, Orpheus-like, walks in the shadows with characters who belong to the world of perdition. As he does so, the author takes on a role comparable to that of Christ in his descent into hell. He thus draws attention to the Cross as the true measure of that world of evil dream whose inhabitants would laugh at heaven as at a childish game.

> The Crucified renounced heaven in order to be annihilated along with sinners; and, precisely for this reason, the Cross is the reality that measures and judges both nothingness and hell.[25]

(ii) Mission

Despite a degree of critical 'eisegesis', Balthasar has certainly whetted our appetites for an account of the *mission* of Georges Bernanos. From what has been said above it appears that writing fiction is a dangerous business. How can one create such a world of dream without incurring guilt? Balthasar accepts this as a valid question and answers it on Bernanos' behalf: *by a call of*

22 *Ibid.*, p. 143.
23 *Ibid.*, p. 146.
24 *Ibid.*, p. 150.
25 *Ibid.*, p. 153.

grace. For Balthasar the notions of artistic vocation and literary inspiration do not represent the secularization of theological concepts. At the very least, they draw attention to a close analogy with the prophet and the hagiograph. More: Balthasar claims they are modes of participation in a strictly charismatic and thus ecclesial reality. Abundant texts show Bernanos did indeed regard himself as carrying out a vocation in the Church. The writer is a steward and depository of truth, for the sake of others. What was his providential subject-matter? Certainly not the moods of the self. Far more important, so he told a correspondent in 1933, were 'duties to be fulfilled, sorrows to be suffered, injustices to embrace'.[26]

Evidently, he stands at the opposite extreme, in this regard, to the English Bloomsbury school, themselves (significantly) agnostics to a man or woman. The sign of his vocation was: burning zeal for God, and it led him to take up a position equidistant from revolt against the order of reality on the one hand, and resigned acceptance of the current state of affairs on the other. For Balthasar, such an attitude is

> the pathos that alone makes the art of Christian literature possible … [by] participating in the unfathomable identity of love and wrath in God, that is, in the gesture whereby God both chooses out of grace and spews out of his mouth in condemnation.[27]

For Bernanos, truth is to be found only by looking at characters from the perspective of divine grace – which is why Balthasar can assert in his regard an 'ultimate identity between the truth of literary creation and the truth of salvation'.[28] The 'truth of salvation' is when the creature, through fallen nature a prey to dissolution, by a free gift attains (not without painful confession) its gracious truth in God. Prayer is the atmosphere of all conversion; other discourse leaves in shadow what the self does not wish to see.

As witnesses to the truth, Bernanos appeals to the Mother of Jesus, to the saints and angels and to the *child* – but to all of these only as 'transparencies' for the 'gaze of God'. The truth of the Word which judges and redeems human personalities is

> [that] Word who can contain and embrace man's whole way from childhood to death because he became weaker than a child and more despoiled than a dying man.[29]

It is the infinite, eternal dimension of this kenotic truth that the Resurrection reveals. The writer's creative activity must be a humble sign pointing to this Word. Here at last is the true poetics. When he was dying, Bernanos said he would have liked to write a life of Christ, to 'speak about him at a church entrance or from behind a pillar, since I am no less poor than the rest of them'.[30]

26 'To a Woman Friend', in *Bulletin trimestriel de la Société des Amis de Georges Bernanos* 2–3, p. 16.
27 *Bernanos*, pp. 166–67.
28 *Ibid.*, p. 169.
29 *Ibid.*, p. 177.
30 The testimony of the abbé Pézeril in *Cahiers du Rhône. Georges Bernanos: Essais et témoignages* (Paris, 1949), p. 345.

Only in the context of such Christocentrism does the role of the saints appear in its true proportions. Admitting that Bernanos never formulated this theoretically, Balthasar does it for him.

> He envisioned the saint as someone who had been prepared by God to become an image of divine truth and revelation for a specific moment in the history of the world. The saint is thus a person commissioned to represent a particular divine task, and this mission asserts itself in his life in such a way that the saint becomes its servant without knowing it and even though he may refuse to obey.[31]

This definition, it must be said, corresponds conveniently closely to that found in Balthasar's own hagiological work! More indebted to Bernanos is another Balthasarian assertion: the charism of sanctity can encounter collaboratively another charism, that of the creative (human) word.

> What the saint has lived – even though he himself has not perhaps received from God the gift of expressing it in words – may be put into the hands of a craftsman of language who is rooted within the same ecclesial sphere as the saint, which is where God appoints his messengers.[32]

While not abolishing the distance between saint and writer this explains the remarkable *convenientia*, fittingness, of the words Bernanos put on the lips of such saints as Jean-Marie Vianney, Thérèse of Lisieux, Joan of Arc. In other words, 'Bernanosian discourse occurs ... at the level of the ecclesial missions'.[33]

Bernanos placed at the centre of such ecclesial missions *witness to suffering love*. He considered that divine suffering love for the earth is the defining characteristic of Christian belief, since the suffering love of the Son of Man, central to the Gospels, points onwards, to the wounded heart of the Father. Crib and Cross define Bernanos' iconographical world, just as the recurring phrase *la douce pitié de Dieu* anchors his theological rhetoric.

(iii) The themes
What, then, of the actual content of Bernanos' work? Balthasar deals first with the wider world it conveys – under the headings of 'cosmos and salvation' and 'the Church', before treating of the sacramental structure of the Christian life and what is perhaps the main thematic outcome – at any rate for a theologian-preacher – of Bernanos' world-view: the Christian – and the Church – 'in time'.

a. Cosmos and salvation
The word 'cosmos' in 'cosmos and salvation' must be taken with a pinch of salt. Balthasar's discussion has in mind chiefly the nature–grace relationship, not quarks or hippopotamuses. It begins with anthropology, where, more yet than we have seen, Bernanos is kitted out in unmistakably Balthasarian dress. Human 'nature', declares Balthasar, summing up for the readers of his

31 *Bernanos*, p. 186.
32 *Ibid.*
33 *Ibid.*, p. 188.

Bernanos book the theological metaphysic adumbrated a decade earlier in *Wahrheit*, is immutable. But not so the

> concrete 'essence' or 'idea' that the living Creator entertains concerning his living Creature, and which both Creator and creature together unfold within a living history.[34]

Inasmuch as Bernanos certainly treats historical epochs and situations as crucial for human possibilities for and against God – and man in God – Balthasar's distinction may be thought a not unilluminating comment on Bernanos' texts. A similar crux arises with the relation of nature and grace. The layman writes plain prose when in *La France contre les robots* he says of despair that it leads people deliberately to degrade themselves, to exact vengeance on their immortal souls. Balthasar glosses this theologically by invoking the nature–grace relationship.

> The possibility of an internal contradiction in man first arises because man in reality is more and must be more than simply himself (his 'nature'), and when man denies this his destiny he is actually trying to abolish himself.[35]

Few writers have exalted human nature more than Bernanos, and yet

> he cannot tolerate our thinking about man for a single instant bereft of his supernatural and 'superhuman' divine goal.[36]

Balthasar shortens the distance from the texts when he speaks of the 'summit' at which man surpasses world and nature and which Bernanos calls by a trinity of names: freedom, love, simplicity. Bernanos maintains that the free venture of love is meant to lead to *holiness* (this is why it escapes the limits of the natural), while the genius of holiness is simplicity. Bernanos had insufficient historical knowledge of the tradition of Christian asceticism to realize how true was the chord he struck. Unwittingly, he placed himself in a tradition going back to the earliest monastic sources (as well as the Gospels) when he made the 'secret' of all his saints lie in this 'seamless unity of supernatural and childlike singleness and simplicity'.[37]

Purity, understood in its sexual sense, is for Bernanos a crucial precondition of such simplicity. He links its contrary – lustful obsession – not only with unbelief but also with madness. In a negative sort of way, these linkages testify to the call of body, as well as spirit, to go beyond itself towards God.

This vocation of the flesh obliges Bernanos – and Balthasar after him – to deal in some way with the cosmic nature in which our bodies are embedded (and not just, then, with human nature as theologically conceived, that is, vis-à-vis grace). Bernanos has little if any description of landscape for its own sake. In his work landscape is symbolic, even pathetic: it takes on a spiritual form cognate with the situation of his characters. A rather incompetent farmer, his accounts of the land are sparing. Only in the *Journal d'un Curé de*

---

34 *Ibid.*, p. 218.
35 *Ibid.*, p. 220.
36 *Ibid.*
37 *Ibid.*, p. 226.

campagne does Balthasar find nature recovering a 'consistency' of its own, but even then this is in an understated way, 'in keeping with the work's chamber-music quality'.[38] Not much sense here that, owing to the theocentrism of all reality, cosmic nature (and its species) cannot *simply* be described as the locus and companion of man. Balthasar's own tendency to treat a cosmic view of reality as now culturally displaced by an anthropic one (at least in the early and middle sections of his career) palliates any slight note of criticism in these pages.

Bernanos had more to say about the 'world' in the sense of the human city. And what he says is stimulating. On the one hand, he rejects the cherishing of the Church as a safe haven from the world. The Church *is* – in union with Christ – responsibility for the world. This is not a matter of finding a moral common ground (Bernanos rejects what he sees as the 'American' solution: a mere republic of virtue). With the redemption, civil society either moves closer to the new paradise or further away from it. Bernanos accepts learning from the world – but rejects dialogue with it.

> Bernanos builds no bridges; what he does is tear down all the sham linkages between the world and the Church in order to make these face one another, each as its clean self.[39]

b. The Church

This naturally raises the question of how Bernanos sees the *Church*. He has some ingredients for a theoretical ecclesiology, and Balthasar spares no effort to provide these with suitable complements. For instance – and the example is foundational – Bernanos clearly distinguishes the visible from the invisible Church. While not allowing these to be counterposed, he takes pleasure – unusually – in the thought of their disparity. In an amusing section of *La liberté, pourquoi faire?*, he treats their non-coincidence as a wonderful divine favour. If to every step of the Church's hierarchy there coincided the appropriate degree of holiness, what neophyte, or even layperson, would not be overawed?

> Would you feel at home in such a place? Allow me to laugh! Instead of feeling at home, you would stop at the threshold of this congregation of supermen, turning your cap in your hands, like a poor beggar at the door of the Ritz or of Claridge's.[40]

That is certainly letting Bernanos speak for himself. More Balthasarian is the way *Bernanos* (the book) presents the interrelation of the Church of sanctity and the Church of office, considered, this time, as two elements *within* the visible Church. It is nonetheless a point that is key for the novels.

> The connection between the saint and the priesthood and its sacraments, the transposition to the former of the divine holiness objectively contained in the latter, so that it becomes subjective, personal holiness: this is the exact point where Bernanos' saintly heroes begin to emerge.[41]

38 *Ibid.*, p. 241.
39 *Ibid.*, p. 253.
40 G. Bernanos, *La liberté, pourquoi faire?* (Paris, 1953), p. 285.
41 *Bernanos*, p. 260.

The priest 'launches' the saint by his ministry of the (Word and) sacraments. If Bernanos' ecclesiology, indeed, is an account of the Church as the communion of saints, Balthasar ascribes this to a 'theological and ecclesiological aesthetics' that has nothing to do with aestheticism. Drawing thereby a distinction which will play a major role in the opening volume of *Herrlichkeit*, he considers that in the saints' purity of form, Bernanos found combined a humane beauty with a supernatural counterpart. The difference from the 'normal' literary hero is that where the saint, like the hero, goes beyond the mediocre he does so, unlike the hero, in conscious obedience to divine vocation – an obedience, Balthasar stresses, which always takes him or her deeper into the Church, and not away from it. This is signalled, in Bernanos' oeuvre, by the role allotted to priest-confessors, spiritual directors, prioresses, all of whom act as 'ecclesial representatives'. Balthasar describes this somewhat brutally as 'a precisely aimed punch in the face of modern personalism, both inside and outside the Church'.[42] This is not an adverse criticism: personalism, he holds, unlike ecclesial obedience, actually fails to draw from persons their best, or at least their best under grace. Balthasar talks of Bernanos' director figures as 'precipitating' their *dirigés* into oblative love, and in a rather horrid passage can find the same true of the representatives of the Church of office in the trial and execution of St Joan: 'the hierarchical Church, doing sinfully what she should have done out of love – namely, offering up what is holy to God'.[43]

From the heart of the Church there overflows what Bernanos termed in his life of St Dominic 'mystical blood', running down in atonement, in communion with the Redeemer, the Solitary One on the Cross. Balthasar even speaks of the saints as belonging to 'the sacrificial matter of the Holy Mass that the Church publicly and sacramentally offers up to God'.[44] As these comments may indicate, in his sense of the Church Bernanos constantly crossed the boundary into the mystical. The saint is granted full experience of the Church precisely as a 'divine and ecclesial mystery', thus disclosing to others the truth of their own Christian lives.[45] As the 'mystical Body of Christ' – the principal description of the Church in the Catholic ecclesiology of Bernanos' lifetime – the Church's whole life is sacramental in an extended sense. Leaving aside, in Bernanos' prose, the parodic or deliberately inverted uses of the language of sacramentality to refer to the degraded or frankly demonic, he invokes that language for all kinds of positive aspects of discipleship, seeing them as, in Balthasar's words;

> existential reflections, as it were, of the actual sacraments of the Church: ... their exegesis through concrete living ...[46]

c. The Christian life: mystical

What interests Bernanos, thinks Balthasar, is a level of experience midway between the psychological (which has nothing *directly* theological about it) ·

42 *Ibid.*, p. 269.
43 *Ibid.*, p. 279.
44 *Ibid.*, p. 273.
45 *Ibid.*, p. 284.
46 *Ibid.*, p. 287.

and the mystical (which is for him the fullest theological penetration of the 'total sacrament' of revelation-derived Christian truth, salvation-derived Christian life).

By 'mysticism' Bernanos understands not isolated privileged experiences in 'spots of time' à la Romanticism but something more radical, as well as distinctively Christian. Mysticism is living in a thoroughgoing fashion by participation in Christ's life – accessible as that is through faith and the sacraments of faith – as from a 'centre'. Bernanos hated the very different – and, surely, statistically far more common – approach of his fellow-novelist François Mauriac. With Mauriac, New Testament *faith* represents an ideal we sometimes manage to touch but are usually unable to, with the corollary that New Testament *love* becomes essentially compassion for an incapacity. (By the same token, Bernanos also strongly disliked casuistry: the 'social value' of someone who wants to know the amount starting from which theft may be considered mortally sinful, he wrote, is nil, even if that person refrains from stealing.[47]) The only Christian who is really interesting is the saint, the person who, not questioning the basis of 'normal ecclesial existence', grows 'out of the ground of the Church's sacramental life'.[48] The alternatives are (supernaturally) dishonourable, and honour – difficult though it be to define – is essential to being human.

The upshot is a view of the mystical Balthasar finds deeply sympathetic. For Bernanos mysticism

> refers to the extraordinary path of a particular vocation to sanctity; but this 'oath' is conceived only as the full-blown exposition and extrapolation of ecclesial normalcy itself, which means it is a function of the community.

And in case we are inclined to think that last clause signifies being 'common or garden', Balthasar adds

> To be more precise still: mysticism involves a vicarious sacrifice offered up by the ecclesial community in a direction that can be none other than that defined by the *Via Dolorosa*, the way of the Passion of Jesus Christ.[49]

What Bernanos inveighs against is mysticism as a flight to security from risk, a pursuit of sublime experiences in splendid isolation from the community of the Church. What he commends is mysticism as a being cast out of all safe existence into an unsoundable abyss. For reasons of his own, Balthasar is all in favour of a mysticism of identification with Christ in his descent into hell, in solidarity with sinners. But even he thinks Bernanos has gone a mite too far when he asserts the controlling presence of Satan in the trials of mystical saints who freely offer themselves in substitution for mortal sinners.

> The 'hell' that must be gone through is just as often a hell in which no 'devil' is encountered; it is, rather, an experiential confrontation with the interminable monstrousness of the world's guilt.[50]

47 G. Bernanos, *Nous autres Français* (Paris, 1939), p. 239.
48 *Bernanos*, p. 299.
49 *Ibid.*, p. 303.
50 *Ibid.*, p. 307.

Sous le soleil de Satan is in danger of erecting one possible kind of 'dark night' experience into a universal norm. Not till his final works is this danger wholly past, and the interior suffering intrinsic (so Balthasar believes) to mysticism takes on a different form. In *Le Dialogue des Carmélites* Blanche, whom the Revolutionary events expel from her cloister, has to learn detachment from herself – that is, even from her own detachment. And, as with all the other Bernanosian spiritual figures, that is precisely for the sake of ecclesial mission. Which is why Balthasar so approves of it: it conforms to his own theology of mysticism as *a risk-filled mission in the Church*.

d. The Christian life: sacramental
Given Bernanos' view of Catholic existence as essentially sacramental, it is not surprising that Balthasar structures his next chapters on the basis of six out of the seven sacraments. (Marriage alone is not treated here.) Since only the sacrament of Confession plays a major role, in any explicit way, in the fiction of Bernanos, the sacramental patterning of themes is to some extent Balthasar's own contribution. But it never lacks a Bernanosian peg on which to hang.

Baptism and Confirmation
The chapter on the 'world of Baptism and Confirmation' serves above all to introduce readers to Bernanos' doctrine of spiritual childhood (Baptism) and its spiritual weapons (Confirmation). For Bernanos, baptismal regeneration is birth to spiritual childhood. Since baptismal grace is the foundation of sanctity, the way of holiness is necessarily the way of such childhood. The life of every saint has a

> simple centre [which] is the love that consists in being perfectly pliable in God's hands and permanently available to his good pleasure.[51]

Beginning from a doctrine of sanctity as dramatic spiritual violence wreaked on the self and its environment, Bernanos gradually adopts the account of holiness as a 'little way' classically expressed by Thérèse of Lisieux, whose life overlapped with his. (She died in 1897 when he was nine.) Baptism creates a new start. It is a mystery that triumphs over time. It grounds the soul in supernatural hope. It gives the secret of eternal youth. Bernanos, so Balthasar points out, loves young saints – not only Thérèse but also Joan of Arc. But this is because they make vivid something true of sanctity *as such*. During the 1920s, Bernanos introduced a number of typical Theresian phrases into his novels, but eventually he found his own way of insinuating Theresian concerns. Thus in the sermon by an unbeliever for Thérèse's feast day found in *Les grands Cimitières sous la lune* he has the preacher say to the surprised congregation: 'Hurry up and become children again, that we in turn might do the same!'[52] Significantly, Balthasar will address himself to this very theme in his last book.

Confirmation, by contrast, equips the Christian child to face a world of wolves. In an excellent definition of its relation to Baptism, Balthasar sums

51 *Ibid.*, p. 317.
52 G. Bernanos, *Les grands Cimitières sous la lune, op. cit.*, p. 272.

up: 'It transforms the Christian's hope and love and self-surrendering faith into weapons of the spirit'.[53]

Typically, Bernanos emphasizes how the grace of Confirmation allows one who sees through the illusions of optimism to have 'desperate courage', or 'desperate energy'. For him, these are the antidotes to resignation and cynicism. This is pertinent to the destiny of culture as well as the soul. Our civilization can only be renewed if baptismal grace rejuvenates it, and enables people to see, for instance, that Chartres cathedral is 'younger' than many of the monuments of architectural Modernism.[54]

Bernanos was under no illusion that the average Christian, clerical or lay, exemplified the requisite virtues. The scandal of the Church for Bernanos is not the scandal of lurid sinfulness. It is the scandal of mediocrity. The world expects much from Christians but receives little. Too often they are not so much its salt as its syrup. But Bernanos also makes observations that complicate this picture. First, disappointment with the Church does not seem to figure in the lives of those whom one might expect to be most conscious of it, namely: the saints. Secondly, insofar as the mediocre are pitiable, the incarnate God who took up and sanctified all human miseries may take them as his dwelling-place. Thirdly, to avoid ecclesiastical pharisaism, one must suspect the virulence of one's own indignation. One must lay it at the feet of the God who, in Christ, constantly suffers in this world. Fourthly, he saw it as part of Christian endurance to remain in solidarity with 'imbeciles' – by which he meant not the clinically insane but those who without realizing it are abjectly spiritually poor.

Holy Orders and Confession

Balthasar's chapter on 'the world of Holy Orders and Confession' in Bernanos gets off to a good start. Or rather, a quite deliberately *bad* start: it links to evil the world of meaning these two sacraments define.

> ... the sacrament of orders, which equips a man in a special way for battling with the Evil One, is conceived by Bernanos primarily as the conferral of a supernatural grace of office that bestows vision, insight into the essence of guilt ... This battle with the Evil One, furthermore, often specifies itself in the sacrament of confession, which is par excellence the 'sacrament of struggle'.[55]

Bernanos' (and Balthasar's) account of the sacrament of Order reflects a period in Western Catholicism when more of a priest's time was given to hearing confessions than is usually the case now. It remains doctrinally the case, however, that, in confession, the act of the penitent is itself the sacramental 'matter' so Bernanos is onto something when he considers that here a psychological state, and the action that issues from it, enjoys a 'transpsychological' – indeed, a directly sacramental – significance.

Bernanos believed that only with the assistance of sacramental grace (whether in Order or Penance) could one know evil, from within, not only safely but objectively as well. As Balthasar interprets him, Bernanos wanted

---

53 *Bernanos, op. cit.*, p. 334.
54 G. Bernanos, *Lettre aux Anglais* (Paris, 1946), p. 179.
55 *Bernanos, op. cit.*, p. 370.

to show the existence, depth and 'suction-power' of the 'satanic abyss'. But only gradually did he find the appropriate novelistic tools for the job. In *Sous le soleil de Satan* he is still too much under the influence of Romanticism, and the attempt to portray a human relationship with a Devil who, however scary, tells the truth about things, anthropomorphizes and in the last resort sentimentalizes the evil Power. What Balthasar expects from Bernanos and finds in the 1927 novel *L'Imposture* is (in the former's terms) a 'trans-psychological' account of evil which does it, to the degree possible, meta-physical justice.

> Little by little, consciousness returned to the Abbé Cenabre ... What was taking shape in him was quite beyond the reach of the intellect. It was wholly unlike anything he had known and remained distinct from his life, even though his life was shaken by it at an astounding depth. It was like the exultation of another being – its own mysterious *realization*. He wholly ignored both the meaning and the goal of this process; but this passivity of all his higher faculties, at the epicentre of such massive agitation, was, to tell the truth, a delectation that made his body quiver to the very roots. He admitted and welcomed the mysterious force into his own nature, enduring it with a terrible joy ...[56]

Grasping evil more fully, Bernanos abandoned the attempt to portray evil persons in their individuality. The effect of conscious surrender to evil, expressed above all in denying God not in his justice but in his love, is best evoked, he now thought, *either* as dissolution into anonymity *or* petrifaction to the condition of a thing. *Monsieur Ouine*, written during the Second World War, takes further the depiction of transpersonal evil. When Bernanos describes Ouine's death, he aims to convey the dead man's damnation. What he actually portrays is the

> irruption of the absolute nothingness that was always present in radical evil yet only now [in the moment of death] reveals itself as the façade of the person is demolished.[57]

This 'nothingness', Balthasar explains, is not that of the philosophers. It is a *hunger that ingests without ever doing more than desiring.*

Bernanos' 'mysticism of sin' is chiefly concerned with the kingdom of evil as such, in its very essence. But he does not neglect its symptomatic mani-festations in particular sins, a number of which he highlights as its eloquent emblems. These include: lying, which draws attention to the self-disin-tegration of being; injustice, the rejection of the most elementary laws and requirements of human existence; and sexual violence or perversion, since these bring about a contradiction between the sign of love and the love that should be present in its sign. Especially striking is Bernanos' account of suicide which, as Balthasar interprets him, fascinates precisely because it lacks all reason, all foundation. It 'incarnates the magnetic power of the abyss', suction by the void.[58]

---

56 G. Bernanos, *L'Imposture* (Paris, 1929), pp. 55–56.
57 *Bernanos*, op. cit., p. 381.
58 *Ibid.*, p. 399.

When Bernanos portrays evil with 'sacral' traits this is because (Balthasar proposes) its attack on being is above all an attack on the 'all-encompassing supernatural mystery of purity and grace'.[59] The 'abolition' of evil would require the 'restoration' of God. The need to state this clearly is what underlies Bernanos' disapproval of the physician as analyst – at least when psychiatric medicine is approached as an *alternative* to seeking out the priest as confessor. The one transcends guilt by analysing it away; the other transcends it by making of his own person the instrument of God's 'judgment of mercy', for the sinner's benefit. Only 'sacramental humility' can cope with the extreme forms pride takes. Bernanos was far less interested in what Balthasar rather snootily calls 'mechanical bourgeois confession'.[60]

Bernanos expects priests to be hated – they are so much the antithesis of unbelieving society – and tends to suspect something is wrong if they are not. The priest is akin to the imaginative writer in that both must know evil in a clairvoyant way. Bernanos' portrait of the good priest largely reflects the historical features of St Jean-Marie Vianney, the mid-nineteenth-century pastor of Ars, near Lyons. In the novels of the 1920s, notably *Sous le soleil de Satan*, Christian and notably priestly existence is utterly dramatic, a continued encounter with despair from which only constant 'transport' to a transcendent salvation can rescue it. Balthasar compares this period of Bernanos' writing to the dialectical theology of Karl Barth, which was more or less contemporary. But then Bernanos' outlook undergoes a softening. Grace becomes more human, just as happened in Barth's writing too. Eventually, he comes to portray the extraordinary in the humdrum and unselfconscious, to the point that the *curé de campagne*, hero of *The Diary of a Country Priest*, dies sublimely unaware of the humiliations he has suffered and in love with life as well as with the God he hopes for in death.

For Bernanos the priest's task as sacramental minister of the Word is to 'transfer the sinner into [the] sphere of the Word's truth'.[61] This requires supernaturalized insight. Basing himself on the life of Vianney, Bernanos took the view that by his ordination the ministerial priest has a special share in the divine light which sees and judges souls by the grace of God in Jesus Christ. (Not, in fact, a claim that the Catholic theology of Order makes.) Balthasar was, for reasons of his own, fascinated by this proposal. His readings in Scholastic philosophy had left him with a question. When someone knows some reality with full justice, and not according to some relative perspective, does the light in which he thus knows derive from the active mind's openness to divine light? Or does it derive – yes – from that source but also from an intelligibility intrinsic to the object itself? This sort of question – it is important in the opening volume of the theological aesthetics – became even more urgent, he felt, when asked in connexion with the supernatural life of souls. Not that Balthasar wholly approved of the way Bernanos dealt with it. As the name of the 1926 novel 'Under Satan's Sun' sufficiently shows, Bernanos was in danger of treating such a share in divine judgment as simultaneously a share in diabolic understanding. Seeing souls from within: this has about it the allure of Hell. The *same act* which holy

59 *Ibid.*, p. 401.
60 *Ibid.*, p. 411.
61 *Ibid.*, p. 420.

priests carry out in the utmost purity and humility of intention, the 'anti-priest' who gives his name to the 1943 novel *Monsieur Ouine* likewise performs in the name of the vampire-like voraciousness of the Infernal One. Knowledge of this kind is a dreadful temptation to concupiscence. For this Bernanos has an antidote which Balthasar *does* approve. It is looking *after the fashion of a little child*, with a gaze of simple love. Here is how Balthasar puts the theistic metaphysics involved.

> Without expressing his intuition in theoretical terms, Bernanos has here entered the innermost sphere of his epistemological and ontological convictions. A subject's penetration through knowledge into the openness of another's spiritual being can be defined as an act of truth, in the strict sense, only by being grounded in love – the love of God, which God makes available to his creatures. In the absence of such love, the medium of knowledge can only be love's opposite: the concupiscence of hell. Here there can be no neutral middle ground. The knowledge of another's spirit must either be creative through love or destructive through greed: for the other's spirit, as spirit, necessarily stands before God and is therefore inaccessible without God.[62]

Such knowledge has a function. It is to enable souls to win the 'battle' of confession. When the confessor's judgment coincides with divine judgment (so Balthasar insists the priest must never interpose a norm for judgment that is not that of Christ's Church), the grace of his sacramental office brings about an extraordinary effect. Insofar as the penitent's personal history and ancestral inheritance is a guilty one, it is 'unreal' – for all evil is an absence of the good that is another name for *being*. But by evaluating her confession in the light of Christ's Passion, death and descent (from which there emerges the might of his Resurrection), the priest's words confer on it 'the only truth it can have in the sight of eternity'.[63]

Balthasar makes the strong claim that 'perhaps more than any other Catholic in modern times', Bernanos was 'crucial in reviving the ecclesial meaning of the public confession of guilt'. Confession is made to a priest, but to a priest as representing not only God but also the communion of saints. Within that communion, there is no such thing as 'private' guilt. Likewise there is no such thing as 'private' absolution either. Bernanos seems to have drawn an analogy in this respect between public life and the domain of sacramental grace. Just as nothing can substitute for the obligation of confession – not even interior repentance, so, by analogy, there is an ineluctable necessity to acknowledge the misdeeds of agents in history. For Balthasar at least, all Bernanos' polemical writings about society, culture, politics have to be seen in a sacramental context.

Every sin is a bud of which, unless it be nipped, the flower is spiritual death. Bernanos excels in portraying the hellish aspects of human personality, the sense in which this world is already the portal of hell. He portrays the hellish as degraded, disintegrated, cold, passionless, insipid. Hell is: no longer to love. Like his predecessor Péguy – and indeed like his interpreter Balthasar – Bernanos was extremely worried by the issue of final damnation.

---

62 *Ibid.*, p. 429.
63 *Ibid.*, p. 435.

How is it compatible with human solidarity? Or with the universality of the divine salvific will? Balthasar finds in Bernanos a distinction between the 'Hell of misery', occupied or, if one prefers, constituted, by those who do not know love, and the Hell of the second death, which consists of those who do not *want* to know it. Kenotically, Christ and the saints descend into the first hell, stretching out a hand, as in the Byzantine Easter icon, to the dreadfully miserable. But those in the second Hell are 'woodlike'. They have petrified. They are reduced to the condition of things, not persons. They are but living memories of what they once were.

There is no doubt about the importance of the first Hell in Bernanos' oeuvre, or of the strikingly Christological way in which he treats it. It is, precisely, the situation of the miserably damned (those damned in the first sense) that suggests to the mind the idea of redemption. Theologically, for Bernanos, the thought of divine redemption is inexplicable without the abject wretchedness of such souls. What he made of the fate of the wantonly damned (those damned in the second sense) does not emerge so clearly from Balthasar's account. At times he moves close to a thesis of negative pre-destination – just as not all those who want to kill themselves can manage it, so not all those who would like to go to Hell can make it. At times, too, he suggests how the dimensions of Christian hope exceed the limits of formal eschatological doctrine: 'the Cross surpasses all possible hells; the hope of the Christian, therefore, is by its nature unlimited'.[64]

Anointing and Eucharist

When Balthasar embarks on the last theme drawn from the particular sacraments, 'the world of Anointing and Communion', his accent remains firmly eschatological and Christological. The Church, he writes, 'stands under the sign of a death agony' – and so Baptism, the sacrament of Christian initiation, is intrinsically related to Last Anointing, the sacrament of passage through death, just as the Holy Eucharist, the Christian's most typical act in the meantime, is the oblation of a love that persevered to the end. As this formulation may indicate, the term 'death agony' must be taken in its widest sense. As Balthasar's American translator notes, the Greek word *agôn* originally meant an assembly brought together to witness a contest. It then began to denote any kind of contest, not just sporting but (it might be) judicial. The psychological state of anguish is a further derived sense of 'agony'. The hierarchical order of these meanings is uppermost in Balthasar's mind. As Erasmo Leiva-Merikakis puts it:

> Christ's *agon* is one fought by the divine and human Hero in the presence of heaven and earth, to regain the divine image in man that has been lost through sin and Satan's trickery. The form this contest takes in Christ's life is his Passion, Cross, death and Resurrection, and hence it is the specifically Christian context that henceforth associates 'agony' with suffering and death, in union with Christ's paschal mystery.[65]

Still, the fact is that anxiety about dying preoccupied Bernanos from an early age. Balthasar considers it possibly pathological. That would not

64 *Ibid.*, p. 455.
65 *Ibid.*, p. 462.

prevent it from being divinely used to allow Bernanos to pursue the theme of death in accordance with his charism as a Christian author. Partly under the influence of *Action française*, he tried for a while to master this anxiety by adopting the cult of heroic death. He started to think of the moment of death as a privileged opportunity to see the self as in a mirror: hence his fascination with the French idiom for 'to realise one is dying', *se voir mourir* – literally, to 'see oneself die'. Balthasar's fear about all this is that Bernanos was turning death into its own brand of exalted egoism. Later, Bernanos corrects this. He stresses the helplessness of the expiring person, the likelihood that the attendant circumstances will be humdrum or even sordid, and – in striking contrast to his earlier portrayal – the element of incomprehension of what is happening. That is emphasized in his lives of St Dominic and St Joan of Arc. The subprioress in *Les Dialogues des Carmélites* voices his changed doctrine:

> Courage could very well be one of the devil's phantasms ... Only one thing matters: that, whether brave or cowardly, we should always be exactly where God wants us, entrusting ourselves to him for all the rest.

Bernanos has many death scenes, and the later ones are meant to confound those sold on heroics.[66]

Eschewing all death-bed theatricality, then, he begins to see death, and the death agony, in a fully Christological fashion. If the death of Christ *is* the redemption, then in it the destinies of all sinners are recapitulated. This is not the rejection of proper preparation for death, the *ars moriendi*. Rather is it another version of it. The weakness of man in the face of the terrible mystery of death *can* be made strong – but only in Jesus Christ. In the early Christian centuries, writers in the martyr-rich North African church drew a contrast between the dying Christian, fortified by the grace of Christ co-agonizing with her, and Jesus himself – who went to his death in a defencelessness that was deliberately absolute, seemingly God-forsaken, with no one to help. In *Les Dialogues des Carmélites* Bernanos recovers just this insight.

He still maintains that death is a great adventure, that it stamps a life with a unique seal. But he is inclined to compare it not to the feats of Titans but to the fearful wonder of a baby's birth. Birth and death entail 'chidlike self-entrusting to another and deepest shuddering in the act of surrender'.[67] They incorporate wonder and anguish in equal proportions. A strange combination, and the ground of its unity, theologically speaking, is the agony of God's eternal Child in Gethsemane garden. One must be denuded, naked before the Father, if one is to share the fruits of the Cross. Heidegger and Sartre thought that experiences of dread and alienation were ontologically revealing. This, for Bernanos (and Balthasar) shows how they actually *are*.

As we know, the Swiss theologian was fascinated by the theme of vicariously atoning, substitutionary representation. Already in this early study of a French writer he both finds it sounded and orchestrates it himself. In a nutshell: 'If a Christian is robbed of life, it is only that he might radiate light all the more abundantly'.[68] So grace acts in the communion of (sinners and)

---

66 G. Bernanos, *Les Dialogues des Carmélites* (Paris, 1949), p. 149.
67 *Bernanos, op. cit.*, p. 479.
68 *Ibid.*, p. 490.

saints, not least in dying. In *Sous le soleil de Satan*, the author remarks of Donissan: 'He gave out with full hands the peace he was deprived of'.[69]

For Bernanos, as for Balthasar, the Anointing of the Sick is a balm for spiritual wounds on the threshold of eternity. In Balthasar's lifetime the Western Catholic ritual of the sacrament was revised to make plain that it is celebrated not simply for those *in extremis* but for the wider clientele of the seriously ill. But Balthasar had no sympathy with any attempt to extend the range of its recipients. In his Bernanos study, he ignored the call already being made for a broader pastoral use of the sacrament, and after the Second Vatican Council continued to treat it as essentially a *rite de passage* for the dying. There is no need, accordingly, mentally to revise his text. In any case, in the concluding pages of 'The world of Anointing and Communion', Balthasar's Bernanos has little to say about the specifically sacramental dynamics of *either* Holy Anointing *or* the Holy Eucharist. He has little comment to make on their distinctive sacramental symbolism, which is, through the power of God, the means of their efficacy. Instead, he takes them as departure points for reflection on the solidarity of human beings in grace or sin, and the way the Redemption Christ won by his Passion can be mediated through the vicarious activity – or passivity – of Christians.

Thus Holy Anointing crystallizes Bernanos' accounts of the death agony, so different for the unrepentant sinner, for whom it is meaningless and the saint who 'plung[es] into the death agony like a cataract into a gulf of light and tenderness'.[70] And yet all human anguish is somehow contained within the redeeming anguish of God incarnate, of which this sacrament is the ecclesial vessel. Thanks to Christ, anguished fear and death itself, the most extreme solitude, become the 'wellspring of deepest communion'.[71] Thanks, again, to Christ's vicarious act of substitutionary representation in his Passion, the communion of saints has entry into the communion of sinners which it is to redeem. An awesome exchange takes place. Faithful disciples become responsible for the consequences of the sins of others. Hence Balthasar's emphasis on sympathy in its philological sense: 'suffering with'. This is the sense he gives to the Christian as 'salt of the earth'.

Not that there is a neutral notion of communion realized diversely in saints and sinners. The solidarity produced by the entangling of sinful destinies can only be delusory. And yet:

> The darker the dusk of solidarity in guilt, the brighter the dawn descending from the much more unfathomable abyss of *vicarious atonement*.[72]

Balthasar's theological dramatics, anticipated in *Mysterium Paschale*, will offer a supremely *objective* account of the Atonement. Chapter 8 of the present study has observed how Balthasar was in no way frightened by the language of *substitution* considered by some twentieth-century Catholics an Evangelical preserve. We saw how, at the same time, as a Catholic theologian he is, very naturally, also interested in the *subjective* appropriation of this

69 G. Bernanos, *Sous le soleil de Satan, op. cit.*, p. 206.
70 *Bernanos, op. cit.*, p. 502.
71 *Ibid.*, p. 504.
72 *Ibid.*, p. 514. Italics original.

Atonement, and the role played in this by the 'sub-mediatorial' activity of others. Hence the sustained attention devoted in these pages to *Dialogues des Carmélites* where this is *par excellence* Bernanos' theme. At the end of his account of how the spiritually fragile Sister Blanche is enabled to go singing to her martyrdom by the willing sacrifice for her of the stronger nuns, Balthasar remarks:

> Bernanos wants us to see ... that life and death are interchangeable within the one Body that must truly be called mystical.[73]

One consequence is that 'communion' – in general Christian usage, a term for happy fellowship – has for Bernanos (and Balthasar) something of the night about it. Only those who are prepared to let their essence bleed away enjoy the full communion of the wounded God. Only they allow his Blood to circulate through them into the whole solidarity of man. Being used, being used up, giving oneself in futile ways, squandering one's efforts on others: this is for Bernanos the true coin of mediated salvation. At the heart of it lies the Holy Eucharist: the broken Body, the outpoured Blood of the divine–human Failure, Jesus Christ, in his sacrificial oblation. Audaciously, Balthasar speaks of Judas's sacrilegious communion as the 'primal Cross' of Christ. Love wasted and betrayed, this is the ultimate archetype for the sacramental life of the Church'. Its acceptance is the secret of the saints. Such utter vulnerability produces humility, and especially – for Bernanos found self-love difficult, self-hatred terribly easy – the ability to love oneself humbly 'like any other of the suffering members of Jesus Christ'.[74] Bernanos sometimes spoke of the message of salvation as a letter which seemed to have arrived at the wrong address. He was unworthy of divine grace. The antidote was to be indifferent to the question whether one was worthy or not. For grace is gift. Only God exclusively *gives*. We *exchange*.

e. The Church and the Christian in time

In Balthasar's conclusion to *Bernanos* he looks at how the latter pictures Church and Christian *in time*. Balthasar was always interested in the question how salvation enters and affects the temporal flow. But here he was chiefly concerned with the way Bernanos exemplifies the Christian – the Churchman – taking responsibility for civil society: the 'temporal mission' of Catholicism.

Bernanos sees man as imperilled – first and foremost by his very existence, the way in which he inhabits his nature, but secondly by the terms of life in the modern world. Nothing much could be done about the first, except divinely, through God's grace and power. But the second was a matter of human willing – or default in *not* willing. It aroused Bernanos' righteous anger, especially where it touched the fate of the poor.

Balthasar provides a checklist of Bernanos' *gravamina* against mid-twentieth-century society. In themselves they differ very much: slavery to technology; overt or covert totalitarianism; philistinism; the tendency to conceal self in group anonymity. But they have a common theme: the threat to personal freedom and a sense of honour. Man is ceasing to be a sacred

---

73 *Ibid.*, p. 517.
74 G. Bernanos, *Journal d'un curé de campagne, op. cit.*, p. 529.

person and becoming a higher animal. Balthasar's explanation of Bernanos' continuing attachment to monarchism is instructive:

> [Bernanos] did not fight for the monarchy but rather for a type of man who would be free enough to want a monarchy: such a man would not perceive monarchy as oppression – as our democrats do – but as the liberating space within which something like human greatness could once again thrive.[75]

Neither Bernanos nor Balthasar seem to offer a definition of honour, a term which has largely disappeared from ethical discourse. But they do describe it. It is a necessary condition for splendour or sublimity in moral action. It can take a specifically Christian form, which it does when natural honour is synthesized with charity. Honour provides the distinctive ethos of the laity because they are the ones encharged with Christianity's mission to the world. The hierarchical Church must at all costs survive if she is to preach and administer the sacraments. Opportunistic compromise with *de facto* Governments or, more widely, the powerful, may have to be her way. But woe betide the ordinary Christian man if he goes down this path. The consequent forfeit of honour will destroy his Christ-given capacity to be salt for the earth. Honour requires that the 'temporal fidelity' of Christians be given in the 'visible' realm to 'princes' – those who by the services they render the citizen and the faithfulness they elicit have won legitimacy, and in the 'invisible' realm to 'the poor, the weak, the widow, the orphan, the forsaken'.[76]

The secularization of the soldier by the modern State has sapped chivalric honour; machine industrialism has marginalized the honour of the craftsman; and often enough economic conditions render family honour almost impossible as well. 'Christian man' – not the same as being a faithful member of the Church, for the Church teaches charity, not honour – will have to be reinvented. Bernanos saw *France* as called to testify to *Christian honour* – to be distinguished from its vainglorious Roman-imperial competitor and from a detached piety (two temptations to which he considered the French particularly prone). The French Revolution failed as a Christian revolution and became monstrous. It need not have. Like the Comte de Chambord, the Pretender to the French throne, Bernanos embraced 1789, rejected 1793. The revolution could have been a national renewal within the ambit of the ancient Christian monarchy and the Catholic civilization it housed, not over against them. Instead, French history produced a Church dominated by a bourgeoisie that had not become less materialistic in exchanging Voltaireanism for a refound Catholicism, while the poor – who should be the spiritual kings at the sacramental banquet – had been left to Marxism to corral.

Bernanos insisted that the Church was not enough. There must also be Christendom. As Balthasar puts it:

> The shrinking of 'Christendom' to 'the Church' and the loss of Christianity's self-evident claim upon and possession of 'temporal existence'

---

75 *Ibid.*, p. 551.
76 G. Bernanos, *Nous, les Français, op. cit.*, p. 138.

represented a colossal and irretrievable loss whose effects permeated the whole of Christian life and thought.[77]

Is all lost, then? No, for the Christian man or woman can still make the spirit of the old Christendom live in them and their actions, and this can be to potent effect. Christians must avoid the spirit of conformity, which would translate the virtue of obedient discipleship into terms of servility to the social mass. Balthasar also distinguished between lay obedience in the Church, and the obedience of monastics and other consecrated individuals. For layfolk, it is not a good thing to encourage a general disposition of docility to everything an ecclesiastical superior is minded to say. The pastoral office should not be over-extended into realms where individual Christians have their own responsibility to exercise.

This should take the form, though, of responsible obedience to the word of Church authority – and so bear a *relation* to monastic obedience. Likewise, so Bernanos thought, the vowed poverty of Religious ought to be reflected in a spirit of poverty in the lives of laymen. Balthasar's reading of Bernanos confirmed him in the view that

> the most authentic Christian locus ... is the place where the two con-
> trary forms and ideals of Christian life – that of the cloister or the
> religious orders and that of the laity in the world – open up to one
> another.[78]

The notion that the Christian existence most worthy of the name takes place at the intersection between the three evangelical counsels and full commit-ment to life in the world was conveniently implicit in Bernanos' writings. I write 'conveniently' because it neatly suited Balthasar's pursuit, with Adri-enne von Speyr, of the idea of the *Weltgemeinschaft* or 'Secular Institute'. Chapter 9 of this book showed how that was so.

Of course no institutional form can guarantee the realization of the spirit of the Beatitudes. And it is by an encomium of that spirit that Balthasar ends this work. More particularly it ends with Bernanos' references to its embo-diment in St Francis. Bernanos never wrote a life of Francis, as he did of Dominic. That did not stop him believing that if only the Christian people had listened to this saint, the history of Europe would have been altogether different, and for the better.

Schneider

Few English (or, more generally, Anglophone) readers are likely to have heard of Reinhold Schneider. Balthasar's focus on him may be explained in part by his Germanist enthusiasms. Though happy to be Swiss, and even happier to be a Luzerner, Balthasar was enamoured – as *Apokalypse der deutschen Seele* tells us – of German literature, thought, culture. There was, he regretted, no obvious German equivalent to Shakespeare, Calderón, Cor-neille, Pascal, Péguy, Claudel, Unamuno, Cervantes: a writer who would

77 *Ibid.*, p. 584.
78 *Ibid.*, p. 598.

serve a 'Catholic *Weltbild*, interpreting all reality in the sense of Christ'.[79] (It is interesting that Balthasar seems to assume Shakespeare was a Catholic, not a widely held view until the beginning of the twenty-first century.) Alas, Goethe – in principle Balthasar's great love among the German classics – had not the slightest idea of a German Catholic past. In this perspective, Schneider, wrote Balthasar in acclamation of his fiftieth birthday, was a star. Schneider's series of historical recreations – so many attempts to express the historical tendencies of different epochs in symbolic form, offer the 'holy German *Reich*' as a 'primordial expression' of the City of God.

This Schneider did not in any narrow nationalist spirit. He always saw that 'realm' in its sympathetic affinities with the entire Christian West: notably Portugal and Spain, France, England and Russia. More importantly still, Schneider sought to draw out the 'entire spiritual-intellectual order from the spirit of the Gospel'.[80] To a theologian of sanctity like Balthasar it could only be appealing that Schneider presented solidarity, and therefore peace, as positively requiring holiness – his 'world' was formed, thought Balthasar, 'from the saints of all lands'. Balthasar did not hesitate to use the phrase 'Schneider's penetrating and forceful theology', to be found not only in his explicitly religious writings – a commentary on the Our Father and the Way of the Cross, a book of meditations for priests, and the numerous hagiological short stories or scenes embedded in longer works – but also in his thousands of letters, many of them attempting to give a sense of spiritual orientation and support to soldiers at the front.[81]

Looking at history as he did from the standpoint of *value*, Schneider's literary aim was indeed to draw the spiritual profile of each age with which he dealt. This is not so extraordinary a phenomenon. Wilhelm Dilthey, the founder – or at least *namer* – of the 'human sciences', *Geisteswissenschaften*, in Germany, had considered that the *imagination* shows the historian the direction in which his proper mode of reason will seek to investigate and verify. History, the real process, is only intelligible, meaningful, through the human practice of 'history' – historiography, itself as much an art as a science.

Schneider's symbolic manner might be thought more appropriate to the exploration of ages when forms of power – and it is the conditions and exercise of power that especially interested him – were themselves symbolically ordered. The affinity for such epochs helps to explain his brief dalliance with National Socialism, spurred by the 'Potsdam Ceremonies' whereby Hitler sought to reconnect the post-First World War history of Germany with that of Prussia and, more widely, the Second Reich. That seemed to Schneider a desirable re-possession by the Germans of their own past in its significant continuities.[82] Schneider was a Legitimist and an aristocratically minded traditionalist but hardly a militarist and certainly not a Nazi. If his *Die Hohenzollern* (1933) was suppressed shortly after publication,

79 'Reinhold Schneider. Zu seinem 50. Geburtstag am 13 Mai', *Der christliche Sonntag* 5. 19, 10 May 1953, p. 149.
80 *Ibid.*, p. 150.
81 'Reinhold Schneider', *Internationale Bodensee Zeitschrift* 3. 2–3 (1953), pp. 17–22 and here at pp. 17–18.
82 See J. Steinle, *Reinhold Schneider (1903–1958). Konservatives Denken zwischen Kulturkrise, Gewaltherrschaft und Restaurantion* (Aachen, 1992), pp. 90–91.

and his book about England *Der Inselreich. Gesetz und Grösse der britischen Macht* (1936) had to be withdrawn, both on political grounds, this was followed by his expulsion from the 'Chamber of the Writers of the Reich', and continuing harrassment throughout the Second World War. That of course does not make him a man of the Left. Balthasar's interest in him, however, is not fuelled by political conservatism so much as by a desire to exploit what Schneider could offer as *materials for a theology of mission*, and notably in the sphere of the world.

More specifically, as Balthasar reports in his preface to the second edition of his Schneider book:

> What was most fascinating in [Schneider's] work was the omnipresent drama of the encounter between two missions that are equally original and yet stand in a deadly mutual conflict: the mission of the one who is entrusted with the task of administering the earthly realm and the mission of the saint as the real symbol of the kingdom of God that descends into the world.[83]

(Indeed, Balthasar saw this 'drama' as applicable to the case of the Secular Institutes like his own *Johannesgemeinschaft*: these too were meant to be worldly – in the best sense – yet radically evangelical.) Balthasar points out how Schneider had never been autobiographical until the appearance of the first edition of Balthasar's own essay in theologico-literary criticism of his work.[84] Hitherto Schneider had determined, rather like Kierkegaard a century earlier, to 'argue' by means of his own existence. Balthasar implies that the publication of his Schneider book, which prescinded from all biographical data so as to concentrate purely on the *form* of his work, may have been a stimulus to Schneider to write his life-story down. Under the section-title 'Curtain', Balthasar will consider how the last, somewhat painful, autobiographical works fit into the Schneiderian scheme.

In the introduction to the first edition – which, apart from the major addendum just mentioned, he left largely unchanged nearly forty years later – Balthasar emphasizes the Carlylean aspect of Schneider. Schneider is a writer for heroes: poets, kings and saints, in that order. But the difference from the Scottish Victorian sage also leaps to the eye:

> The leaders are justified, not by their personality, but only by their mission and their humility in the presence of a truth that they themselves are not.[85]

Schneider judges his figures and their conjunctures by reference to a criterion only faith makes possible: the standard of holiness. That said, dominating Schneider's work are figures of world-historical significance set against their landscape. Balthasar takes his cue from that in laying out his Schneider study at once chronologically and topographically.

83 H. U. von Balthasar, *Nochmals: Reinhold Schneider* (Einsiedeln-Fribourg, 1991); ET *Tragedy under Grace. Reinhold Schneider on the Experience of the West* (San Francisco, 1997), p.11.
84 H. U. von Balthasar, *Reinhold Schneider. Sein Werk und Weg* (Einsiedeln, 1953).
85 *Idem, Tragedy under Grace, op. cit.*, p. 17.

(i) Portugal

Schneider's earliest literary expedition (both in fact and in imagination) was to Portugal, whose golden age he conjured up in his study of *The Lusiad*, the Portuguese national epic. In 1918, the Second Reich collapsing about him, the young Schneider took refuge in Portugal. As Balthasar comments, melodramatically:

> he takes up his position at the point where the continent descends into the ocean, and he absorbs into all his pores the oozing away of the West.[86]

As yet unreconciled to his ancestral Catholicism, Schneider, in his Iberian period, fell under the spell of the Spanish Existentialist author Miguel de Unamuno. Unamuno's 1913 study *Del sentimento tràjico de la vida* is a somewhat lugubrious celebration of 'noble pride' as the proper bearer of the tragic dimension of life. But Schneider appears to have taken it as the key to Portugal's century of greatness and failure to which the massive poem by Luís Vaz de Camões (c. 1524–1580) bears witness. Schneider's 'The Passion of Camões or the Decline and Fulfilment of Portuguese Power' investigates the materials that went into the making of Camões' work.[87] Schneider shows how the ruthlessness of Portuguese colonization removes plausibility from its claim to be inspired by the Christian idea, and how too the mother country was impoverished through intoxication with the thought of far-off realms and their riches. Portugal's 'greatness' was a dream. Camões' poem transfigured the historical events imagistically but could not change their historical actuality. Even a great poet could not transform into pure quixotry the 'greedy, tragic passion for power and possession'. This was the kind of common (universal?) existential contradiction in human experience which served as a typical starting-point for Schneider's spiritual–intellectual journey, as (in Balthasar's comparison) 'idea and concept' for Plato or 'reality living through form' in Aristotle.[88] For Schneider at this stage of his aeneid, 'existence was incurable'.[89] Yet even at this early date, Balthasar divined in Schneider's work something that went beyond such philosophical pessimists as Schopenhauer (and Unamuno). And this was a sense for:

> the Catholic 'ordering of being', the possibility of uniting heaven and earth (and idea and existence) that is portrayed best in the Incarnation of God.[90]

In fact, this judgment anticipates Schneider's development. At the time of writing his main preoccupation was nihilism and the way some kind of positive form might be established by starting from zero. He explained this miracle in Nietzschean terms: it comes from the will of life for power. Only gradually, and without at first any credal commitment, would he abandon this position. Nietzschean will is immanent in the world, but, Schneider came to think, form comes to be only through a world-transcending transposition

---

86 *Ibid.*, p. 35.
87 R. Schneider, *Das Leiden des Camoes oder die Untergang und die Vollendung der portugie-sischen Macht* (Hellerau, 1930).
88 'Reinhold Schneider', *art. cit.*, p. 18.
89 *Tragedy under Grace*, p. 133.
90 *Ibid.*, p. 45.

of life. One could call that 'faith' on the understanding that in this case the word is essentially a metaphor.

Meanwhile, Balthasar sought to stand back from Schneider's study of Portugal and its poet to reflect on the presuppositions of the German author's writing. For Schneider, as a culture declines, the historical process tends to produce images which transcend their own origins and function as 'representations of eternal meaning'.[91] In an essay collection published ten years later, Schneider spoke of history forming 'images that stand above the ages with the power of allegories'. Comparing such images in their seeming inexhaustibility to the power of the revealed word, he saw them as earthly media for expressing a trans-worldly reality. They 'make visible the substance of an epoch in its relation to eternity'. Might it be possible then, to 'summarize' via such images 'the history of peoples, and the salvation history hidden in this'?[92]

Schneider was fascinated by decline as well as flourishing. This was pertinent to Portugal, not least. But the remarks just cited contain nothing on its especial significance. It may have been, then, under the influence of Oswald Spengler's 'The Decline of the West', that Balthasar generalizes the decline theme in Schneider's study and adds:

The price paid for the supratemporal validity of the image is the life that belongs to time: life must die to itself in order to become an image; indeed the image itself is most eloquent precisely when it is in the process of arising out of death, as the perpetuation of the life that sacrifices itself, as tragedy that has taken on form.[93]

If so, Spengler's culture pessimism has been brightened by the 'die and become' theme in which Balthasar found the secret evangelicalism of the German Romantics. In any case, circumstantial evidence supporting Balthasar's 'take' on Schneider are found in the rôle that images of life-in-death play in the latter's work. Kings – major symbolic figures for Schneider – are portrayed supremely in their dying. Balthasar lauds Schneider's imagism.

All the images are completely open, unlike the symbolism that understands them as something ultimate; they are as open as the wound of existence from which they flow. The concept (as its name indicates) is something that closes; the image is something that opens, because it points to what is depicted in the image.[94]

That chimes with the approach of Balthasar's theological aesthetics.

But back in conclusion to Portugal, the 'land at earth's margins', 'the land of the dreamers and of the poet satiated with suffering' whither Schneider fled, 'the inheritance of German dialectics as the thorn in his heart'. Balthasar gives us a clue to the nature of his interest in Schneider when he writes:

91 *Ibid.*
92 R. Schneider, *Macht und Gnade. Gestalten, Bilder und Werte in der Geschichte* (Wiesbaden, 1940), p. 262.
93 *Tragedy under Grace*, p. 47.
94 *Ibid.*, p. 49.

Here it was possible to combine classical humanism with an eschato-logical-utopian radicalism and thereby to lay the foundations of an interpretation of existence in extreme terms as historical struggle.[95]

Congruently with the above judgment, Balthasar notes Schneider's lack of enthusiasm for St Thomas, whose work he considered insufficiently indebted to the Johannine Apocalypse, the final book of Scripture, the starting-point for Balthasar's own theological dramatics. Thomas remains attached to 'creation and its ordering'. But the 'most concrete historical ordering' is more like that revealed in the Book of Revelation, with its 'tensions and cata-strophes'. And these, wrote Schneider in his retrospect on his own literary career at mid-century, 'shatter the world of St Thomas'.[96] Schneider is counterposing to Thomist creation-thinking a thinking based on eschatology (and Christology). For Balthasar, however, these positions are not so much opposed as complementary.

(ii) Spain

Schneider's account of Spanish 'form' turns crucially on Philip II, and its main lines are laid down in the subtitle of his study 'Philip II, or Religion and Power'.[97] The heart of the book is a philosophy of kingship – which in Bal-thasar's hands *qua* Schneider expositor becomes a theology of the same. But, as we shall see, both Schneider and Balthasar treat kingship as the key to a metaphysic for Everyman. Schneider writes about Philip of Spain's mind-set but in a way so hostile to psychological reductionism that it leaves psy-chology behind. As Balthasar explains:

> Philip must be misunderstood by all who do not live out of faith as he does. His existence is the end of psychology, because the force out of which he lives and constructs lies beyond his soul.[98]

Schneider cites approvingly Novalis' claim that in modern times the 'masks of psychology' have been erected in the sanctuary where by right the 'images of the gods' should be. Specifically, no one who is unprepared to die to himself and to the 'claims and abilities of his own soul' will ever understand the greatness of 'existence as office and representation'.

Now 'office' and 'representation' are recurring terms in Balthasar's ecclesiology and theology of the saints. For his part, Schneider was more inclined, in his early period, to express what was happening in Fichtean terms. The 'idea' (key Fichtean term) so took hold of Philip that nothing was left of his personality save continuous sacrifice thereto.[99] Balthasar cites tellingly from Schneider's nearly contemporary work on the Hohenzollern dynasty to make the point that 'spiritual, metaphysical decision', and not a Legitimism of blood, lies at the heart of Schneiderian royalism.

> The mystery of this appearance does not lie in the blood but rather in the demand made; this is the genuine nobility of kings. Where the

95 *Ibid.*, p. 50.
96 R. Schneider, *Rechenschaft. Worte zur Jahrhundertmitte* (Einsiedeln, 1951), p. 75.
97 *Idem, Philipp II oder Religion und Macht* (Leipzig, 1931).
98 *Tragedy under Grace, op. cit.*, p. 53.
99 For Schneider's interest in Fichte, see his *Fichte. Der Weg der Nation* (Munich, 1932).

greatest demands are made, the greatest fruit will be borne, and there is only one presupposition for this: that this demand is completely understood and is grasped as a new life ... A king is never bourgeois; his task is to live out in the eyes of his subjects that which is most rare and uncommon: the consuming service of the idea.[100]

The king is essentially tragic, and the nature of the world appears vicariously in him. He represents all his subjects, and is 'expropriated' (a capital term of Balthasar's Mariology) into their universal dimension. So the king lives out a *vicarially representative existence* – which is why kingship can be, in the Son of David, the 'vessel for the archetypical revelation of the God-man'.[101]

At Schneider's (and Balthasar's) time of writing, the European intellectual scene was increasingly dominated by the 'historical metaphysics' of Existential philosophy – being as time and becoming. Balthasar was not wholly against this, as his Nyssa book demonstrates. But he knew it was not enough. An 'aristocratic metaphysics' suggested by the practice of kingship 'transcends' such historical metaphysics, so Balthasar suggested, in the

> only direction that is creative of values and of the world, which unintentionally justifies the highest culture and past and overcomes nihilism.[102]

The prince is to be himself in such a way that all are included in him – the whole people in its historical being, in past, present and future. Hence Schneider's doctrine of the mutuality of the people's will and the king's will. As Balthasar explains:

> The genuine king is possible only when a country thinks in kingly terms, and this thinking leads it to demand the corresponding image of its ruler. Then the visible crown would be so strong that it would make the secret, invisible crown shine in all hearts.[103]

Kings in a kingless time (above all in a post-Christian time) are truly to be pitied. This is the burden of Schneider's account of Frederick William IV of Prussia in 'The Crown that was Saved'.[104]

Balthasar considers one can almost go so far as to speak of the crowning of kings, in Schneider, as an *opus operatum*, an infallibly given grace, as in the Catholic sacraments. In Schneider's own words: 'Offices have a force that continues to work even when the bearers do not correspond to their offices' – a comment made in his study of English history, 'The Island Realm'.[105] More particularly, Philip II rules at the Escorial in close symbiosis with the monks of the palace monastery. He rules 'with the experience of the monk'. As Schneider puts it:

> This is the only form of life of the Catholic monarch, the form now discovered at last: as his kingdom is a fief received from God so he

100 *Idem, Die Hohenzollern. Tragik und Königtum* (Leipzig, 1933), pp. 10–11,
101 *Tragedy under Grace, op. cit.*, p. 55.
102 *Ibid.*
103 *Ibid.*, p. 62.
104 R. Schneider, *Die gerettete Krone: Erzählungen* (Munich, 1948), pp. 120–38.
105 *Idem, Der Inselreich. Gesetz und Grösse der britischen Macht* (Leipzig, 1936), p. 379.

himself dwells in God's house together with men who are subject to God, not to him.[106]

Here highest pride and deepest humility coincide. Personality is instrumentalized – yet does not become anonymous in the modern sense, for it is 'the essence of the personality to stand before the Absolute and be under obligation to it'.[107] Clearly, Schneider is ascribing to kingship an objective form of holiness – to which, adds Balthasar (and this is a characteristic emphasis of his entire theology of office) 'personal-subjective holiness' should conform.[108] Fortunately, nearly every European people has seen in history at least *one* saint among its kings and queens. Though Schneider was not yet, at this time of writing, a convinced Catholic, he had discerned a great truth.

> He has been affected by the overwhelming truth of the form of the expression and, in search of its source, has stumbled on humility.[109]

The king is close to the monks, and as Schneider's later meditation on St Louis of France suggests, to the priest. 'Priest and king, the chosen distributor of heavenly grace and the one installed in office to administer the fragile earthly power', are interrelated. They 'encounter one another in the mystery of the crown of thorns, the sign of kingly priesthood hidden in history'.[110]

It will irritate some people, says Balthasar, that Schneider is uninterested in the abstract philosophical doctrine of the State, which Balthasar himself is happy to define in a Thomist way as the '*bonum commune* and the various constitutional possibilities of realizing this'.[111] Schneider is concerned with the ideality of human existence in history – and that cannot prescind from eternal destiny, however rare the connexion in politology.

For the traveller in Castile, Philip is inseparable from the Escorial – at once palace, church, monastery and funerary monument. Balthasar gives the building a philosophical interpretation. 'The spirit of representation demands in terms of its own concept that it become an image.'[112] The king is not forbidden to turn his palace into a place of perpetual prayer, just as the mystical saints of the period (Balthasar mentions Teresa of Avila and Ignatius Loyola) are allowed to turn to the world to change the face of the earth. Balthasar's spirituality of 'holy worldliness' recurs here with force. On the statues of the royal dead set up alongside those of the saints in the Habsburg mausoleum he comments:

> The king knows that he does not negate life by looking thus into death: the dead kings and saints are living, and they join the work of shaping the future in the communion of saints.[113]

Secular power, like art, can transcend itself in the direction of grace.

---

106 *Idem, Iberisches Erbe* (Olten, 1949), p. 294.
107 *Idem, Weltreich und Götterreich. Drei Vorträge.* (Munich, 1946), p. 46.
108 *Tragedy under Grace, op. cit.*, p. 60.
109 *Ibid.*, p. 61.
110 R. Schneider, *Der Priester im Kirchenjahr der Zeit* (Freiburg, 1946), p. 109.
111 *Tragedy under Grace, op. cit.*, p. 61.
112 *Ibid.*, p. 75.
113 *Ibid.*, p. 67.

The connexion of Philip II with Schneider's Portugal book is that a like melancholy passes over it. But theologically considered, in the Spain book the melancholy discloses hidden triumph.

> The mystery of the Spanish power is the faith. Its power becomes most visible where the secular power begins to dwindle; where earthly certainty sees decline and doom as inevitable. It is here that its line intersects the sinking human curve and draws up out of it what must be salvaged.[114]

Just so Philip has a Mass of thanksgiving celebrated in all the churches of Spain when he hears the news of the Armada's failure, which itself followed on the loss of the Dutch Provinces. Comments Balthasar: 'Despite all its booty, the North, which abandoned the form of the faith [by adopting Protestantism], has won nothing, and despite all its losses, the South has lost nothing [essential]'.[115] For the Portuguese dream, the world was only appearance. By contrast, Spanish faith is

> the penetration from appearance to being, from the apparent power of men to the power of the Lord, from the apparent glory of the earth to the glory of the kingdom of God.[116]

Pace Philip II's response to the Armada disaster, a faith whose law was *not* the 'night of the Cross' could hardly be the 'folly of Christ'. In saying as much, Balthasar anticipates Schneider's later Catholic turn, but there were already straws in the wind. It is through the Cross that Schneider would find his way back to the faith, writing his book on England. But meanwhile there was Prussia.

(iii) Prussia

Here Schneider was still concerned with power and its tragic entailments. Written in 1933, the year Adolf Hitler became German Chancellor, 'The Hohenzollerns, Tragedy and Kingship' is a drama in three acts.[117] The foci are: firstly, the rise of the Order of Teutonic Knights, ascetic militants, Christian organizers of the sands and steppes of heathen Prussia; then, after the Protestant Reform, the expansionist Elector of Brandenburg-Prussia Frederick William I; and finally, his even more successful son, the enlightened despot and strategist Frederick II, 'The Great'. Schneider's book, culminating in its portrait of the 'heroic nihilism' of Frederick the Great, is a study in the dynamics of power, power's inherent restless drive. As his foe the Austrian empress Maria Theresa learned to her cost, 'the perfect army demanded to be put to the test'.[118] Here Schneider's book on Fichte may be considered a fitting epilogue. To interpret the soul, as Fichte does, under the sign of will – and therefore power – is typically Prussian and indeed, so Balthasar adds, thinking no doubt of the Nominalist background of the German Reformation, Protestant. The pity about Fichte was his inability to

---

114 *Ibid.*, p. 70.
115 *Ibid.*, p. 71.
116 *Ibid.*, p. 74, citing R. Schneider, *Stunde des heiligen Franz von Assisi* (Colmar, 1941), p. 15.
117 *Idem, Die Hohenzollern, Tragik und Königtum* (Leipzig, 1933).
118 *Tragedy under Grace, op. cit.*, p. 84.

experience the infinite as an overwhelming that comes from outside
himself because he only feels it in himself as a burning summons to the
deed.[119]

Hence the charge of covert atheism levelled against him. But hence too, more
widely, the way his philosophy encapsulates the 'German achievement' –
what Schneider calls 'a deification of becoming, in thought, in word, in
sound, in deed, carried through to the last sacrifice'.[120] The Fichtean 'I' is
primal history portraying itself in the world, and through that 'I' God portraying himself there. It is God 'taking on form in the material of destinies
and kingdoms'.[121] Schneider seems to underwrite at least an element of this:
the Absolute is life pouring itself into and through forms in order to break
them. Not this nisus towards contradiction does Balthasar admire in him but,
rather, another feature of the Fichte study:

> the admiring vision, full of compassion, of the great soul that sacrifices
> itself to give its testimony in the sphere of history, constructing its
> order and disclosing its eternal meaning.[122]

But more and more – and this is the key to Schneider's imminent return to
Catholic belief and practice – Schneider realized that *what* he admired in this
'vision' was really:

> a primordial Christian experience that could find its appropriate lan-
> guage only in a Christian *theology* of history under the sign of the
> Cross.[123]

What was necessary was to retrace the path followed by that secularized
theology which is German Idealism, reversing specifically first secularism,
then Protestantism, and finally Nominalism. What Schneider had to overcome was the antithesis posed with such sharpness by Max Scheler in his
later (post-Catholic) period: power itself is devoid of value, value in itself
devoid of power. Schneider had to set his face against the great anti-Christian
'renunciation' by 'modern thought and life' of the 'organic unity between
spirit and body, between God and man'.[124] Through his book on England
when he rediscovers traditional Christendom, Schneider's vision becomes,
for Balthasar, fully valid. But two insights of the earlier works remain: the
'Iberian' insight that greatness lies in self-forgetful service, the 'Prussian'
insight that the 'source of all history is an invisible decision in the inner space
of the soul'.[125]

(iv) England
When he came to write 'The Island Realm', Schneider's mind was made up.
History is to be viewed from the vantage-point of faith. He had conceived, so
Balthasar maintains, a theology of history in an Augustinian mould. With the

119 *Ibid.*, p. 87.
120 R. Schneider, *Die Hohenzollern, op. cit.*, p. 197.
121 *Ibid.*, p. 170.
122 *Tragedy under Grace, op. cit.*, p. 92.
123 *Ibid.*, p. 93.
124 *Ibid.*, p. 94.
125 *Ibid.*

foundering of his three-volume project on the German Reich (he feared it would only too easily suffer misinterpretation after Hitler's coming to power), 'The Island Realm' is the only complete example of such a 'theology of history' we have from his hand. Schneider's concern is for 'demonstrable ethical-religious guilt, ... particular wrong decisions taken in history'. Schneider held *guilt* to be the single strongest motif in English literature. He claimed he had identified three structural moments of its dominance in English history – the Conquest of England by William of Normandy, Henry VIII's separation of England from Rome, and the official murder of Charles I. The revolt of the American colonies, in Schneider's opinion, was the island realm reaping what it had sown, and sown too well. What were those dragons' teeth? They were, for Schneider, *the betrayal of unity*. As Balthasar explained on his behalf, it is not that the English were more guilty than other peoples. Rather, their history is 'symbolically representative for history, indeed existence, at large'.[126]

Schneider's approval of the peaceful circumstances of the conversion of England to the faith and the quasi-unification of much of its territory under Alfred (the 'perfect Christian king') drives his disapprobation of William the Conqueror. 'Cunning', so Balthasar reports, 'forces the law onto its side; power subjects to itself the Rome of diplomacy, the episcopacy, the monks, the faith'.[127] The Conquest marks a 'decisive leap from justice to power'. The question recurs of the terms on which kingship is held. The decision of the barons in forcing Magna Carta onto King John may have been correct. Yet it opened a 'wound' that one day will lead Charles I to mount the Whitehall scaffold. Schneider claims to detect in mediaeval England a deficient feeling for the sacred character of the crown. 'The king had sinned against the spirit of his office; was this an argument against the office?'[128] Refusing to distinguish the idea of the crown from the one who bears it permitted Henry VIII's fateful decision to follow his conscience. That meant withdrawal to an internal dimension, unverifiable from without, while abandoning the external sphere to 'pure power'. Shakespeare proceeded to write the epilogue of the old England; Marlowe, with his amorality, the prologue for the new. As for Charles I, in Schneider's hands, the highest tragic pathos surrounds the martyr-king's 'expiatory death' – though in the burning of the old London in the Great Fire the Tower will survive, 'gloomy symbol of guilt and of power, and of their unity'.[129] The Tower of London is the 'decisive counter-image to the monastic palace of Castile'.[130]

Before leaving Schneider's England, Balthasar adds a magnificent excursus of his own. Only faith can be the ultimate guide for reason in a world both sinful and redeemed – the true faith, which is in God incarnate and the mediation of his grace that is Mary/the Church. Schneider himself would explore that claim by means of a constellation of figures around the time of the writing of *Inselreich*. In *Kaiser Lothar* there shines St Otto of Bamberg,

126 'Reinhold Schneider', *art. cit.*, p. 19.
127 *Tragedy under Grace, op. cit.*, p. 100.
128 R. Schneider, *Das Inselreich, op. cit.*, p. 101.
129 R. Schneider, *Macht und Gnade* (Wiesbaden, 1940), p. 8.
130 *Tragedy under Grace, op. cit.*, p. 103.

pacific missionary in Pomerania.[131] In 'Scenes from the Age of the Con-quistadors: Las Casas before Charles V',[132] Schneider takes as his hero the Dominican friar who 'overflowed with Christian rage', denounced the crimes of the Spanish conquerors in Latin America, and took the part of 'father of the humiliated children of nature'.[133] All three books, but especially the last, raise the question: which is prior, grace (the law of Christ) or power (the law of fallen nature)? When a Christian theologian is speaking the answer might seem obvious. But things are not so simple. As Balthasar asks:

> Was it not the fatal great renunciation, the apostasy from the real Christian task, when the State was relativised as merely the work of men and refuge was sought in the absolute sphere of 'grace'?[134]

There seems, then, to be a contradiction in the heart of Christian existence. How might it be resolved?

Balthasar himself starts from the axiom that through the soul's orientation to eternity history is what it is. It is in history that the fruits of spirit's contemplation are shown (a distinctively modern spiritual perception which for Balthasar – ever since the early 'Patristik, Scholastik, und wir'– marks an advance on ancient and mediaeval thought). In this sense, the soul itself is 'radically historical'; 'the body is its history, and so history becomes its body'.[135] That is why the individual in history is now given more weight by Schneider, alongside the 'representatives': the king, and the saint. Balthasar refers to a study by Schneider of holy women which proposed to indicate the *historical* fruitfulness of their prayer, from Hannah in the books of Samuel to Joan of Arc.[136] Thus is Scheler's 'fateful system' overcome: the spirit is 'not powerlessness vis-à-vis the dark depths of the mighty world of the instincts, for the primary power lies with the spirit'.[137] But the power of the soul must always be seen in its immediate relation to the God of eternal grace: there is, after all, only one goal for humankind and that is not natural but super-natural in kind.

> Man's true power, as God intends it, is power derived from the rela-tionship to what is ultimate, to the goal of grace, that is, power in subordination to the one who reveals God's eternal power in the world, Jesus Christ ..., and in union with the Church that has received his communion. ... In the case of Christ this is a power that enters the sphere of darkness and of the demonic powers to take up the struggle against them and to extend the power of God on earth.[138]

What we always have to ask is, In some given case, does power assist people to move towards *caritas* or towards *cupiditas* – closer to the supernatural goal of life or further away from it? Here Schneider's Augustinianism enters into

---

131 R. Schneider, *Kaiser Lothars Krone. Leben und Herrschaft Lothars von Supplinburg* (Leipzig, 1937).
132 *Idem, Las Casas vor Karl V. Szenen aus der Konquistadorenzeit* (Leipzig, 1938).
133 *Tragedy under* Grace, *op. cit.*, p. 105.
134 *Ibid.*, p. 107.
135 *Ibid.*, pp. 110, 112.
136 R. Schneider, *Pfeiler im Strom* (Wiesbaden, 1958).
137 *Tragedy under Grace, op. cit.*, p. 113.
138 *Ibid.*, p. 115.

its own. Is power serving the *civitas Dei* or the *civitas terrena sive diaboli* (the 'city of earth and the Devil'), intertwined as their stories are till the end of time? Hence the need for the discernment of spirits, vigilance and prayer.

Exercising such discernment in regard to the principles involved, Balthasar explains:

> Schneider often comes close to asserting, in the sense of the earlier [heroic-tragic] dialectic [of the Iberian studies] that collaboration in the earthly kingdom means that one becomes guilty out of necessity; in such passages, to be guilty seems to be a quality attaching to action within history. But Christ did not become guilty when he acted, nor did his Mother. The Cross can be called tragic because the ultimate contradiction is fought out to the end in this suffering, but the Incarnation itself cannot be called tragic, for the human nature of the Son does not stand in antithesis to his divine nature... It is not Being that is tragic; the tragic has a boundary. Schneider knows this: 'Tragedy ends in the presence of humility, as it ends in the presence of perfect love'.[139]

In the death on the Cross lies the victory – and so the contradiction explodes.

In effect, Balthasar criticizes Schneider for excess of dualism whereby power is neutral for man until it bears the sign either of heaven or hell, grace or rebellion. For Balthasar, man's power is 'not only a relation to God's power; it is, to begin with, a quality of his being'.[140] When considered on the basis of creation, and in its potential, it is, in the words of Genesis, something 'very good'.[141] Balthasar was more sorry than surprised not to see in Schneider greater respect for natural law.

> Through sin, of course, a shadow has been cast on the 'natural law' that is as deep as the shadow cast on the nature of man himself, which falls into guilt, misery and death. But no matter how profound the degenerations of the 'primary natural law' (that of paradise) may be supposed to be in the 'secondary natural law' (corresponding to the fallen human condition), they do not justify us in hopping over man's essential structure, both in his individual aspect and in his social and political aspect; the State, too, whose coercive character has been made necessary by the fall is not per se evil, but rather good.[142]

It is best, thinks Balthasar, to see Schneider's reflections as starting where natural law thinking ends. The word of the Gospel reveals in Cross and Resurrection the Creator's *ultimate* intention which cannot be read off from the natural structures of this world (especially under sin). Such structures do not give human life its *full* meaning. That is why they must remain open to the realm of grace, to positive revelation in both grace and judgment. A natural law doctrine of the State, for instance, needs complementing by an account of its historicity within the single supernatural order. The principles of natural law take us a certain way, but the immediate decisions on which

---

139 *Ibid.*, pp. 118–19, with an internal citation of R. Schneider, *Corneilles Ethos in der Ära Ludwigs XIV. Eine Studie* (Leipzig, 1939), p. 97.
140 *Ibid.*, p. 123.
141 'Il potere dell'uomo seconda la rivelazione biblica, I', *Humanitas* 18 (1963), pp. 113–22, and here at pp. 114–15.
142 *Tragedy under Grace, op. cit.*, pp. 123–24.

the good (or ill) of peoples turns require more. Such decisions call for evaluation as 'decisions of humility or of pride, of piety or of godlessness'.[143] For
Schneider, by Christian reflection on our accumulated historical knowledge
of war and its effects, we can tell that a Gospel of non-resistance is what the
Church ought to be preaching in civilized society today.

(v) Russia

As a counterpart to the historical guilt explored in 'The Island Realm', three
concepts now receive fresh emphasis in Schneider's work: truth, conscience,
confession. Henceforth they will constitute his chief response to history's
demands. In the words of the *starets* (an Orthodox spiritual guide) in
Schneider's evocation of Napoleon's contemporary, Tsar Alexander I: 'The
truth displays no grace. It is grace itself'. To which Alexander replies, 'It
judged me without any accusation. It *was* the accusation itself.'[144] The
'missing piece' in Schneider's scheme is supplied from Russia – Holy Russia,
or at least the Russia that is the

> homeland of the naked souls, of the sinners who make their confession
> without restraint, of the solidarity passionately grasped in guilt and in
> grace.[145]

Balthasar calls Russia 'The Good Thief', the one who 'bows before the verdict
and is exalted above all imagining'. Dostoevsky and other Russian authors
knew this. In their novels, 'the guilty person admits before everyone the deed
he has covered up and thus becomes everyone's brother'.[146] As Balthasar
comments:

> Thus confession takes on its social dimension not only because the
> individual receives new tasks and strengths for the fellowship through
> being purified but, on a much deeper level, because it is completely
> impossible for him as an individual to submit himself to the judgment
> of grace without at the same time involving in a mysterious manner the
> fellowship with which and because of which he became guilty and
> which fell into new and alien guilt through his guilt.

And he concludes:

> If guilt is in its most profound essence the lack of love, which creates
> isolation, so that there is in the deepest sense no fellowship in guilt,
> then the paradoxical fellowship in guilt becomes a true fellowship
> within the act of confession.[147]

And what transpires is a 'clarification and cleansing' of the realm of history
which in this way shares in the judgment of the world by God and Christ as
does in a different modality (compare Bernanos) sacramental Confession.

Schneider's 'Russian' writings raise in Balthasar's mind the question of
vicarious atonement and thus the issue of readiness to suffer. It was

143 *Ibid.*, p. 126.
144 R. Schneider, *Der Traum des Eroberers. Zar Alexander: Zwei Dramen* (Wiesbaden, 1951),
     pp. 110, 113.
145 *Tragedy under Grace, op. cit.*, p. 134.
146 *Ibid.*, p. 136.
147 *Ibid.*, p. 136.

apparently from the culture of pre-Revolutionary Russia that Schneider picked up a teaching on non-resistance – from Avvakum and the Old Believers, from Alexander I at the end of his reign, from Nikolai Leskov's *On the End of the World* and the anonymous author of *The Way of a Pilgrim*. Balthasar lists a long catalogue of Western non-resisters whom Schneider lauded – and their Old Testament archetype, Daniel in the lions' den. (Schneider has a loving description of the sculpted Romanesque image of Daniel at Worms.[148]) Balthasar, however, finds himself unable to travel with him all the way. Schneider's

> non-resistance extends to the cosmos that fell through man's sin and has been caught up against its will into violence: he has the Franciscan compassion with the suffering animal but also with the cruel animal, and he suffers even when plant and stone are ravished by man. It is logical that he speaks against the murder of tyrants.[149]

That included those who laid the abortive July plot against Hitler.

For Balthasar, there is here a failure to hold together in a Catholic frame all relevant partial truths. Christ, after all, 'took care not to enter the hour of darkness on the basis of his own judgment'.[150] His non-resistance was not chiefly vis-à-vis his enemies, but vis-à-vis his Father. His essence was total availability for the Father's will. His remedy for sinful structures is deeper than mere non-resistance to external superior power. Moreover:

> the State – which is not the Church – has no eschatological goal: the human beings who form the State will rise from the dead, not the State itself. This means that the laws it follows cannot be governed primarily or exclusively by the law of the Cross, which finds its justification at Easter from beyond this world.[151]

Balthasar judges Schneider's pacifism against the witness of Scripture and Tradition and finds it wanting. The Lord, it seems, does not want

> the situation of bloody martyrdom, to which only the individual can be called by the Holy Spirit, to be forced on the generality of his disciples by those who hold the reins of society, for otherwise these rulers would presumptuously lay claim to the prerogatives of the Spirit.[152]

So nothing is left but to bear certain harsh antitheses through the ages. And once again Balthasar has recourse to his beloved 'Secular Institutes' where we ought to find those 'non-resistant' people who take their stand on the life of the counsels (supremely non-resisting in their refusal to have goods, eros, power at their disposal) yet 'solidify' their effective power so as to become a 'model for the rulers of this world and those who bear responsibility'.[153] Balthasar finds it very 'Russian' in Schneider that he is so obsessed with the fate of the 'thief on the left', the 'bad thief', rather than the good thief on the

148 R. Schneider, *Und Petrus stieg aus dem Schiffe* (Baden-Baden, 1946).
149 *Tragedy under Grace, op. cit.*, p. 144.
150 *Ibid.*, p. 145.
151 *Ibid.*
152 *Ibid.*, p. 147.
153 *Ibid.*, p. 150.

right. As Schneider wrote in his war-time meditation on the Way of the Cross:

> We cannot give up the hope that even those who use their last strength to turn away from you die within the circle of salvation and that you find ways to the lost and build bridges where we only see gulfs.[154]

Balthasar agrees that just as prayer *must* embrace all, so hope *may* do so.

(vii) Germany

Returning to Germany in the appalling years of the end of the Weimar Republic and the beginnings of Nazidom, Schneider wanted not so much to describe as to help. He managed to bring out some tracts in Alsace-Lorraine where censorship was less rigorous, but only with the collapse of the Third Reich was publication possible for him again in Germany itself. He besought his countrymen for confession and repentance, asking them to stand firm in the judgment of truth which alone could free the flow of grace from the inexhaustible reserves of the Cross. On the basis of Schneider's immediately post-war writings, Balthasar put his appeal like this:

> The people are now to do what the individual does in sacramental confession. They must begin by seeing their 'Führer' and taking good note of his figure, not forgetting him – they must see his facelessness, how the word rotted and perished through him, how he corrupted every silence and contemplation. Then they must consider his collapse into the abyss, the end of a continuous, unstoppable collapse, of a cataract of all good things and all values. In this revelation of the abyss each one should recognize the demons as a reality and learn to fear them as a power that also has the force to take possession of a people and use them as a body ... No one should dare to deny his share in guilt ... The closer one stands to the truth – the saints are the closest – the more willing is one to recognize one's share in guilt.[155]

Schneider appealed too for an unmasking of the demons at work in German history, not least artistic and intellectual history, and the exorcism of the lying spirit which treated these as irrelevant to what was done with power. He proclaimed indeed the need for German culture to return to Christ, who is the only reliable Tester of spirits.[156] Rather as Balthasar had done with *Germanistik* and eschatology in the 1930s, Schneider now went through a huge quantity of works in the German literary tradition, evaluating them in Christomorphic fashion.[157] His conclusion: to allow certain non-Germans – above all the Greek tragedians, Dante, Calderón, Shakespeare – to help in the criticism of the German writers. 'Only that which is highest and purest can help us: through looking on it we shall be healed.'[158]

154 R. Schneider, *Der Kreuzweg* (Colmar, 1942), p. 55.
155 *Tragedy under Grace, op. cit.*, p. 160.
156 R. Schneider, *Die Heimkehr des deutschen Geistes . Über das Bild Christi in der deutschen Philosophie des 19. Jahrhunderts* (Baden-Baden, 1946).
157 For examples, see *Tragedy under Grace, op. cit.*, pp. 163–73.
158 *Ibid.*, p. 173.

That critical work was accompanied by new creative writing on Schneider's part, the aim being to establish some elements of a 'radical Christian poetics'.[159] The danger for Germans was that poetic images no longer exerted pressure for historical action. Schneider wanted to change that. 'A word that does not compel us to ask, "What ought we to do?", is not worth uttering.'[160] It is no echo of the eternal Word that bears up the world. Furthermore, as Balthasar remarks:

> A life that did not reveal the will to accept responsibility, to politics in the classical sense of the word, would not be capable of giving birth to responsible art.[161]

The Christian artist in particular is a commissioned man, with a heightened responsibility. Schneider emphasized the priority, in the post-National Socialist world, of restoring respect for the word, and the awareness of the duty to carry out truthful words.

Hence, thinks Balthasar, his post-war preference for drama. Schneider called drama 'the carrying out of the truth' as agents are summoned to a Yes or No: not just to reflection but to action. We can surely find much of the inspiration for the opening volume of Balthasar's own theological dramatics in Schneider's *Rechenschaft* where we read:

> The dramatic-tragic substance of the Christian life and faith has not yet formed its exhaustive expression; this may in large part be due to the fact that in the period of the highest creative power of the English, the Spanish and the French, the drama, misunderstood as 'theatre', was not acknowledged by the Church.[162]

Schneider's yearning for a 'meeting between the Church and drama' was answered in some fashion in Balthasar's *Theodramatik*. For his own part, he selected and re-published with his own introductions classic plays from *Oedipus at Colonus* to Grillparzer's *Ottokar*, as well as writing between 1946 and 1962 a half-dozen dramas of his own. Several of these deal with the issues of specifically ecclesial existence to which Balthasar now turns.

(viii) Rouen

Basically, Balthasar wants to present Schneider's account of subjective and objective holiness – the saint and the man in apostolic office – and to speculate on the relation between them. Though Schneider always discusses people in the Church, and not the Church in her generality – just as he speaks by preference of the king and not of the State, he works nonetheless with a tacit ecclesiology. The Word of the holy God become flesh bestows on the world his abiding presence, and the space and time of that presence is the Church. The Church is

159 *Ibid.*
160 R. Schneider, *Der Priester im Kirchenjahr der Zeit* (Freiburg, 1946), p. 60.
161 *Tragedy under Grace, op. cit.*, p. 175.
162 R. Schneider, *Rechenschaft, op. cit.*, p. 226.

a dying to the world and a mission into the world, and this makes her both the redemption itself and the place where the fighting for the sake of this redemption is keenest.[163]

The saint is the 'exemplary person in the Church, thanks to grace'; the pope is the 'exponent of the holy form in time'. Balthasar unabashedly intercalates his own ecclesiology when be explains that the two hierarchies (those of subjective and objective holiness) exist for one another rather as the disciples John and Peter yield to each other's primacy in the Fourth Gospel – since office knows it serves love while love renounces what is its own and submits to office. In this, 'the Church's existence is perfected in an act of transcendence beyond herself to the unity that is Christ'.[164] Somehow, Balthasar implies, Schneider has to show the convergence of the 'one who sits on the cathedra' and the 'one who is raised to the honours of the altar'.

Why not take, then, the example of Joan of Arc? What saint reveals more tellingly that subjective sanctity has a *mission* just like the objective holiness of the successor of the apostles? In more Schneiderian terms, the saints are the 'real symbols' and 'mighty forces' of the Kingdom of God, and Schneider interprets them on the principle that 'nothing is more active than contemplation'.[165] Typically, the saints burn – as Joan at Rouen – not only because God kindles a fire that enlarges their souls but also, alas, owing to the Church, or more precisely, to the sinners in her who make her live in discord with her essence. Too often – as with Thomas Becket – the truth is proclaimed but makes no impression. Yet what is this but the imitation of Christ before Pilate?

Not that the opposing of saint and ruler should be taken as the norm in Christendom. Rather the contrary, in fact. Balthasar writes:

> As the king lives the destiny of his people, so the saint lives to a much greater degree the destiny of the Church; but as the kingdom of God in the world, the Church contains in a mysterious fashion the State in herself and cannot dispense herself from her maternal responsibility. The struggle of the saints on behalf of the kings is a situation that can never be bypassed.[166]

Bartolomé de las Casas before the king of Spain is a favoured Schneiderian example. Office in the Church for Balthasar (as for Schneider) has a terrible mien. The officer cannot be what the office demands. If he wanted to be, he would 'exalt himself in arrogance and want to be the equal of Christ'. On the other hand, if he wanted to soothe himself with the reflection that of necessity he must fail, then 'he would have betrayed the essence and the unquenchable demand of the office'.[167] No man in the Gospels is rated more harshly by the Lord than is Peter, the first pope. So too for Peter's successor, the tension is killing. The vicarial Peter – the pope – is to pasture, which means:

163 *Tragedy under Grace, op. cit.*, p. 185.
164 *Ibid.*, p. 186.
165 *Ibid.*, p. 189.
166 *Ibid.*, p. 196.
167 *Ibid.*, p.216.

He is to wield his power of grace in an earthly form and this is a form that is not simply alien to the earthly administration of power. As he pastures a Church visible on earth, he necessarily comes into the force field of earthly power ... [Y]et measured against [that earthly power], his power will ... always appear to be powerlessness, even where it is the reflection of Christ's omnipotence in heaven, but a fortiori where it is the presence of the power of his Cross.[168]

Schneider poses the dilemma: can the Church of office administer earthly (civil) power without guilt in the service of heavenly power and power-lessness – and can she, if contrary-wise she deprives herself of all civil power, avoid betraying her commission in the world? Schneider resolves the dilemma, to his own satisfaction at least, by minimalizing the significance of the latter threat. Despite all the guilt of her office-bearers, chronicled in numerous disgraceful (or putatively disgraceful) cases, Balthasar begs to disagree.

[T]he Lord did not send his disciples in his omnipotence to the peoples so that they might suffer and perish there but so that the peoples might see their light and come to conversion ... Her commission means that the Church is to be active and conquering ... But to be active means coming into contact with power, being familiar with its working, possessing not only the simplicity of the dove but also the cunning of the serpent.[169]

This is surprising, coming from the author of 'The Razing of the Bastions'.

In two different studies, Schneider compares the hermit-pope who abdi-cated, Celestine V, the power-driven pope Boniface VIII, and the pope who combined the inner mindset of Celestine with the firm political intention of Boniface – Innocent III. In 'The Great Renunciation', subjective holiness takes flight from the realm of office so as to remain itself – thereby abandoning office to distorted power.[170] In simple terms, the wider Church was guilty for not helping Celestine to bear his rôle. More deeply, however, there is also ecclesial guilt wherever action and contemplation are experienced as exclu-sive one of the other. In 'Innocent and Francis', Schneider portrays a pope who inwardly identifies with Francis of Assisi but outwardly uses the weapons of the world.[171] Is, then, the contradiction between Rouen and Rome, subjective and objective holiness, final? Schneider's concisely written piece on Gregory the Great suggests not.[172] Like Celestine, Gregory is chosen pope against his will. Like Innocent, the basis of his work is *contemptus mundi*. Yet through gentle strength he has a powerful effect on his age.

(ix) Marienburg
Marienburg is Balthasar's last halt on his tour of Schneider's world. In 1274 a castle was built on a channel of the Vistula some thirty miles south of Danzig,

---

168 *Ibid.*, p. 208.
169 *Ibid.*, p. 220.
170 R. Schneider, *Der grosse Verzicht* (Wiesbaden, 1950).
171 *Idem, Innozenz und Franziskus* (Wiesbaden, 1952).
172 R. Schneider, 'Papst Gregor der Grosse', in *idem, Gedanken des Friedens: Gesammelte Kleinschriften* (Freiburg, 1946), pp. 119–33.

an outpost of Christendom in pagan Prussia. In 1309 the Order of Teutonic Knights transferred their headquarters there from Venice. The *Marienburger Schloss* is a mighty fortress, towering over its landscape like some Eastern Mont Saint Michel. Inspired by Schneider, Balthasar calls the vocation of the knights the 'gradual subjection of the earth to the law of the Cross and of culture',[173] and the last chapter of Balthasar's Schneider book, as originally conceived, is a paean to the spiritual knighthood which underlay secular knighthood and presented itself in pure form – at any rate in principle – in the knightly Orders. The paean is raised not in a spirit of historical nostalgia but with a view to resurrecting it in the modern world and Church. Something analogous was happening indeed in the French Catholic renaissance in the effort to invest scout associations with the spirit of chivalry.

> Knighthood changes its form, depending on whether Christians and the world are willing or unwilling to receive the imprint of its spirit; but it does not change its soul.[174]

In the modern world, Catholic Christians must find, despite that world, a 'form' compatible with the 'form of service and representation'. As Balthasar understands it, this will be a new culture-creating form of monasticism.

> The spirit that must inspire monasticism at the present hour must bear in itself the entire span that goes between renunciation and making use (on the basis of one's mission), and it must also have the span between Spain and Russia, between Ignatius with his form and John with his all-embracing love, and this tension must be lived in the ecclesial form that, as Marienburg shows, offer a place to the most exposed positions of the Christian in the world.[175]

While on the one hand, we must not spiritualize the visible Church to the point that we remove all boundaries between the states of life within her, there should be on the other the 'highest compenetration' of office and holiness. So the new body of knights Balthasar seeks

> is called to this intimate encounter between the monk who bears responsibility for the world and the man of the world who administers State and culture out of the spirit of renunciation.[176]

Certainly Balthasar was deeply concerned that no culture worthy of the name could survive the levelling down of the individual, since on the individual turns the quality of ethical and spiritual life.[177] With this anxiety for the humane future of technologically proficient, media-invasive mass democracy (despite the material advances and increase of equity which he acknowledged), was married a second which also echoed Schneider's concerns. As Balthasar wrote, 'In the long term, no culture lives from its past, however rich that past may be'.[178] Individuals, no matter how creative and

173 *Tragedy under Grace, op. cit.*, p. 247.
174 *Ibid.*, p. 248.
175 *Ibid.*, p. 259.
176 *Ibid.*, p. 264.
177 'Sur les conditions d'une culture', *La Revue de Culture européenne* 4 (1954), pp. 11–21, and here at p. 14.
178 *Ibid.*

responsible, cannot form a culture without 'community and comprehension'.[179] What sort of unity, then, should contemporary Europe seek? Balthasar drew his readers' attention to a 'mysterious spring which, in principle higher than any culture, has irrigated the entire domain'. It is, of course, the Catholic faith. Of this culture-making faith he writes:

> It is not because it has existed that it must continue to be accorded value, but because it is the truth which at the same time possesses the power of active grace.[180]

Among critics who had followed Schneider's career, a number thought that particular Christian had reached a crisis point in his own faith around the time of Balthasar's 1954 essay 'On the Conditions of a Culture' whence these remarks are drawn.

(x) Schneider's finis
There remain to be considered, accordingly, the autobiographical writings of Schneider's last years. 'Winter in Vienna' (1957–1958) was read by some as a reconversion to Schopenhauerian pessimism and a 'sensational apostasy' from the fervent Catholicism embraced ever since the writing of *Das Inselreich*.[181] But Schneider always had difficulty, comments Balthasar, in embracing the Resurrection (not the Cross). There was nothing really new, therefore, when he wrote: 'I know that he [Christ] is risen; but my vital force has sunk so far that it is unable to reach out beyond the grave'.[182] Schneider continued to make a daily prayer in church even though 'the Father's countenance has become wholly obscured in darkness'.[183] It would be on his way back from the Liturgy on Holy Saturday 1958 that he collapsed and died. That is Balthasar's cue to interpret Schneider's 'crisis', if such it was, in terms of the Paschal Mystery.

> When Schneider allows himself to sink down wearily, this is a pious (though hidden) following of the crucified Christ, who no longer sees or understands, into the hands (which can no longer be felt) of the Father who created this terrible world and bears the responsibility for it.[184]

Balthasar will not have it that Schneider was in this regard a mystic, nor will he concede he was simply a depressive. Schneider's grasp of some of the difficulties of theodicy, the rational justification of an all-good and all-powerful God who nonetheless allows the world's pain, was the problem's root. But despite this, Balthasar still thinks Schneider's work radiates a 'Christian nobility' – one reason he finds fewer readers today. Words like 'freedom', 'conscience', 'responsibility', so easily abused, are only proper received, so Balthasar suggests, by nobility of heart.

179 *Ibid.*, p. 20.
180 *Ibid.*, p. 21.
181 R. Schneider, *Winter in Wien. Aus meinen Notizbüchern 1957–1958* (Freiburg, 1958).
182 *Ibid.*, p. 79.
183 *Ibid.*, p. 119.
184 *Tragedy under Grace, op. cit.*, p. 277.

Coda on Claudel

But let us end this *tour d'horizon* of Balthasar on Catholic literature with light
and joy. In the 1930s, at the Jesuit study-house at Lyon-Fourvière, Balthasar
began, with passion, to translate the poems of the diplomat, dramatist and
'maker' Paul Claudel. As Dominique Millet-Gérard notes, Balthasar and
Claudel were to be united by 'the hope of giving Europe a theology of divine
glory and a literature worthy of it'.[185] Claudel entertained that hope before
Balthasar. In 1935 he is found writing to Père Marie-Vincent Bernadot,
Dominican director of *La Vie intellectuelle*:

> *Beauty* is an idol which cannot be the goal of art. That goal is the glory
> of God and the teaching of the faithful *by relation to the latter*.[186]

For Claudel was already borne along by the aesthetic current of the Thomist
revival, the 'Thomist aesthetic' whose 'keystone' was the 'theory of the
splendour, *le rayonnement*, of the beautiful'.[187] That was one of the sources of
Balthasar's theological inspiration too. His ontological concept of beauty, as
the radiance of being bestowed on creation from God, drew on the same kind
of reading of Thomas as is found in the Maritain of *Art et Scolastique* and in
Claudel himself.[188] Theological aesthetics haunt Claudel's biblical commentaries and dramas, and have left their mark in the prevalence in his writing of
the language of 'form' and 'figure', two key terms of Balthasar's own vocabulary. Balthasar found Claudel's poetic idiom characterized by the highest
clarté, not only lucidity but luminosity, 'like an irresistible revelation of
highest joy'.[189]

Looking back, in his 1981 'Petit mémoire sur Paul Claudel', he considered
Claudel claimed – as poet, not philosopher – to 'see all things at the same
time – or to see in one thing all others'. This makes it hard, one might think,
to decide whether the supernatural revelation of God in Christ is the true
origin of Claudel's 'catholic vision of the universe', or whether, alternatively,
it was through this 'catholicity of things' that he reached 'the Christological
centre of the cosmic Poem and Drama'.[190] Actually, Balthasar deemed this set
of alternatives false.

> The essentially Catholic poet has the right and even the duty to take his
> flight from the starting-point of the concrete, to consider its symbolism
> … and thereby to discover the coherence of all the elements that form
> together an immense sentence which is only intelligible, however, in
> the Logos incarnate.[191]

185 D. Millet-Gérard, 'Paul Claudel lu par Hans Urs von Balthasar. Continuité de la Tradition culturelle européenne', in *Claudel et l'Europe. Acts du Colloque de la Sorbonne*
(Lausanne, 1997), pp. 28–51.
186 Cited *ibid.*, p. 29.
187 Millet-Gérard draws attention to the influence of the historian of mediaeval thought
Maurice de Wulf, author of 'Les théories esthétiques de saint Thomas' in the *Revue Néo-
scolastique* for 1896.
188 See for Claudel's Thomism the evidence brought forward in D. Millet-Gérard, *Claudel
thomiste?* (Paris, 1999).
189 'Nachwort', *P. Claudel. Der seidene Schuh* (Salzburg, 1939), p. 403.
190 'Petit mémoire sur Paul Claudel', in *Claudel Confesseur de la Foi*, I, = *Bulletin de la Société
Paul Claudel* 82 (1981), pp. 1–3, and here at p. 1.
191 *Ibid.*, p. 2.

It was 'in all these marvellous objects reflecting their beauty in each other' that Claudel perceived the glory of God of which Christ will be the supreme revelation. Even in his biblical commentaries, however, the 'Christic glory' can appear 'drowned in the cosmic glory': Balthasar would have preferred Claudel to have written more on the glory of the Cross – though the theme certainly appears for instance in the poetic cycle entitled 'Le chemin de la Croix' and, elsewhere in *Corona Benignitatis Anni Dei*, the 'Hymne du Sacré Coeur'.[192]

In January 1940 Claudel made an entry in his diary.

> The weather is rather better. Journey to Einsiedeln with Father Urs von Balthasar, a translator attracted by my works, a very distinguished Jesuit. Einsiedeln a prodigious paradisal cave, an architectural bouquet, a paradise of gold, imagination, colour. Gold that falls on us in con-cavities of blue and rose. The chapel of St Meinrad's Black Virgin in the middle of the church. A meal in the refectory. Everything covered in snow. The beatification of Brother Meinrad Engster in progress.[193]

By this time, Balthasar had already translated *Les cinq grandes Odes* but also, at far greater length, Claudel's most celebrated drama, *Le Soulier de Satin*. This was clearly a labour of love: the postword to the first edition implies as much.[194] In effect, he read the play through the lens of Scripture's Song of Solomon, interpreting it as telling of the interlacing of the beauty of the soul, the glory of God, and the insatiable need of the creature for the love of God. Repaying in advance Claudel's compliments to the abbey church at Einsie-deln, home of Balthasar's publishing house, and his own adopted spiritual home, Balthasar calls the play 'timeless Baroque', lauding its 'light, air and freedom'.

By his own confession, Balthasar spent 'months, indeed virtually years' translating Claudel – in effect, the greater part of the poetic oeuvre.[195] He claimed that this work paid his debts to the 'catholicity of the natural world' which for Claudel was itself a disclosure of a 'supernatural Christian cath-olicity'. Balthasar's own task was a different and complementary one. At a time when German-language theology had 'turned to transcendentality' – he has in mind the Transcendental Thomists with their focus on the universal 'horizon' of being' – Balthasar's own task was to point up the uniqueness of the 'categorial' epiphany of Jesus Christ. Balthasar was faced with thinkers who treated the religious self-expression of humanity in its widest gamut as already reflecting the universal divine will to communicate and reveal. In this context, his duty was to point to the crucial otherness of the biblical revelation.

> If in the cosmic domain Claudel was right to insist on the mysterious fact that each created form included the existence of all the others, one could not say so much of the world religions. If there can be analogies – for example, for the idea of sacrifice in a number of religious systems, it does not follow that the Sacrifice of Calvary is only the highest form of

---

192 P. Claudel, *Oeuvre poétique* (Paris, 1967), pp. 477–87, and pp. 404–407.
193 P. Claudel, *Journal* II (Paris, 1969), p. 54.
194 'Nachwort', *art. cit.*
195 'Petit mémoire sur Paul Claudel', *art. cit.*, p. 2.

a cultural usage common to most religions. This led me to study the question of uniqueness more than that of analogy.[196]

Balthasar's focus was on that uniqueness of Christ for which the best comparison, he held, was the uniqueness of a work of art. Claudel, thought Balthasar, should have approved his project. 'His poet's eye always had a sharp sense of the specific difference of a phenomenon, a dramatic situation, a landscape, a painting.' Claudel did not think it necessary to develop theoretically what by connaturality for all practical purposes he could see anyway. But just because he possessed that connaturality 'I can consider him one of my masters who, in the selfsame religious faith, taught me to *see*'.

> If his religious and Christian aesthetic differs somewhat from mine, that is because it lingers so long over nature in all its dimensions – that immense basement of Christianity. He is the cosmic poet and in his dramas the anthropological poet with always a final aim in view that is theological, Christian. The theologian, by contrast, who does not dispose of so exceptionally rich a nature and whose métier is to announce salvation in Christ, seeks for a method that goes right to the heart of his subject.[197]

It is to a last evaluation of Balthasar's method and task that we must, in conclusion, turn.

---

196 *Ibid.*, p. 3.
197 *Ibid.*

Conclusion: Fruitful Reflection

How then are we to conclude? Perhaps by suggesting the character of the impulse Balthasar has given to Catholic theology for its use – if it be wise! – in the future. Balthasar considered his own theology as an attempt to place his finger, 'a kind of finger like St John had' he hoped it might be, on the fullness of divine revelation. Congruently with *Dei Verbum*, the Constitution on Divine Revelation of the Second Vatican Council, he took that to mean the fullness of revelation *in Jesus Christ*. That cannot be identified without entry in depth into the biblical witness, wherever possible understood, as that Conciliar text puts it, in the same Holy Spirit who inspired it. That implies then, reading Scripture in Tradition, from the standpoint of the wondrous amplitude of the Bible's reception in the Church. In Balthasar's eyes, that in turns means seeing divine revelation with the eyes of the saints. As he himself remarked, when interviewed: 'I have to say that only the saints among the theologians truly interest me'.[1] And he went on to explain that by that he meant not only the canonized doctors, from Irenaeus, through Augustine to Anselm and Bonaventure (his own examples). He was also referring to what he called 'forms which make holiness stream out'. Naming not only Dante and Newman, both Catholics obviously, but also Kierkegaard and Solovyev, a Lutheran and an Orthodox respectively, he suggested there an ecumenism of the thinking spirit which may be more valuable, actually, than the official ecumenism of bilateral dialogues. His remarks indicate that there can be holy form in a literary *oeuvre* that comes directly out of Christian life, even when the individual is not – for whatever reason – a candidate for canonization. (Of course Newman might pass from the second category to the first, but hardly the others.)

One thing Balthasar commonly looks for in the work of holy men, or at least holy forms, is integrity in the sense not only of the integration of life and thought but in its root meaning of *wholeness*. (An 'integer' is a whole number.) As Medard Kehl has put it:

> Balthasar is always concerned, before and in all particular theological questions, to get a view of the *whole* of Christian faith as such. That 'whole' is more than the (subsequent) sum of its parts because it represents primordial unity which precedes every 'critically' dissecting

1 M. Albus, 'Geist und Feuer. Ein Gespräch mit Hans Urs von Balthasar', *art. cit.*, p. 73.

analysis and every simple listing of elements one after the other. The *one* fundamental Christian mystery – God's love for the world in the gift of his Son and the sacrament of his Church – should be recognized in its original 'infold' (*Einfalt*), so that it can then also be continually recognized again in its detailed 'un-foldings' ...[2]

We can see how that operates in the main adverbial 'takes' he performed on the same divine subject-matter: theo-aesthetically, theo-dramatically, theo-logically, and lastly what I would call theo-mystically.

Thus *theo-aesthetically*, Balthasar would re-concentrate our loving gaze on the primordial beauty of Christ. His sharpest criticism is directed to a practical (whether pastoral or political) theology that has mislaid the primal Icon. As he put it:

> No beta can be explained other than in terms of its alpha. The alpha always presupposes everything else, yet we can never take it for granted as a premiss just to be left behind, like that.[3]

But as Balthasar makes plain, the 'alpha' he is speaking about is not, after the manner of rationalism, a conceptual initial axiom. The governing premise of a theological aesthetic is the understanding that the radiant beauty of the Incarnate Word, the 'form' on whom the Father confers the glory of the Godhead, is, precisely as the majesty of crucified and hell-harried love, evidence enough to elicit the adoring witness of the heart. As he put it very simply in *Love Alone*, the summary of *Herrlichkeit*:

> 'Aesthetics' has for us a purely theological sense: the perception in faith of the self-authenticating glory of God's utterly free gift of love.[4]

So is this 'eliciting' our witness in some delicate, refined, sense? Or, more roughly, is it *compelling* it? Despite contemporary Western humanity's withdrawal from Christian believing, Balthasarian theo-aesthetics uses the strong language of the overwhelming grandeur of divine love. We needed and still need to be shaken from complacency in our little world. Balthasar's theology seeks to mirror for us the way divine revelation intends to do so. Citing *Love Alone* again:

> The totally-other, the ever-greater, *appears* and seizes hold of us *in* the very act of overwhelming us through the ultimately incomprehensible character of that love. Precisely when the creature sees and feels him-self clearly drawn towards the heart of God, he sees clearly the irre-vocable and inescapable nature of that primary, universally valid relationship between the relative and 'absolute, worldly and divine being?' And he can only endure this frightening shaking of the foun-dations of his finite being when he has learnt to decipher the figure of revelation – not formally as 'word', but really, as absolute love.[5]

2 M. Kehl, 'Hans Urs von Balthasar: A Portrait', in *idem* and W. Löser (eds), *The Von Balthasar Reader* (New York, 1982), pp. 34–35.
3 'Why I am still a Christian', in H. U. von Balthasar and J. Ratzinger, *Two Say Why* (ET Chicago, 1971), p. 14.
4 *Love Alone: the Way of Revelation* (ET London, 1968), p. 9.
5 *Ibid.*, pp. 48–49.

Then *theo-dramatically*, we are to let the divine drama have its full scope in all its dimensions, positioned as we are between earth and heaven, with the powers of Hell at our gates, and positioned too between time and eternity, our time and the Age to Come, the absolute future of the world. Innumerable divine missions are given to enable people to play their parts in this drama. The overall dramatis personae is the great thing, but it cannot work aright unless we ourselves know what is our role.

Again, *theo-logically*, Balthasar knows that, though revelation is not doctrine, it has an essential doctrinal aspect. As Christ put his experience of the Logos into language, so the apostles did to their experience under the clarifying action of the Holy Spirit. This goes on in the Church, notably in doctrinal definition. Balthasar wants to situate theology firmly within that ecclesial process. As he has shown, it is not simply a matter of honing doctrinal statements, which become more and more narrowed in their focus if also more and more precise. It is also a question of letting them find their place time and again in the Christian intellectual totality, with at its centre, the descending Word of God.

Lastly, *theo-mystically*, if we may coin a word, the situation is much the same.

> Today we must investigate in what way the Christian wealth ... relates to its origin: to the ineffable poverty of the divine incarnate, crucified love. We draw close together, near to the source and beginnings, in order to hear the 'Word that was in the beginning'. We unite ourselves outwardly; the question is whether the grace will be given us to collect ourselves inwardly as well.[6]

Balthasar never ceased to call for a renewal of contemplativity in the face of the divine form, the self-disclosure of the triune God.

Some people, doubtless, will not appreciate the *tone* of much in Balthasar's writing. Even when most consciously at the service of the contemplative, it never excludes an element of the polemical. This is a theological oeuvre written against as well as for: its author was too conscious of the *conjuncture* of his lifetime to do anything else.

> Today the Christian people (or what is left of it) is searching with a lamp for persons who radiate something of the light, something of nearness to the source. It has long since had enough of the modernities, lacking all religious instinct, which trumpet at it from the press, the radio, and often enough from the pulpit. It is sad because it is unintended, and an all too justified fear torments it that the 'one thing necessary' could be totally blocked off and made inaccessible by the 'experts', or the many dilettantes and apostates who pose as such. Often these are poor wretches, who must shout so loud in order to justify to themselves their inner predicament of no longer being able to pray.[7]

Hard words for hard times. But possibly, therefore, pastorally well-conceived hard love.

---

6 *Convergences, op. cit.*, p. 14.
7 *Ibid.*

The future of Balthasar's influence on Catholic theology turns principally of course on the reception accorded his own work. But it turns secondarily on the destinies of the corporate project represented by the review *Communio* of which he was the principal co-founder and whose authors constitute a significant network in modern Catholicism worldwide. In launching the *International Catholic Review*, soon to be known as *Communio*, Balthasar had asked what standpoint the new review was to adopt so as to scan aright the clash of ideologies and philosophies of the day. The crucial section of his answer is found in the words:

> In order to be of universal importance, [Christianity] has to be something special, definite, unique, as opposed to what falls within everyone's range of vision. And not only 'something' special among other special things, but *the* special thing, so much so that it can claim universal importance precisely on the ground of its uniqueness.[8]

By invoking the word *communio* as his – by no means obvious – marker for what is at once unique and universal, Balthasar could lay out not only a Trinitarian and Christological ecclesiology of a kind that would soon be adopted by the highest levels of Church authority but also a whole programme for Church life through authentic reform and spiritual, social, cultural renaissance.

This is no mere ecclesiology in a technical sense; in fact, the essay that sets out the Balthasarian sense of 'communio' is virtually unplaceable. The primary meaning of the term for him is that people do not enter community by their own initiative. They are in it from the start, they are *a priori* mutually dependent. The challenge is not to get into this kind of situation but so to act as to perfect its pattern. The chances of that happening are obviously affected by how solid the primary foundations turn out to be. What are the plausible candidates for a well-grounded communication in reason, freedom and human nature at large? Balthasar's discussion thereof is rendered somewhat dated by his assumption that the principal contenders must be Christianity and what he terms 'evolutionary communism'.

That does not greatly affect his apologia for the Christian version. The latter has two strengths in its community project. One is

> in God himself, who could not bestow personal communion with himself and among men if he were not already in a profound sense a community in himself: loving mutual inherence, loving exchange, which presupposes loving consent to another's freedom. Wherever the divinatory vista opening out on the divine Trinity, which alone discloses God *concretely* as absolute love, is blocked, the idea of perfect community can never develop.[9]

The other plus comes from humanity itself, as the Gospel sees us.

> If man were not created in the image of God, and for him, he would not experience in himself the urge to look for a more perfect communion among human beings than he is capable of picturing within the setting

8 'Communio – a Programme', *International Catholic Review* 1 (1972), p. 3.
9 *Ibid.*, p. 5.

of more earthly conditions. For contact, dialogue, community of goods are only means, not the reality itself, which remains unimaginable, transcendent.[10]

The strength of Christianity lies in the fact that its 'communional' foundations stand on a priori real principles, rather than being received (as it is the case with evolutionary communism) from a relation to prospective, ideal states of affairs.

> If communion is made a mere object of eschatological hope for mankind and not a real antecedent gift ... then all generations which were only on the way to it are left behind, they are only material and have no access to the great communal festival.[11]

The Christian *communio* is realized in the communion of Eucharistic gifts in the Holy Spirit – which means its community is

> established antecedently by God on the grace of the abasement, humility, acceptance of poverty by Jesus Christ in loving dedication,

and so lives by an ethos of 'spontaneous, pre-psychological, pre-methodical, helpful brotherly love', which Balthasar contrasts favourably with the 'evolutionary communist' alternative.[12] It is no recipe for self-satisfaction:

> The fact that even though we have received the gift of communion with God we remain at God's disposal, is a continually renewed experience of the divine judgment: which of us opens himself to the love of God and thereby to true fraternal love? We recognize it to a certain degree, then the criteria escape us; judgment belongs to God alone.[13]

For Balthasar, this is the reason why we should never anticipate the Last Judgment by consigning others to certain perdition. We can, then, hope – but not know – that all may ultimately be brought within the divine–human communion.

Meanwhile, great tensions sear the world and the Church. For Balthasar the greatest of these is that between Jews and 'Gentiles' – placed in inverted commas because, presumably, the category as used here includes (not very happily) Christian Jews. Peter's speech in Acts (3.20–26) opens the prospect of eventually Jewish–Christian communion in the common hope for the returning Messiah. Then there is the rift in communion with separated Eastern Christians, for whose prospective (again) healing Balthasar proposes a reversal of the trend of Western Catholic theology in the 1970s to become

> more and more rapidly alien, in its understanding of tradition, liturgy and ministry, to the venerable Church of the origins, as though the latter no longer seriously counted ...[14]

---

10 *Ibid.*
11 *Ibid.*, p. 7.
12 *Ibid.*, p. 6.
13 *Ibid.*
14 *Ibid.*, p. 9.

That did not prevent him being exercised by the tendency of Catholic ecumenists to ignore the Oriental Catholic churches in favour of the Orthodox. 'There is such a thing as genocide among Christians.'

So far as relations with Evangelical Protestants and Anglicans were concerned (the placing of Anglicans last in this list may or may not be significant), he affirmed that these dialogues also are 'within our communion in Christ'. But he warned against 'tinkering away to unions in calculating and politic fashion' rather than 'recognizing the demands made by the communion which has already been bestowed on us by God's communication of himself'.[15]

In his programme Balthasar sought to recognize some kind of communion too with non-Christians and even with opponents of Christianity. He pointed out that the atmosphere of world society retains certain effects of the global penetration of Christianity. The enemies of the faith may sometimes be opposing its caricature, not the real thing. Be that as it may, the Christian for whom communion is the watchword does not abandon anyone, not even outright apostates.

Throughout, Balthasar's stress lies on the way communion is divine gift not human origination. It is not at the disposal of the Christian, or even of the Church. That said, Balthasar enters a caveat against the contemporary tendency to reduce the Church to a framework of institutions and make small groups the criterion of Christian vitality. Whatever the hopes of regeneration from below such groups offers, they cannot be made into the Church without disintegrating her into an array of charismatic sects. The roof is not to be detached from the house, the *Catholica* from cells of enthusiasts or 'base communities'.

Communion so understood will be demanding for the one who understands it.

> Buddhists and Stoics train themselves to enter a sphere without suffering and hate; the impact of contradictions does not affect them, for they communicate with the enemy in a supra-personal absolute. The Christian, however, must open his heart and allow himself to be most intimately affected, challenged, hurt.[16]

Only completely humble faith in what God's love has already done will work, 'without any kind of triumphalism', says Balthasar, 'even of love'. People today, he had written, 'would like a Church of love'. But, he warned:

> It will become a Church of mere human love – and thereby be indistinguishable from the world – unless it is seriously a Church of faith: faith in the love of the triune God who in the Cross of Jesus Christ 'loved me' [and all of us] and gave himself for me' (Galatians 2: 20). For simple co-humanity no one will enter a seminary or novitiate and all the Bishops' Conferences and Synods in the world will not alter that fact. And very soon all the churches will stand empty, if only co-humanity is preached and Jesus Christ no longer proclaimed.[17]

15 *Ibid.*
16 *Ibid.*, p. 11.
17 'Zwischen Scylla und Charybdis', *Vaterland* 153 (5 July 1969).

Of course Balthasar knew perfectly well, and stated often enough, that faith entails love. But for the New Testament, love of one's brother is the *criterion* for the authenticity of one's love of God, 'not a *substitute* for [that] love, or indeed simply *identical* with it'.[18] Here Balthasar pinpoints one kind of demand and, clearly, it is a call to let the theological virtues flower. The other challenge Balthasar highlights is more intellectual. It involves bringing into play the 'gift of critical discernment and all dialectical arts of thought and eloquence'. There is a contest going on, a contest of philosophies of life, and we are not to be afraid of taking part. For Gospel reasons, obviously.

Despite his great intellect, at once capacious and analytic, and his equally formidable learning, Balthasar did not suffer from bigheadedness. The story is told of Hilaire Belloc that, making his confession, he asked the priest's counsel for his intellectual pride. 'Mingle with your intellectual superiors', was the confessor's advice. 'But Father', replied a bewildered Belloc, 'where are they?'[19] The five books of this *Introduction to Hans Urs von Balthasar* suggest an answer for any of us afflicted with a like ill.

18 'Die Struktur der Kirche in einer säkularisierten Welt', *art. cit.* There is a polemic here against the manner of interrelating the two love commands found – or at any rate thought to be found – in Karl Rahner's work.
19 P. Hunt, 'Belloc – Fifty Years Later', *The Chesterton Review* XXIX. 3 (2003), pp. 353–66 and here at p. 353.

Bibliography

The fundamental bibliographical guide to Balthasar's own writings is C. Capol, *Hans Urs von Balthasar: Bibliographie 1925–1990* (Einsiedeln 1991). The Archiv Hans Urs von Balthasar at Arnold Böcklinstrasse 42, CH 4051 Basel, Switzerland, puts out a regularly updated guide to secondary literature under the title 'Hans Urs von Balthasar – Sekundärliteratur – Monographien – Dissertationen – Habilitationsschriften'. The same Archive also provides guides to pertinent journal articles and essay collections.

Index of Names

Abelard, P. 171
Abraham 18, 233
Adam 40, 63, 87, 99, 102, 135, 152, 155, 169, 185, 209, 214
Adam, K. 74
Albert 165, 242
Albrecht, B. 116
Albus, M. 14
Alexander I 326, 327
Alfred 323
Ambrose 26, 111
Anselm 88, 89, 211, 337
Anthony of Egypt 9
Anthony of Padua 240
Aquinas, see Thomas Aquinas
Aristotle 44, 73, 214, 316
Athanasius 26, 170, 171, 270
Athenagoras, apologist 27, 28
Athenagoras, patriarch 14
Augustine 4, 26, 31, 41, 51–6, 57, 63, 64, 65, 76, 103, 192, 231, 238, 337
Avvakum 327

Bach, J. S. 250
Baius 63, 99
Balas, D. 38
Barth, K. 2, 5, 15, 19, 24, 27, 31, 32, 33, 40, 57, 66, 72, 74–107, 112, 114, 146, 147, 149, 154, 172, 177, 247, 254, 263, 291, 306
Basil 26, 43
Bauhofer, O. 102
Bay, M. du, see Baius
Becket, T. 330
Béguin, A. 293
Bellarmine, R. 148
Belloc, H. 343

Benedict XVI 12, 17, 25, 233
Bernadot, V.-M. 334
Bernanos, G. 3, 103, 104, 113, 114, 199, 273, 289–313
Bernard 238, 269
Bérulle, P. de 3, 156
Blondel, M. 3, 59, 60, 101
Bloy, L. 289, 290
Bonaparte, N. 157, 326
Bonaventure, 165, 238, 242, 337
Boniface VIII 331
Borromeo, C. 225
Bossuet, J.-B. 277
Bouyer, L. 33
Bremond, H. 242
Brunner, E. 85, 89, 90
Buber, M. 5, 139
Bulgakov, S. 174
Burckhardt, J. 111

Cabasilas, N. 170
Cajetan 59
Calderón, P. de 4, 313, 328
Calvin, J. 75, 178
Camões, L.Vaz de 316
Carlyle, T. 315
Casas, B. de las 324, 330
Casel, O. 159, 160
Catherine of Siena 117
Celestine V 331
Ceppède, J. de la 175
Cervantes 313
Chambord, Comte de 312
Chardon, L. 175
Charles V, emperor 324
Charles I, king 323
Chesterton, G. K. 260

347

John XXIII 6, 60, 68
John the Baptist 207, 257
John Chrysostom, see Chrysostom
John of the Cross 122, 179, 187, 234, 242, 252, 256, 263, 283
John of Scythopolis 41, 42, 43
John Paul II 12, 14–19, 72, 122, 183, 208
Joinville, J. 290
Joseph 207
Journet, C. 113
Judas Iscariot 311
Jude, apostle 112
Julian of Norwich 117
Justinian 32, 41

Kaegi, W. 111
Kant, I. 26, 62, 128
Kehl, M. 179, 337
Kierkegaard, S. 62, 78, 81, 163, 315, 337
Knox, R. 136

Laberthonnière, L. 101
Labourdette, M.-M. 96
Las Casas, see Casas B. de las
Leahy, B. 202
Leira-Merikakis, E. 308
Leo, pope 231
Lessing, G. E. 131
Lestov, N. 327
Lewis, C. S. 3
Löser, W. 23, 24, 38, 51
Louis IX 290
Lubac, H. de 3, 11, 18, 23, 24, 27, 30, 31, 56, 57–73, 87, 101–2, 113, 135, 137, 138, 139, 169, 192, 200, 254
Lustiger, J.-M. 66
Luther, M. 40, 75, 103, 178

MacDonald, G. 3
Magdalene, see Mary Magdalene
Marcel, G. 113
Marchesi, G. 57
Maréchal, J. 59, 64
Margaret of Scotland 240
Maria Theresa 321
Maritain, J. 173–4, 203, 334
Marlowe, C. 323
Marmion, C. 277
Martha 208, 257, 273

Martin, T., see Thérèse
Mary of Bethany 208, 257, 273
Mary, Blessed Virgin 6, 17, 52, 71, 81, 103, 110, 116, 119–20, 137, 154, 161, 165, 193, 197, 198, 200, 201, 202, 203, 204, 205, 206, 207, 208, 215, 219, 220, 222, 224, 229–36, 257, 258, 271, 282, 297, 323, 325
Mary Magdalene 39, 207
Marx, K. 61
Matthew, evangelist 12, 182
Mauriac, F. 113, 289, 302
Maximus the Confessor 4, 24, 31, 32, 37, 41, 42–50, 55, 57, 84, 103, 104, 128, 211, 282
Meinrad 335
Menasce, P. de 113
Mercier, D. 226
Mersch, E. 100
Michelangelo 139
Millet-Gérard, D. 334
Möhler, J. A. 138
Mongrain, K. 30, 64
Monica 53–4
Moses 284
Müller, G. L. 245

Newman, J. H. 13, 57, 60, 77, 138, 139, 266, 291, 337
Nietzsche, F. 61, 62, 69, 130
Novalis 318

Origen 4, 23, 24, 30, 31–7, 39, 41, 43, 44, 57, 60, 61, 66, 68, 137, 186, 280, 282
Otto of Bamberg 323

Pannenberg, W. 132
Pascal, B. 3, 313
Paul, apostle 76, 81, 82, 112, 141, 153, 175, 176, 177, 184, 186, 200, 203, 217, 221, 226, 238, 253, 254, 266, 285, 286
Paul VI 9, 14, 106
Paulinus of Nola 51
Péguy, C. 3, 7, 289, 290, 307, 313
Peter, apostle 17, 43, 52, 112, 184, 190, 200, 203, 205, 206, 207, 224, 230, 330, 341

Index of Subjects

Christ as the true man 145–9
Fall of 48, 169, 215 *see also* original
    sin
human nature in Barth's theology
    81, 88
human nature in Bernanosian
    literature 298–9
incompleteness of 127–9
original nature of 63–4, 214
as servant and friend of God
    99–100
split between nature, with its
    desire for human love, and
    spirit, with its desire for being
    128–9, 133
transcendent nature and need of
    127–9
transformation from primal image
    to final likeness 213–17
uniqueness of the individual 128
wholeness possible for man only
    through Son's incarnation
    131–2
see also anthropology
Marian theology 6, 72, 119–20, 154,
    229–36
Christo-Mariological criterion for
    Church state of life 208,
    218–22
Christology and 230–2, 233
the Church and 17, 116, 197–8,
    200–4, 234–5
the Marian *fiat* 202, 229–35, 268,
    282
'Marian liberation' 207
Mary as pray-er *par excellence* 263
Mary as Virgin, Mother and Bride
    232–3
phases of consent 233–5
the placing of Mariology 235–6
marriage 48–9, 221
sacrament of 160, 222
Mass *see* Eucharist/Mass
meditation 13, 239
see also contemplative prayer
mission, theology of 91, 114, 227–8
encounter of worldly and spiritual
    missions 314–15
exemplified in Elizabeth of Dijon
    252–8

exemplified in Thérèse of Lisieux
    238, 245–52
hagiology of mission 237–45, 298
holiness and 237–40
individual 'Christian missions'
    157–8, 283, 339
literary mission of Bernanos 296–8
salvation and the temporal
    mission 311–13
monasticism 120, 224–5, 251
Christian secularity and 217–22
monastic obedience 313
need for new culture-creating
    form of 332
Monophysitism 99
mystery
and the attitude of prayer 142
of the Church 70, 195
fruitfulness and 46–7
of God as Love 191
Paschal Mystery *see* Paschal
    Mystery
Presence in 160–1
as root of mysticism 33, 282–3,
    339
sharing of 'exoteric' saints in
    divine mystery 240
mysticism
of Adrienne von Speyr 112, 118,
    281–3
in Bernanosian literature 301–3
Chalcedon and 44, 46
dark nights 179, 187, 234, 243, 267,
    302–3
de Lubac 58, 69–70
as ecclesial grace 104
of Elizabeth of Dijon 255–8
inseparability of history and 34
Jesus as archetype of the mystic
    266–7, 283
moving beyond Thomistic
    teachings 283–5
natural 286
pagan ecstatic mysticism 130
passion mysticism 112, 118
of radiance 35, 267
rooted in the Christian mystery 33,
    282–3, 339
of sin (Bernanos) 304–8
see also contemplative prayer